THE STORY OF
IRELAND
A History of the Irish People

NEIL HEGARTY

THOMAS DUNNE BOOKS
St. Martin's Press
New York

They are begging us, you see, in their wordless way,
To do something, to speak on their behalf
Or at least not to close the door again.

Derek Mahon

HÉG
402-1922

THOMAS DUNNE BOOKS.
An imprint of St. Martin's Press.

THE STORY OF IRELAND.
Copyright © 2011 by Neil Hegarty.
Introduction copyright © 2011 by Fergal Keane.
Maps © 2011 by Encompass Graphics.
Afterword copyright © 2012 by Neil Hegarty.
All rights reserved. Printed in the United States of America.
For information, address St. Martin's Press, 175 Fifth Avenue, New York, N.Y. 10010.

This book is published to accompany the television series entitled *Story of Ireland*,
first broadcast on BBCNI and RTE in 2011.

www.thomasdunnebooks.com
www.stmartins.com

ISBN 978-1-250-00289-1

First published in Great Britain by BBC Books, an imprint of Ebury Publishing,
a Random House Group Company

First U.S. Edition: March 2012

10 9 8 7 6 5 4 3 2 1

CONTENTS

LIST OF MAPS

INTRODUCTION

THE INTERNATIONAL ISLAND

As a foreign correspondent I am naturally inclined to view the world as a place where the histories of different peoples continually bump up against each other; where trade and culture, great migrations, revolutions, the rise and fall of empires constantly alter the patterns of settlement, belief and identity. Whether standing in a remote Angolan town looking at the ruins of an old Portuguese cinema, watching the British flag being lowered for the last time in Hong Kong, or listening to the Inuit in the Canadian high Arctic recall the stories told by their ancestors of the coming of the white man, I am struck by the connections, both intimate and grand, that are braided through the histories of vastly different peoples.

When asked to write and present *Story of Ireland* for BBC Television and RTE I wanted to describe the role of events beyond our shores in creating the Ireland of today. In recent times the multi-billion euro international bailout highlighted the intermeshing of Ireland's economy with the rest of Europe. This is not to claim the Irish narrative has been entirely directed by outside forces. As those who read this book and watch the television series will see: this is above all the story of Ireland. But that story repeatedly intersects with, and is shaped by, the story of other peoples and nations.

Nothing reduces me to despair more than a vision of Irish history that reduces the debate about the past to a simple paradigm of the Irish versus the English, who was right and who was wrong, as if history could be reduced to a crude morality play. As this book will show, it is not only misleading and reductive but profoundly self-limiting. The real story of Ireland and the Irish is so much bigger.

How can one possibly understand the violence that traumatize Ireland during the Elizabethan era without understanding the passion of the religious wars that devastated Europe in the mid to late sixteenth century? English terror of the Counter Reformation becomes both motive and alibi for atrocities in Ireland. Come forward to the age of revolution in the eighteenth century and witness the impact of the American and French revolutions on Irish political thinking, or three decades later the influence of Daniel O'Connell's mass political movement on a generation of European reformers, including the English Chartists.

In America the Scots–Irish community would help to frame the American constitution and give the new United States one of its most famous presidents, Andrew Jackson, the son of Presbyterian immigrants from Ulster, who went on to lead America in a war against Britain. Jackson's bitterness against the British, stemming from the Revolutionary War, was as vivid as anything expressed by the Catholic enemies of the king.

In the aftermath of the Famine of 1845–8 Catholic migrants became one of the largest populations in the cities of America's east coast. In New York, at the famous Cooper Union, a building synonymous with great American political rhetoric, the Irish who had arrived as ragged peasants a decade before were commanding large audiences, and the attention of the *New York Times*, for their rallies against British rule in Ireland.

By the middle of the 1850s there were more Irish living in New York than in Dublin, and they brought with them the techniques learned in Daniel O'Connell's campaigns, creating the machine politics that helped the Democratic Party control many of the country's major cities. A century later this community would also provide one of the most notable American presidents of modern times, John Fitzgerald Kennedy.

In the modern age we can see how the Anglo-Boer war, World War I, and the advent of the European Community in the aftermath of World War II, would all play a part in making the Ireland of today. The most dramatic event of recent modern history – the attack on the Twin Towers in New York on 11 September, 2001 – changed utterly the international environment in which militant nationalism operated. After that, any lingering attachment to the bomb and the gun on the part of Sinn Féin and the IRA became an impossible prospect.

At every turn I took while making the television series I was aware of international connections. The first Irish were people who had come from elsewhere, probably around 8000 BC, part of the great human migrations that first reached Britain, and then crossed the Irish Sea. The elaborate passage tombs they built at Newgrange in County Meath belong to an Atlantic pattern stretching from Spain to Scandinavia; the amber with which Ireland's bronze age jewellery is so beautifully decorated reached the island via a Baltic trading route, perhaps from as far away as eastern Germany or Poland; resin from the Pyrenees was used to style the hair of an Irish king born 2500 years before Christ.

Our ancestors were nomadic peoples with highly developed hierarchies, whose struggle for survival was underpinned by their faith in a spiritual world. They worshipped the gods of nature as they drove their cattle in search of grazing. Along the same routes that brought precious materials such as amber came stories and ideas. Standing in the gloom and damp air of a Newgrange tomb, I heard Dr Gabriel Cooney, one of Ireland's leading archaeologists, describe the information superhighway of 3000 BC.

'I think that, like today, people would have tended to put things in their own context, these early farmers building this monument would probably have had stories of places that were far away, and would have realized how things worked in other areas.' We shared a Celtic culture with peoples in Britain and continental Europe. The Irish Sea witnessed a burgeoning exchange of trade and ideas with the peoples who inhabited Cornwall, Wales and Scotland. It was far easier to sail to a Welsh coastal village from County Wexford, or from the Antrim coast to the Mull of Kintyre than it was to travel from the east to the west of Ireland by foot.

One of the great historical absolutes of my childhood was that because Ireland had never been conquered by the Romans she somehow remained aloof from the changes that radically altered British society. It was Julius Caesar who invented the myth of Hibernia, a land of winter into whose mists civilized men dared not venture. There may have been a self-serving element to this, the future emperor of the Romans justifying his own reluctance to embark on a potentially costly conquest. And while there is no evidence of any large Roman military operation against Ireland, there were plenty of traders willing to ignore the grim warnings and visit Ireland's east coast. Harbours grew up to service the boats that carried Irish leather to clothe the Roman legions. The Irish cattle barons of the plains became rich in the process. As Ned Kelly, keeper of antiquities at the National Museum of Ireland, told me: 'The cattle barons start getting notions of grandeur and they become the important provincial kings of early medieval Ireland. You have the establishment of dynasties at that time, and they continued in power for hundreds of years afterwards. They were looking to model themselves on the Roman emperors.'

The traffic in goods and ideas was a two-way process and the greatest Roman export to Ireland was spiritual. The faith that would come to be seen as an indivisible part of Irish identity was carried across the seas from Roman Britain, where it had become the state religion on the orders of the Emperor Constantine. Through the efforts of saints such as Patrick, Declan of the Decies and a host of others, the Roman faith was spread through the island, creating monastic centres around which faith and commerce could thrive, and where an aesthetic revolution would take place. Scholars came from the continent to be educated at the great monastery of Clonmacnoise in County Westmeath.

The exquisite *Leabhar Gabhaile* – the Book of Invasions – is an example of the artistic and literary magnificence that emerged from the scriptoria of the Irish monasteries. This seventh-century account of the roots of the Irish weaves us into the stories of the ancient world and emphatically, and with considerable self-satisfaction, concludes that the Irish are a people of many origins, the best possible combination of numerous peoples! The Book of Invasions fuses legends, oral history, biblical stories and no end of vivid imagination to create an overarching myth of Irish origin. Its historical significance is what it reveals about how our ancestors saw their place in the world: they did not see themselves as cut off, or insignificant, and they were confident of their identity.

That cultural confidence would be challenged by the Vikings in the nineth century, and by the Normans two hundred years later. I travelled to Normandy and to Norway to understand the dynamics that had propelled the invaders towards Irish shores. It is too tempting to see them in familiar stereotype, as the demons who prowled the texts of our primary school history lessons, violent louts who despoiled our land of saints and scholars. They were certainly all of that, but there was more to these rough warriors than rapine and pillage.

It is also worth remembering that the lot of the Irish peasant varied little whether it was a Gaelic, Viking or Norman boot upon his neck. Warring Irish kings inflicted hideous damage on the monastic settlements, and monasteries themselves went to war over the control of land. In one notable battle between the monks of Clonfert and Cork there was, according to the Irish annals, 'an innumerable slaughter for the ecclesiastical men and superiors of Cork'.

Labelling the Vikings or Normans as evil foreigners is poor history. How much more fascinating to journey into the world that made them, and to see their descent on Ireland as a process inspired by the imperatives of their own societies. In the snow-dusted fjords of the Norwegian autumn, I met Professor Jon Sigerdsson of the University of Oslo, who described a Viking society straining under economic pressures in the sixth and seventh centuries AD. As one of the world's foremost experts on Viking culture, he believes a lack of resources in Norway, and the ingrained Norse habit of wanting to be better than the next man, helped inspire the attacks on Ireland.

'The Vikings loved to compete. They competed about almost anything. Who could travel the furthest, who was the bravest in battle, who could eat the most and who drank the most. Competition was actually the key element in this society, so it was important for the local chieftain or the petty kings to be able to give good gifts to their followers and friends, or to throw big parties. But there was not a lot of wealth in Norway so I think that one of the main reasons they actually left for Ireland was just to plunder some Irish monasteries and churches, steal the goods and bring them back to Norway.' These Vikings changed their spots with the passing of years, becoming traders and settlers, establishing Ireland's most important cities and ports, and becoming entangled in the power struggles of Irish kings. Near my home village of Ardmore in County Waterford lies the fishing port of Helvick Head. Driving there last summer with a Swedish friend, I noticed a look of puzzlement on her face.

'Why do you have a Scandinavian village name here?' she asked. 'You know it "means where the rocks come down to the water"?'

'The Vikings settled that place,' I replied. She was genuinely astonished. Lest anybody think we Irish are alone in often failing to grasp the international dimension to our history, my friend, an educated woman who grew up in a fishing village that had likely been founded by Vikings, knew nothing of the impact of her ancestors. Other Norsemen would found the mighty kingdom of Normandy. These iron-clad warriors, who developed the use of cavalry to humble armies as far away as Sicily, would impose their will on the English and the Irish.

With the arrival of the Anglo–Normans came a long conquest that ushered in a new language, system of laws, parliament, the division of the land into thirty-two counties, and a reshaping of the landscape into the patchwork pattern of fields we see today. As Norman knights became Irish dynasts, the relationship with the local Gaelic chiefs changed; for all their immense power on the battlefield and the scope of their political and cultural influence, the Anglo–Normans could never feel entirely confident of their identity, hence the laws, described in detail in this book, aimed at achieving separation between Gael and settler. In crude terms there would never, with the exception of the Ulster plantation, be enough settlers to achieve a complete cultural separateness. Even in Ulster, some similarities between the world of the Scots settlers and that of the native Irish were inevitable, given the long history of trade and migration between the northeast part of Ireland and Scotland, and the dependence of the planters on native labour supply.

As a child growing up in the Republic of Ireland, I was aware that I lived on a divided island. I knew that three of my grandparents received pensions from the State for their service in the IRA during the fight against the British between 1919–1922, and that after that conflict they had taken the side of Michael Collins in the civil war. It was only later that I became aware of the complex nature of familial attachments and allegiances. My paternal great-grandfather, whose son had fought for the IRA, spent his life as a loyal servant of the British Empire. Sergeant Patrick Hassett joined the Royal Irish Constabulary from a poor farming family in County Clare and served all over Ireland, including Belfast, before retiring on the king's pension. He died in 1921, just as his son took up arms against the empire.

The stories I was told as a child cast the struggle with the British in a manichaean framework. My heroes were Cúchulainn and Patrick Pearse, and I saw the ancient Celtic warrior and the modern revolutionary as part of an unbroken chain of resistance to foreign invasion. One of my earliest recollections is of the great parade through Dublin on the fiftieth anniversary of the 1916 rebellion.

My memories of that particular day survive as a handful of images. Somewhere beyond the heads of the crowd a band was playing. I begged my father to lift me up so that I could see what was happening. As I was borne on to his shoulders, I saw soldiers marching past and the music became louder. There were lines of old men with medals on the opposite side of the street. I remember that they all seemed to be wearing hats.

I was five years old, so I have no recollection at all of what my father might have said, how he would have explained the scene to me. It would be several years before I discovered that he had brought me to witness the fiftieth anniversary celebration of the Easter Rising of 1916. Looking back from the vantage point of the twenty-first century, from an Ireland traumatized by financial crisis and loss of economic sovereignty, it is difficult to convey the great surge of patriotic sentiment inspired by the anniversary.

As an old schoolteacher of mine, Bean Ui Cleirigh, put it: 'We all felt as if we were walking two feet taller, as if we really had taken our place on the stage of nations.' Bean Ui Cleirigh was the kindly headmistress of a school founded by the sisters of Patrick Pearse, the most famous of the rebel leaders executed by the British. We were taught through the medium of Irish, and the history we learned stressed the sufferings of the Irish and their ultimate triumph over the foreign invaders. We had also been visited at school by the President, Éamon de Valera, a veteran of 1916, who only escaped execution because he had been born in America.

Now it is possible to see that great celebration of revolution as a ceremonial coda to the story of the revolutionary generation. The Ireland de Valera had known and that he had devoted his life to shaping was changing rapidly. International Ireland had been reborn. The soldiers I watched marching down O'Connell Street on that Easter Sunday in 1966 belonged to an army that had recently taken part in its first United Nations missions; the Catholic Church in Ireland, so long the bastion of conservative clergy, was experiencing the effects of the liberalizing agenda of Pope John XXIII and his Second Vatican Council; the economy was expanding under the leadership of a former revolutionary turned technocrat Seán Lemass, who had replaced the ageing and nearly blind de Valera in 1959; and the country had applied to join the European Economic Community, precursor to the European Union.

My father was a romantic nationalist. His was the Ireland of lost battles and sad poems, of martyred heroes like Theobald Wolfe Tone and Robert Emmet. He recited stories of Cúchulainn and the Knights of the Red Branch to me at bedtime, and as an actor he won awards for his television portrayals of rebel heroes. Yet for all his attachment to the Ireland of martyrs he welcomed the change. The Ireland of 1966 was noticeably more self-confident and outward looking than the country in which he had grown up. My father was born in the immediate aftermath of a civil war in which an estimated 4000 people were killed, a conflict characterized by fratricidal atrocity and bitterness that of which endured well into my own generation. He came to adulthood during the economic stagnation, strict religiosity and cultural claustrophobia that permeated the newly independent Irish State. Eamonn Keane was ten years old when, on St Patrick's Day 1935, President de Valera spoke on radio to remind his people that as well as being Gaelic, 'since the coming of St Patrick, Ireland has been a Christian and a Catholic nation, she remains a Catholic nation'. Of this single-identity nation the poet Louis MacNeice, an Ulster Protestant, witheringly observed:

> *Let the school-children fumble their sums in a half-dead language;*
> *Let the censor be busy on the books; pull down the Georgian slums;*
> *Let the games be played in Gaelic.*[1]

But MacNeice was clear-eyed and objective enough to recognize that in Unionist-ruled Ulster there existed another land of small horizons.

Free speech nipped in the bud,
The minority always guilty.
Why should I want to go back
To you, Ireland, my Ireland?
The blots on your page are so black
That they cannot be covered with shamrock.

MacNeice published his great poem 'Autumn Journal' in 1940 as Europe was convulsed by war. His bitter tone needs to be understood in the context of its time. MacNeice nurtured the anguish of the exiled intellectual for whom Ireland represented both a prison and an inspiration. In this respect he followed a tradition of exiled Irish writers, including Samuel Beckett and James Joyce; indeed, the latter famously wrote of Ireland as 'the old sow that eats her farrow'.

For MacNeice the imagination needed distance if it were to be unfettered. Yet Ireland and its preoccupations followed him. He believed that the Irish, north and south, had become trapped in a narrative of atavistic slogans: 'A Nation Once Again' or 'No Surrender'. Identity was defined in ever narrowing circles of Catholic or Protestant, nationalist or loyalist, Irish or British. Take your pick according to tribe. The debate about an Irishness that might transcend such proscribed identities or even be a mixture of them, or a view of identity that might at least embrace the complexities of our history, was a long way into the future. The ground has widened now, the shrill voices of certainty are less voluble, but it is still a painstaking work in progress.

Earlier I described Irish internationalism as something 'reborn'. In fact the period of our isolation from the mainstream of world affairs was comparatively short, and it was almost overwhelmingly a psychological rather than a physical drawing inwards, beginning for both northern and southern states after 1922, and continuing in the south until the arrival of Lemass as taoiseach in 1959. My own speculation, based on my experience of other war-ravaged nations, is that the men who took over the twenty-six counties of the Irish Free State after the civil war were, besides being inherently conservative, too exhausted by the physical and moral cost of the conflict to have a vision that extended beyond creating stability and balancing the books. The country was broken, the bitterness coursed through every political debate, and the people could justifiably wonder what freedom had brought them.

Yet even in that period, Ireland was not isolated on the international stage. The Free State government was actively engaged in the politics of the British Commonwealth, and even during World War II, Irish neutrality did not mean the country was entirely unaware or untouched by the great catastrophe unfolding across the seas. After the declaration of a republic in 1949, the country pursued an assertively independent foreign policy, gaining UN membership in 1955 and upsetting her American allies by declaring support for Chinese membership of the UN. During this period, Irish towns and villages witnessed the departure of hundreds of thousands of people for Britain and America. But when these emigrants returned on holiday visits they brought accounts of other worlds and ways of living. Along with the celebrated 'American parcel' and its flashy ties, button-down-collar shirts and loud check trousers, came uncles and aunts who described tantalizing freedoms in the cities across the ocean.

For all the efforts of the censors, the customs men could not search every bag or blockade the ships and planes that brought in books that were morally dubious in the eyes of the Church or the 'Committee on Evil Literature' established by the government in 1926. Nor could the likes of Archbishop John Charles McQuaid of Dublin, a self-appointed moral conscience of the nation, stifle the minds of writers such as Flann O'Brien (Brian O'Nolan), whose comic masterpieces included *An Beal Bocht* (*The Poor Mouth*, 1941), a merciless satire written in Irish about stereotypes of native misery and the Gaelic language ideologues whom the writer loathed. A representative sequence involves a Gaelic revivalist from Dublin addressing the country folk at a festival.

Gaels! It delights my Gaelic heart to be here today speaking Gaelic with you at this Gaelic feis in the centre of the Gaeltacht. May I state that I am a Gael. I'm Gaelic from the crown of my head to the soles of my feet… If we're truly Gaelic, we must constantly discuss the question of the Gaelic revival and the question of Gaelicism. There is no use in having Gaelic, if we converse in it on non-Gaelic topics. He who speaks Gaelic but fails to discuss the language question is not truly Gaelic in his heart; such conduct is of no benefit to Gaelicism because he only jeers at Gaelic and reviles the Gaels. There is nothing in this life so nice and so Gaelic as truly true Gaelic Gaels who speak in true Gaelic Gaelic about the truly Gaelic language.

In *The Hard Life* (1961) O'Brien reflected on, among other things, Irish piety and the lack of a proper public toilet for women in central Dublin. One of the principal figures is a sanctimonious German Jesuit by the name of Father Kurt Fahrt, who is taunted throughout by the fractious figure of Mr Collopy, who believes the matter of proper facilities for women should be placed before the pope in Rome. It is anarchic, surreal and brave, and belonged to a decidedly European post-modernist tradition.

The pace of change accelerated throughout the 1960s and 1970s. Television had arrived in 1961, the same year I was born. Until then, dissent was articulated by a comparatively small intellectual elite whose views rarely reached beyond a limited audience. But the cultural commissars of the republic could not control the flow of debate on television and radio.

I did not grow up in the tyrannical isolation of General Franco's Spain, and was part of the first Irish generation that could travel widely simply for the 'experience' as distinct from economic necessity. I recall the pride of seeing Van Morrison – who embraces British and Irish identities – walk on to a stage in America and be greeted for what he was: one of the great figures of twentieth-century music.

The sense of coming from an 'international island' was something I experienced in ways both profound and seemingly trivial: the victory of the singer Dana in the Eurovision Song Contest in 1970; the importation of American blues to Cork city by *our* local guitar legend, Rory Gallagher; the arrival of the first non-white pupils at my school later in the mid 1970s. They had come on scholarships organized by Irish missionary brothers, who had gone to the West Indies during the heyday of British imperialism. Our headmaster, Brother Jerome Kelly, was one of the most far-sighted men I have known. He went to the West Indies as a missionary, having grown up on a poor farm in one of the most remote parts of Ireland, a place in which I doubt a black or brown face was ever seen.

Brother Kelly witnessed the decline of British colonialism and taught many of the boys who would go on to become prime ministers and chief justices under the new dispensation. He returned determined to encourage in his Irish pupils an attitude of openness. Although a proud Irish nationalist himself, he was too clever and had seen too much of the world to live or teach according to slogans. He hired men who would challenge our preconceptions. Among them was a warm, and occasionally fiery, history teacher, Declan Healy, who spoke beautiful Irish and caused our heads to spin with his gift for asking troubling questions. On one occasion Healy challenged his class with the proposition that Sir Edward Carson, the Ulster loyalist leader and pet hate of Irish nationalists, was in fact an Irish patriot. As he reminded me recently: 'I remember one kid saying, "Sir that doesn't make any sense." I said, "How do you mean that doesn't make any sense?" I said, "Carson wanted the union of Ireland and Britain, he wanted what for him was the best thing for Ireland. Now can you say that he's not a patriot because he doesn't agree with you?" I was trying to do that kind of thing, it was a bit awkward and sometimes you'd be afraid they might use it as answers to questions in examinations and find themselves in trouble. But as I always said, we'll have a go.'

*

Those words, 'we'll have a go', came back to me throughout this journey into history. Trying to tell the story of thousands of years in five hours of television was a daunting task. Yet it was easily one of the most rewarding journeys I have undertaken in my career. I have always yearned for stories that challenge the way I see the world and that turn my own prejudices on their head. The *Story of Ireland* told in this book and in the television series is far more than a recitation of old battles. But I have to acknowledge the impact of war as a motive in wanting to tell the Irish story. The lesson I learned from covering the wars of Africa, the Balkans and the Middle East is that the greatest single cause of conflict is our fear of the other, of 'them'. Fear that they will rise up and kill us; fear that they will take our jobs; fear that they will erase our identity, that we will be eradicated entirely as a people or forced to become like 'them'.

In Portadown, County Armagh, I was once told by a loyalist demonstrator that he would like to see 'you and all your bloody priests on top of a bonfire'. I was happy that the presence of the police prevented his aspiration becoming tangible. To this man my southern accent and name marked me as the enemy. I represented a threat to his home and his sense of himself as a Protestant subject of the Queen. He knew nothing of my history and I, at that time, could see him only as a cartoon character, the walk-on bigot in a drama from the seventeenth century.

Soon afterwards I was posted permanently to Northern Ireland and I covered the conflict day in and day out. I also read every book I could on the history of the previous four centuries, and I made it my business to talk with nationalists and unionists and, above all, to listen. The world that had seemed so simple from the other side of the border turned out to be a very complicated place indeed. I learned, slowly and at times painfully, the virtue of trying to put oneself in the other man's shoes, and of looking beyond rhetoric to the history that made him. If the telling of history, for nationalists and unionists, for Irish and British, is a mere matter of computing wrongs in the hope of a final moral victory, then we miss the point entirely. The story must be a means to greater understanding.

Perhaps this idea is best expressed in a poem written by a good friend of mine, Michael Longley, an insightful and civilized voice throughout the years of the Troubles. In the best tradition of outward-looking Irish writers, Longley reaches across the oceans and draws from the classical tradition for a work he wrote to commemorate the IRA ceasefire of 1994. In the poem 'Ceasefire' Longley evokes the death of Hector at the hand of Achilles before Troy, and the visit to the victor's tent by King Priam, father of Hector.

Put in mind of his own father and moved to tears
Achilles took him by the hand and pushed the old king
Gently away, but Priam curled up at his feet and
Wept with him until their sadness filled the building.

Taking Hector's corpse into his own hands, Achilles
Made sure it was washed and, for the old king's sake,
Laid out in uniform, ready for Priam to carry
Wrapped like a present home to Troy at daybreak.

When they had eaten together, it pleased them both
To stare at each other's beauty as lovers might,
Achilles built like a god, Priam good-looking still
And full of conversation, who earlier had sighed:

'I get down on my knees and do what must be done
And kiss Achilles' hand, the killer of my son.'

Fergal Keane, 2011

PROLOGUE

The human history of Ireland begins very late in European terms: humans first appeared there a mere ten thousand years ago, in the wake of the last ice age. These first settlers may have come from western France or Iberia, hugging the curving European coastline before making a final jump north and west. Or they may have crossed the narrow North Channel from Britain: indeed, some of the earliest evidence of human activity in the island has been uncovered in the northeast of the Country at Mount Sandel on the banks of the river Bann in what is now County Derry. Here, archaeologists have discovered mute testimony – in the form of charcoal and ash, salmon bones and the hazelnut shells that are ubiquitous features of these early sites – of a mesolithic culture dating back to 7000 BC. Similar sites have been excavated across the island: an aerial view reveals a wealth of other artificial ripples and furrows in the landscape, all of them silent but eloquent memorials of nameless and untraceable ancestors.

These first settlers were far from static. They were beginning to trade, to travel, to explore the land and exploit its rich resources: venturing across to what is now Scotland, for example, to barter hides and their superior hard flint for seed, cattle and other novelties that would transform their home surroundings. At the same time, the dense forests that succeeded the ice ages began to be hacked away for firewood, to provide access to grazing land on the bald uplands and to carve out small fields in which the first primitive strains of rye, oats and especially barley were grown. More newcomers came, and more, as a result of these contacts between this society and the world outside, slowly but unceasingly feeding new ingredients and genes into the Irish scene: and as the mesolithic age passed into the neolithic, so levels of sophistication rose in agriculture, in pottery and sculpture and in science.

And in architecture: for these are the ancestors that began, definitively, to leave a built legacy across the island. In what is now the windswept and bleak littoral of north County Mayo, for example, lies that patchwork of tombs, dwellings and ancient stone-walled agricultural land called the Céide Fields, which were grazed by cattle and planted with cereal crops five thousand years ago when the climate was a good deal warmer than it is today. It was only by flukes of climate change that this landscape came to be covered in a thick, pickling layer of peat bog that preserved it for posterity; there is no reason, therefore, to think that what was accomplished in Mayo was not equally undertaken elsewhere. Or take the remarkable megalithic monuments that began to appear at this time too, of which the astronomically aligned passage tombs at Newgrange, Dowth and Knowth on the bend of the river Boyne in County Meath remain the most famous.

Later, metals were fashioned into shapes beautiful and practical: smiths worked bronze into tools, horns and ornaments for the country's elite; and gold into fabulous collars, torcs, necklaces and bracelets. A model boat fashioned in pure gold – 'that small boat out of the bronze age / Where the oars are needles and the worked gold frail / As the intact half of a hollowed-out shell'[1] – was an element in the Broighter Hoard, stored carefully in a wooden box and unearthed by a farmer ploughing his fields on the shores of Lough Foyle in 1896. Human history, then, began to unfold and to score itself on to the land – but a modern map of the island is equally impressed with traces of a parallel mythical past: the modern cathedral city of Armagh that is named for the goddess Macha; Faughart in County Louth where the hero Cúchulainn accomplished his mighty deeds; the hexagonal stones of the Giant's Causeway in County Antrim that geologists surmise were forged by volcanic action millions of years ago, but that myth declares to be the work of supernatural hands.

History and myth have thus been much mingled, and the result is that the story of this pre-Christian land is still the subject of a good deal of conjecture. Of course, tales handed down from generation to generation can preserve a version of history that would otherwise be utterly lost – especially when dealing with oral cultures that leave few or no written records for posterity. In this case, tales of invasions of the island by the Milesians of Iberia and other mythical entities seem to glimpse an ancient past, when repeated waves of new settlers came from over the sea. Such events were not formal military expeditions as we would understand the term, but they had immediate cultural and political implications on the island itself: it was divided and divided again among various groups and tribes, in a pattern that would continue well into the Christian era. These later migrations, however, did not erase the earlier, culturally sophisticated societies already established. Persistence and consistency characterize this island's history – and these earliest human civilizations were no less dogged in this regard than their successors would prove to be. Rather, it is much more likely that newcomers, discovering as they did a country already settled, adapted their old ways to the new land. In the process, they added both their genes and – more immediately usefully – their own layers of vital cultural experience to an increasingly complex society. And as the centuries passed, so the population of the island slowly rose: by 700 BC, it may have risen above the one hundred thousand mark.

By the fourth century BC, Ireland had appeared on maps of the classical world. Although the Carthaginians had long maintained a blockade of the Strait of Gibraltar, the better to maintain control of their trading routes, at least one mariner managed to dodge the patrolling ships and sail north and west in search of the tin and other metals that formed the wealth of the western islands. The navigator and cartographer Pythias of Massilia – modern Marseilles, but originally a Greek colony – named the far-flung island Ierne, a name clearly derived from Ériu, the Irish matron goddess. Three hundred years later, as Julius Caesar swept through Gaul and landed in Britain, the name had been Latinized: the Romans unflatteringly knew the island that hovered just over the western horizon as Hibernia, land of winter. They gradually accumulated all the knowledge they needed about this Hibernia, as with all the territories that fringed their empire: ample evidence exists, in the form of Roman coins and material goods, that imperial scouts and traders crossed the water in search of butter, cattle and Irish wolfhounds; and that Roman merchants and enterprising tourists fetched up in the valley of the river Boyne to marvel at the already ancient tombs. Conversely, Hibernian contacts with Britain and further afield, in search of gold, wine and agricultural produce, were equally common and ongoing. Roman control of its province of Britain was never as deeply rooted and all-encompassing as has sometimes been supposed – Romano–British towns were invariably walled, in sharp contrast to the situation in, say, Gaul and Spain – and it is reasonable to assume that repeated Hibernian incursions in search of booty and slaves were one good reason for this state of affairs.

But this land of Ierne or Hibernia was only ever of marginal economic and strategic interest: there was never enough at stake to make a Roman invasion worthwhile. Only once, in AD 82, do we have a fascinating glimpse of a moment in history when a decisive Roman intervention might have been possible. The historian Tacitus describes an embassy in that year in the form of a Hibernian princeling, 'expelled from his home by a rebellion', who sailed across the water to Roman Britain. The intentions of this prince were to negotiate with Agricola, the all-conquering Roman governor of Britain (and father-in-law to Tacitus himself, which is why we know so much about him), who maintained a fleet in the Solway Firth, less than a day's sail from the northeast coast of Hibernia. He 'was welcomed by

Agricola, who detained him, nominally as a friend, in the hope of being able to make use of him'.[2] The embassy, in other words, would have provided a convenient pretext to enter and conquer Hibernia, had the political will been present.

The identity of this petty king has never been established, but some of the recurring themes of our story are set at this point. The first is of the disenfranchised or otherwise put-upon exile seeking foreign aid – with potentially momentous consequences. The second is of a relationship between the two islands that is already close and mutually significant. 'I have often heard Agricola say,' Tacitus remarked, 'that Hibernia could be reduced and held by a single legion … and that it would be easier to hold Britain if it were completely surrounded by Roman armies so that liberty was banished from its sight.'[3] But Agricola was diverted by rebellion in Scotland and his alternative invasion plans were shelved – for good, as it turned out: Hibernia may have been clearly visible from points on the coast of Roman Britain, but the empire's legions would never cross the sea in force.

By the fourth century, Roman control of Britain was visibly waning and Irish influences began to increase in potency. Although these contacts continued to take the form of pillaging, skirmishes and slaving raids, there were also sustained attempts at planting communities along the western seaboard of Britain. Such settlements were made in Cornwall, in west Wales and later in Dál Ríata, a long-enduring and politically successful kingdom straddling the narrow waters of the North Channel; the existence of such colonies underscores the sense that the seas at this time were as much highways as barriers to movement. These increasing contacts, of course, also impacted profoundly on the situation at home: goods and materials seized or traded in Roman Britain were carried back across the sea, helping to effect shifts of balance on the domestic scene.

This was an intensely hierarchical society. The country's many tribal kings were at the top of the structure, while grinding poverty without hope of betterment was the lot of the landless serfs at the bottom. There was no state, nor anything resembling it, in this politically fragmented land of *túatha* or petty kingdoms and endlessly fluctuating borders. Neither was there a firm division of the country into larger units: the provincial pentarchy of Ulster, Munster, Leinster, Connacht and Meath might have been in existence at certain periods in history, but was certainly not a constant presence in political affairs. The nearest the country came to a degree of unity was in its structure of federations of *túatha* that had submitted to the authority of an overlord – and such federations were apt to change all the time. By the fifth century AD, when a documented history of the island begins, the forms of the modern provinces of Munster and Connacht were more or less recognizable, but those of the others were not: Laigin in the southeast occupied a much smaller territory than the modern province of Leinster; the ancient dynasty of the Ulaid ruled over a now-shrunken kingdom in the north and east of modern Ulster; and the northern and southern branches of the Uí Néill dynasty governed a wide and fluctuating area that stretched from the fertile eastern plains to the island's rugged northwestern tip.

Power was concentrated in the hands of a number of dynasties, flowing down from a king or patriarch into the rest of society. Emphasis, in this oral culture, was placed upon learning: poets and scholars were the conservators of tradition and convention. And so, in spite of the enduring rivalry between these kingdoms, Ireland was not characterized by anarchy: this society was abidingly conservative, its members tending to know their place in a complex and carefully calibrated scheme of things. Life was ordered by dense mazes of laws: these were extraordinarily pervasive and covered every issue under the sun, from marriage, murder and inheritance rights through to the perils and minutiae of beekeeping; the system was collated and written down after the arrival of Christianity heralded the shift from an oral to a written culture. As for the sense of political fragmentation, here too the roots of a larger collectivity could be discerned – and so the political disunity of these years ought not to be equated with the absence of a shared, if nebulous, identity. After all, it is significant that the Gaelic word for a province is *cúige*, meaning a fifth – and the presence of a fifth implies the existence of a whole.

PART ONE

GODS AND WARRIORS

CHAPTER ONE

CHILDREN OF GOD

How wonderful it is that here in Ireland a people who never had any knowledge of God – who until now have worshipped idols and impure things – have recently become a people of the Lord and are now called children of God. You can see that the sons and daughters of Irish kings have become brothers and virgins for Christ.[1]

According to the legends, Christianity first arrived in Ireland on a spring night in AD 433. The pagan high king Laoghaire (Lóegaire) had ascended the hill of Tara, and now he stood on its summit, surrounded by druids and vassals. His task was to light the sacred fire of Beltane, which would usher in summer, and the ancient law dictated that no fire could be lit on this feast day before that of the king himself. But suddenly, on the hill of Slane nearby, a flame flared in the darkness and the old codes were in a moment exploded. The druids pleaded with Laoghaire to 'extinguish this flame or it will burn forever'; and, hastening through the spring twilight to Slane, they found on the summit of the hill the man called Patrick. An epic battle of magic followed, during which Patrick lifted a druid into the air and dashed his brains out; and in the aftermath of the newcomer's victory, the fearful Laoghaire saw the truth: 'It is better that I should believe,' he said, 'than die.' On Easter Day the high king converted to Christianity; and at Tara, Patrick set about converting all the chieftains of Ireland in their turn.

It is a captivating tale: and it sweeps the national saint, endowed with unprecedented power and authority, to the centre of the stage of Irish history. Yet, for all that it mingles legend with the rhythms of pagan Ireland, it pays scant attention to the historical reality – for Patrick was not in fact responsible for carrying Christianity across the Irish Sea. This new religion had taken root well in advance of his ministry: certainly an established Christian community existed in the south and east of Ireland as early as the last decades of the fourth century. This early Christian community did not exist in isolation: indeed, with the Pelagian heresy posing a substantial threat throughout much of Europe, the doctrinal wellbeing of the Church in Ireland, as elsewhere, was a pressing issue for the papacy itself.* In 431, then, the first Christian bishop was dispatched by Rome to Ireland – and his name was not Patrick. The theologian St Prosper of Aquitaine records the event: 'to the Irish believing in Christ, Palladius, having been ordained by Pope Celestine, is sent as first bishop'.[2]

Few details are known about this first bishop or his visit to Ireland. Palladius – most likely a Briton or Gaul of aristocratic background – made landfall on the coast of what is now County Wicklow, and most of his time in Ireland was spent ministering in this corner of the country: he is traditionally associated with Baltinglass, where he is said to have deposited his writing tablet, together with certain relics of St Peter and St Paul. His stay was of no great duration – within three years he had moved on to Scotland – and though his mission was symbolically important, it has essentially vanished from the Irish collective memory. Palladius's successor, by contrast, has attained an iconic presence in Irish history – though the irony is that precious few hard facts exist about the life and times of either man. As we shall see, however, the championing of Patrick and erasure of Palladius from the story of Ireland came about largely for reasons of political expediency.

---

* The Pelagian model posited that humankind was born without original sin, and was therefore capable of attaining grace without the need of Divine intervention.

Much of what is known about Patrick derives from his own writings, which provide a number of insights into his character but – since they were never written as autobiography – hardly any into his movements and travels. In the centuries that followed, other historians made various claims and assertions – and as a result, we come to Patrick as through a thicket of half-truth, myth and falsehood to discover that he was born (it is not known exactly when) into a well-off Romanized family in a small trading town somewhere in western Britain (it is not known exactly where); and that he grew up comfortably enough amid the growing decay and fragmentation of the Roman world. Although the remnants of the Roman province of Britain had by now Christianized, this young man was certainly not in close communion with God. He had already committed a misdemeanour frequently referred to but frustratingly unspecified throughout his writings: it was perhaps a sexual crime or had something to do with the sin of idolatry. Patrick had received the bare bones of an education: although he could read and write in Latin, he lacked that polished grounding in philosophy and the classics that many of his male peers might have enjoyed. Just short of his sixteenth birthday, however, Patrick's life would take an unexpected and violent turn.

The Irish Sea had long been considered not as a barrier between Ireland and the outside world, but rather as a highway; and the established Irish settlements in west Wales, southwest Scotland and Cornwall enabled commodities and ideas to flow easily both east into Britain and west into Ireland. Some of these commodities were human: indeed, it seems likely that among the first Christians in Ireland were slaves taken in Irish raids on the increasingly undefended British coast. The adolescent Patrick was captured by one such party of slavers, torn from his comfortable provincial surroundings and brought to Ireland. This, he notes in his *Confession*, was no more than he deserved: 'we had abandoned God and did not follow his ways ... so God poured out his anger on us and scattered us among the hordes of barbarians who live at the edge of the world'.[3] He spent the next six years herding animals – most likely in what is now County Mayo – and here both his destiny and his relationship with God were sealed:

> *After I came to Ireland I watched over sheep. Day by day I began to pray more frequently – and more and more my love of God and my faith in him and reverence for him began to increase. My spirit was growing, so that each day I would say a hundred prayers and almost as many each night, even during those times when I had to stay overnight in the woods or mountains. I would get up each morning before sunrise to pray, through snow and frost and rain. No harm came to me because of it, and I was certainly not lazy. I see now looking back that my spirit was bursting inside me.*[4]

Eventually the young Patrick escaped, got on board a ship and fled Ireland, prevailing upon a pagan crew (who grumbled but happily soon came to their senses) to return him to his home in Britain. The heathen Irish, however, continued to be present in his thoughts; eventually he resolved to return there as a missionary – a move that was very much against the wishes of his family. His plans were also opposed by the local clerical establishment, which did not altogether approve of the idea of evangelizing in what was still a partially pagan society; Patrick was even accused of harbouring base financial motives. Nor was he free of other, private anxieties: in particular, his relatively uneducated status in relation to undertaking such a task is referred to throughout his *Confession*.

He certainly faced daunting challenges in Ireland – not least because Christianity so firmly denied the existence of other gods. It was for this reason that later writers were at pains to demonstrate Patrick's authority over his pagan enemies: it was only by smashing, humiliating and generally vanquishing them that he could repeatedly prove the authority of his God over all other gods. In some ways, though, the Christian mission resonated: pre-Christian devotion was characterized by, for example, the worship of gods in groups of three, by sayings collected in threes (triads), and so on – from all of which the concept of the Holy Trinity was not so very far removed. Against this backdrop the myth of Patrick and his three-leafed shamrock fits quite neatly. The concept of heaven and hell also struck a chord, given that pre-Christian Ireland had a deep and constant sense of communion with an invisible other world.

The new religion's central image – the crucified Christ who had sacrificed himself for the common good – would have meant much to a society where human sacrifice was still practised. The warrior caste in particular must have found such symbolism appealing; and the saints and missionaries of the early Church were recast as 'warriors for Christ' with relative ease. But Patrick's message was also directed explicitly at those who were marginalized in society: at the young and especially at women, who had little enough to gain from preserving a status quo in which they had no independent rights of their own. Certainly, many women in his following – including members of the nobility – took the veil, and in the process handed over their precious things to enrich the Church. Given that females were themselves viewed as commodities, to be married off in whatever way best served their family circle, it is easy to imagine the hostility that a mission such as Patrick's aroused.

The story of his life, however, pivots on the writings of a host of later supporters and hagiographers – and it is largely as a result of these works that he was moulded into a miracle worker and prophet, his story intersecting with that of the heroes of ancient myth. In later centuries, sites scattered across the country took stakes in his life and reputation: his traditional burial place at Downpatrick held a tooth, for example; Dublin possessed the Bachall Íosa or crozier supposedly given to Patrick by Christ himself; and pilgrimage sites at Croagh Patrick and Lough Derg became famous across Europe.

From the very earliest times his life and legacy were being shaped towards specific ends, and this can best be seen in his long-standing association with Ulster. According to tradition, Patrick's ministry was at its most active in the northeast of the country: in particular at Armagh, close to the ancient political centre of Emain Macha (Navan Fort), and at Downpatrick. From the seventh century onward, the ecclesiastical authorities at Armagh were intent on asserting ownership of this saint and his legacy, the better to bolster their claim to supremacy over the Irish Church – and they did not hesitate to resort to invention when the facts of Patrick's life let them down. Parts of the Book of Armagh, for example, were claimed to have been written by Patrick himself – although the earliest passages in the volume in fact date from the ninth century, long after the saint's death. Other sections contain copies of narratives – originally written in the seventh century by the clerics Muirchú and Tírechán – which set out to glorify Patrick and his mission. Yet another section – entitled *Liber angeli*, or the Book of the Angel – describes a celestial messenger proclaiming Patrick's status both as apostle of all the Irish and as first Bishop of Armagh, thus underscoring the monastery's claims to primacy. In the face of this urgent political quest, the less politically relevant story of Palladius was bound to be set aside.

The developing cult of Patrick swept all before it – and yet aspects of the man's personality can still be glimpsed. He was nothing if not worldly: very keen, for example, to emphasize his status as a bishop. Nor did he underplay the dangers he faced as a missionary in a land that was only tentatively opening up to his message: he was physically threatened, and came to understand the importance of 'gifts', or bribes, in smoothing his relationships with a plethora of petty Irish kings. Patrick was a pragmatist, in other words – one of many practical figures and budding politicians who dominated the dangerous world of the early Christian Church. He fully understood the importance of political patronage and of alliance-building with the myriad rulers of each *túath* or small Irish kingdom; an early tradition speaks of Patrick and St Declan of Ardmore, in what is now County Waterford, coming together to select the new king of the region. And Patrick was well matched in this world by these same political rulers, who recognized that the new religion could be turned to other uses. For such tribal kings, the arrival of the new faith held out the prospect of connection with a wider world, with its new ideas and potential for advancement. They could also work in conjunction with the Church to pass laws, legitimize their authority and control the people for their own purposes. The aims and aspirations of Church and local rulers began to fuse.

The new Church ploughed the energy of his supporters into the foundation of churches – hundreds of them, established at local level all over Ireland. These first places of worship may have been very small, simple affairs – buildings of wood or stone that could accommodate no more than a few dozen people – but they were instrumental in maintaining and extending Christian influence: such churches began to form the focus of local identity, their priests able increasingly to wield power over their communities. A machinery of governance thus came gradually into existence, as the Church began the long process of defending and advancing its own aims in a variety of ways.

The physical evidence of a pagan Ireland began to fade and was smoothly absorbed into the new Christian rite. The distinctive aspects of Irish society – its tribal kingship, its clannish culture, the place of the druids, the honoured role of the poet class – were utilized as points of contact between the new religion and the immeasurably old. The result was that a template of new belief was laid upon the ancient one, with results that can still be discerned today. The figure of the Christian patroness Brigit, for example, was grafted on to an older pagan entity – and places of spiritual potency and pilgrimage were similarly recycled and remoulded to a new

Christian use. 'There by dim wells', writes the poet Austin Clarke, 'the women tied/A wish on thorn'[5] – and, indeed, the holy wells and wishing trees that still exist today across the landscape of Ireland offer good examples of such ideological colonization.

Patrick died late in the fifth century, with the Church already deeply rooted in Irish society. The legends of the patron saint's magical duels and miracles have persisted throughout the centuries – but, although this 'most adaptable of saints' has been a consistent focus of propaganda, his material legacy owes little or nothing to spin.[6] Instead, it is a substantial thing in its own right, and Patrick himself emerges as a complex and compelling character: at once a relatively unpolished man of provincial stock, a former slave with an unparalleled insight into the culture of his former captors, a passionate evangelist and a canny political operator who was able to establish foundations of tremendous durability for his Church.

Patrick's status as a foreigner, a newcomer on the Irish cultural scene, moreover, places him within what was already a long-established tradition in Irish culture: one of porousness, of openness to overseas influence – a tradition that sprang from long years of inward migration, travel, and human and economic relationships. In the centuries preceding Patrick's abduction Ireland had already been thoroughly probed, with the Greeks and later the Romans coming to a good understanding of its geographical position, topography, resources and relative worth. Irish exports of butter and cattle were prized; and merchants and entrepreneurs crossed from Gaul and Britain in search of trading opportunities. In the second century the island appears in the *Geographia,* the famous and influential atlas of the world compiled by the Alexandrian scientist and cartographer Ptolemy (Claudius Ptolemaeus). Ptolemy certainly never visited Ireland, but he was able to access the reports of sailors, traders and policymakers that circulated through the Roman Empire; and the island's presence in the *Geographia* signifies its secure place in the Roman imagination.

In their turn, the Irish imported Mediterranean wines, oils and other indicators of ease and luxury; and they slowly absorbed, too, over the centuries, aspects of the culture of the outside world. In so doing, they altered inexorably the history of their own island – a process that finds its apotheosis in the coming of Christianity. As Patrick was setting out on his mission in Ireland, however, this outside world was itself transforming: and, as the Roman Empire imploded in the course of the fifth century, so the Irish began the process of writing a new cultural history – one that would stand the test of time.

The decline of the Roman Empire in the west had been slow, but the end when it came was relatively sudden and shocking: within a century of the first Germanic invasions across the Rhine, Roman civilization was barely a memory; Rome itself had been sacked by Alaric and his Visigoths in August 410. Across the continent of Europe, a patchwork of small feudal kingdoms fought with each other; the citizens of Italy and Gaul were now serfs; and even the Church faced a struggle to survive. The great continental libraries and repositories of knowledge began to decay and literacy to decline, as this epitaph from the bishop historian St Gregory of Tours in the sixth century testifies: 'In these times when the practice of letters declines, no, rather perishes in the cities of Gaul, there has been found no scholar trained in ordered composition to present in prose or verse a picture of the things which have befallen.'[7]

Relatively few written accounts of contemporary life survived these centuries in Europe. In Ireland, however, the cultural tides were running in the opposite direction, as the oral tradition began, from the sixth century onward, to give way to the written word. It was at this time that the most detailed records of everyday life began to be maintained, listing everything from tribal conflict to the weather, from outbreaks of plague and its fatalities to laws, poetry, hymns and prose. And as literacy throve, so too did

Patrick's Irish Church, assisted by its ability to adapt smoothly to local circumstances. Each Irish *túath*, for example, had its own bishop to oversee affairs; these arrangements replaced the structure of dioceses that were the basic building blocks of Church administration in Europe. This differing Irish practice was one of many that would cause persistent grumbles in Rome in the centuries to come. Moreover, these bishops were not, as was the case elsewhere, the ultimate wielders of authority – for in Ireland, final authority lay elsewhere.

From the beginning of the sixth century a network of monasteries began to develop in the Irish countryside, and the abbots that ran them became increasingly powerful figures. The earliest monastic foundations tended at first not to be of the church-and-cloisters model that would appear later, in the Middle Ages. Rather, they would consist of an enclosure with a small stone chapel and a number of cells in which the monks lived individually. By their nature, some were in the most remote areas imaginable: Skellig Michael, for example, which clung to its crag of rock in the stormy Atlantic 20 km (12 miles) off the coast of County Kerry. But other monasteries were rather more worldly: although ostensibly places of retreat from the world, they frequently had ample resources at their disposal. As a result, they attracted the patronage of kings and the wealthy: their abbots became wielders of temporal power in their own right and many lived in the style of the country's temporal rulers, in the midst of wealth and (relative) comfort. Many monasteries also owned great swathes of land, thus controlling the economic destiny of much of the population and providing employment and distributing alms to the inhabitants; the monks of Armagh, for example, had a good deal of land not only in Ulster but across Munster and Meath too.

In the process, these institutions were responsible for a novelty on the Irish scene: prototype towns. After all, a good many hired workers, craftsmen, farmhands and artisans were employed by the monasteries, all of them requiring working and sleeping quarters; there were in addition populations of serfs – little better than slaves – bound to each institution; and as a result, clusters of buildings developed around each site. These settlements would typically contain orchards, beehives, physic gardens and all the paraphernalia of large farms, as well as markets, housing and places of instruction and incarceration. A seventh-century description of the wealthy monastery at Kildare offers an insight into the form and nature of such places:

> And what words are capable of setting forth the very great beauty of this church, and the countless wonders of that monastery which we may call a city [civitas], if it is possible to call a city that which is enclosed by no circle of walls? However, since numberless people congregate within it and since a city acquires its name from the assembly in it of many, this is a very great city and the seat of a metropolitan. No human foe nor enemy onset is feared in its suburbana, the clear boundaries of which the holy Brigit herself marked out. But it (together with all its church lands throughout the whole of Ireland) is the most secure city of refuge for its fugitives. The treasures of the king are kept there...[8]

The fusion between religious and civil authorities in these localities is a theme that would recur throughout Irish history, with the nobility integrating the monastic institutions they established into their royal houses and domains. Each abbot was a powerful figure: as well as being the spiritual father of his monks, he was also the ruler of the community and the heir to the property. Family succession increasingly became the norm, the role of abbot passing to a member of the local ruling family. Such secularization saw certain abbots behaving like petty kings, declaring war on other monastic communities. Over a four-year period, for example, the monks of Clonmacnoise are recorded as going to war with the monasteries at both Birr and Durrow, in the process leaving more than two hundred dead. These conflicts tended to arise not from dry doctrinal dispute but from dynastic quarrels. And tribal connections also meant that monasteries were drawn into larger political conflicts: as the ambitious Uí Néill clan vied with the Ulaid for control of Ulster in the late eight and ninth centuries, so control of the abbacy of Armagh became a key political objective. During this period the rolls recording significant ecclesiastical positions provide a window into a wider political history, reflecting simply and clearly the shifting power balance between the ruling families in a given district of Ireland.

The growth of monasticism also has legal ramifications, as the monks' connections to powerful clans helped bind secular and ecclesiastical law closer together. The educated, literate elite – though by no means always clerics themselves – now invariably received their education in a clerical context, and their world view was shaped accordingly: the law of the land would now be bound up with the law of the Church. The result was the creation of comprehensive legal works such as the *Collectio canonum hiberniensis* (700–750) with its views on everything from property and theft to marriage and inheritance rights. The country's intricate collection of oral laws was now transcribed on to the page, and interpreted through an ecclesiastical prism. At the same time, the pre-Christian world – still so tangible in a newly Christianized Ireland – began to be interpreted and shaped in a different light: it was now regarded as the Old Testament past to a fully enlightened New Testament present.

In these turbulent years the monasteries managed to balance their political and economic roles with a flowering of creativity; and their workshops and dimly lit scriptoria became sites of remarkable industry.

Throughout the country, monks laboured over great manuscripts and books, and many of them rapidly achieved a very high level of scholarship, mastering Greek, Latin and the rudiments of Hebrew. Crucial to this process was the fact that Ireland had never been a part of the Roman Empire: its people had not been systematically Romanized, and Irish culture had therefore preserved ancient history, legend and stories intact. The character of Patrick's distinctively *Irish* Church, moreover, now proved decisive: just as the saint and his followers had been adept at absorbing pagan ritual and feasts into the new Christian canon, so now Irish monks freely and enthusiastically drew on local language and idiom. The first written grammars and alphabet in Irish were devised, the ancient tongue in the process becoming the first written vernacular language in Europe.

By means of these monastic writings, therefore, a literary tradition evolved in Ireland centuries before it appeared elsewhere in Europe. Irish monks transcribed biblical texts and sermons, the Gospels, the Psalms and the lives of saints, before moving on to the great works of late antiquity, including many of the classics from Greek and Latin pagan literature. Ireland's oral tradition now found a new and powerful expression. The sprawling oral epic of the *Táin* – the dramatic tale of the clash between Queen Medb of Connacht and the youthful Cúchulainn, hero of Ulster – was written down for the first time during this period, for example, and became fixed in a way that would have been inconceivable in a non-literate age, when stories would have altered endlessly in the telling. Pagan and Christian narratives, Gospel and heroic tale were thus subjected alike to interpretation and codification, and the legacy of this attention lies in the remarkable illuminated manuscripts produced in these centuries. The seventh-century Book of Durrow and the more famous and 'magnificently comic' Book of Kells that was likely produced on Iona are the most luminous examples – but there are many such, relating Gospel and biblical stories in extravagant and glowing detail.[9]

Such industry has had a profound effect on our understanding of Irish history. Virtually everything written and presented as historical fact under the auspices of the early Christian Church was manufactured, calculated and driven by political and ideological agendas. As we have seen, the monks working in the scriptorium at Armagh were in the business of producing carefully crafted propaganda in order to help their institution gain lasting primacy over the Irish Church. But the clerics of Armagh were not alone in their endeavours. The Church as a whole was intent on convincing potential converts that they were already part of a wider Christian faith; and as a result, its representatives now set about inscribing the Irish into a much greater narrative that encompassed the whole Judaeo-Christian tradition. Turning their attentions to the Book of Genesis, which described the creation of the world, early scribes and clerics noted that it neglected to mention the Irish – so they undertook, as compensation, the formation of a whole new story.

The result was the *Lebor Gabála Érenn*, the Book of the Taking of Ireland, begun around 700 and ranking among the most successful works of propaganda ever produced in the country. Inspired by the biblical history of the Israelites, the narrative recounts the histories of all the peoples who ever settled in Ireland, weaving a new genealogy that stretched all the way back to Noah and in the process establishing the legitimacy and lineage of the Irish people. In connecting these myths of origin to the Old Testament, the *Lebor Gabála Érenn* succeeded in portraying all the Irish dynasties and peoples as descending from a single set of ancestors. This proved to be a powerful and all-pervasive myth: race, language, land and landscape were utilized as the basis for ethnic unity; and Ireland and the Irish were placed on a par with the great classical cultures of the known world.

There was, of course, nothing unusual about the formation of such an origin myth, which was characteristic of any culture wishing to legitimize itself. Rome, for example, did precisely the same thing when its early writers invented a connection with ancient Troy, in the process underpinning a new position of authority within the classical Mediterranean world. In addition, genealogy was central to Irish culture. The role of the *filid* or caste of respected poets was to remember and celebrate the lineage of the king. They were figures to be feared as much as admired: with his power over words, a

poet might damn a miserly or unappreciative noble in the eyes of the world
– and in the process taint his future.

With the evolution of the *Lebor Gabála Érenn*, the monastic order in
Ireland thus demonstrated its ability to shape the world: in reinventing the
past, it might also change the present and influence the future. The monks
could create a great and glorious genealogy, altering their destiny in the
process: the same clerical spin doctors at Armagh who had used the figure
of Patrick to further their own ambitions now became adept at putting
forth their propaganda skills on behalf of their powerful patrons in the Uí
Néill dynasty. Muirchú's *Life* of Patrick had described Lóegaire of the Uí
Néill clan as 'a great king, fierce and pagan, and emperor of the Irish';
Niall, the ancestor of the Uí Néill, was from 'the family that rules almost
all the entire island', invoking the institution of the high kingship; yet
another Uí Néill king would be named as 'ruler of the whole of Ireland
ordained by God'.

The ecclesiastical authorities at Armagh were keen to develop the idea
of an ordained and consecrated king; and they were able to draw on the
Old Testament in their efforts to do so. The Book of Samuel notes that
'Yahweh judges the ends of the earth, he endows his king with power, he
exalts the horn of his anointed'; and the phrase 'ordained by God' occurs
again and again in manuscripts written by clergy connected with the Uí
Néill dynasty, which during this period had steadily expanded its power
base.[10] One result of this process of dynastic ascendancy was that it put
some flesh on the bones of the ancient Uí Néill claim to the high kingship
at Tara. This was a shadowy institution, with little in the way of practical
application – there had never been a king at Tara who was in a position
to govern the entire island – but its symbolic power was naturally envi-
able. The exalted claims made on behalf of the Uí Néill dynasty were by
no means fully reflected in the political situation on the ground; but this
fact was largely irrelevant to the great game being played out. With the

assistance of the powerful clerics at Armagh, the Uí Néill were in it for the long haul.

The first record of a king being crowned in western Europe long predates this phase of activity at Armagh. The coronation was that of Aedán MacGabráin of Dál Ríata in 574, and the monk who consecrated his reign was himself a prince of the Uí Néill clan. He was also a warrior, a poet, a natural historian, a diplomat, a kingmaker, a founder of the monasteries at Derry, Durrow and the Scottish island of Iona, and a thoroughly industrious historical figure; we know him as Columba or Colum Cille (521–97).*

Colum Cille was born at Gartan in what is now County Donegal. Tradition tells us he was named Crimthann or 'Fox'; it was only later, when he entered the monastic life, that he was given the name Colum Cille, 'dove of the Church'. But he was rather more hawk than dove: he left Ireland for Scotland in 563 to found Iona, and it is fairly certain that his part in instigating the bloody battle of Cúl Dreimhne (in what is now County Sligo) was one reason why he abandoned Ireland relatively late in his life. A century later, however, his biographer Adamnán – abbot of Iona and the ninth Uí Néill to succeed Colum Cille as ruler of this powerful and influential monastery – begged to differ, claiming in his *Vita Columbae* ('The Life of Colum Cille') that the saint took to the road to become an exile for the Lord. This *peregrinatio pro amore Dei* was certainly common enough among the more devout Irish monks, who would sever all links with their secular identity and leave their community in order to become born again in Christ: by the ninth century, such monks were fetching up in locations as remote and inhospitable as the Icelandic coast. But Colum Cille did not propose going so far, nor even abandoning his own

---

* In addition to his other activities, Colum Cille is also credited with the sighting (and banishment) of the Loch Ness Monster.

people: Iona, off the west coast of Scotland, was part of the kingdom of Dál Ríata that spanned the narrow seas between Ireland and Scotland – to all intents and purposes, a part of Ireland itself.

The arrival of Colum Cille brought political complications for the rulers of Dál Ríata, who were allied to the ancient rivals of the Uí Néill clan, the Ulaid of northeast Ulster. Once established on Iona, Colum Cille began to bring his considerable diplomatic influence to bear on the situation, not only consecrating MacGabráin as King of Dál Ríata but accompanying the new leader across to Ireland in 575 to a summit conference with the Uí Néill in what is now County Derry. This summit is said to have resulted in a pact binding the Scottish Dál Ríata to the Uí Néill – at the expense, needless to say, of the Ulaid. And, just to ensure that the agreement was duly honoured, Adamnán tells us that Colum Cille prophesied dire disaster to Dál Ríata should the alliance be broken. Adamnán's *Life* is firmly hagiographical: although one takes from it a sense of Colum Cille as a flesh-and-blood individual, the text is manifestly designed to secure the reputation and international fame of its subject:

> *And this great favour also was conferred by God on that man of blessed memory, that, although he lived in this small and remote island of the Britannic ocean* [i.e. Iona], *he merited that his name should not only be industriously renowned throughout our Ireland, and throughout Britain, the greatest of all the islands in the whole world; but that it should reach even as far as three-cornered Spain, and Gaul, and Italy situated beyond the Pennine* [sic] *Alps; also the Roman city itself, which is the chief of all cities.*[11]

In spite of Adamnán's glowing testimony of a Christ-like man who loved children and spoke with the birds and animals, Colum Cille emerges from history as rather more the politician than the saint – and thus very much in keeping with the nature of the Irish Church in this era. Through his extensive federation of Irish monasteries he kept a very close eye on events on his home island, especially those relating to the fortunes of his Uí Néill kin; and it is clear too that he bound his church on Iona very closely to the affairs of state in Dál Ríata, in the remainder of Pict Scotland and later, in the neighbouring kingdom of Northumbria.* For Colum Cille and his followers, it seems, politics and spirituality went hand in hand.

Certainly he was one of the most important figures in the early Irish Church. Through his efforts, the monastery on Iona would become one of the great centres of Christian learning in the early medieval world: from Iona, his followers would help to expand a literate, Christian society among the Scots and Picts of northern Britain; and after his death, a new wave of his disciples would effect the same radical cultural change across England.** St Aidan, for example, left Iona to evangelize among the pagan Angles of Northumbria and to found the island monastery at Lindisfarne in 635; the dazzling Lindisfarne Gospels would be created here at the beginning of the eighth century. Other figures would press further south and into an ever-wider world, heeding the call to 'go out of thine own country, and from thy father's house, into a land that I shall show thee'.[12] In the eighth century the Venerable Bede, from the Northumbrian monastery at Jarrow, wrote approvingly of scholars travelling across to Ireland. Here they were welcomed gladly by the inhabitants, who 'without asking for any payment, provided them with daily food, books and instruction'.[13] Such stories and such education and zeal would seal Ireland's reputation as a land of saints and scholars – and the deeds of one wandering monk in particular would

---

* A confederation of Pictish tribes had inhabited parts of what is now Scotland since before the Roman conquest.
** Colum Cille was not the first missionary to Scotland. St Ninian, about whom little is known, was evangelizing there at the end of the fourth century. His Casa Candida in Galloway was the country's first Christian chapel, and his shrine at Whithorn attracted pilgrims from Ireland itself until the Reformation.

have a decisive impact on the future course of western European language and culture.

The Antiphonary of Bangor, with its pages of Latin hymns, psalms and chants, is the oldest surviving written service of the Irish Church, and a testament to the influence of Irish monks on European Christianity. It is likely to have been compiled at Bangor in what is now County Down, founded by St Comgall in the middle of the sixth century as one of Ireland's most austere teaching monasteries. Significantly, this small prayer book is held today not in Ireland but in the Ambrosian Library in Milan. It was taken from Bangor by St Dungall early in the ninth century – as the abbey faced devastation from Viking raiders – and brought to the monastery at Bobbio, high in the Apennines in northern Italy and home to one of the great libraries of the medieval world. Bobbio was significant for another reason too: it was the final resting place of St Columbanus (540–615), among the most influential of the Irish *peregrinari* and the founder of Bobbio. Columbanus was a Leinsterman by birth: early in his life, however, he had travelled north to study at Bangor; and here he discovered that the starkness and intensity of the monastery's regime suited him. But the call of exile would eventually prove too strong, and in 590 Columbanus sailed for France.

Columbanus is a compelling figure in early Irish history. He was the first of the *peregrinari* whom fate would direct to the European mainland; and he was, moreover, a man both of remarkable scholarship and of firm and uncompromising opinion. He died at Bobbio some twenty-five years after setting foot in Europe, by which stage Ireland's first and most striking brain drain was already in progress: for several centuries to come, the cream of the island's scholars would similarly set forth into exile, imprinting an extraordinary Irish cultural influence upon western Europe and in the process securing their home island's potent reputation as a centre of learning and literature. Not that Columbanus regarded himself principally as a saint or a scholar: he saw himself rather as a sinner and as a result lived a markedly stark life, striving always to get the better of a flawed nature. Such an austere interpretation of their calling won Columbanus and his followers a wide following among a population who could not possibly feel threatened by holy men who subsisted bleakly on a starvation diet and a lack of sleep.

Among the first of these admirers was Guntram, the Merovingian Frankish King of Burgundy, who permitted Columbanus to found a monastery at Annegray, in the Vosges Mountains. Within a short time, the new institution proved so successful that two further monasteries were founded nearby, at Luxeuil and Fontaines. Columbanus inspired his followers with powerful sermons, many of which survive to this day as decidedly stern testaments to the man himself: 'one thing which I know I shall say: the man who here battens, here sates himself, here makes merry, here smiles, here is drunken, and here plays, shall hereafter hunger, thirst, mourn, wail and lament.'[14] Building on the lessons learned at Bangor, Columbanus now drew up his own Rule: a set of forbidding regulations for monastic life built around fasting, obedience, corporal punishment and confession. It was far more austere than the Benedictine model, and for almost two centuries it became the cornerstone of monastic communities founded by the Irish and the European monks they trained. Perhaps its most lasting influence was in the application of the Irish penitential practice in Europe. Traditionally, European penance was performed in public, complete with sackcloth and ashes; in Ireland, however, confession and penance were private rites. The Irish version, moreover, had been thoroughly codified: it was guided by a horrifying series of texts that listed every conceivable sin nothing that could be imagined was excluded, with masturbation and bestiality ranked equally as the wickedest sins of all. This *medicamenta pænitentiae*, or 'medicines of penance', proved a good deal easier to swallow than the public mortifications prescribed in Europe; and, as a result, it began to spread throughout the continent. By the thirteenth century, the Irish practice had become standard throughout Europe; indeed, it remains the norm in the Catholic Church today.

The success of Columbanus's new monasteries, complete with monks tonsured in the Irish style, proved unsettling to the bishops of the Frankish Church. Resentment simmered until the tension finally came to a head in a major ecclesiastical dispute over the precise dating of Easter. Calculating the correct and proper date of Easter was (and remains) a complicated process: and in the sixth and seventh centuries, although the European Church had come to a degree of accord on this vexed matter, the Irish Church continued to work along different lines. A century later, Bede would remember an epistle from Honorius I (pope from 625 to 638) to the Irish, whom 'he found to have erred over the keeping of Easter ... urging them with much shrewdness not to consider themselves, few as they were and placed on the extreme boundaries of the world, wiser than the ancient and modern Church of Christ scattered throughout the earth; nor should they celebrate a different Easter contrary to the pastoral tables and the decrees of the bishops of all the world met in synod'.[15] Columbanus held to the Irish model, with the result that his European monasteries celebrated Easter at a quite different time from that of their neighbours. In an age when the smallest degree of ecclesiastical difference could be regarded as heresy, his major deviation from European tradition gave Columbanus's enemies an opportunity to attack.

Columbanus himself, displaying his trademark scorn for diplomatic niceties, had in fact already challenged Pope Gregory the Great to abandon the European model of calculation in favour of the Irish one – and in 603 he was summoned to account for his heresy before the Frankish bishops. Columbanus viewed these clerics with the utmost contempt: to him they were a caste of soft, self-important churchmen, satisfied with ministering only to the elite. So he simply refused to go, sending instead a letter that was stinging and calculated to offend: 'I, Columba the sinner, forward greetings in Christ. I render thanks to my God, that for my sake so many holy men have been gathered together to treat of the truth of faith and good works, and, as befits such, to judge of the matters under dispute with a just judgment, through senses sharpened to the discernment of good and evil. Would that you did so more often….'.[16] In such texts, Columbanus proved his reputation as an abrasive and confrontational personality. His letter, employing beautifully crafted Latin, went on to take the bishops to task for their materialism, adultery, lack of industry and interference with his holy mission.

> But someone will say: Are we really not entering the kingdom of heaven? Why can you not by the Lord's grace, if you become as little children, that is, humble and chaste, simple-hearted, and guileless in evil, [yet] wise in goodness, easy to be entreated and not retaining anger in your heart? But all these things can very hardly be fulfilled by those who often look at women and who more often quarrel and grow angry over the riches of the world.[17]

Having flayed the bishops thus, Columbanus appealed again to the pope, reaffirming his loyalty to Rome and asking to be left in peace. The dispute between the Irish and European Churches over the dating of Easter would not be completely settled until the Synod of Whitby in 664, but it appears that the resolve of the papacy cracked first. Columbanus's monasteries continued to follow the Irish tradition; and their leader maintained an erudite and sometimes familiar correspondence with various popes, who seem to have permitted him to live and work as he pleased.

The local situation, however, became increasingly difficult. Columbanus had already offended the clergy; and eventually his uncompromising morality would result in offence to the civil authorities too. In particular, his refusal to bless the bastard offspring of the Merovingian monarch Theuderic ('You ought to know that they will not receive the royal sceptres, because they have been born to whores'[18]) had serious consequences: he not only offended the king but threatened the stability of the realm – and his comments appear to have been the last straw for the authorities, already irked by Columbanus's insistence on having his own way in every single matter, large or small. His loyal converts would continue to live by the Rule (although in the years following his death his monasteries quietly fell into line in the much-disputed matter of the timing of Easter) but the Irish monk himself – after a threat of deportation to Ireland was eventually lifted – was banished from Burgundy and forced once more into exile.

Columbanus spent two years wandering through what are now France, Germany, Austria and Switzerland; and as he went, he continued with the Lord's work by conducting a campaign of destruction of pagan sites and disruption of ceremonies. His decision to direct his footsteps towards Italy, however, eventually created dissension amongst his followers. He quarrelled bitterly with his oldest friend, Gall, who would, as a result, remain in the Alps to spread the Christian message and become in the process the founding father of the Swiss Church. After his death, the great monastery named in his honour – at St Gallen, in northeast Switzerland – would play a crucial intellectual role in the evolution of the Swiss nation. Columbanus himself reached Milan in 1612 and, after interceding in a dispute between King Agilulf of the Lombards and Pope Boniface, was granted by a grateful monarch a piece of land in the Apennines between Milan and Genoa. Columbanus transformed a cavern here at Bobbio into a small chapel and his last days were spent in prayer.

His legacy would prove to be an enduring one. Possessed as he was of a harsh view of faith, Columbanus had been, in his own words, a 'dissenter whenever necessary'. But he also exemplified the rigorous levels of scholarship that could be found in the Irish monasteries of the day, and he bequeathed an extensive body of work: his masterful scripts and sermons testify to his education, paying homage as they do to such classical writers as Virgil, Ovid and Juvenal. He was the first to conceive of Europe as a cultural entity in its own right; the first to express in writing a sense of a specifically Irish identity; and the first Irishman to leave a lasting impression in the world beyond his native island.

Bobbio itself became the greatest of his monasteries, developing in time into a centre of learning and scholarship. In its scriptorium, surrounded by books and manuscripts illuminated in Ireland, generations of European scholars would learn to read and write in Latin. His teaching monastery at Luxeuil, meanwhile, would produce hundreds of young scholars, who would follow his example and spread the gospel throughout pagan Europe; twenty-one of its students would be canonized. At least sixty monasteries were founded in his name across the continent: by the ninth century, Irish scholars had begun to follow the pioneering missionaries and to gain important academic roles in the courts of monarchs such as Charlemagne; and Irish foundations could be found across a great swathe of western and central Europe. The work accomplished by Columbanus and his evangelizing successors helped to disseminate Latin literature in western Europe, and in the process to underpin the future development of Europe's rich array of national languages and literatures.

The sea which carried the monks from Ireland to Europe from the sixth century onward, however, would in later centuries carry other travellers too: warriors sailing from the cold north to haunt the sleep of Christians throughout the continent . The experience in Ireland would be no different.

CHAPTER TWO

LANDFALL

This year came dreadful forewarnings over the land of the Northumbrians … terrifying the people most woefully: these were immense sheets of light rushing through the air, and whirlwinds, and fiery dragons flying across the firmament. These tremendous tokens were soon followed by a great famine: and not long after, on the sixth day before the ides of January in the same year, the harrowing inroads of heathen men made lamentable havoc in the church of God in Holy-island, by rapine and slaughter.[1]

In the year 793, the monks on Lindisfarne off the Northumbrian coast looked out to sea and saw a fleet of small, nimble ships come swiftly out of the northeast. The authorities at Lindisfarne, if the hysterical accounts of the *Anglo-Saxon Chronicle* are to be believed, must have been anticipating some horror or other to fall upon them – and so it came to pass. These ships were filled with warriors from western Scandinavia, who landed on the stony shores of the island and proceeded to burn the buildings and plunder the store of precious goods that had been built up at the monastery in the century and half of its existence. It was but the first of many such raids, which resulted in the forced abandonment of Lindisfarne a century later and marked the advent of the Viking age in northwestern Europe.

Until this time the people of Scandinavia had had their own rich resources of timber, cattle and fish to exploit, and had tended to keep themselves to themselves. Now, though, they were bursting from their homelands and moving east into the heart of Russia, south towards Germany and the Mediterranean, and west into the Atlantic. There were a variety of reasons for this change: in the case of Norway, overpopulation combined with an increasing sense of the fragile fertility of their sea-girt valleys; new ship-building technologies that enabled longer and more ambitious voyages to be undertaken; and a gradually warming climate that stretched the sailing seasons and made these voyages less perilous. Norway, moreover, was the poorest region of Scandinavia and – like Ireland itself – lacked any degree of political unity. The mariners overseas, therefore, were individuals impelled by family and local loyalties and were seeking wealth and stability for themselves and their communities. In the end, then, it was the Norwegians of all the Scandinavians who made the most spectacular voyages, pressing west through bitter seas to Iceland and Greenland and finally across the Atlantic to Newfoundland.

Word of the cataclysmic raid on Lindisfarne spread quickly from community to community, from Northumbria to Iona and across the water-knit territory of Dál Ríata to Ireland. The records speak of a rising apprehension and of similarly strange phenomena as noted in the *Chronicle*: a blood-red moon; heavy snows falling after Easter. Two years after the raid on Lindisfarne, Viking longships appeared in Irish waters. Centuries later, when the tale of these years was written down, unceremonious chroniclers memorialized the event. 'Devastation of all the islands of Britain and Ireland,' noted the *Annals of Ulster* laconically on the burning of the monastery on the island of Rathlin. And so began a pattern of attack and plunder on the hosts of monasteries built on indefensible sites all along the coastline.[2] In 802 and 806 the Vikings attacked Iona itself: in the latter raid sixty-eight monks were killed, and in response the Columban federation of monasteries began construction of a new Irish foundation well inland in County Meath, carrying from Iona the precious Book of Kells.

By the middle of the ninth century, Viking ships had scouted out the entire coast of Ireland – even Skellig Michael, the most isolated and austere of Ireland's monasteries, found itself under attack in 824. Little wonder that a clerical scribe could look out across a wintry sea and smile:

> *Bitter is the wind tonight,*
> *It tosses the ocean's white hair.*
> *Tonight I fear not the fierce warriors of Norway*
> *Coursing on the Irish Sea.*[3]

And as in Ireland, so it was across northwestern Europe: in France, where in 843 the dreadful sack of Nantes by the Norsemen led to slaughter on a vast scale; in England, where Saxon London was attacked and burned in 851; in Wales, where the Vikings fell upon fertile Anglesey in 853; and in many other places besides. And there were other consequences to this Viking activity. The political cohesion of Dál Ríata, for example, had long been under strain: the increasing sense of the island of Ireland as a distinct cultural entity was loosening the ties that bound northeastern Ireland and southwestern Scotland; the Scottish half of the kingdom was becoming an increasingly important player in specifically British affairs; and the increasing Viking control of the sea lanes now made communications between Scotland and Ireland more and more difficult. Before long, the two halves of the territory had gone their separate ways; and the Scottish half would gradually coalesce with Pictish society to form the embryonic kingdom of Scotland.

It proved almost impossible at first to defend against the Vikings' tactics. Their small, agile ships could appear and disappear rapidly, long before any resistance could be mustered against them. They were, moreover, shallow-draughted and thus able to nose up many of Ireland's rivers: soon, they had made the Shannon and other waterways their own; fleets were based on lakes across the country, and not even such wealthy and powerful inland monasteries as Birr, Clonfert and Clonmacnoise – the last of which was torched in 835 – were safe from assault. In 837, two great fleets of sixty-five ships sailed up the rivers Liffey and Boyne; and at the end of the summer of 841, for the first time the Vikings on Lough Neagh did not go home but instead pulled their longships out of the water, signalling their intention to winter on the lake. Nor were the treasure and grain stores of the monasteries their only goals: in 821, Viking ships raided the harbour at Howth on the northern edge of Dublin Bay and seized great numbers of women – slaves and thralls being as valuable to the Vikings as they were to the Irish.

These ferocious Norsemen have come down to us as very demons from hell – for so they must have appeared to the monks and scribes who recorded the history of these years and who saw their achievements and their very civilization suddenly under attack. The shock of the Viking arrival had much to do with the expansive nature of their warfare: the wars carried by the Irish from *túath* to *túath* were often highly localized in nature, often involving no more than cattle raiding, and the local inhabitants became adept at getting quickly and quietly out of the way. The Vikings, on the other hand, were driven implacably by economic survival, and their methods were much more brutal.

While the monks may have been largely defenceless against the axes and swords of the Viking raiders, they had to hand a weapon that had been fine-tuned for decades. Just as they had set in stone a cultural and political history of Ireland that suited their interests and those of their political allies, so now the monasteries fought the Vikings with ink and scroll. They castigated these newcomers for any and every harshness, injury and oppression witnessed in Ireland in these years; and added a variety of satanic flourishes for good effect, presenting the northern onslaught as divine retribution for Ireland's sinful ways. Like the Irish annals, the clerical accounts of the *Cogadh Gaedhil re Gallaibh* – the War of the Irish and the Foreigners – were

written retrospectively, yet they came to be viewed as eyewitness testi-
monies; in the process, they imprinted themselves on to the collective
consciousness, doing much to create the image of the Vikings that has come
down through the centuries. Take the following passage, which portrays a
much put-upon Ireland struggling under the Viking yoke:

> *There was an astonishing and awfully great oppression over all Ireland,
> throughout its breadth, by powerful azure gentiles, and by fierce hard-
> hearted Danes, during a lengthy period and for a long time, namely for
> the space of eight score and ten years .... The whole of Munster became
> filled with immense floods, and countless sea-vomitings of ships, and
> boats, and fleets, so that there was not a harbour, nor a landing port,
> nor a fort, nor a fortress, nor a fastness, in all Munster without fleets
> of Danes and foreigners; ... and they ravaged her kingdoms and her
> privileged churches, and her sanctuaries; and they rent her shrines and
> her reliquaries and her books....*[4]

Such passages contain a great deal of historical truth: they record and
preserve the *sense* of the Norse impact on the Irish scene. Violence was of
course an accepted aspect of monastic life: since the monasteries of Ireland
were significant centres of population, wealth and political power, with
strong ties to local Irish dynasties, they had always been drawn into the
island's many internal conflicts. The raiding and burning of monasteries,
however, was certainly stepped up by the Vikings, who were a good deal
more thorough in their application of such strategies: to judge from the
unearthed contents of many a grave in Norway itself, they did not hesitate
to loot as many monastic treasures as they could get their hands on, with
jewelled missals, Bibles and altar treasures carried away as booty.

However, the notion of a solid Irish front against these Norsemen –
regardless of the cultural affinities that existed within the collective Irish

population – is not borne out in fact. There was no sense of united resistance: the internal disputes between dynasties meant that the Irish were too devoted to fighting amongst themselves to consider general alliances in some notional common Irish good. Indeed, Irish leaders were not averse to forging local alliances with the Vikings themselves in order to further their own position or to mount a successful attack upon the monasteries of their opponents. Nor can the lurid accounts of Viking savagery obscure the resilience of the Irish monastic system in the face of this onslaught. In Britain and France whole monastic settlements disappeared as the Norsemen began to take and govern great tracts of land for themselves. In Ireland, on the other hand, it was possible for monasteries and Viking settlements to develop in close proximity, as demonstrated at Cork. Such a state of affairs points to a rather different version of history from that propagated by the Irish monks; and it finds its best expression in the example of Dublin, which at this point in history begins its evolution into the principal city of Ireland.

At the dawn of the Viking age, twin settlements existed side by side close to the mouth of the river Liffey. At a site a little way inland, a low hill rose on the southern bank of the river and around its base a little tributary stream – the Poddle – curled to form a tidal lake before joining the main flow of the Liffey. At this point the river could be forded, though with some difficulty: here a settlement named Áth Cliath – the hurdle ford – grew up and throve on trade coming in from across the island. At the same time a monastic settlement had developed on the edge of the little lake, from which it took its name: *dubh linn*, the dark pool, today the site of the gardens of Dublin Castle. Patrick himself was reputed to have come here to christen the district's first converts on an island in the Poddle; later, St Patrick's Cathedral would be built on the spot. The two settlements, though different in character, naturally had much in common and much to gain from communication and cooperation; and gradually the population and prosperity of the district grew. It was this growing wealth, of course, that drew the Vikings, whose fleet of sixty longships entered Dublin Bay and made landfall on the Liffey's shingled banks in the spring of 837.

The Norsemen built their first fortified stockade on the shores of the dark pool itself: the area provided anchorage, and the nearby hill was a safe place from which to survey the district. A good deal of archaeological evidence exists to show that these new settlers had rather more on their minds than rape and looting. While dark layers of ash and charcoal in the digs provide evidence of burning and destruction by fire, it is also known that Christian churches in the Dublin area continued to function throughout this period. Although we can only guess as to the nature of everyday society in this place and at these times, there is evidence enough that life carried on in the aftermath of the Viking landings. As the newcomers acculturated, trade inevitably took the place of pillage.

More and more of them arrived in this promising place, and the Dublin settlement would eventually become a principal colony of the Vikings in Ireland. At suitable spots along the southern and eastern coasts – at Arklow, Wicklow and Waterford, Youghal and Cork – similar colonies arose, and would in time become Ireland's first full-fledged towns. Only in Ulster would the Vikings ultimately fail to overcome local opposition and establish any stronghold: the Uí Néill and Ulaid were tough fighters and their landscape was rough, remote and mountainous.

The Scandinavians brought with them no domestic traditions of city-building. They founded and fortified their ports because they were obliged to do so, not because of some cultural imperative carried with them from the north; and therefore it is a reflection of the opposition to their presence in Ireland that Viking towns were such sturdy, solid places. For the Norsemen did not by any means have everything their own way. From the middle of the ninth century they had begun to suffer serious reversals: the Uí Néill ambushed a force of Norsemen in County Meath in 848, for example, and put some seven hundred of them to the sword; and such attacks were far from uncommon. In 849, Danes were added to the cultural mix – appearing in Ireland not to join forces with their Norwegian kin, but rather to struggle with them for mastery of valuable turf; and the Danes too were not beyond making temporary, expedient alliances with local Irish kings.

The most serious of the Norse military defeats came at the beginning of the tenth century. Having ostensibly consolidated their power bases in Ireland, they had begun to turn their attention towards Britain in an attempt to hamper an increasingly powerful rival presence across the island. By the late ninth century, Danish kingdoms had been established at York and across the east of England; Danish forces were probing deep into Wales and Scotland; and the relative fragility of the Norsemen in Ireland itself had been demonstrated in 853, with a devastating naval defeat at the hands of the Danes on Carlingford Lough. But the decision of the Norsemen of Ireland to focus elsewhere proved costly: stronghold after stronghold was ransacked by an array of Irish forces; and after a period of localized civil war the Norse rulers of Dublin were expelled by the native Irish (acting, for once, in concord) in 902 and driven into exile in Scotland and the Isle of Man.

It seems unlikely that the general Norse population of the town, having put down roots and begun the process of integration, was thrown out with the city's rulers. Instead, such potent, binding ties changed the situation, for Dublin was no longer merely a strategic Norse stronghold on the Liffey: its population was increasingly Hiberno-Norse through bonds of kinship, trade, intermarriage and friendship. The Norsemen had settled in Dublin, built homes, developed trade, married into prominent Irish families and produced offspring of their own. Olaf, King of Dublin in the middle of the ninth century, for example, had married the daughter of Áed Finnliath, King of the northern Uí Néill, and had become a Christian as part of the deal. Dublin, in other words, was home to the Norsemen – and they intended to take it back. After twelve years in exile, a large fleet of Viking ships recaptured Waterford and over the course of several years built up their strength in the town enormously. By 917 they were ready to make their move: they advanced north and recaptured Dublin, and their expansion in Ireland began again.

This new nexus of Viking power was by any standards a place of wealth and industry. New fortifications were constructed to protect the town, which was now increasingly referred to as Dubhlinn – the Dyflinn of the Icelandic sagas – and within the city walls the markets throve through trade in slaves, leather and jewellery; the city's artisans began to deal in glass and jet; weavers, blacksmiths and shipwrights were hard at work; and the authorities struck the first coins. Dublin now lay at the centre of a vast semicircular trade route that ran from Constantinople (modern Istanbul) and Russia through the Baltic to Norway, Iceland and Greenland: wine and silver from southern Europe were funnelled through the city and north to Scandinavia; furs, walrus ivory and amber flowed south through Dublin and into a wider world. And in Dublin, as in the other Norse seaports, cultural mingling became increasingly the order of the day: in the decorative work that survives from the period, for example, Norse symmetry and interlacing begins to replace the Anglo-Saxon detail that had previously influenced Irish design. This influence was, moreover, gradually disseminated throughout the country: both the Crozier of Clonmacnoise (fashioned in bronze in the first half of the twelfth century) and the Cross of Cong (created in the same period to house a fragment of the True Cross) would be unmistakably influenced by a Scandinavian aesthetic.

In the wider hinterland of these ports, meanwhile, other cultural changes were beginning to be felt. Shortly after the recapture of Dublin, the ports of Wexford and Limerick were founded; and the Vikings began to act as economic middlemen between the native Irish and overseas markets, helping to funnel Irish timber and hides through their harbours for export. The sharp dividing line between Gall and Gael – foreigner and Irish – as

IRELAND, c.1014

ATLANTIC
OCEAN

Rathlin Island

CENÉL
CONAILI
Derry

DÁL
RIATA

Lough
Derg

CENÉL
NEÓGAIN

NORTHERN
UÍ NÉILL

Lough
Neagh

DÁL
NARAIDE

Armagh

DÁL
FIATACH

AIRGIALLA
Downpatrick

UÍ BRIÚIN
BRÉIFNE

CONNACHT

CONAILLE
MUIRTEMNE

Croagh Patrick

SOUTHERN
UÍ NÉILL

Hill of
Slane

Hill of
Tara

Clonmacnoise

Durrow

Clontarf, 1014

Dublin

Birr

Baltinglass

Wicklow

DAL CAIS

LAIGIN

Arklow

River
Shannon

Limerick

OSRAIGE

UÍ FIDGENTE

DÉISI

Wexford

DESMUMU

Waterford

Youghal

Cork

Skellig
Michael

N

0   miles   50

Key

DÉISI   Kingdoms
         and territories

✠   Monastic Sites

o   Viking towns

⚔   Battle sites

delineated by medieval propagandists, then, became increasingly blurred in eastern and southern Ireland; and in the major ports it began to vanish entirely. Human economic and emotional imperatives now began to forge a new culture, a new world.

In the latter half of the tenth century, the great power game in Ireland began to shift. Norse influence reached its zenith in eastern and southern Ireland, while the Uí Néill retained supremacy across the north and held the nominal kingship at Tara. But other figures were eyeing the glittering prizes too: in particular, the Dalcassian clan of central Ireland, which possessed the great virtue of straddling the river Shannon. The river was the country's communications highway and the key to the expanding seaport of Limerick; and the Dalcassians, observing the Viking control of Ireland's waterways, had in the process absorbed important lessons. The tide was running in favour of the clan: the Uí Néill were expending their strength in a bitter internal power struggle; and in the south, the Norse of Dublin had engaged the Danes of Limerick on Lough Ree in 937, destroying their fleet and capturing their king. Weakened by this defeat, the city was now fair game.

In 976 the Dalcassian leader Mathgamain was assassinated by the Danes, and in retaliation the Dalcassians immediately stormed Limerick. Ímar, the leader of the city, and his sons sought sanctuary in the monastery at Scattery Island, but Mathgamain's brother Brian broke into the church (violating all the laws of sanctuary in the process) and slaughtered them all. *Túath* after *túath* now yielded to Brian's might: within four years he had seized control not only of Limerick but of the entire province of Munster, and was pushing his men into Leinster and Connacht. He had become a legend in the process, taking to himself the name Brian Bóruma – Brian Boru, the lord of cattle tributes. Such tribute was an indication of social status: it was now evident to all observers that Brian was making a bid for even greater dominion.

Certainly, to the watching Uí Néill and their leader Máel Seachnaill, the Dalcassian move was a naked land grab and the most serious threat in centuries to the authority of their clan. The two power blocs fought each other to a standstill; finally they realized that there was little to be done but to tread water and conclude a fragile peace, to last only until both sides could renew their strength. The Treaty of Clonfert in 997 declared the Dalcassian leader King of Munster and Leinster, while the Uí Néill retained control of their traditional lands in the north and west. Both blocs would cooperate against the dominance of the Norse at Dublin.

This outcome was deeply disagreeable to the leaders of Leinster, in whose eyes Brian was no more than a provincial upstart with intolerable pretensions to the kingship. A year after the treaty, Maelmordha MacMurchada seized the kingship of Leinster from the Dalcassians and launched an open rebellion against this new political order. Brian's response was rapid and decisive: he gathered his forces and made for Dublin, which was ruled by Sitric Silkbeard, Maelmordha's Norse ally and also his cousin – a sign of the mingling of cultures that was now standard across the east and south of Ireland. Rather than risk a siege, Maelmordha and Sitric decided to march out and fight at Glenn Máma, in what is now County Wicklow: it would be a ferocious and bloody battle, but once again Brian proved the better strategist. Centuries later, the *Annals of the Four Masters* would describe the engagement:

> *From the victorious overthrow they shall retreat,*
> *Till they reach past the wood northwards,*
> *And Áth-cliath the fair shall be burned,*
> *After the ravaging the Leinster plain.*[5]

The armies of Leinster and Dublin retreated in disarray from the hills and into the city, harried by Brian's forces as they went. Nor would Dublin's walls avail the defenders: Brian plundered the city and burned the fortress, taking Maelmordha hostage until sufficient tribute had been paid to secure his release. As for Sitric, it was said that he managed to escape the city and flee north to Ulster to seek refuge with the Ulaid – but they denied him assistance, and he was forced to return south and submit in humiliation to Brian. With an eye to the future, however, he was permitted to remain ruler of the city as Brian's vassal.

With the southern half of Ireland now pacified, Brian turned his attention north. Suspending his temporary peace treaty with the Uí Néill, he mustered the forces of Munster, Leinster and Dublin and in 1000 led them north into the rich farmland of Meath and towards the Uí Néill seat of power. The records are unhelpful at this point: they do not say how or why, but what is known is that by 1002 Máel Sechnaill had surrendered; the southern branch of the Uí Néill had fallen; and the symbolic seat of power at Tara belonged to Brian. Nearly all of Ireland, however unwillingly, had been subdued, and only Ulster still refused to bow to his authority. It would take a further ten years of campaigning, the combined military forces of the southern half of the country and a large degree of canny politicking to subdue the province: it is recorded in the Book of Armagh, for example, that in 1005, Brian donated twenty-two ounces of gold to the monastery and recognized Armagh's claim to primacy over Ireland. Once more, Church and State were formulating a mutually beneficial arrangement: Armagh's ambitious clerics were now entitled to tithes from all of Ireland's other monasteries, and they in turn named Brian Boru 'Emperor of the Irish'.

In the opening years of the eleventh century, then, a semblance of political cohesion existed in Ireland for the first time. The high kingship at Tara had attained a degree of actual meaning; the Vikings of Dublin and Limerick had been subdued; and hosts of petty kingdoms had been forced to recognize Brian's authority. But this achievement had taken a campaign lasting several decades, and had left bitterness and resentment in its wake. The political unity of Ireland, in other words, was no more than the thinnest of membranes stretched across a scene of seething discontent. Rebellion inevitably erupted once again and, with all the principal actors remaining in place, opposition to Brian's overlordship was led by Sitric of Dublin and Maelmordha of Leinster. Brian's army ravaged Leinster, and Dublin was besieged yet again – but this time, the onset of winter forced his armies back into Munster. This bought the rebels the time they desperately needed. Maelmordha dispatched Sitric to seek Viking aid from abroad, and in the meantime Brian's kingdom, so recently stitched together, was beginning to unravel. The leaders of recently conquered Ulster agreed not to take sides but, sensing weakness, they also refused to provide men and arms in support. As a result, Brian too was obliged to seek the help of Viking mercenaries.

In the spring of 1014, Brian's army gathered outside the walls of Dublin. On Palm Sunday, a fleet sailed into Dublin Bay: it was a formidable force, with representatives from Viking Europe among them. At a stroke, Brian had lost his numerical advantage; and five days later, on Good Friday, 23 April, battle was joined. Brian, now over seventy years old, is said to have prayed in his tent while his son Murchad led the army – comprising the Irish of Munster and Connacht, the Hiberno–Norse of Limerick and Waterford, and a force of Manx mercenaries – out into the wide, flat fields on the northern bank of the Liffey. Facing them were the forces of Leinster and Dublin, together with their own Manx and other Viking allies – and these took their stand at Clontarf, with their backs to the longship fleet moored in the bay. Sitric, meanwhile, stayed in the city to organize its defence.

The battle was ferocious, but late in the afternoon the balance began to shift in favour of Brian. His Leinster and Viking opponents were forced to retreat towards the sea, with Brian's men in pursuit; and there on the edge of the water they were defeated. By nightfall, bodies were drifting on Dublin Bay, and the field at Clontarf was strewn with the corpses of men and horses, commoners and nobles; among them were both Maelmordha and Murchad.

Nor did Brian escape: it is said that the Manx leader Brodar extricated himself from the massacre and hacked his way through the lines to reach Brian's tent; and there, with one blow of his battle-axe, he swept the old king's head from his shoulders. This was a powerful climax to a battle that has been mythologized as the triumph of the Irish over the foreigners; and this version of the story is topped off by the removal of Brian's remains for burial not in his Dalcassian homeland, but at the cathedral at Armagh. Even in death, it seems, Brian was playing a potent game, underscoring his claims of kingship and national unity by being laid to rest in sacred ground in the ecclesiastical capital of the country.

The Norse sagas remember events at Clontarf thus:

The men of Ireland will suffer a grief
That will never grow old in the minds of men.
The web is now woven and the battlefield reddened;
The news of disaster will spread through lands.[6]

In truth, however, Clontarf did not mark the defeat of Norse power within Ireland: rather, it was the climax of a specifically Irish civil war in which foreigners had participated only as minor players or paid mercenaries; and in its aftermath, a power vacuum opened up. Brian had demonstrated that the kingship of the country was no mere symbolic office: on the contrary, the will and the military muscle could be found to make it tangible. As a consequence, the provincial kings of Ireland now fought each other to follow in Brian's footsteps and become the next ruler of the whole island.

Subsequent leaders began, insofar as they were able, to concentrate yet more power into their hands and to channel as many resources as possible into military campaigns against their rivals. A caste of administrators grew up as these changes took hold: in the long absences of their kings in the field, they became increasingly vital both in maintaining a stable sense of authority and government and in guarding against the treachery of potential usurpers. Newly acquired lands were used as bargaining chips or gifted to sons and allies and to the Church; taxes were imposed to pay for the wars; and the common people of the country suffered accordingly. By the beginning of the twelfth century the map of Ireland had changed substantially, with power being hoarded in fewer and larger kingdoms. The province of Connacht was now in the ascendant, and was building a hefty power base across the west and south of the country.

At the same time, the Irish Church was setting about its own changes: in a move to bring about greater concord between it and the wider European Church, representatives of the papacy devised a new, countrywide system of dioceses. St Malachy, appointed Archbishop of Armagh in 1132, was instrumental in imposing the changes – together with a new code of clerical celibacy and morality – across the country, thereby cementing the primacy of Armagh. Simultaneously the monasteries were stripped of their lands, possessions and much of their role in Irish society. The autonomy and power of their abbots passed now to the Irish bishops, who began to wield the temporal power that their continental equivalents had long enjoyed. Gradually, monastic industry ceased; the scriptoria and schools began to close; and ownership passed into the hands of European orders such as the Augustinians and Cistercians, who established themselves in Ireland for the first time. The effect of this ecclesiastical reform was to end much of the educational and cultural activity that had taken place for centuries: the monks might not always have been busy with their prayers and their bottles of ink, but they had undoubtedly filled a space in Irish life that would now increasingly be left empty.

As for the place of the Vikings in this rapidly changing domestic scene: the power games being played across Ireland did much, ironically, to ensure that the Norse presence would remain intact. Their trade with Europe continued to prosper and their Irish seaports to grow. Sitric himself continued as King of Dublin in the aftermath of the battle, and his influence and power were amply demonstrated by the foundation, at his behest, of Christ Church Cathedral in the city some twenty years after Clontarf. The Scandinavian presence in Irish affairs, which had never in any case been dominant or universal, continued its process of slow evolution into a distinctive Hiberno–Norse civilization founded on borrowings from both cultures and from further afield; and this process continued throughout the eleventh century and into the twelfth. An end would indeed come to Norse influence in terms of thriving seaports and trading routes – but this end would come courtesy of yet another cultural and military shock administered by newcomers to the Irish scene.

PART TWO

THE LONG CONQUEST

CHAPTER THREE

THE LORDSHIP
OF IRELAND

By the middle of the twelfth century, the rulers of Ireland were looking out into a rapidly changing Europe. The political structure of the continent was altering, with a political mosaic of minor duchies and fiefdoms now giving way to larger and more centralized realms. In the southern half of the neighbouring island, a patchwork of minor Saxon and Danish territories had by the tenth century begun to coalesce into a unitary kingdom of England: and with the invasion of William of Normandy in 1066, this new land was stitched into an even larger and more potent political entity. Brian Boru's adventures in eleventh-century Ireland could, with hindsight, be seen as just one element in a much wider European political shift.

The Irish elite was well acquainted with events elsewhere in Europe. It is true that some aspects of life in Ireland appeared ostensibly unchanging: those on the lowest rung of the social ladder, in particular, would have continued to live out their lives without travelling very far from the place of their birth. But a great many merchants, soldiers and politicians were well acquainted with the wider world. The sea remained a communications highway: indeed, in a country cut with forest, highland and bog it was sometimes easier to travel abroad than within the island itself. And now the Church – which had linked its flock to the European mainstream since the dawn of the Christian age – was increasingly falling into line with Rome, and the European monastic orders that were establishing themselves across the country were bringing goods and ideas with them. The coming of the Vikings and their swift fleets of nimble, shallow-draughted ships made the potential of the sea as a means of communication and of exchange even more vividly realized. As a result, cultural and economic connections between Ireland and neighbouring lands were becoming ever more tangible.

Within Ireland, the struggle for political supremacy was ongoing. Rory O'Connor of Connacht (?1116–98) had been inaugurated high king at Dublin in 1166. In carving out his notional supremacy, O'Connor recognized that his triumph was inevitably fragile, to be sustained only by endless political, diplomatic and (as the need arose) military effort. Dermot MacMurrough (1110–72), the other crucial character in this great game, did not hold a position of military dominance, but his kingdom of Leinster was of great strategic importance. The canny and farsighted MacMurrough had long understood the importance of investing time and energy into his political relationships beyond Ireland: he could not hope for domestic political ascendancy without foreign aid. For a time he had been successful, gambling and backing the right horse in the race for the English succession. For, while one political game was underway in Ireland, a bitter struggle had been fought out for the English throne between Matilda, granddaughter of William of Normandy, and her cousin Étienne de Blois – better known in English history as Stephen. Between 1135 and 1153 the throne had been disputed between their two factions and English society was riven by civil war. Eventually, Matilda's son would secure the throne: in 1154, Henry Plantagenet (1133–89) was crowned Henry II at Westminster Abbey.

MacMurrough had declared for Henry early in this bitter internecine struggle, and in the process had earned the young monarch's favour. In the opening years of Henry's reign, the alliances he had forged in Ireland and Scotland helped to influence Irish politics, and MacMurrough's political fortunes waxed accordingly: to his territories in Leinster he added more in the fertile lands of Meath; in 1162, the Norse of Dublin had acknowledged his lordship; and his brother-in-law had been consecrated as the new arch-bishop of the city. All this, in the finely balanced world of Irish politics, had to come at the expense of someone else: in this case, both Rory O'Connor and his ally Tiernan O'Rourke, the one-eyed King of Breifne, had been weakened, losing both territory and prestige.

As Henry's reign continued, the pendulum would swing back: in 1166 MacMurrough's enemies launched a joint attack, taking him by surprise; he was driven from Meath, repudiated by the Norse of Dublin and forced to seek refuge in his own fastness of Leinster. Yet even here he would not be secure: his allies rejected him and he fled Ireland barely in time to save his life, taking ship for Bristol. He had been humiliated – and, already desper-ate to regain his lands, he turned now towards Europe for succour.

Much of the story of these times has come down to us courtesy of Giral-dus Cambrensis (Gerald of Wales, 1146–23) – clergyman, writer, traveller and observer of this complicated contemporary cultural scene. Giraldus is an ambivalent figure in Irish history: his portraits of the country are among the earliest comprehensive accounts that have survived, but they are far from objective and as a result make for bracing reading. He was himself partly of Norman stock, partly of Welsh; he was a fervent supporter of the Anglo-Norman newcomers to the Irish political scene; and he makes no bones of his opinions. 'I have been at pains,' he declares, 'to unfold clearly the story of the subjugation of the Irish people, and of the taming of the ferocity of a very barbarous nation in these our own times.'[1] He writes scathingly of the barbarity and uncouthness of the Irish: their refusal to mine or till the soil correctly or to trade as they ought to trade, their cunning and violent ways, their lack of honesty. He does remark on their fine stature and their way with music – but in general, compliments are thin on the ground. These harsh portrayals may, however, be seen as carrying a little less weight when one remembers that he was equally scornful in his atti-tudes towards the Welsh, the English and even, on occasion, the Normans themselves. Endlessly curious and probing, fascinated with every detail of language and culture, partial, political, 'self-admiring, highly critical of others and therefore quarrelsome and a mean enemy', Giraldus is a gripping but dangerous guide through this early period in the story of Ireland.[2]

In his account written seventeen years after Dermot MacMurrough's death, Giraldus describes him as one who 'preferred to be feared by all rather than loved …. He was inimical towards his own people and hated by others. All men's hands were against him and he was hostile to all men.'[3] Giraldus was certainly no admirer of MacMurrough: such descriptions have, as a result, done much to establish the Leinsterman's poor reputation in Irish history. Not even Giraldus, however, could fully encapsulate the complexities of MacMurrough's personality. Here was a foster-child of common birth, who rose to power in his own right; a man who curried favour with a foreign king, but who was very far from standing in awe of the noblemen of his native Ireland: 'from his earliest youth and his first taking of the kingship,' Giraldus notes disapprovingly, 'he oppressed his nobles, and raged against the chief men of his kingdom with a tyranny grievous and impossible to bear', on one occasion blinding and killing seventeen noblemen of Leinster. He 'loved the generous, he hated the mean', and yet was as bloodthirsty and violent as they make them.[4]

Giraldus was quite correct: those who stood in MacMurrough's way tended to pay a heavy price, with massacre joining ritual blinding as his favourite means of laying down the law. And, while he had lavished financial favours upon the Church in Leinster, not even its representatives were immune from his violence. Take, for example, the scene in 1132 at Kildare – at this time, the effective capital of Leinster. A rival dynasty had appointed their candidate, Mór, as abbess of the influential monastery, in the process thoroughly upsetting MacMurrough's political machinations. Rather than agonize unduly on his next move, however, he moved swiftly, ordering the abbess to be abducted by his men and raped: Mór, divested brutally of her virginity, was in the process disqualified from her position. MacMurrough now completed the job to his satisfaction: the abbess's house was burned, many of her followers were killed – and a MacMurrough appointee was installed in the post in her stead. In another episode, he had seized Tiernan O'Rourke's wife Dervorgilla – although the records imply that she was a willing refugee from an ugly and loveless marriage – and kept her at his headquarters at Ferns for a year before sending her home. It was an act calculated to humiliate and weaken his adversary. Such was MacMurrough's style, rooted in a political climate that was positively Sicilian in its intensity and nastiness. His special hatred of Dublin, for example, can be explained by the fact that its people had murdered his father and buried him in the court of their assembly hall in the company of a dead dog – a potent and humiliating mark of disrespect. As MacMurrough did, so had he been done by.

In the traditional telling of the tale, MacMurrough is uniquely wicked and treacherous: the forerunner of every back-stabbing sucker-up to the English that has ever roamed the pages of Irish history. But in seeking the help of the powerful, he was merely doing what ambitious or desperate chieftains have always done. The crucial difference in this case was that he was asking for assistance from what was – in spite of recent disputes over the English succession and in spite of occasional reverses in policy and arms – the most organized and brutal expansionist power in western Europe. It was not a connection to be exploited carelessly.

Henry II had inherited an English kingdom that had already been in Norman hands for over a century. Its ruling class was cultured: its members may have been descended from Vikings who once ravaged western Europe, but they were now part of a sophisticated French-speaking community. This was a paradoxical society: a world of sword and blood and shocking brutality, but one too of legal and architectural advances, of chivalry and courtly love. England, moreover, was but one component in a wider civilization: that loose entity that historians have named in retrospect the Angevin (Planta-genet) Empire. This was not a state in any modern sense of the word, but rather a jigsaw of kingdoms and duchies that stretched from southern Scot-land to the south coast of England and from Normandy itself along the Atlantic seaboard of France to the Pyrenees. These lands were bound together not by a cohesive government or administration or civil service but rather by force of arms and by the fealty of a host of local rulers to Henry Plantagenet himself, the French-speaking and French-based ruler of a conglomeration that dominated northwestern Europe.

Norman civilization was defined by a hunger for land – just as their Viking ancestors had exploded out of Scandinavia to wreak havoc across Europe, so too the Normans began fanning out across the continent centuries later, establishing kingdoms in Sicily and southern Italy and the eastern Mediterranean, as well as in France and Britain. This movement was part of a wider trend, brought about in part by the climatic event called the Medieval Warm Period that spans several centuries at the end of the first millennium. Temperatures rose during this era, agriculture flourished and populations exploded; from Russia, Poland and the Balkans through Germany to France, people were on the move searching for new homes and new sources of food. It was inevitable that, as they pressed from their own territories into those of their neighbours, tensions would be inflamed and blood spilled. And it is against such large tapestries – spanning cultural development, climatic conditions and politics – that the first Anglo-Norman incursion into Ireland must be viewed. It was not a unique or even especially remarkable event, simply one that ties Ireland directly into the experience of the European mainstream.

MacMurrough, his wife, his daughter Aoife and a handful of support-ers landed at Bristol in the summer of 1166. The party then made its way across the Channel to Normandy and from there travelled southwest to the court of Henry II in Aquitaine; and here MacMurrough offered Henry homage and fealty.* The Norman verse poem entitled *The Song of Dermot and the Earl* describes the explicitly feudal nature of the contract between the two. Dermot addresses Henry:

> *Henceforth all the days of my life*
> *On condition that you be my helper*
> *So that I do not lose everything*
> *You I shall acknowledge as sire and lord.*[5]

In exchange for an army, in other words, MacMurrough would give land. Henry had by now been on the throne for twelve years, and he was a match in cunning and ruthlessness for the Irish chieftain who came seeking his help. Though doubtless pleased to accept MacMurrough's fealty, Henry was still cautious about becoming directly involved in what might prove to be a risky Irish adventure. So he prepared to enter the debate by proxy, providing MacMurrough with a letter authorizing his subjects to enter the fray. This in itself was more than enough to raise an army, and a well-pleased MacMurrough left France for England, intent on mustering a force as soon as possible.

Henry had engineered a situation that suited him well. He was a leader with restless and acquisitive knights to satisfy – and one, moreover, whose authority rested on fragile foundations. The Angevin Empire was certainly a power to be reckoned with in Europe, but it was also subject to continual pressure on its borders. In the north, Scotland could be handled by treaty and diplomacy, but Wales had proved impossible to pacify completely, its colonists increasingly pinned down in the chains of castles and fortresses that pockmarked the mountainous terrain. In the east, the ascendant French monarchy had designs on Normandy and Anjou; and in the south, the

---

* Henry had married the formidable Eleanor of Aquitaine in 1152; she had brought to the marriage additional vast French territories as her dowry.

papacy represented another, highly potent, focus of political power. Henry would attempt to deal with this last problem by bringing the English Church to heel: the Archbishop of Canterbury, Thomas Becket – that turbulent priest who refused to bend his will to that of the king – would be murdered in his own cathedral in 1170. In this wide geopolitical context, then, the presence of a still-autonomous Ireland on the empire's northwestern wing was a threat and an irritant: Henry wanted to secure the unruly flanks of his own realm; and he wanted to achieve this by bringing these flanks once and for all within his own sphere of influence.

Once again, the interests of the political and the ecclesiastical coincided. Henry had, in fact, entertained the idea of pulling Ireland into his empire well before the arrival of MacMurrough at his gates. As early as 1155, in fact, at a council at Winchester, the young king had discussed this very possibility. There was a strong clerical body of opinion in favour of such a move: the English Church at Canterbury had been riled by the papal decision three years before that rejected its claims to ecclesiastical control over Ireland; Pope Eugenius III had ruled that Armagh could perfectly well take care of its own affairs. The meeting at Winchester, therefore, had been an opportunity for Canterbury to grasp what it had previously lost. In the event, Henry had set aside the idea of entering the Irish political scene – but only for the moment, and the groundwork for such an intervention had already been laid.

The Plantagenet claim to Ireland was further underscored in the form of *Laudabiliter*, an edict ostensibly issued to Henry II by Pope Adrian IV, who reigned from 1154 to 1159. In twelfth-century Europe, with its united universal Church, the papacy stood at the apex of the feudal power structure: it was, therefore, always a good idea to have the pope on side; and *Laudabiliter* certainly appeared to demonstrate a cordial understanding between the papacy and the Plantagenets. The edict assented to the occupation of Ireland, both for the good of the Irish themselves and in order to reform the Irish Church further and bind it more closely to Rome; as a result, the edict and its contents have always played a fraught role in Irish history. It is accepted nowadays that a papal bull entitled *Laudabiliter* certainly existed and that it was indeed issued on behalf of Adrian. The original contents of the document, however, are much less clear: it is unlikely that they will ever be known for certain, and the text that exists today is probably a concoction of some kind. For one thing, it does not conform to the style of papal records from that period; nor is there any record of such a text in the papal archives. Furthermore, the original text known as *Laudabiliter* comes down to us from Giraldus, who claimed to have copied out the original faithfully: he may well have done so, of course, but as an Anglo-Norman historian and propagandist of note, he had obvious motives for fabrication. Yet the crucial fact is that people at the time believed in *Laudabiliter*: as a text, it generated its own mythology within the medieval period.* Nobody – not even the Irish themselves – contested the pope's right to grant possession of Ireland to Henry. In a tradition dating from the time of the fourth-century Emperor Constantine, it was popularly believed that the western islands of Europe were the property of the pope, to bestow on whomsoever he chose. Contemporary opinion was clear: Henry had a papal licence to invade.

The motives and actions of the papacy in this case stemmed from its opinions over the state of the Church in Ireland. Adrian's predecessors may have been of the opinion that the Irish clergy could be trusted to run their own affairs; but Adrian and his advisers had become convinced that their flock in Ireland had strayed too far from the Roman straight and narrow and required a degree of realignment – and he was prepared to ally himself with the Anglo-Normans in order to bring this realignment about. Adrian

---

* There are several later copies of the bull, including a fourteenth-century document now preserved in the UK National Archives.

would have been influenced, perhaps, by the fact that the system of tithe – 'Peter's Pence', by which taxes went to the Church – was not adhered to in Ireland. His opinions would also have been coloured by scandalous tales that had begun doing the rounds: it was claimed that Ireland, far from being a land of saints and scholars, was in a state of scandalous moral disarray. 'Never before had he known the like, in whatever depth of barbarism; never had he found men so shameless in regard of morals, so dead in regard to rites, so stubborn in regard of discipline, so unclean in regard of life. They were Christians in name, in fact pagans.'[6] Such comments had the effect of spreading throughout Europe the idea that the Irish were little more than barbarians: it was all a far cry from the message disseminated by Colum Cille and Columbanus, and it helped to establish a school of anti-Irish literature that was as influential as it was persistent.

Reform, of course, was already being implemented in Ireland, rippling out from St Malachy's seat of power at Armagh and demonstrating in the process that powerful elements in the Irish Church in these years were by no means averse to further changes. Resistance to tithe had still to be overcome, however, and some elements of a modern ecclesiastical administrative system remained absent: while Ireland now had a network of dioceses, for example, it did not possess a system of parishes, as in England and across western Christendom. In any case, if *Laudabiliter* is to be believed, Pope Adrian knew exactly what he wanted: 'for the purpose of enlarging the borders of the Church, setting bounds to the progress of wickedness, reforming evil manners, planting virtue, and increasing the Christian religion,' Henry II was ordered to enter Ireland, 'and take possession of that island…'. This, then, was the state of affairs when Dermot MacMurrough arrived in Aquitaine.

MacMurrough, understanding the mindset of his putative new allies as he did, imagined that he could tempt them easily with what must be a tantalizing prospect: acres of lush land in Ireland for the taking. He and his entourage, therefore, made their way to west Wales in order to recruit assistance from the colonial barons of Pembrokeshire, who were hard pressed in the face of persistent native Welsh unrest and revolt. This was a promising prospect: surely the colonists would happily trade their unprofitable situation in Wales for a brighter future in Ireland. Yet MacMurrough's blandishments did not at first fall upon eager ears. While his quest appeared reasonable enough – it was not unusual for such emissaries to seek the help of mercenaries in this way – the colonial barons were obliged to weigh up their prospects carefully: their present situation may have been vexing, but the prospect of future riches in Ireland was doubtful, prey as it was to a host of incalculable factors. In the end, though, MacMurrough found his man.

Richard de Clare (1130–76), the second Earl of Pembroke and a man of restless ambition, was a French-speaking aristocrat of substantial wealth, dynamism and clout, with great landholdings and local roots in Wales but a power base in England. He was not French but neither was he explicitly English; and he was certainly not Welsh. He and his fellow colonists were referred to as Anglo-Normans, and were the product of a long and complicated mingling of cultures and histories. In the middle of the twelfth century Pembrokeshire was already 'Little England beyond Wales', its population a multilingual and heady mix of English and Norman landowners, Flemish workers and artisans, and the remnants of a native population dispossessed of their lands. The region was blessed with fertile farmland and superb natural anchorages; and it was a natural jumping-off point for any voyage to Ireland.

De Clare – better known in Irish history as Strongbow – decided to take MacMurrough up on his offer of land in exchange for men. The latter was doubtless pleased to have at last established an alliance of sorts; Strongbow no doubt hoped the arrangement would deal with certain difficulties of his own. In the bitter English struggle for the throne between Stephen and Matilda he had backed the former and, although he had subsequently come to terms with the victorious Henry and pledged loyalty to him, bad blood remained. The king had consistently withheld the royal patronage required at that time to guarantee prosperity. Yet despite his position Strongbow drove a hard bargain, for he insisted on the hand of MacMurrough's daughter Aoife in marriage – and thus the kingship of Leinster itself on MacMurrough's death. This was problematic, for such a deal assumed the existence of primogeniture in matters of inheritance. This was a principle then beginning to gain acceptance across western Europe, but it remained quite alien in Irish law. Nevertheless the deal was duly agreed: MacMurrough was signing over lands that were not legally his to bestow.

In August 1167, MacMurrough sailed from Milford Haven in the company of a small band of Norman-Welsh soldiers – in effect, the first Anglo-Norman military landings on the Irish coast. He re-established himself easily enough at Ferns. Rory O'Connor and Tiernan O'Rourke came down from the north and assaulted his position; perceiving his present military weakness, however, they merely extracted a tribute of gold in recompense for the taking of Dervorgilla years before; and set about more conflicts of their own in other parts of Ireland. They even agreed, before departing, that MacMurrough could once more take the title of King of Leinster. In the aftermath of this attack, MacMurrough settled down at Ferns to await the coming of his new allies from across the sea. He would, as it turned out, have to endure a fretful two-year delay before his saviours arrived.

Three ships sailed from Pembrokeshire in the spring of 1169, landing on 1 May between Wexford and Waterford, at what was then Bannow Island; the channel dividing the island from the mainland has since silted up. MacMurrough quickly came down from Ferns to join them and this combined force attacked Wexford, forcing the town to surrender on 5 May. The civic leaders acknowledged MacMurrough's overlordship; and MacMurrough in his turn showed his *bona fides* by giving control of the town and its harbour to the newcomers. MacMurrough was clawing back the prestige he had lost; and the Anglo-Normans were secure in their new Wexford base.

In the months that followed, Anglo-Norman ships ploughing the waters from Pembrokeshire and anchoring in the now friendly port of Wexford would become a common sight – and yet the next wave of landings was momentous. In May 1170, an advance force landed on the rocky and easily defensible headland at Baginbun, east of Waterford. It was a modest contingent – a ship or two, containing one hundred-odd men – yet adequate for the job in hand. Additional forces came out from Wexford to meet them; a fort was established on the headland; and cattle – not the invaders' cattle and thus a potent provocation – were rounded up and driven on to the headland too, thus guaranteeing a food supply. The intention of the supremely organized Anglo-Norman force at Baginbun could not have been clearer: Wexford had been secured and Waterford would be next. So the Norse of Waterford, in alliance with local Irish rulers, put together a force with the aim of overwhelming the newcomers and driving them back into the sea.

The Irish and Norse substantially outnumbered the small Anglo-Norman force. But this did not avail them, for the newcomers boasted superior weaponry and strategic skills: their archers, for example, rained death upon the Norse and Irish from above. They were able even to deploy the stolen cattle to deadly advantage: as the disorderly mass of Norse and Irish soldiers advanced towards the Anglo-Norman stockade, the panicked beasts were driven through its gates into their midst, trampling and killing many and causing chaos; and at this point, the Anglo-Normans advanced with deadly efficiency and routed their enemies. Within a short time, it is estimated that, of the Norse-Irish force of a thousand men, half were dead – and a mass of executions followed, in contravention of the usual contemporary European rules of war. The captives had their legs broken and were beheaded, and one source describes a certain Alice of Abergavenny, a camp follower who carried out many of the decapitations (though probably not the seventy of lore) in retaliation for the death of her lover in the battle. The bodies were then thrown over the cliffs into the sea.

This was a suitably arresting curtain-raiser for the sack of Waterford that summer. Strongbow himself now decided to join the action and made his way to Milford Haven, raising a substantial expeditionary force as he went. As he was about to set sail, however, word came through from Henry: the king – perturbed, maybe, at the notion of a potentially autonomous kingdom being established in Ireland – had forbidden the force to depart. But Strongbow could not now back down without fatally losing face. He sailed from Milford Haven on 23 August 1170, established himself at the river crossing at Passage, below Waterford, and arrived at the walls of the city on 25 August. Waterford's Norse rulers were not prepared to surrender; and their resolve to hold out could only have been strengthened by the news of the bloody violence at Baginbun a few months previously. However, the city walls were breached rapidly and, after a period of intense street fighting, Waterford fell that same day. 'A great slaughter of the foreigners at Port Láirge by the overseas fleet' was how the *Annals of Innisfallen* records the siege and battle, implying that the conflict had nothing to do with the Irish themselves.[7] The truth, of course, was very different.

That the sack of Waterford still resonates in the annals of Irish history is in part due to the work of the nineteenth-century Irish painter Daniel Maclise, whose vast canvas of *The Marriage of Strongbow and Aoife* (1854) hangs today in the National Gallery of Ireland. This painting portrays the couple in front of a throng of pseudo-Graeco-Roman divinities; stacks of corpses lie piled all about and the streets of the city run red with blood. Aoife and her female companions are lit sharply and glaringly, while Strongbow and his knights stand in deep shadow. The painting exemplifies the extent to which a representation of a historical event can be interpreted in fundamentally different ways. In the nationalist tradition, the painting is a moving evocation of complete subjugation – the forced marriage of England and Ireland. This interpretation, however, ignores the fact that

Maclise himself was a Unionist and that his painting was designed to celebrate the vigour of the British Empire in all its Victorian might.

Yet the material point is how Strongbow and his men regarded both the events at Waterford and the marriage itself. They saw their expedition as the beginning of a land grab: this, after all, was the reason they had come to Ireland in the first place. The taking of Waterford was instrumental to these plans, for it enabled them to upgrade their status in Irish affairs: no longer a peripheral force, they were now a significant power and one that would be able – up to a point – to control its own destiny. Similarly, the marriage of Strongbow to Aoife raised the possibility of a new bloodline, a new dynastic order in the land – a shocking change in such a conservative and tightly regulated society: 'and Dermot gave [Strongbow] his own daughter,' noted the *Annals of Loch Cé* with shrill outrage, 'and a part of his patrimony; and Saxon Foreigners have been in Erinn since then'.[8] This was a situation pregnant with the potential for yet greater Anglo-Norman influence in Ireland – though it did not as yet signify a done deed. The next move must be the capture of Dublin.

Strategically situated, wealthy and confident, Dublin remained the key to Ireland; and MacMurrough himself had long understood that his rule in Leinster could never be properly secure without control of the city too. It is at this point that MacMurrough – who had not even been present at the capture of Waterford, so rapid had been the advance and onslaught of Strongbow – came into his own. The Hiberno-Norse rulers of Dublin might have felt relatively confident that they could withstand the Anglo-Norman onslaught: the city's defences were stout, and the overland route from Waterford and the southeast was squeezed between the sea and the granite mass of the Wicklow mountains, which were considered impassable to any substantial army. Nevertheless, they knew what had happened at Waterford and hastily sent word to Rory O'Connor, requesting aid. It was forthcoming: O'Connor could see as clearly as everyone else that these new arrivals presented an imminent threat if he did not act. O'Connor's army – very large, if perhaps not quite as large as Giraldus subsequently claimed – gathered at Clondalkin, southwest of Dublin, to await the enemy.

As it turned out, both O'Connor's army and the men of Dublin had not accounted for the local knowledge of MacMurrough and his men. Rather than march along the coast, as had been anticipated, the combined force of MacMurrough and Strongbow traced a path through the mountains and so came down upon Dublin unawares. Seeing that they were suddenly cut off from their allies in the city and sensing defeat in the air, O'Connor's army melted away; a few days later, with negotiations over the fate of the city still ongoing, the Anglo-Normans launched a sudden attack, took the city walls and streamed into Dublin. Asculph, the last Norse ruler of the city, fled rather ingloriously in a ship made ready for just such an eventuality; and Strongbow seized control on 21 September 1170. In the aftermath of the taking of the city, he and MacMurrough set out to press home their advantage in a campaign across Meath and into O'Rourke's territory in Breifne, burning and destroying as they went. O'Connor's army withdrew across the Shannon into his native Connacht and the year ended as well as it could have done for Strongbow. In the spring of 1171 MacMurrough died unexpectedly at Ferns, 'without the body of Christ', as the *Annals of Ulster* thundered, 'without penitence, without making a will, through the merits of Colum Cille and Finnen and the saints whose churches he had spoiled'.[9] Strongbow was now King of Leinster.

But his position, though strong, was far from unassailable. The Hiberno-Norse launched a counter-attack on Dublin shortly after MacMurrough's death, gathering in a fleet of over sixty ships at the mouth of the river Liffey. Giraldus describes the Norse as 'warlike figures, clad in mail in every part of their body after the Danish manner. Some wore long coats of mail, others iron plates skilfully knitted together, and they had round, red shields protected by iron round the edge.'[10] For some time the outcome of the battle rested on a knife edge – but these warriors, 'whose iron will matched their armour', were repulsed in the end and Asculph, who had returned with his fleet to reclaim the city, was captured and beheaded.

This attack on Dublin – formidable though it was – represented only the preamble to a larger assault that summer, in which Irish armies took up their stations north, south and west of the city and Norse fleets blockaded the harbour. There followed a prolonged process of attrition: O'Connor sent word that the Anglo-Normans might keep Dublin, Wexford and Waterford but would have to relinquish Leinster and their other territorial gains – and there is little doubt that at that moment he was in a position to make such a favourable deal with the newcomers. But Strongbow would have the last word: an Anglo-Norman sortie was sent out in stealth from Dublin and attacked one of the Irish encampments at Finglas, northwest of the city. In the slaughter that followed, over a thousand Irish soldiers were killed, though O'Connor himself escaped and fled westward. This, his last throw of the dice, had been unsuccessful: the protracted siege was broken; the remaining Irish armies dispersed once again to their own territories; and Strongbow himself hastened south to relieve an attack on Wexford.

At last he was master of the Irish territories he had won by marriage and by force of arms. But Strongbow remained a vassal – and his overlord was far from pleased with the pace of events. For Henry II, observing from mainland Europe, the unfolding story in Ireland was both good and bad news. It suited his purposes well enough to have the problematic Strongbow removed for a while from Wales, to face whatever fate awaited him across the Irish Sea; and it was equally important to have a bridgehead secured in Ireland. He was less than content, however, with the playing out of subsequent events; and especially displeased at the news that Strongbow had assumed, on the death of his father-in-law MacMurrough, the title of King of Leinster. Such a title was all very well in Ireland, where kings remained numerous: the concept in Europe, however, was beginning to cohere and become very restricted; this was not a club that just anyone could join. That a vassal of the Crown might himself set up as a monarch was anathema to Henry: there must be one pivot only in his realm, one centre of power; and Strongbow's activities merely served to underscore the fragility of the king's own authority.

Strongbow was no mere uppity provincial: he was a potential rival to Henry. And he was, like his liege lord himself, a descendant of William of Normandy: Henry needed no history lessons to remind him of what might happen should an alternative focus of power build up on the margins of one's land, should a rival seize the opportunity to invade and occupy. William had given a master-class on this very subject at Hastings in 1066; and while Henry owed his throne to his great-grandfather's daring, he would not permit Strongbow the same opportunity. Instead, the Anglo-Norman adventurers in Ireland would be kept firmly in line, lest the country develop into a safe haven for his rivals and enemies. This is the beginning of a theme that would become dominant as the centuries passed: Ireland would be persistently represented as a base, a springboard, a back door. Successive English governments in particular would imagine Ireland as a temptation to enemies eager to destabilize from afar, to invade from the rear, to overthrow the English state from a position of safety and proximity. But for Henry at this time, these fears were related to his whole power base, not merely to England.

It was against such a fraught geopolitical backdrop that the king now resolved to assert his rule and authority in Ireland. He had already begun to do so, in fact, issuing a series of decrees that signalled his engagement in Irish affairs and announced his determination to clip Strongbow's wings: all Anglo-Norman ships in Ireland, for example, had been ordered to return to their home ports or risk the confiscation of their cargoes. Strongbow had responded by sending messages professing fealty to the king, and emphasizing that all that had been gained in Ireland was ulti-mately the possession of the Crown. Such a display of public grovelling was most welcome – but Henry knew well enough that they were merely fine words. He remained intent on coming to Ireland himself: and in advance of his journey he ordered Strongbow to a meeting in Pembrokeshire, where he might lay down the law once and for all.

In the event, there could be no mistaking the nature of the power rela-tionship between the king and Strongbow. Had the latter ever contemplated the idea of an independent kingdom in Ireland, Henry's show of strength would have put paid to such a fancy. Giraldus portrays a meeting that shifts gradually in tone from apoplectic rage to benevolent amiability. The nature of the feudal relationship between the two men was underscored: Strong-bow once more offered the king his public loyalty; and Henry recognized Leinster as his servant's possession by right. But he would not go further than this; Strongbow's most recent acquisitions in Meath were not mentioned, nor were the vital seaports of Dublin, Wexford and Waterford. And, on 16 October 1171, an imposing fleet sailed from Milford Haven, carrying some thousands of soldiers together with a force of archers and a good deal of sealing wax – the uses of which would soon become apparent. This fleet landed near Waterford the following day, and the city was formally surrendered to Henry.

This was another significant milestone in the history of the Anglo-Norman presence in Ireland, although later Irish annalists strove to suggest it was no such thing: the *Annals of Inisfallen*, for example, declines even to mention Henry's name, instead implying that he was in some way still tied to the apron strings of his mother, Matilda: 'The son of the Empress,' it sniffs, 'came to Ireland and landed at Port Láirge.' But the Anglo-Norman barons, newly enriched with Irish lands, could be under no such illusion. They gathered at Waterford to greet the monarch – whose first act in response was an assertion of his own authority over his vassals. This was the beginning of the Crown's formal presence in Ireland. Henry asserted the Plantagenet possession of Dublin, Wexford and Waterford and their immediate hinterlands; and Strongbow was confirmed in his authority over Leinster. These were the first edicts the monarch issued in Ireland, but there would be a good many more during his stay, the royal seal stamped in wax on all of them. He was in Ireland, in other words, not to shed blood but to legislate and to order the country's affairs in his own interests.

It was not only these new Anglo-Norman landowners who came to submit to Henry – the native Irish were also eager to pay homage. Dermot McCarthy, king of the territory of Desmond in the southwest, was the first to arrive, and he was soon followed by others. Giraldus records these events with faithful loyalty:

> [King Dermot of Cork] was drawn forthwith into a firm allegiance by the bond of submission, an oath of fealty and the giving of hostages; an annual tribute was imposed on his kingdom; of his own free will he submitted himself to the King of England. The king moved his army from [Waterford] and went first to Lismore, where he stayed for two days, and from there continued to Cashel. There, on the next day, Donal, King of Limerick, met him by the river Suir. He obtained the privilege of the king's peace, tribute was assessed on his kingdom ... and he too displayed his loyalty to the king by entering into the very strongest bonds of submission.[11]

As the royal progress moved towards Dublin, so a succession of Irish rulers – including Tiernan O'Rourke, much weakened by the upheavals of recent years – came to pay homage to Henry and submit to his rule. This rapid and apparently unproblematic submission may seem striking, but the Irish elite of the twelfth century had no particular philosophical problem with the concept of a foreign king – especially if he might well rein in the power of freelancing Anglo-Norman adventurers. The Irish rulers would also have hoped that Henry would depart as quickly as he had arrived: it would be a good deal more agreeable to be a vassal to a distant, absent king than to a neighbour always on the hunt for additional taxes and tribute – a neighbour such as Rory O'Connor, for example, who delayed his own submission to Henry and who remained the nominal high king. There was a good deal more to be gained from being loyal servants of Henry than from offering futile resistance to him.

Moreover, the size of the army that Henry had brought to Ireland – the largest force that had ever been seen on the island to that point – also played its part: pragmatism would always win the day in such a situation. Much better, the thinking went, to buy Henry off with a little flattery and conventional displays of loyalty. Such a formula cost very little; and was, moreover, by no means an unfamiliar cultural phenomenon, either in Ireland or in Europe as a whole. Dealing in such a way with another ruler created a personal bond; it was sealed practically and symbolically with hostages and tribute. And crucially, the power, lands and wealth of the subordinate all remained intact. It was a good deal – at least for the moment – and this was thoroughly understood by both parties to it.

The Irish bishops were also content to accept Henry as the country's leader. The synod held at Cashel early in 1172 was the king's work: his official reason for being in Ireland, after all, had been to implement the pope's orders and regularize Church affairs along Roman lines; and he had, therefore, to be seen to do something in this direction. At Cashel, the bishops agreed the introduction of tithe in Ireland, along with firm rules governing marriage, property rights, church attendance and much else: the full introduction, in other words, of the Church's Gregorian reforms (initiated by Pope Gregory I in the sixth century). Again, however, there were fine distinctions: authority over Ireland might have been ceded to Henry, but at no time did the pope – now Alexander III – or the Irish bishops cede their own ecclesiastical authority to the king. The Irish Church would continue to be answerable to Rome, and to Rome alone.

Henry now moved on to Dublin, where he spent the winter of 1171–2. Rather than stay inside the walled city – where Christ Church Cathedral on its hill was already more than a century old – he decided that he would establish his court just east of the city walls, close to where Trinity College stands today. This location was chosen presumably because of its historical resonances: the Norse Thing or gathering mound, where laws had been read and disputes settled in the days of the Viking supremacy, remained a prominent feature of this district of the city. Henry was signalling that he would take up where the Norse had so lately left off: that he, and nobody else, would henceforth be legislating for Dublin. He also ordered the construction of a large palace of wattle, in the Irish manner; and here he celebrated Christmas of 1171 with a feast, to which were invited the Irish great and good. But Henry's stay was certainly not all festive cheer: he had Dublin's Hiberno-Norse population forcibly removed to what would become the suburb of Oxmantown on the opposite bank of the river Liffey. And in the aftermath of this expulsion, measures to separate the two peoples became a feature of the social and political landscape. The women of Anglo-Norman Dublin, for example, could be fined sixpence for wearing kerchiefs dyed in saffron in the Irish style: it became imperative to display signs of cultural difference from, and superiority over, the surrounding population.[12] Taking this civic engineering a step further, Henry now also made over the city itself to the traders of Bristol. Dublin already had, of course, long-standing trade links with the southwest of England, but Henry's edict had the effect of decisively reorienting the city. No longer could Dublin foster its potent economic and cultural links with northern Europe and the Scandinavian world. Henceforth it would be formally an English colony, with its destiny and its economic vitality tied to the English market and the English Crown.

Henry sailed from Wexford in April 1172, his departure hastened by a stormy, icy, disease-ridden Irish winter and by troubling and long-feared changes that had taken place in his sprawling empire. His three eldest sons had risen against him, and Louis VII of France had taken advantage of his long absence to attack Normandy. The king would never return to Ireland, but his expedition had been a triumph and he had achieved what he had set out to do: Anglo-Norman authority had taken root firmly in the east and southeast; the vital seaports had been secured; potent connections had been made with the Irish kings and his own authority was now accepted by them; and he was now Lord of Ireland in addition to the long list of his other titles.

In the aftermath of Henry's departure, skirmishes at once began on the shifting border between the new colony and Gaelic Ireland. In one such, Tiernan O'Rourke was killed: his head was brought back to Dublin and displayed on the city's battlements. The Anglo-Norman position was further compromised by revolts against Henry's rule in Brittany, Gascony and on the Scottish borders, and by yet more French attacks on Normandy. The king called on his Irish vassals to come to his aid and they obeyed, thus weakening their position in Ireland itself. The result was a period of political and military conflict, marked by attack and counter-attack across the south of the country and the expulsion of the Anglo-Norman garrisons from Waterford and Limerick. Once more the future of the newcomers appeared uncertain, and it took a formal document to bring a measure of order to Ireland.

The Treaty of Windsor, signed by Henry and Rory O'Connor on 6 October 1175, carved up the country between the Anglo-Normans and the Irish, with the former confirmed in their possession of Dublin and the southeast; outside these lands the high king's authority was accepted, and O'Connor was also obliged to keep the peace among the Irish. The treaty looked sensible on paper – but within two years it had failed. Henry was too far away to curb the rapacity of his own Anglo-Norman knights, who were now pushing the borders of the colony north along the eastern coastline of Ulster, and O'Connor was simply incapable of wielding authority over the Irish. Meanwhile, the recent troubles throughout his empire had convinced Henry that a radically new direction was needed. The result was a marked change in policy: the Angevin entity would be split into units that would henceforth be governed directly by the king's four sons; the youngest, John (1166–1216), would be the new King of Ireland. It was a decision that, like the Treaty of Windsor, made perfect sense: Henry's vast lands were knitted together only by allegiance to a common lord and a common family; and by hiving off the empire's component parts into family hands, Henry hoped to bequeath an empire that would outlast him. But from a practical point of view the new kingship of Ireland made no more sense than had the treaty that preceded it, for it presupposed that Ireland was, or at any rate soon would be, a united polity – when in truth it was nothing of the sort.

It would be eight years before the young John visited Ireland. In the interim Henry appointed a series of lieutenants, tasked with bedding down royal power. When John eventually arrived in his realm, in the spring of 1185, his visit – if the accounts are to be believed – proved to be a diplomatic disaster. Giraldus was on hand throughout and his chronicle is spiced with details of his lord's failings, of his disrespect and arrogance, of an expedition that was doomed from the very first. John and his companions, he tells us, abused the Irish who came to submit themselves on his arrival at Waterford: 'our newly arrived Normans treated them with contempt and derision, and showing them scant respect, pulled some of them about by their beards, which were large and flowing according to the native custom.'[13] The Irish leaders, claimed Giraldus, left and began instantly to plot revenge. Furthermore, John and his uncouth entourage went to some pains to treat the resident Anglo-Norman lords with equal disrespect – with the result that anger and bitterness followed the young man wherever he went.

Although such colourful tales improve in the telling, Giraldus would not have had the inside track on any Irish plots and intrigues. Instead, it seems clear that he viewed as an affront John's policy – sensible though it was from the Crown's point of view – of granting lands to new settlers whose loyalty was not in doubt. It is highly unlikely – beard-pulling notwithstanding – that common cause was suddenly forged among the Irish lords; and rather more likely that the original Anglo-Norman settlers were by this stage so embedded in Irish society and so intent on following their own agenda that John could make no military or administrative impact on what was nominally his lordship.

John eventually left in December – a time of year when no ship would normally brave the crossing to Wales – and returned to his father with tales of the ungrateful and rebellious residents of Ireland. Nevertheless, Henry persisted in his plans for a separate kingdom; and to this end, an envoy arrived from Pope Urban III in January 1187 carrying permission to establish such a state in Ireland and a crown of peacock feathers for the new King John. This prospective new kingdom stands as one of the great 'what ifs' of Irish history. What if Henry's plans had come to pass? Would Ireland have evolved into a state separate from, and equal to, England? If so, how would its varied society have developed? But Henry's great plan was to unravel: one by one, John's elder brothers died; and instead of becoming King of Ireland in due course, John succeeded to the throne of England in 1199. Ireland would remain a lordship, in a position subservient to the English Crown, for another four hundred years.

John has been popularly regarded as one of England's worst monarchs. His record as an excellent administrator – overhauling the civil service, for example, and in the process laying down the foundations of a modern state – has traditionally been overshadowed by the rather more interesting litany of his sins, which range from losing control of Normandy to sparking a civil war in England, from mislaying the Crown Jewels in the East Anglian fens to being cruel, capricious, murderous and (worst of all) the arch-foe of Robin Hood. Yet he left a deep imprint on Irish affairs. It was during his reign (1199–1216) that the basis of royal government was created, with strongholds established at such strategic locations as Athlone and Clones, influencing events in Connacht and Ulster respectively. He is remembered too for ordering the construction of Dublin Castle, the foundations of which were laid in 1204: this complex would for centuries function as both the symbol and reality of foreign authority in Ireland. John's reign also brought, in 1207, the first national coinage, and the application of English common law in the Irish colony. The interpretation and traced consequences of these facts have inevitably been disputed down the years, but their impact cannot be doubted. It was also the case that John, like his father before him, was at least as concerned by the actions of his independently minded Anglo-Norman landowning subjects as he was by those of the Irish; as a result, he learned to treat the latter as a group that might be wooed to keep the colonists in check, putting a final stop to the freewheeling adventuring that had gone before. Moreover, John's misfortunes elsewhere in Europe impacted directly and immediately on Ireland: as his European territories shrank and the Angevin Empire began to focus on England, so the energy available for Ireland increased. It was a sign of events to come.

John's lightning final trip to Ireland in the summer of 1210 demonstrates that, while in English history he is known disparagingly as 'Lackland', he understood well how to conduct a thoroughly effective military campaign. He landed at Waterford on 21 June and, in the course of a two-month stay, managed both to build bridges with Irish chiefs (and extract hostages from them too, in order to be certain) and to settle the main Anglo-Norman issue of the day, the rebellion of Hugh de Lacy in Ulster. De Lacy's strings of castles on the northeast coast and on Lough Neagh were popularly regarded as impregnable – but John swept all before him and de Lacy fled to Scotland. With all issues settled, the king departed Ireland in a swirl of efficiency and was back in England by the end of August. These were not the actions of a conqueror, in spite of what Giraldus might have claimed: what John sought was a stable, trustworthy and revenue-producing polity on his western flank.

The death of John six years later had immediate and long-lasting repercussions for Ireland. He had inherited from his father Henry the concept of his realm as a federation of kingdoms and duchies bound by loyalty to their ruler – and he was, therefore, instinctively open to the Gaelic concept of the high king as a loose overlord to whom one owed allegiance in return for a good deal of flexibility in running one's own affairs. So long as John remained on the throne, this delicately poised status quo remained in place: with his death, however, it broke down, and new policies began instead to highlight the chasm between native Irish and colonists. Almost immediately, for example, the new statutes of Magna Carta came into effect: the rights of landowners and nobles in the lands settled by the Anglo-Normans were thus guaranteed – but the charter did not extend to the Irish themselves. At the same time, Irish appointments to the Church were forbidden. In a letter to the Irish Church, Pope Honorius reacted sharply:

> It has come to our knowledge that certain Englishmen have, with unheard-of audacity, decreed that no Irish cleric, no matter how educated or reputable, is to be admitted to any ecclesiastical dignity. We are not prepared to allow so temerarious and wicked an abuse to pass in silence, and we command you by authority of this letter to denounce the decree as null and void, forbidding the said Englishmen from enforcing it or attempting anything of the kind in future. You are to make known that Irish clerics, whose merits are attested by their lives and learning, are to be freely admitted to ecclesiastical dignities, provided they have been canonically elected to their posts.[14]

While the Crown might from time to time call upon the Gaelic lords to provide manpower and weapons – in 1244, for example, the men of Connacht turned up to fight for Henry III in Wales – it was generally happy to emphasize vital distinctions between Irish and non-Irish in the colony. One source describes 'two races, one of which … dwells in the towns, castles and seaports; the other is a wild people … who speak a strange language … which have neither town, house, castle nor dwelling and dwell always in the woods, and on the mountains of the country, and have many chiefs among themselves, of whom [even] the most powerful go barefoot and without breeches, and ride horse without saddles.'[15]

These new policies find their best expression in the application of the law. Although the common law of England had been extended in theory to Ireland, it was not applied in the distinctive Angevin manner – that is, with reference to already existing local law and mores. Time and experience had demonstrated the sense of this Angevin custom, which made the existence of a new regime, a new ruling elite, much easier to digest. In Wales, for example, it was common practice to hear cases according either to the laws of Wales or to English common law, depending on where the court was sitting – and this in spite of the Crown's persistent difficulties in asserting its rule in the country. In Ireland, however, traditional Irish laws were not permitted any place in the workings of the new colonial administration. This state of affairs had much to do with the fact that certain aspects of Irish law – those permitting vendetta, for instance, or calling for material compensation in reparation for an act of homicide – were regarded by the English authorities as another example of the barbarism intrinsic to the Irish nature. As a result, the indigenous aristocracy was without legal protection for the lands they still held; simultaneously, the common Irish labourer, tied to his landowner, was denied legal protection simply as a result of his status. Individuals would on occasion be granted the protection of the common law – but the situation remained fundamentally discriminatory.[16]

This gradual assertion of colonial authority in the thirteenth century also found physical expression: the large-scale construction of castles and keeps, many of which survive in one form or another to the present day, transformed the countryside. Giraldus, noting the strategic and military utility of the castle in the Irish landscape, muses that:

> the less remote part of the country, as far as the river Shannon, which divides the three eastern parts of the island [i.e. Ulster, Munster and Leinster] from the fourth [Connacht], should be secured and protected by the construction of many castles … it is far, far better to begin by gradually connecting up a system of castles built in suitable places and by proceeding cautiously with their construction, than to build large numbers of castles at great distances from each other, sited haphazardly in various locations, without their forming any coherent system of mutual support or being able to relieve each other in times of crisis.[17]

These infrastructural changes were altogether new: Irish kings, even the most powerful, tended not to live in what one would call castles or elaborate forts. Instead – largely because each local or provincial economy revolved to an extent around the herding of cattle and other livestock – they lived a partially nomadic life; the creation of large centres of power in such a milieu would run contrary to cultural norms and political reality. The newcomers, on the other hand, were firmly invested in the principle of creating buildings that were meant to last. They believed in them not only for defensive purposes, but also symbolically: a great man needed a great residence in which to live and dominate the surrounding countryside. The flip side of such vast works of encastellation, however, lies in the clear understanding that they were so urgently *needed*: the colonial expansion across the country was constantly opening up new areas of conflict and dispute; and the colonizers' grip on their lands could never be taken for granted.

At the same time, new agrarian practices were being implemented in Ireland. It would be wholly inaccurate to imagine the landscape of Gaelic Ireland as purely pastoral: land continued to be given over, as it had for many hundreds of years, to the production of oats and barley, with a little wheat and flax for the production of linen. But the twelfth century in Europe had witnessed an agricultural revolution, and now the Anglo-Normans transferred the rudiments of this sophisticated agrarian economy into Ireland by means of the cultivation of cereal crops on a much larger scale. This conversion to more intensive agriculture was driven by the recognition that much of Leinster and Munster were ideally suited to these methods of farming. It was given added urgency by the loss of the fertile plains of Normandy to the French in 1204: the English were obliged to make up the difference with a more thorough exploitation of land elsewhere.

In the middle of this changing rural landscape, new communities began to develop: most of the market towns in the south and east of Ireland can trace their beginnings back to this period, as full urbanization took root in the country. The aim of the colonists in establishing what was sometimes quite a dense network of towns and communities was to re-create a familiar country beyond the Irish Sea. They wished to replicate in Ireland the familiar paraphernalia of life that had existed back home: the crops and castles joined by parish churches and monasteries, by priests and labourers, by merchants and tradesmen and farmers. And in consequence, the colonial presence was no longer a matter of adventurers on the make; it became a story of cultural transformation, as men and women and children by the shipload began to arrive in Ireland, as towns and countryside were moulded into a more comfortable form. This gradual expansion of the English colony at the expense of the Irish in the course of the thirteenth century was culturally and economically shocking. As the boundaries of the colony extended outward, the Irish were left increasingly with the marginal and less agriculturally viable land. It would create a powerful imperative in the Irish mind to hold whatever territory was left.

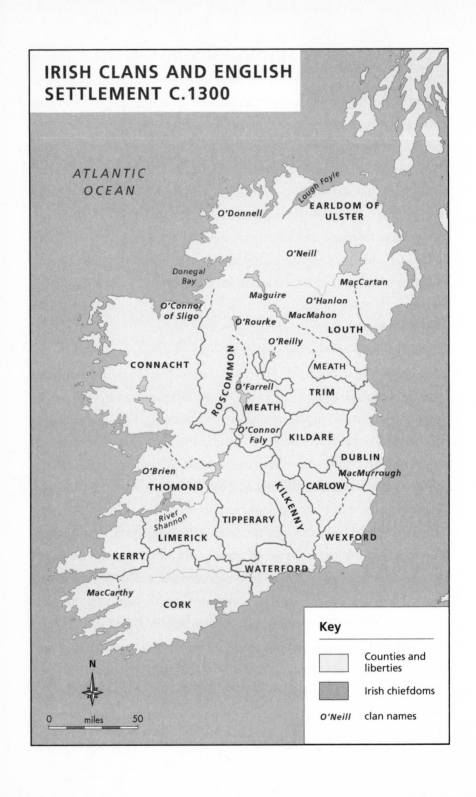

IRISH CLANS AND ENGLISH SETTLEMENT C.1300

ATLANTIC
OCEAN

Lough Foyle

EARLDOM OF
ULSTER

O'Donnell

O'Neill

*Donegal
Bay*

MacCartan

Maguire

O'Hanlon

*O'Connor
of Sligo*

O'Rourke

MacMahon

LOUTH

O'Reilly

CONNACHT

ROSCOMMON

MEATH

O'Farrell

TRIM

MEATH

*O'Connor
Faly*

KILDARE

DUBLIN

O'Brien

MacMurrough

THOMOND

KILKENNY

CARLOW

*River
Shannon*

TIPPERARY

WEXFORD

LIMERICK

KERRY

WATERFORD

MacCarthy

CORK

N

0   miles   50

Key

Counties and
liberties

Irish chiefdoms

O'Neill clan names

CHAPTER FOUR

WASTED AND CONSUMED

In the century that followed John's campaign in Ireland, the authority of the lordship became firmly recognized across the south and east. The names of counties that are familiar today – Carlow and Kildare, Kilkenny and Tipperary and Kerry – were already inscribed on the maps; established settlements and fortified strongholds had spread along the coasts of Ulster and Connacht as far as Donegal Bay and Lough Foyle; and no part of the island of Ireland was immune to the influence of the colony. Yet the maps and records tell only one side of the story: in practice, the political situation was curiously unresolved. The authorities at Dublin were engaged in a game of checks and balances with a host of rulers up and down the land – local powers in any number of hues, both Irish and Anglo-Irish, all of them able to command the attention and loyalty of swathes of the population. The power of the lordship on the ground was far from undisputed, and the fragility of colonial authority in Ireland was becoming increasingly apparent.

This feeling found its clearest expression in what might be called the first formal articulation of Irish alienation from English rule. Written in about 1318 from King Donal O'Neill in Ulster to Pope John XXII, the *Remonstrance of the Princes* expresses the rising sense of grievance and outrage felt by the Irish against the English community in the country.

There is no hope whatever of our having peace with them. For such is their arrogance and excessive lust to lord it over us and so great is our due and natural desire to throw off the unbearable yoke of their slavery and to recover our inheritance wickedly seized upon by them, that as there has not been hitherto, there cannot now be, or ever henceforth be established, sincere good will between them and us in this life. For we have such a natural hostility to each other arising from the mutual, malignant and incessant slaying of fathers, brothers, nephews and other near relatives and friends that we can have no inclination to reciprocal friendship in our time or that of our sons... .[1]

The *Remonstrance* is a powerful statement of Irish cultural identity. Far from being a piece of proto-nationalist propaganda, though, it does not overtly reject the English right to rule Ireland. Instead, it internationalizes its focus by referencing the original papal decision to grant the rule of Ireland to the English Crown; a copy of *Laudabiliter* was even included in the dispatch to clarify the point. The pope gave Ireland to the English, the *Remonstrance* argues, on the understanding that the country would be governed well and with justice; and the Irish were willing to become loyal vassals of the Crown on the same basis.

The Crown, however, never kept its side of the bargain:

Their regular clergy dogmatically assert that it is no more a sin to kill an Irishman than a dog or any brute …. They have striven with all their might and with every treacherous artifice in their power, to wipe our nation out entirely and utterly to extirpate it …. In order to shake off the hard and intolerable yoke of their slavery and to recover our ancient liberty … we are compelled to wage deadly war with them … rather than to bear like women their atrocious outrages.

Equally, the Remonstrance was not antipathetic to the English *per se*. Rather, its grievances were directed towards those colonists who had crossed the sea and settled as an Anglo-Irish 'middle nation' in Ireland, in the process taking the best land and reducing the Gaelic economy to near destitution.

In rejecting as legally void the English authority over Ireland, O'Neill was naturally asserting his own claim to the country based on his lineage. But he also had a larger political agenda: rather than press this claim in his own right, he wanted to pass his notional throne on to another claimant, Edward Bruce (*c.*1280–1318), the brother of King Robert Bruce of Scotland (1274–1329). By 1318, in fact, Edward had already been involved in Ireland for several years, having landed at the head of a Scottish army on the Antrim coast in the spring of 1315. For O'Neill, the invitation made political sense: in offering the throne of Ireland to Edward, he could protect his own local interests in Ulster from a host of rivals; his calculations followed a time-honoured Gaelic model of placing local needs and local power structures first and foremost.

Scottish intervention in Irish affairs was by now commonplace. The Norse city-state of Dublin had had strong and enduring ties with the Norse of Scotland; later, the new English colonial authorities in Ireland had become accustomed to playing their part in the wars with the Scots; mercenaries from Scotland were long-established players on the Irish military scene; and at this very time, Robert Bruce himself had married an Ulster noblewoman. Fresh from an indecisive victory over the English at Bannockburn in June 1314, Bruce understood the importance of Ireland to the future of Scotland. At best, he could safely install Edward on the Irish throne, wrest the country from its English orbit and secure a valuable ally to the west. Even if the conquest of Ireland could not in the end be accomplished, he might hope for a secure base along the eastern seaboard of Ulster and control of the northern half of the Irish Sea. At worst, it would distract the English on his southern border by opening up a second, expensive flank in the battle; and it would disrupt the flow of Irish manpower and grain that hitherto had helped to maintain the wars between England and Scotland.

The Scottish invasion of Ireland was particularly savage. Having pacified much of eastern Ulster and created a safe Irish base, Edward led his men south, the intention being not to capture and subdue the fortified bases of Leinster but to burn communities, lay waste to the countryside and create anarchy for the Dublin government. It was, from their point of view, a sensible strategy – the Scots had besieged the castle at Carrickfergus at the heart of their Ulster base for over a year before finally capturing it, and they had presumably learned a lesson or two in the process – and it worked too: the rich farmland of Leinster provided the economic pulse of the lordship and the Scots' depredations did indeed create economic turmoil. But it was unfortunate for the invaders – not to mention the civilian population of Ireland – that the three-year campaign in the country coincided with a Europe-wide famine. While the Scottish troops might be able to seize what provisions they could find, a succession of bitter winters and cold, stormy summers meant that there was simply no food to be had.

Ultimately, Edward Bruce's campaign failed because, in spite of the Crown's increasingly tenuous hold over Ireland, the authorities' control of Dublin was never seriously compromised. In 1317 the Scots briefly threatened to take the city, and the authorities responded by setting fire to the northwestern suburbs in an effort to hamper the advance; this strategy worked, even if in the process the fire spread and burned down much of the centre of the city. Nor did the Irish come together in an alliance against the Crown; and the Anglo-Irish barons, rooted in their own cultural identity, saw clearly that the English connection offered more than a Scottish one ever could. Edward withdrew once more into Ulster and, on 14 October 1318, he was killed in battle near Dundalk; parts of his dismembered body were brought to Dublin as evidence of his death.

The invasion was eventually stemmed, then, but at great cost. The slowness of the Dublin authorities in meeting and defeating the Scots was evidence of their own underlying military and fiscal weakness; and their sluggish and limited response to the destruction wrought by the Scottish armies exposed further what was clearly the threadbare nature of the English presence in Ireland. Put frankly, governance of much of Ireland was increasingly beyond the administration's strength. Vast tracts of countryside lay wasted following the Scottish campaigns, and would remain unproductive in the decades ahead. The castles, keeps and fortifications built during the thirteenth century were decaying; on the eve of the Scottish onslaught long sections of the walls of Dublin were crumbling; highways, causeways and bridges were increasingly in a state of ruin. The story was the same in towns across the east and south of Ireland. The treasury in Dublin simply did not have the funds to undertake the necessary repairs. The countryside was depopulating too: in these years, many of the smaller communities established in the first years of the lordship vanished from the records for ever; and the English government, involved now in expensive and debilitating war with France, was in no position to invest attention, much less hard cash, in its Irish colony. And, to complete this litany of woe, outbreaks of smallpox and influenza swept through Ireland in the 1320s.

The arrival of the Black Death in Ireland, although it did not mark the culmination of these misfortunes, certainly added to them. The disease had first arrived in southern Europe in the spring of 1348, coming to Sicily from the Black Sea aboard Genoese trading vessels: following long-established trading routes, it had then spread with terrifying speed across the continent. It was first recorded in Ireland in the late summer at the eastern ports of Drogheda, Howth and Dalkey – ferried on ships from Chester and Bristol, maybe, or from France on vessels carrying wine to the Irish market. At Kilkenny, Friar Clyn recorded the frightful impact of the plague before himself being struck down:

More people in the world have died in such a short time of plague than has been heard of since the beginning of time …. The pestilence was so contagious that whosoever touched the sick and the dead was immediately infected and died, so that penitent and confessor were carried to the grave … that pestilence deprived of human inhabitants villages and cities, so that there was scarcely found a man to dwell therein …. Many died of boils and abscesses and pustules which erupted on their shins or under their armpits; others died frantic with pain in their head and others spitting blood … this plague was at its height in Kilkenny during Lent; for on the sixth day of March eight of the Friars Preachers died. There was hardly a house in which only one had died, but as a rule man and wife with their children and all the family went the common way of death.[2]

The Irish chronicles give the plague only glancing mentions. Its effects on the society of Gaelic Ireland remain elusive; but it is clear that its impact was much greater on the crowded and urban world of Anglo–Ireland. It is estimated that the population of Dublin – approximately twenty-five thousand before the onset of the plague – shrank by more than half in its immediate aftermath, and had fallen to less than five thousand a century later.[3]

Such records as have survived report the gloom of these years in the lordship. By the 1360s Ireland had become a charge on, rather than a net contributor to, the coffers of the English exchequer. A circle of decay set in, as agriculture diminished, government revenues fell away, and the reach and clout of the authorities declined. Dublin itself became increasingly detached from the life of the lordship in Munster and Leinster: it became difficult and dangerous to travel from the city to other parts of Ireland; and such urban centres as Limerick and Cork once more became the *de facto* self-governing city-states that they had been in Norse times.

The situation for the colonists became increasingly straitened. In 1349, the citizens of Carlow are recorded as complaining that their lands were being attacked and plundered to within the shadow of the town walls, and the extinction of the settlement itself seemed likely; in 1388, the people of Cork expressed an identical grievance. It is tempting to see these as ploys designed to extract more money from a reluctant treasury – and, indeed, this was doubtless sometimes the case. But not always: by the 1390s, Carlow had truly been plundered and its people had for the most part fled; security had further deteriorated to such an extent that a strong military escort was needed to venture between one town and another; protection money was paid to the Irish chieftains by those colonists who could afford to do so.

It was not, however, all a tale of woe. These same surviving records, for example, detail an export trade in rude health. Ireland may have been more isolated now than it had been for years, but it was by no means wholly adrift from the shipping lanes, and contact with other parts of Europe continued apace. Trade with England, Scotland and Flanders throve; ships called at Irish ports from as far away as the Baltic, the Mediterranean and Portugal, bringing wine, silks and other luxuries in return for Irish wool, timber, hides, fish and corn – ample evidence that parts of the Irish countryside were productive in spite of the prevailing political uncertainty. There are glimpses of an export trade in linen – that most Irish of products – to the markets of Bristol. Sometimes, indeed, there are even records of investment and new building in the southern and southeastern ports. And, although this export trade slackened gradually – most dramatically in the aftermath of the Black Death – it continued through the course of the fifteenth century, even as the economic and political strength of the lordship continued to wane.

Significantly, one reason for this vitality lies in a measure of cooperation that, at certain times and in certain places, existed between the cultures of Ireland. As central control diminished, for example, it made sound economic sense for the trading ports (that handled the export trade) and the hinterlands (that controlled the supply of raw materials) to come together on occasion to assure the flow of trading goods to their mutual benefit. For all that violence and bloodshed were common features of Irish life, then, it was also true that the Irish and the English settlers would sometimes be obliged – increasingly – to communicate in non-confrontational ways. Collision could not be the norm always and everywhere: notions of cultural exclusiveness and purity could vanish rapidly amid the rough and tumble of everyday life; and for both sides, this slow process of acculturation manifested itself in the adoption of certain customs, forms of dress, food and drink, and language when it was prudent or profitable to do so.

As a result, Irish appointees began to take up positions in the civic administrations of the coastal ports, often to the chagrin of the local grandees; and there were settlers in parts of the countryside who were scarcely distinguishable, in dress or language or manner, from the Irish alongside whom they lived. The great settler families, such as the earls of Ormond in Leinster and of Desmond in Munster and (most influential of them all) the FitzGeralds of Kildare, continued to identify strongly with England and to consider themselves English – legally, indeed, they could have held no place in the English hierarchy in Ireland had they not done so. Yet even these dynasties were, to a greater or lesser extent, partly gaelicized – they belonged to both cultures and to neither.

The Statutes of Kilkenny, formulated by the Irish parliament sitting at Kilkenny in 1367, had been an early response to this blurring of the cultural lines in Ireland. The statutes had themselves been anticipated in previous legislation governing the relations between the Irish and colonists, but the laws enacted at Kilkenny were much more clearly directed, seeking to impose a solution to the problems of the colony in Ireland and stating baldly why stern measures were necessary:

Many English of the land forsaking the English language, dress, style of riding, laws and usages, live and govern themselves according to the manners, dress and language of the Irish enemies and also had contracted marriages and alliances with them whereby the land and the liege people thereof, the English language, the allegiance due to our lord king, and English laws there are put in subjection and decayed ....[4]

The colonists had become 'degenerate' and the first aim of the statutes was to stamp out this sickness and renew the colony's essential Englishness.

A host of measures was proposed to this effect. Irish poets and musicians, for example, were forbidden from moving among the colonists, for fear they would spy out their secrets and ways; and the colonists themselves were to be subject to a whole raft of new legislative restrictions. The Irish language was singled out for attention: a colonist caught using Gaelic faced the penalty of being removed from the safeguard of the common law and treated as Irish – a serious penalty, in that the sentence for killing an Englishman was death, whereas the punishment for killing an Irishman was only a fine. This particular clause, in fact, had a broader cultural resonance: simultaneously, the English government was championing the use of English over French as part of its struggle against France in the Hundred Years' War. But the statutes had much more than the Irish language in their sights:

It is ordained and established that no alliance by marriage ... fostering of children, concubinage or sexual liaison or in any other manner be made henceforward between English and Irish on one side or the other ... Also, it is ordained and established that every Englishman use the English language, and be called by an English name abandoning completely the Irish method of naming and that every Englishman use English style in appearance, riding and dress, according to his

position in society …. And that no Englishman worth one hundred
shillings a year in land, holdings or rent shall ride otherwise than on
a saddle in the English style ….

Some of the statutes seem trifling today: the playing of a game called *horling*
– which appears in fact to have been a precursor to modern hockey, rather
than to modern hurling – was forbidden, with colonists enjoined to prac-
tise archery or throwing the lance instead. Taken together, however, they
demonstrate the degree of foreboding in the administration of the lordship
at the time: if the colony were to survive, it was essential that such drastic
measures be adopted.

The statutes also betray the fear that the authorities felt for the colonial
population itself – in particular for its elite, now governing its lands in its
own interests and in its own way, regardless of the wishes of the Crown.
The great irony here is that this population as a whole, regardless of the
manner in which they lived their lives, continued to regard themselves as
culturally English. The statutes were simplistic in the extreme and were
handed down by administrators who seemed to have little true sense of the
intricacies and subtleties of Irish society.

The Statutes of Kilkenny resonate in Irish history, but they also have a
place in the broader context of the evolution of greater state control and
the slow rise of central government in England itself. While they are distinctively racial in their preoccupations and cultural anxieties, they can also be
related to the Statute of Labourers that was passed in England in 1351 with
the intention of curbing the social and economic mobility of those former
landless serfs who had been newly empowered, following the Black Death,
by the dearth of available labour. The Statute of Labourers sought to reim-
pose the power of the aristocracy over this class of peasants; like the Statutes
of Kilkenny, it reflected an anxiety to maintain certain structures of power
and authority in what was a rapidly changing world. Most striking of all,

perhaps, is the understanding that both sets of laws were essentially unenforceable: legislators were gazing Canute-like at the advancing tide, powerless to act. In the case of the Statutes of Kilkenny, the evidence speaks for itself, for they would be enshrined, adopted – and duly ignored. As the fourteenth century ended and the fifteenth began, intermarriage continued; ecclesiastical offices came into the hands of Irish clerics because Englishmen could not be found to fill them; and Irish tenants moved on to the settlers' manors in the absence of anyone else to till the land.

Further attempts would be made to shore up the position of the colony. The expeditions of Richard II – the third and last English monarch to visit medieval Ireland – in 1394–5 and 1399 seemed to achieve their aims, in that a number of Irish chieftains submitted to the king; the colony may have seemed set fair now for a revival. But it was not so: Richard 'gained but little; for the Irish, then feigning submission to his will, straight away after his departure were in revolt, as all men know'.[5] Furthermore, Richard's absence in Ireland resulted in the loss of his kingship (usurped by Henry Bolingbroke) and subsequent death.

Meanwhile, the borders of the Pale – that zone encompassing Dublin and its hinterland in which the Crown's writ more or less ran – had shrunk by the middle of the fifteenth century to within a few miles of the city, and the authorities were obliged to fortify the roads running into Dublin from the west in order to protect it from attack. Stories were told of corn stolen from the fields of the Pale and of buildings attacked and looted by the Irish under cover of darkness. It was not until the very end of the fifteenth century, with the Tudor dynasty more or less established on the throne of England, that the administrations in Dublin and London would at last be in a position to address the situation in Ireland anew. Power would be centralized ruthlessly by the Tudors – and both the freewheeling English barons of Ireland and their Irish neighbours would meet one of history's immovable forces.

*

On 13 October 1494 an English delegation put in at the harbour of Howth, just north of Dublin, and made its way into the city. At its head was Sir Edward Poynings, the king's new representative in Ireland.* Poynings's spell in the country was brief – he would be gone again by 1496 – but what happened in these few years symbolized the renewed English determination to order events in the Irish colony. One of Poynings's first acts was to sweep away the entrenched caste of administrators at Dublin Castle and replace it with English-born officials – representatives of an Old English culture were being supplanted by New English loyalists; it was a decision that set off a wave of unrest and violence in the countryside of the Pale. Very soon, however, Poynings felt secure enough to summon the Irish parliament to meet at Drogheda, on the northern edge of the Pale: the session opened at the beginning of December 1494.

The parliament would sit at Drogheda for several months, and during this time it promulgated a series of thirty or so acts known today as Poynings' Law. Of these, the best remembered is the ninth, which declared that the Irish parliament could no longer legislate independently: all laws would now have to be approved by the English monarch or his representative in Ireland; furthermore, the parliament itself could henceforth not even meet without the monarch's consent. Other provisions – for example, regulating the hiring of certain servants (that is, Gaelic Irish servants) employed by Old English families within the Pale – were reminiscent of the Statutes of Kilkenny in their intentions; others – such as those banning the keeping of private firearms – spoke of a determination to end the private wars and legal and military free-for-all that had characterized life in the lordship. As a whole, there was a clear intentionality behind Poynings' Law: these measures, designed to imprint themselves on the political life of the country,

---

* Poynings was in fact the second-in-command to the official Lord Deputy of Ireland, Henry, Duke of York – who at the time was four years of age.

were drafted and pushed through by the will of a new regime that had just taken power in England.

Henry VII, the first of the Tudor monarchs, had come to the throne in 1485. His first pressing task was to reconcile a state torn apart for three decades by the chaotic Wars of the Roses fought between the Houses of Lancaster and York, and thus to copper-fasten the dubious Tudor claim on the throne itself. Ireland had already played a significant part in one early threat to Henry's power. In late 1486 or early 1487 one Lambert Simnel, a pretender to the throne, escaped from imprisonment in the Tower of London and made his way to Dublin. Here he was supported covertly by Gerald FitzGerald, the eighth Earl of Kildare and first Lord Deputy of Ireland – and thus the king's official representative in the country – and crowned at Christ Church Cathedral on 24 May 1487. Simnel's supporters in Ireland raised an army that was dispatched to England a few weeks later, only to be annihilated at Stoke Field in Lincolnshire on 16 June.*

Simnel's activities had the effect of once again concentrating minds on the state of Ireland. The country may have held no intrinsic allure for the Crown, but the English authorities remained alive to the strategic possibilities of Ireland and to the potential threats it posed. This unease was given further impetus by the subsequent efforts of another pretender, Perkin Warbeck, who paid several visits to Ireland in the 1490s in the course of a campaign of destabilization. There was a perception that the evident neglect of English interests in Ireland, the political drift that had become such a feature of life in the lordship, could not be permitted to continue – that, when circumstances allowed, something had to be done. Poynings's brief visit symbolized this energy: it is significant for the sense of engagement and knowledge of Ireland that it brought. But there would not be any

---

* Simnel was pardoned by Henry VII, who recognized that the pretender had been a pawn in the hands of others: and rather than hand Simnel over to the executioners, the king gave him a job in the royal kitchens.

further sweeping changes in Ireland just yet: at Christmas 1506, to be sure, Henry appears to have arranged for a large and well-organized military force to be sent across the Irish Sea in the following year with the objective of conquering the whole island once and for all – but this plan never materialized, the king's still fragile position making such a great gamble distinctly unwise. He had to be content with already having left a mark on the Irish political scene.

For the moment, then, the FitzGeralds of Kildare continued to exercise influence in the now much-diminished lordship. Their position was maintained by their value in the eyes of the English monarchy – it was cheaper and usually more straightforward to have a local force in the saddle in Ireland. This reality was reaffirmed when the eighth earl, in spite of his obvious disloyalty, was reinstalled in his position as lord deputy: when told that 'All England cannot rule yonder gentleman', Henry's response had been a dry: 'No? Then he is meet to rule all Ireland.' So the Kildare dynasty began the sixteenth century in an ostensibly strong position: secure in the favour of the Crown, and ready and willing to continue to rule Ireland by means of a now-familiar combination of violence, diplomacy and matrimonial alliance.

Henry died in April 1509, and in June his son was crowned at Westminster Abbey. Henry VIII was a formidable character: over 1.8 metres (6 feet) in height – psychologically significant in an era when people were distinctly smaller than they are today – and possessed of a very distinct idea of his divine right to rule.* His world may have been poised between feudal absolutes and the power politics of a new age, but his was not to be a reign like that of his father, mediating between squabbling barons, endlessly sending armies to crush rebellions, uncertain as to where the next challenge to the throne was going to emerge. Within a decade of being crowned, Henry

---

* In sixteenth-century England the average male height was 1.7 metres (5 feet 6 inches).

was sweeping away all obstacles to his power. He rapidly subdued the independently minded nobles of northern England, and it would only be a matter of time before he turned his attentions to their Irish counterparts.

Henry's feelings about Ireland and his subjects there were essentially ambivalent. At one level, he saw a population of colonists that was essentially part of the English nation; at another, however, he saw degeneracy, with these same colonists over-exposed to the barbarous Irish, even to the extent of speaking their tongue, wearing their garb and following their traditions. His objectives for Ireland – at least to begin with – were measured and implemented slowly: they were concerned principally with bringing its uncouth inhabitants more or less to heel, and with maintaining and entrenching existing English control over parts of the country. After all, there were few other avenues open to him: England at the opening of the 1500s remained a second-rate European power, impoverished by the traumatic defeats and loss of foreign territory that had marked the previous century. Henry was hamstrung by empty coffers: there was no money for a wider campaign for change in Ireland, even if the royal will was consistently there. And it was not: Thomas Howard, Earl of Surrey, who briefly replaced the new (ninth) Earl of Kildare as lord deputy in 1520, sighed that it would be better for Henry if Ireland were simply to sink beneath the waves.*

In the years that followed, indeed, the English presence in Ireland reached its nadir – this in spite of the renewed interest displayed by the Tudors. The country's population had still not begun to recover from the ravages of the fourteenth century; moreover, Henry's intelligence services, controlled by Thomas Cromwell, informed him that Kildare was governing the colony solely in the interest of his own family and faction. In Dublin, the city's infrastructure was crumbling (the castle had to be evacuated for fear

---

* Howard, later Duke of Norfolk, was the uncle of two of Henry VIII's wives: Anne Boleyn and Catherine Howard; ironically, in the aftermath of the Reformation, the Howards would remain one of England's most visible Catholic families.

that its buildings would collapse); the Pale was being raided at will; and Kildare was expending the colony's slender strength in bitter feuds and internal strife. He was recalled to London in the autumn of 1533: before leaving Ireland, he appointed his impetuous son Thomas FitzGerald (1513– 37) – nicknamed 'Silken Thomas' on account of his fondness for fine clothes and trappings – deputy governor in his absence, and a chain of momentous events was set in motion. In June the following year, having heard (false) rumours that his father was dead, Silken Thomas convened a council meeting at St Mary's Abbey on the northern bank of the river Liffey opposite Dublin Castle. Here, on 11 June, he threw down his sword of state – the symbol of his office – and formally and publicly rejected the authority of the king; adding for good measure the public pronouncement that Henry's recent marriage to Anne Boleyn was illegal and that the king was a heretic. He followed this up in July with an assault on the castle and the killing of the loyalist Archbishop Allen.

These events would appear to have marked the point of no return for the FitzGeralds. Yet, remarkably, they may not have been intended as such. Given that the dynasty was adept at brinkmanship and that this strategy had worked well in the past, it may have been that the aim of the exercise was simply to pile more pressure on Henry to end his and Thomas Cromwell's meddling in Irish affairs. Silken Thomas, after all, was merely following his father's orders by whipping up a measure of chaos in order to bring Henry to heel: anarchy in Ireland was expensive, and the FitzGeralds were the one force in Ireland who had proved themselves able to bring disorder in the Pale to an end. Yet Thomas miscalculated: the king chose to treat the events in Ireland as outright rebellion. In London, Kildare was arrested and imprisoned in the Tower, where he died in September; in Ireland, the FitzGerald stronghold at Maynooth, outside Dublin, was besieged and taken by Crown forces in March 1535. The castle's defenders were put to death but Silken Thomas, his safety guaranteed, was dispatched to exile in London – where two years later he too was executed, along with his father's five brothers; their remains were exhibited through the streets of the city. The Kildare hegemony was now, definitively, at an end.

Henry's ruthless reaction had been guided by a vital and rapidly changing political scene, one that encompassed a world far beyond Ireland, yet involved Ireland intimately. The king needed to show that he was in control of his own policies and to demonstrate his resolve: if he backed down in Ireland, a good many factions in England would watch and learn from events. The Reformation, meanwhile, brought about by Henry's complicated marital arrangements that had led to a permanent breach with Rome, had a particular Irish dimension: it was the catalyst for a slow rupture in the relationship between the Crown and the 'degenerate' Old English who had inhabited Ireland now for over three hundred years and who remained culturally secure in the Catholicism that Henry was now intent on sweeping away in England itself. For these families, there was an invidious choice: whether to remain with Rome and risk the wrath of the Crown, or to follow Henry in abandoning this age-old link for a new State religion. Faced with this dilemma, many of the colonists would come to resent their cultural link to England – not only because of their adherence to the old faith, but also the loss of the quasi-independence they had enjoyed in Ireland.

The Dublin administration was intent on demonstrating both its temporal and its ecclesiastical authority in Ireland. In the second half of the 1530s, for example, it embarked on a number of military operations throughout the country from south to north. These campaigns caused a good deal of disquiet in Gaelic Ireland, for Crown forces not only captured strongholds that had slipped from their hands but also probed deep into areas that had traditionally been safe Irish territory, including the marshy lowlands of what is now County Offaly and the rugged valleys of the Wicklow mountains. This new, purposeful policy of the State found its best expression at a meeting of the Irish parliament in June 1541, at which the lordship came to an end. Henry was formally declared King of Ireland – the first English monarch to assume the title – and the proclamation was followed by all manner of celebrations in Dublin. The move was of course a logical political step: Henry and his ancestors had held Ireland as a gift of the papacy; but in the light of the Reformation, such a status could not possibly be defended. He had to move swiftly, therefore, to change the country's status and to declare it, not a gift of anyone (and of a pope least of all) but rather an inalienable possession.

At the same time, the State moved to mould the Church in its own image. To all intents and purposes, two Churches now began to coexist within Ireland: one within the bounds of the English colony and the other in the rest of the country. From 1539 the ancient monasteries began to vanish, one by one, as they had done in England; their lands were confiscated and granted to loyal followers of the Crown, and their material wealth was gathered into the State treasuries. By the end of the year they had almost gone from Leinster, their former inmates for the most part left to make a living as best they could. The cultural shock of these changes cannot be underestimated. Attachment to the old systems ran deep and, as in England, it would be no easy matter simply to jettison centuries of Catholicism in favour of the new arrangements. Whether or not the monasteries had been badly run and administered – and very many of them had been in steep decline for decades, the monks abusing their positions and privileges – they had nevertheless been fixtures in the land and in the lives of the communities who lived around them. Many of them had fulfilled important economic, educational and social functions, all of which now disappeared overnight; and the bitterness of the monks in the face of what they considered heresy was communicated rapidly among their former flock.

In addition, the iconoclasm that accompanied the Reformation was deeply shocking to the devout. Take the scene at Dublin in 1538, for example, when Archbishop George Browne (who had officiated at the wedding of Henry and Anne Boleyn) caused a bonfire to be lit in front of Christ Church: as the fire took hold, the cathedral's ancient relics – including the Bachall Íosa, the crozier of Patrick – were brought out and dumped into the flames. At first, such dramatic statements of intent had little effect: the further from Dublin one went, the less influence the reformed Church exerted. The great majority of the clergy and laity in Ireland were unmoved by its agenda and this resistance inevitably took on a political hue: 'The friars and priests of all the Irishry do preach that every man ought, for the salvation of his soul, [to] fight and make war against our sovereign lord the king's majesty and if any of them die in the quarrel, his soul, that so shall be dead, shall go to heaven as the souls of SS Peter, Paul, and others, which suffered death for God's sake.'[6]

It may have been accepted in government circles that the battle for souls might take some time to win, but the military campaigns of the 1530s convinced many that the struggle for land and temporal authority could more easily be achieved. From July 1540, when Sir Anthony St Leger took the reins of authority in Ireland, there was a clear intent to bring a measure of order to as much of the island as possible. This was the beginning of the policy known as 'surrender and regrant', which was born out of the urgent need to settle matters once and for all. This might be done by a full-scale invasion – but, while one faction at court counselled an all-out assault, Henry was more inclined to listen to those pragmatists who formulated a means by which the island might be coaxed into submission without bankrupting the English state in the process.

Surrender and regrant meant that Gaelic chiefs would give up their lands and their political independence to the Crown. Title to these same lands would then be returned to them together with citizenship, English aristocratic titles and the protection of the law – all in return for loyalty, financial tribute in the form of rent, and an agreement to speak and dress in a way becoming to an English citizen. Surrender and regrant would therefore guarantee both peace in Ireland and at the same time a much-needed flow of revenue into the English exchequer. It was a practical solution but psychologically deft too, acknowledging for the first time the requirement that Gaelic lords be treated both as leaders of society in their own right and as people worthy of legal protection, rather than as outlaws almost by birth.

As such, the policy was highly symbolic. The Gaelic lords of Ireland now had the possibility of becoming part of the status quo, though at a price that would include the relinquishment of the existing Gaelic inheritance laws in favour of the English system of primogeniture. The system had some success in the 1540s: some thirty Gaelic Irish and Old English families, including the O'Donnells and O'Neills of far-flung and hitherto obdurately Gaelic Ulster, submitted formally to Henry. But the relationship between Catholicism and the new reformed faith remained in flux, the object of much cultural negotiation; the sharp and unbridgeable divisions between the two faiths would only later become apparent.

Surrender and regrant would remain a central plank of Tudor policy in the years to come. The reigns of Edward VI (1547–53) and Mary I (1553–8) saw English financial and military subventions stepped up in a bid to force the pace – but increased coercion would prove counter-productive, and the growing levels of violence served only to alienate the local settler populations. In particular, the experiment with limited plantation settlers in the lowlands of Leinster – initiated by Edward and continued by Mary – proved disastrously expensive, requiring large garrisons to repel the expropriated O'More and O'Connor clans after the establishment of their territories as Queen's and King's Counties. The Tudors pondered the experience: to what extent was it in English interests to move slowly towards an accommodation in Ireland, given that violence continued regardless? In religious terms, meanwhile, Mary's passionate Catholicism naturally complicated matters, in Ireland as in England: it was reported that the citizens of Kilkenny marked her accession to the throne with overtly Catholic celebrations that would have raised both the rafters in the city and eyebrows in Dublin Castle: 'They rang all the bells … they flung up their caps to the battlement of the great temple [St Canice's Cathedral], with smiling and laughing most dissolutely … they brought forth their copes, candlesticks, holy water stock, cross, and censers. They mustered forth in general procession most gorgeously, all the town over, with *Sancta Maria, ora pro nobis* and the rest of the Latin litany.'[7] But it would be in the course of the long reign of Elizabeth I (1558–1603) that the defining events would be played out, against the context of a continent now traumatized by religious upheaval.

Beyond Ireland's shores the old Europe of feudal certainties was being rent asunder. The Reformation had induced panic in the Catholic monarchies of Europe, as well as bouts of savage retaliation: when, for example, tens of thousands of Protestant Huguenots across France were killed by Catholic mobs in 1572 in the aftermath of the St Bartholomew's Day massacre, Pope Gregory XIII ordered a *Te Deum* to be celebrated. In England itself, the Reformation remained far from complete: Mary had caused hundreds of Protestants to be burned at the stake for refusing to return to the old faith; and when her half-sister succeeded to the throne in 1558, it was by no means certain which direction policy would take. The cautious and parsimonious Elizabeth was at heart a pragmatist. She was certainly not a fervently committed Protestant in the way that Mary had been a zealous Catholic, and it seems clear that she fulfilled her Protestant destiny for sound practical reasons – as the best means of preserving her throne in a dangerous political world. As the daughter of Henry VIII and Anne Boleyn – the wife who replaced the devouty Catholic Catherine of Aragon after Henry divorced her – and as head of the reformed Church in England, however, Elizabeth became increasingly the focus of the hostility of Catholic

Europe in general and of Spain in particular. The stakes were immeasurably higher than they had ever been for her father.

In 1569, as a Catholic rebellion was brewing in northern England, an Old English revolt erupted in Ireland – partly as a result of the central government's political mismanagement of the situation. It had been the wish of Elizabeth's ministers to install English-born (and therefore politically loyal) colonists, traders and middlemen at strategic points throughout the province of Munster – in the more important coastal ports, for example, where they could be given trading privileges. Their aim was to enable central-ized English power to flow unimpeded throughout the region. Although many minor members of the province's gentry looked forward to this new economic order, Munster society as a whole remained obdurate. For one thing, its circle of Old English families continued to control economic and political life; and a network of local alliances between these families and Gaelic power in the region further consolidated its inaccessibility to outside influence. Breaking these local power bases, then, was a principal govern-ment objective, and it was towards this end that the Earl of Desmond had been summoned to court in 1567. His absence – so the thinking went – would deprive Munster politics of a key leadership figure: the actual effect, however, was to produce a vacuum filled, two years later, by rebellion.

The first Munster uprising, of 1569–73, was also, of course, sparked in part by the arrival of these loyal Elizabethan adventurers, drawn to Ireland by the promise of wealth and success. Sir Humphrey Gilbert was one such: fourteen years later he would claim Newfoundland for the Crown, the first English colony outside Ireland. In the meantime, however, the mining, trad-ing and forestry opportunities afforded in Munster kept him and his fellows more than occupied. It is significant that the rising in the province used religion as a rallying cry: Elizabeth's forces were attempting to compel the residents of Ireland 'to forsake the Catholic faith by God unto his church given and by the see of Rome hitherto prescribed to all Christian men'.[8]

But there was comparatively little force available to counter English military might, which, combined with the systematic destruction of property, crops and livestock in the province, soon proved deadly. Terror became a weapon of policy, directed specifically against the civilian population. Gilbert noted of his actions in Munster that he was 'constantly of the opinion that no conquered nation will ever yield willingly their obedience for love but rather for fear'. The opportunity to surrender was offered only once: he 'would not afterwards hearken to no parley … and put man, woman and child to the sword'.[9] Gilbert specialized in the subjugation of rebel castles and villages and the killing of their inhabitants, and was in the habit of ordering the decapitation of large numbers of men at a stroke. On occasion he would have the path to his tent decorated with severed heads so that relatives of his victims would be made to walk past their late relations' remains. He would boast later that the sight of 'the heddes of their dedd fathers, brothers, CHILDREN, kinsfolk and friends' wrought 'great terror'. It was an easy matter to rationalize such actions: the Irish could readily enough be condemned as mere beasts and vermin who deserved nothing less.

In 1570 Elizabeth was formally excommunicated and Catholics forbidden to attend reformed Church services. Such measures had the effect of removing the last obligation of loyalty to the Crown on the part of the Catholic population of Ireland; and it also hardened yet further the government's attitude to Catholicism, which began to be regarded as treasonous. At the same time the core of local resistance in Munster had not yet been dissolved, and the return to Ireland in 1573 of Desmond provided this resistance with a useful rallying point. Elizabeth's tendency towards prevarication also now intervened in affairs: she ordered that Desmond be restrained by diplomacy, if possible. As it turned out, however, matters had now progressed too far and too many vested interests had been threatened for diplomacy to work. At this moment, a European intervention would prove decisive.

In July 1579, a small papal-sponsored invasion force landed and dug in at Smerwick, near Dingle on the County Kerry coast. Spain and France had declined to support the expedition officially, but its very existence emphasizes the extent to which European governments were alive to the strategic possibilities of Ireland; there were, in any case, Spanish soldiers among the Irish and Italian troops at Smerwick. More Spanish, Irish and Italian troops came ashore in September the following year, by which time revolt had once more spread across Munster and many other parts of southern Ireland. Yet this augmented force at Smerwick lasted barely another month before it was destroyed by the English, who – contrary to the rules of war at the time – beheaded the captives and threw their bodies into the sea. The poet Edmund Spenser, who with Walter Raleigh was present at Smerwick, would later defend the killings on legal grounds: Spain and England were not in fact officially at war at the time, so the normal rules of warfare did not apply.

Spenser, indeed, was among the first to advance cogent arguments for the systematic colonization of the country: he and Raleigh were the *de facto* representatives of a school of thought that reasoned that the inhabitants of Ireland were simply on the wrong side of history. If the Irish would not remove themselves peaceably ('to bring themselves from their delight of licentious barbarism into the love of goodness and civility'),[10] they must be removed by force and if necessary exterminated. And, indeed, in this second Munster uprising, that of 1579–83, widespread civilian deaths were the norm. Atrocities were committed on both sides – when the Irish captured the southern port of Youghal, for example, many of the English citizens who lived there were executed – but Elizabeth's forces had the advantage, once again deploying a scorched earth policy across the province to devastating effect. Cattle were seized and the harvests burned, causing starvation throughout the countryside; it is thought that some thirty thousand Irish – a third of the population of Munster – were killed or died of famine in the four years from 1579.

Elizabeth's private views on this matter are anyone's guess. The recall in 1582 of Lord Grey, who had led the Munster campaign, may hint at royal disapproval of his brutal methods; so too does an irked passage in Spenser's *A View of the Present State of Ireland* that notes the monarch's complaints at the violence taking place in her name even as the Irish tide flowed in her favour:

> So I remember that in the late government of that good Lord Grey, when after long travail and many perilous assays, he had brought things almost to this pass we speak of, that it was even made ready for reformation, and might have been brought to what her Majesty would, like complaint was made against him, that he was a bloody man, and regarded not the life of her subjects no more than dogs, but had wasted and consumed, so as now she had almost nothing left but to reign in their ashes.[11]

Royal disapproval or no, however, the campaign in Munster was carried through to its bitter end without intervention from London; and similar tactics would be employed yet again in Ireland before the Tudor age came to an end.

By 1583, Elizabethan forces had subdued the rising across southern Ireland: its leaders were dead or in hiding, the population largely destitute. This time, it was decided to resolve the issue of Munster once and for all, by means of a large-scale plantation of the province. Accordingly, the territory was now intensively surveyed and charted and its assets calculated; land was confiscated from a formerly rebellious population and handed over to Elizabeth's soldiers; settlers were brought in to populate the countryside and in the process to secure the coastal ports against any possible Spanish invasion; and forts and military strongholds were constructed in key locations. The survey of Munster was a model of rationality, with laws laid down with crystal clarity and Irish tenants prohibited from cultivating the newly created manors.

Yet the new models could never be fully applied on the ground. For one thing, the new arrivals discovered a Munster that was in a state of disarray but certainly not as empty as the survey had implied. The existing inhabitants were promptly pressed into service on the newly planted estates, introducing both a welcome measure of economic productiveness and, in the longer term, a growing sense of rancour. Attempts were made as part of this plantation to re-create the pastoral landscapes of England in the Munster countryside: in the splendid setting of the Blackwater valley, for example, both Spenser and Raleigh were given estates – in the case of the latter, 16,000 hectares (40,000 acres) of land in and around Youghal. This would be a land upon which Elizabethan order and the Protestant faith could be imposed and where the enterprising settler could make a fortune. The colonists were perhaps spread too thinly across the landscape – yet it seemed that control of Munster had at last been sealed, and that a new order had now been established definitively across the whole south of Ireland.

There remained one great obstacle to English dominance of Ireland – in the fourth province, the one that would in time become synonymous with the conflict between the Irish and English. It is no exaggeration to say that the combination of distance, topography and a tradition of independence meant that for much of the time the administration in Dublin had little idea of what was going on in Ulster. The English still held the old fortress at Carrickfergus and the southeastern coastal fringe of the province; but an abortive attempt in 1566 to plant a garrison at Derry was a sign that much of the rest of Ulster lay far beyond their control. The province remained a source of deep anxiety for Elizabeth and her advisers. For one thing, it was the scene of a good deal of potentially destabilizing Scottish settlement. Government forces had attempted to deal with the Scots by strength of arms – one particularly bloody episode, in 1575, saw the massacre of perhaps seven hundred women, children and retainers of the MacDonnell clan who had been billeted for safety on Rathlin Island – but Elizabeth was eventually forced to accept a permanent Scottish presence in northeastern Ulster. The connections with Scotland also brought the province much too close for comfort to the Catholic supporters of Mary Stuart, Queen of Scots and a rival to her throne. Mary's execution in 1587 took care of that particular problem. Almost at once, however, another presented itself, in the form of a powerful Irish chieftain who had become an English-sponsored nobleman – but who was ready now to challenge the position of the Crown in Ireland.

In one telling of the Irish story, Hugh O'Neill (1540–1616) is immortalized as a great freedom fighter. In reality, he embodies the ambiguities and dilemmas of his time. He was Irish and Catholic, but was also a scion of a family that, having accepted the surrender and regrant policy of Henry VIII, had received the earldom of Tyrone; he was prepared to be loyal to the Crown, but this loyalty did not extend to relinquishing his political independence; he had shown himself to be both a subtle politician who could charm Elizabeth herself, and a ruthless killer who, in his own interests, had taken the English side in the terror unleashed in Munster – as a result of which he had become the second Earl of Tyrone, with substantial lands across central Ulster. O'Neill, then, comes down to us as in many ways an incalculable figure: the product of an English assimilationist agenda and yet the gravedigger of that same policy.

However much O'Neill has been mythologized by later generations, it is evident that he did not start out as a champion of Catholic Ireland. At first, indeed, he was quite prepared to employ English political leverage to carve out his own power base in Ulster. Nobody could walk the tightrope between Gaelic interests and those of the English State as well as O'Neill, and it was for this reason that he received the support of Elizabeth for as long as he did; in the eyes of her government, he was the man best placed to keep Ulster peaceful – the key mediator between the two cultures. Yet, to an Elizabethan state intent on establishing for good its control over Ireland, a man such as O'Neill could ultimately never be sufficiently loyal. An Ulster ruled by one or more indigenous barons – even if they did protest their loyalty and hold their lands by the gift of the monarch herself – would ultimately be viewed as an unsatisfactory state of affairs: these lords were Gaelic, and essentially beyond the pale.

O'Neill's transformation into an oppositional figure therefore, was prompted partly by the gradual English destruction of his power base in Ulster. In 1591, English officials began the confiscation of Gaelic land in County Monaghan: the territory was subdivided among English settlers, a garrison was established at Monaghan town and English law was invoked across the new county. The actions of the Crown further disrupted the tenor of Gaelic life in Ulster, and introduced a note of fear and instability. It also, significantly, disrupted the flow of tenant revenues to the likes of O'Neill. He was obliged to act, not least for reasons of political prestige, for if he did not respond, a host of rivals certainly would.

The 1580s had been years of political and military disquiet for Elizabeth, and in particular as Spanish power consolidated itself in Europe while the Tudor monarchy remained cash-strapped and English power as fragile as ever. The defeat of the Spanish Armada in 1588, though a signal triumph for England, was not the overwhelming victory of popular myth: the war that continued fitfully between the two countries was marked by as many important naval victories for Spain as for England, and by increased Spanish investment in Ireland as a means of weakening Elizabeth's regime. It was into this bitter ideological struggle that O'Neill now inserted himself, seeing an opportunity in its religious dimension; he made contact with Philip II of Spain, citing their shared Catholicism as a reason why the Spanish should intervene in Ireland. It was a bold attempt – the first, though certainly not the last – to fuse Catholicism with Irishness, and to harness the potential power of a heady new identity. The Spanish government and the papacy were notably unconvinced by O'Neill's sudden Catholic zealotry, yet as he had once been Elizabeth's man, he was now theirs. In Rome, Pope Clement VIII named O'Neill 'Captain General of the Catholic Army in Ireland'.

When the moment came O'Neill struck first, defeating the English forces in several battles in southern Ulster. These encounters culminated in August 1598 at the battle of the Yellow Ford in County Armagh: the English were routed and some nine hundred soldiers perished alongside their commander (and O'Neill's brother in law), Henry Bagenal, who had been hell-bent on destroying O'Neill's political position. In England, the heavy defeat caused consternation at court and Elizabeth was finally obliged to commit financially to the struggle, pouring into the Irish campaign vast amounts of money that her treasury could ill afford. She rounded furiously on the Earl of Essex, her commander-in-chief in Ireland: O'Neill, that 'base bush kern' [foot soldier], was humiliating English armies and boasting about it abroad. Essex, ruined by his experiences in Ireland, would be executed the following year.

In Ireland, meanwhile, the effect of the battle was dramatic: in Munster, yet another uprising spread like wildfire, undoing the plantation of the province in a matter of days. The colonists were swept off the land and forced to flee for their lives: 'the misery of the Englishry was great. The wealthier sort, leaving their castles and dwelling-houses, and their victuals and furniture, made haste into walled towns, where there was no enemy within ten miles. The meaner sort (the rebellion having overtaken them) were slain, man, woman and child; and such as escaped came all naked to the towns.'[12] O'Neill, meanwhile, called on his co-religionists to rise up and follow him: 'I will imploye myselfe to the utmost of my power in their defence and for the extirpation of heresie, the plantinge of the Catholic religion, the deliverie of our country of infinite murders, wicked and detestable policies by which this kingdom was hitherto governed, nourished in obscuritie and ignorance, maintained in barbarity and incivility and consequently of infinite evils.'[13] Yet in the end, he was unable to bring the people of the Pale with him. Now, victory over the English would more than ever depend upon Spain.

Philip II had died in September 1598 and his successor, Philip III, though interested less in the Irish dimension and more in Anglo-Spanish peace negotiations that were dragging on tediously, nevertheless continued to encourage O'Neill, sending arms and ammunition to assist his cause. Elizabeth, meanwhile, had ordered Charles Blount, Lord Mountjoy, to take the place of Essex in Ireland – and in Mountjoy O'Neill had an opponent who understood what was needed to finish the struggle once and for all and had the will to execute his plans in their entirety.

In 1600 a substantial English naval force of four thousand men, led by Sir Henry Docwra, sailed into Lough Foyle, bound once more for Derry: this time the landing was successful, and a garrison was established in this strategic location at the heart of O'Neill's own territory. At the same time Mountjoy set out to burn the countryside, adopting the scorched earth policy that had earlier paid such dividends in Munster. His tactics worked: large areas of Ulster were reduced to destitution; O'Neill's lands were now being threatened from the north and east by the garrisons at Derry and Carrickfergus and from the south by English soldiers dug in along the line of the river Blackwater. He knew that if the Spanish did not come soon, there would be little point in them coming at all.

On the morning of 2 October 1601 a fleet of thirty-three Spanish ships carrying four and a half thousand troops appeared off the Cork coast, bearing down towards the town of Kinsale. But from the beginning the expedition was dogged by bad luck. Some ships got lost in bad weather and did not reach Kinsale, and the army with which the Spanish soldiers were supposed to join forces was waiting far away in Ulster. Mountjoy quickly moved to flood the neighbourhood of Kinsale with his own soldiers, seven thousand of them boxing the Spanish into the town and laying siege to it. For O'Neill, fearful though he was of leaving his Ulster strongholds denuded of strength, it was all or nothing: as winter closed in, his forces began a long march the length of Ireland. By early November they had reached Kinsale and taken up positions behind an English army now increasingly ravaged by disease.

Although 'turning points' seem to swirl promiscuously through the telling of Irish history, it is evident that what happened at Kinsale would change the political balance in Ireland for ever. On one side were ranged the forces of expansionist England; on the other what remained of an Irish order that had struggled to live with the Crown but was now fighting for its existence. On Christmas Eve 1601 the Irish attacked: O'Neill's army was divided into three unwieldy formations; the Spanish troops at Kinsale never arrived on the field; and before long, the battle had become a rout. In such an inglorious manner the destiny of Gaelic Ireland was settled. Marching in the aftermath of Kinsale through O'Neill's unguarded lands in Tyrone, the English induced both famine, by slaughtering cattle; and panic, by slaughtering men, women and children. In a moment of symbolic destruction, the ancient crowning stone of the O'Neill clan at Dungannon was smashed to pieces.

Even now, however, all was not over for O'Neill. Negotiations concluded at Mellifont in the spring of 1603, six days after the death of Elizabeth, permitted him to retain his lordship in Tyrone, to the disbelief of many both in Ireland and Britain. He was pelted with earth and stones as he travelled through the English countryside on his way to London. Once in the city, however, he was welcomed graciously by the new monarch, the Stuart James I, who was himself lately arrived from Edinburgh. O'Neill appeared to have weathered the storm. It soon became apparent, however, exactly what Kinsale had brought about: the fracturing of what had been the tremendous continuity of the Gaelic order. The old ascendancy had survived in Ulster in ever narrower circumstances, but now it began to collapse, taking with it its social codes and structures of law and inheritance. This decline did not take place overnight: well into the seventeenth century Gaelic traditions and practice could still be seen in daily life across Ulster. Now, however, they were hollowed out, struggling to adapt to the demands of new financial and legal systems that exposed the weaknesses of what had come before. The Irish language, though it would also survive, was now in steep decline, spoken by ever-decreasing numbers of people in smaller and smaller districts of the country.

A good deal of this would become apparent only in the course of time – but even as events were rushing forward, Hugh O'Neill and his supporters quickly realized that they had been swept aside by history and politics. A new fleet from Spain would not arrive: Spanish naval power had been disabled at the battle of Gibraltar in 1604; the Anglo-Spanish peace negotiations had at last borne fruit and the prime objective of the Spanish State was to maintain friendly relations with the new Stuart monarchy; and in the meantime, O'Neill's lands were being subjected to steady encroachment by the English. On 14 September 1607, he and a host of Irish nobles and their families took ship at Rathmullan in County Donegal. This was the Flight of the Earls, one of the great landmark events in Irish history: O'Neill and his followers, beaten and dispossessed, sailed out of Lough Swilly bound for Europe. 'We are a flock without a shepherd,' an Ulster poet wrote. O'Neill would die in Rome nine years later, still dreaming of leading an invasion of his homeland.

PART THREE

FAITH AND FATHERLAND

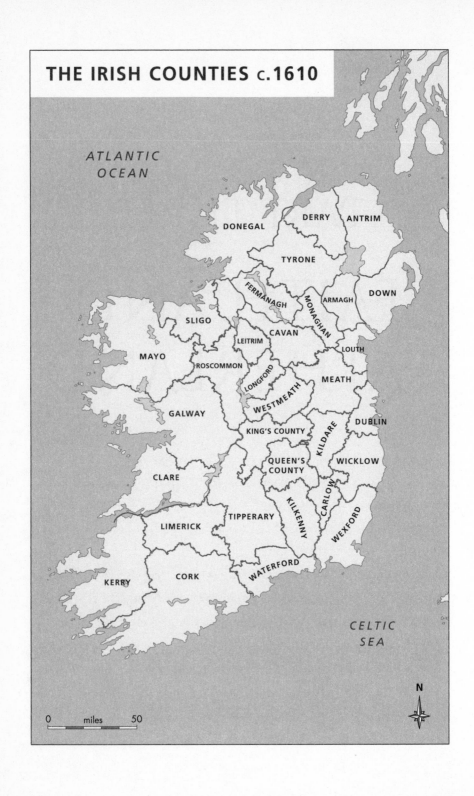

THE IRISH COUNTIES c.1610

ATLANTIC
OCEAN

DONEGAL
DERRY
ANTRIM
TYRONE
FERMANAGH
MONAGHAN
ARMAGH
DOWN
SLIGO
CAVAN
LEITRIM
LOUTH
MAYO
ROSCOMMON
LONGFORD
MEATH
WESTMEATH
GALWAY
KING'S COUNTY
KILDARE
DUBLIN
QUEEN'S
COUNTY
WICKLOW
CLARE
CARLOW
TIPPERARY
KILKENNY
WEXFORD
LIMERICK
WATERFORD
KERRY
CORK

CELTIC
SEA

N

0   miles   50

CHAPTER FIVE

A RUDE
AND REMOTE
KINGDOM

*Ulster Unionists, fearful of being isolated on the island, built a solid
house, but it was a cold house for Catholics. And Northern nationalists, although they had a roof over their heads, seemed to us as if they
meant to burn the house down.*[1]

By the end of the Elizabethan age, a century of Tudor engagement with
Ireland was at last bearing fruit. The country had been subjected to sword
and starvation; rebellion had been stamped out. English influence was once
again spreading across the island, although in some upland areas – for
example, the Wicklow mountains, within hailing distance of Dublin – there
were many districts that had remained largely resistant to government
control. Mountjoy, who was lord lieutenant from 1600 to 1606, reported a
raid into the glens of central Wicklow in 1600, describing how government
troops had 'spoiled and ransacked the counties of Ranelagh and Cosshay,
swept away the most part of their [i.e. the rebels'] cattle and goods, burnt
all their corn and almost all of their houses, leaving them little or nothing
that might relieve them'.[2] Elsewhere, however, the network of administrative counties – so alien to Gaelic Ireland, so familiar an element of life in
modern Ireland – that had gradually developed during the sixteenth

century was now virtually complete. Ulster was carved into nine such units; and the system was rounded off in 1606 with the addition of Wicklow as Ireland's thirty-second county. In Dublin, meanwhile, the foundation in 1592 of Trinity College had symbolized a new cultural confidence: the college's role in the centuries to come would be as a centre of English and Protestant influence in the Irish capital.

The events at Kinsale and at Rathmullan brought to an end the political autonomy of Ulster. Many of the province's Gaelic leaders had gone into exile and their lands were in the hands of the Crown; the notion that the original landowners might maintain possession of their properties – which had taken root with the original lenient treatment of Hugh O'Neill – was now set aside for good. For Ireland might have been ostensibly pacified and its old order unravelled and discarded, but it was still not regarded as loyal; on the contrary, its overwhelmingly Catholic population was, in the eyes of the administrators at Dublin Castle, pledged fundamentally to the papacy. This was a problem that required an altogether new solution – and the English response would be radical.

The Plantation of Ulster was a state-sponsored endeavour, vastly greater in scale than the sixteenth-century plantations that had been undertaken in Munster and Leinster. It provided for the uprooting and removal of the native Irish population from much of the province and its replacement by Protestant colonists loyal to the Crown and to the new order in Ireland. Certain principles underpinned the project: the first was concentration, the English government having learned the lessons of earlier attempts at plantation, when a thinly dispersed population of settlers had not always been able to defend itself; the second was segregation, thus creating an atmosphere in which sparks would be less readily generated.

The government's plans were greeted in some quarters with enthusiasm, and the private sector hastened to take a stake in this new enterprise.

Before the official scheme itself was even underway, indeed, a complex set of negotiations had resulted in an independent plantation being established in counties Antrim and Down. In 1605 the O'Neills of Clandeboye, near the small settlement of Belfast, had transferred two-thirds of their extensive lands into the ownership of two well-connected Scotsmen, James Hamilton and Hugh Montgomery. In return, the family was guaranteed security of tenure and of succession on its remaining possessions. It was a pragmatic decision, in other words, based on a clear understanding of what the future had in store. Sir Arthur Chichester, a former soldier who was lord lieutenant from 1605 to 1615, also received a large grant of land, extending from Carrickfergus west to Lough Neagh.* These were perfect business opportunities: the lowlands of Scotland, so clearly visible from the County Down coast, were overpopulated, while Ulster itself was underpopulated; and what could be easier than ferrying an entirely new population across the narrow sound between the two islands? The first Scottish settlers – farmers, carpenters, stonemasons and other artisan workers – were landed at Donaghadee in May 1606; leases were awarded to suitable settlers, and two years of good harvests and mild winters ensured that the enterprise got off to a smooth start.

The large-scale Crown-sponsored colonization of Ulster was initiated in the following year, with government lawyers asserting royal title to six Plantation counties: Donegal, Fermanagh, Coleraine, Armagh, Cavan and Hugh O'Neill's former seat of power, Tyrone. The Flight of the Earls eased this change of ownership, for the territories of the departed O'Neill and his allies could now be declared forfeit. The Plantation project ordained that three main groups would be granted land: 'undertakers', namely English or Scottish nobility, who received the largest parcels of territory; 'servitors', former

---

* Chichester remains best known for setting in motion the expansion of Belfast from an insignificant settlement at the mouth of the river Lagan into, eventually, the largest city and industrial powerhouse of Ulster.

army officers who were given medium-sized plots of land, both as a reward for their services and to ensure that security in areas of continued native settlement was in reliable hands; and finally those native Irish who had displayed loyalty to the Crown.

The position of this third group was carefully controlled. Although its members would eventually receive between a fifth and a quarter of all land granted in Ulster, few would possess anything like as much as their ancestors had done. In addition, some were permitted to hold their new lands only for their own lifetime and were forbidden to gift it to the next generation. There was also a deliberate policy of granting them land far away from their traditional home areas in an effort to weaken their personal following. And there were yet further restrictions: the native Irish were not permitted to lease land as tenants from undertakers; and while they might lease from servitors or from the few Gaelic clan chiefs left, they were obliged to pay more rent than the newly planted settlers.

Rigid as these restrictions appeared on paper, though, they could not always be applied in practice and – as had been the case in the earlier Munster schemes – the aims and principles of the Plantation began to alter according to the facts on the ground. For example, the scheme envisaged that very many English and Scots Protestant settlers would be drawn to the lowlands of Ulster; in addition, the established – that is, Protestant – Church in Ireland and Trinity College also received large grants of land. Initially, however, not enough of these new leaseholders would come to Ireland to occupy the undertakers' estates; furthermore, in many cases undertakers actually preferred Irish tenants because they paid higher rents and were not obliged to be given security of tenure through a lease. Such circumstances led to a Plantation in which new settlers found themselves living side by side with native Irish, generating the very tensions that the planners had sought to avoid. And of course, to the general sense of cultural displacement that the Plantation brought to many members of the native Irish community humiliation had been added in the form of higher rents and absence of security.*

As a result of the initially slow uptake of land in Ulster, a decision was taken to exclude the county of Coleraine from the overall scheme. The territory was instead offered to the guilds of the city of London as part of a new and very large corporate endeavour: the involvement of such prestigious private corporations in the Plantation – so it was reasoned – would shore up the entire operation and provide long-term stability. The London guilds were distinctly underwhelmed by the offer: they were reluctant to become involved in any way with remote and unpromising Ulster, and it took a fair amount of negotiation and browbeating on the part of the Crown to change their minds. In January 1610, however, agreements were finally reached: the county's area was expanded substantially as part of the deal, to take in sections of the former O'Neill lands in Tyrone and the mouths of the rivers Foyle and Bann, with their rich fisheries and commercial possibilities.[3] The county was renamed Londonderry to reflect its backers, and the guilds set about parcelling up their new territory among themselves. The administration of the new colony was in the hands of fifty-five companies in all, including grocers, drapers, fishmongers, goldsmiths, skinners and tailors. Urging Londoners to come west, a pamphlet declared that Ulster's promised land 'yieldeth store of all necessary for man's sustenance, in such measure as may not only maintain itself, but also furnish the city of London'.[4]

---

* Also at this time, many Gaelic Irishmen were rounded up and dispatched to Europe: some six thousand, for example, were shipped off to serve – rather improbably – in the army of Lutheran Sweden, then beginning its ascent into one of Europe's most influential powers. The Irish presence in Sweden dwindled as men deserted in favour of the armies of Europe's Catholic powers, especially of Spain – but a detectable Irish presence persisted nevertheless in the Swedish army in the following decades, with several individuals carving out significant careers. See, for example, Harman Murtagh, 'Irish Soldiers Abroad, 1600–1800', in Thomas Bartlett and Keith Jeffrey (eds), *A Military History of Ireland* (Cambridge: Cambridge University Press, 1996), 304.

With the establishment of a new county came the foundation of a new city: the old monastic settlement at Derry now became Londonderry, perched on its hill above the Foyle. The city was laid out along sternly rational lines: behind its new walls lay a geometric grid of streets, a design that would be repeated in the years to come in the new English colonies of the New World. The colonists planned to top off their new home with another symbol of changing times, by constructing on the brow of the hill the first Protestant cathedral to be consecrated in Europe since the Reformation. The stone that recorded the cathedral's completion in 1633 emphasized the role played by the city's backers:

> *If stones could speake*
> *Then Londons prayse*
> *Should sound who*
> *Built this Church and*
> *Cittie from the grounde.*

The development of the Plantation in the new city and county of Londonderry signalled both its ambitions and its limitations. The London guilds set to work adapting the territory to their own ends: market towns were founded across the county, and new development grafted on to already existing settlements; Draperstown, for example, received investment from the Company of Drapers. As time went on, however, it became apparent that the London guilds were not always scrupulous in applying the policy of segregation, for in the new county, as elsewhere in Ulster, the planter population was very thinly distributed, and it was clear that the economies of these new settlements would require an Irish presence if they were to function successfully. As a result, many Irish families – some of them regarded as upstarts by the old Gaelic ruling class – managed to carve out a substantial space for themselves in this new order.

In the new colony of Londonderry, however, the new social structure was imposed strictly: Protestant planters dwelt within the new fortifications, while the Catholic population lived in a district – low-lying, marshy and later called the Bogside – below the city walls. It was as potent a symbol of the new order as could be imagined. Across the Plantation counties, the settlers from the very outset adopted an embattled outlook, inhabiting both physically walled settlements and fortresses of the mind. Habitually they worked their fields with a weapon to hand; and tales spread of refugee Irish lurking in the woods and uplands, at all times ready to seize the opportunity to wreak havoc on the planted towns and tilled fields. Gaelic Ireland was imagined intensely by the settlers: brooding beyond their walls, dispossessed, unsettled and threatening.

Because English settlers did not arrive in the expected numbers, the Plantation never assumed the High Church character that had been anticipated by its designers. This was in part due to the well-earned reputation of Ulster as 'a rude and remote kingdom ... the first likely to be wasted [laid waste] if any trouble or insurrection should arise'. As late as the spring of 1608, the old settlement at Derry had been burned in a sudden native Irish revolt: as unattractive an advertisement as could be imagined for the new city of Londonderry that was to follow. But the initial sluggishness of the Plantation effort was also due to the colonization of North America, which began simultaneously with the successful settlement of the Jamestown colony of Virginia. Increasing numbers would be drawn towards the *tabula rasa* of the New World, seeing in its ostensibly empty landscapes opportunities that the confined fields of Ireland could not offer. And people saw liberties too: the *Mayflower* anchored at Cape Cod in 1620, its Puritan passengers craving religious freedoms and prepared to take their chances in an unknown land in order to acquire them. Ireland, with its bloody and chequered past, could never hold the same potential.

Ultimately, planter numbers would swell – augmented not solely by English men and women but increasingly by settlers crossing the North

Channel from Scotland, the kin of those lowland Scots who had already emigrated to Antrim and Down. These new colonists were predominantly (but not wholly) Dissenters: Presbyterians whose cultural attitudes were already profoundly adversarial, having been the object of religious persecution in Scotland itself, and who arrived in Ireland to find themselves once again on the wrong side of a High Church regime. They came determined both to reclaim their new land of Ulster from popery and barbarism and to maintain their own distinct faith and identity in the face of the disapproval of government and established Church. Stories were told of colonists rowing back across the sea to Scotland on a Sunday in order to participate in a true Presbyterian Sabbath, then returning the same day. These newcomers carried with them a religious culture that, with its overtones of egalitarianism and democracy, was wholly different from any that had hitherto existed in Ireland: there was little sense of hierarchy among the Dissenters, no caste of bishops ready to triangulate the relationship between God and the flock. They brought too a fierce certainty that they were a chosen people and that Ulster was to be their promised land; their destiny was to have their faith and resolve tested unceasingly by God in the form of the threat posed by the Catholic population. These settlers were Presbyterian first and Scottish a distant second: and future conflicts in Ireland would increasingly be shaped by religion.

These Scots immigrants helped to establish permanently the Plantation in Ulster: by 1622 a mere thirteen thousand colonists had come to Ireland and taken up their grants of land; but by 1640 this number had grown to more than thirty thousand. For some, to be sure, there was a rude awakening: they arrived in remote Fermanagh and Donegal to find land that was boggy, or still heavily forested; back-breaking work would be required to render the fields productive. Yet the harvests were good and the colony established itself: a ship from Scotland sailed up to the new quays of Londonderry in 1615, for example, carrying a load of 'plaid', 'Scotch cloth' and '27 Scots daggers' – implying the existence of a population that remained armed to the teeth while slowly becoming more sanguine about its prospects.[5] Only a little, though: the sense of embattlement, of imminent threat from both the Catholic population and potentially from the government at Dublin, remained a key characteristic of Scots Presbyterian culture in Ireland.

This sense of isolation among many of the incoming Scots – magnified by the feeling that their English fellow settlers, being insufficiently godly, were essentially no better than Catholics – militated against any notion that the two groups could be meshed into one. And yet, in spite of these deep cultural and religious differences between English and Scots, established Church and Dissenters, a new society slowly took root in Ulster. Peaceful contact, commerce and occasional intermarriage inevitably occurred between the settlers and the native Irish too; and Chichester's hope that 'these counties in a short time will not only be quiet neighbours to the Pale, but be made as rich ... as the Pale itself' seemed a sanguine one.[6] Tensions were nevertheless rising in the province: although displacement did not take place overnight nor at the point of a pike, English and Scottish settlement was inexorably pushing the Gaelic Irish on to the province's most marginal land. In addition, the new order was exploding long-held notions of class and status: it was no easy matter for the leaders of Gaelic Ireland to be reconciled to a grievous loss of prestige; or to be bettered, socially and financially, by individuals they felt to be their inferiors.

Plantation was also implemented in other corners of Ireland in these years, though to a much less ambitious extent than in Ulster. In Wexford, a number of families – both Irish and Old English, but all Catholic and therefore suspect – were ejected from their lands: those who petitioned most strenuously against the seizures found themselves transported to the new colony of Virginia. Other plantations in the midlands seemed similarly designed to entrench new loyal colonists in the landscape; the previous policy of surrender and regrant was now quietly forgotten. At the same time, there was little attempt at evangelization by the newly established Church of Ireland: efforts seemed directed rather at acquiring and tilling the land than at gaining the loyalty of the Catholic population. The notion of anglicization that underlay English policy in the first half of the seventeenth century, then, existed largely on paper only: while the stern grid of streets behind the walls of Londonderry implied a sense of rationalism and cultural superiority that would inevitably win the day, such attitudes and certainties were seldom teamed with attempts to win hearts and minds.

The new political climate proved alarming to the Catholic Old English community in Ireland. Some of its members, in spite of the travails of the previous century, had made the assumption that they would be in close communion with the English administration rather than in opposition to it – but the increasing identification of the State with Protestantism gave the lie to such notions. For James I, it was a political imperative that the established Church be supported wholeheartedly: as the son of Mary Stuart, he remained the object of scrutiny on the part of his Protestant subjects, who were alert at all times to any sign of secret Catholic sympathies. The relatively liberal policies pursued in Ireland in the opening years of his reign, therefore, rapidly gave way to forms of anti-Catholic repression; and the Gunpowder Plot of November 1605 bred an anti-papist sentiment that could not readily be dispersed.

The legislative environment, however, was at first less harsh towards Catholicism than it might have been. James was equally required to foster a sense of unity among the quarrelling component parts of his new realm, and this fact did not permit an outright campaign against the substantial Catholic populations of Ireland and Britain: the legislative programme of 1612, for example, included laws enacted against Jesuits and seminarians, but was in general limited in its anti-Catholic scope. Several years later, though, the campaign was stepped up and directed specifically against the laity: the government now tilted decisively and publicly against the Catholic faith – and this, paired potently with political harassment, had the result of placing both the Gaelic Irish and the Old English firmly on the back foot. As for the Catholic Church itself, it was inevitable that it would emerge as an oppositional political movement.

James died in March 1625 and his son was crowned Charles I in February of the following year. The new king embodied many of the ambiguities of the age: although a shy and diffident man, he was also inflexible in his views and, like his father before him, wholly dedicated to the principle of the divine right of kings. He was no ideologically committed Protestant: rather, he was cosmopolitan and a religious moderate; his consort, Henrietta Maria, was a French Catholic princess. From the very beginning, therefore, the king was in conflict with the increasingly Puritan English parliament. He was required to walk a tightrope at all times, and the increasing fragility of his rule was expressed in the political incoherence of these years. The state's policies in Ireland inclined first in one direction and then in another, reacting to the climate of the world outside as much as to the state of Ireland itself. When, in the 1620s, the long peace between England and Spain ended abruptly, the Old English families in Ireland sought to make political hay by demonstrating their public loyalty to the Crown. The result – the 'Graces' agreed in 1628 between Charles and Old English representatives, guaranteeing existing property rights and an end to land expropriation – symbolized a certain grudging understanding between the two sides. However, when peace negotiations with Spain were once more taken up in the spring of 1629, many of these Graces fell by the wayside and anti-Catholic policies and land confiscations soon began again. To Ireland's Catholics Charles was no ally, but he was a far better bet than the Protestant English parliament that regarded itself as purified and democratic and was now bent on checking the monarch's powers.

Increasingly, the Crown struggled to assert itself in both England and Scotland. In 1639, in order to shore up his declining authority in Scotland, Charles attempted to impose the Book of Common Prayer in the kingdom.

The Calvinist Scots would have none of it: they responded by occupying northern England and demanding autonomy from the Crown; this in turn destabilized English politics and empowered the English parliament, with the result that Charles lost control of the political process not only in Scotland but also in England. The monarch infuriated the Parliamentarian side yet further by ordering the raising of an army of Irish Catholics to cross the Irish Sea and intervene on the Royalist side in England itself – thus tapping into the latent English fear of the Irish arriving in the night to murder them in their beds. Fearful of what might be in store should a vengeful Puritan parliament gain the upper hand, the Irish Catholics made a fateful decision: they would strike first in support of the Crown.

The Irish Confederacy formed at this time was by no means a separatist league. Instead, it brought together what remained of the Catholic elite – both the Old English families and the Gaelic chieftains who had survived Elizabeth's wars – in what was in essence a rising in defence of Catholicism in Ireland. Time would show that this was far from a united group: on the contrary, it was riven with dissent, for its conglomeration of leaders had fundamental differences and varying aspirations. For now, however, a limited degree of common purpose sufficed. Although the leaders of the rising anticipated that support could be gathered from across Ireland, it was clear from the outset that their muscle would come principally from Ulster, where grievances were at their keenest. So when the rebellion began on 23 October 1641, its principal aim was to seize not only Dublin Castle, the seat of English authority in Ireland and stocked with a great store of arms, but also the main forts and centres of power across the north. But the rising was ill planned and disorganized from the outset. In Dublin, the administration was tipped off in the nick of time and the castle reinforced just enough to prevent its capture; and in Ulster, while the rebellion swept across much of the centre of the province, Londonderry and the chain of strongholds stretching south of the city remained in government hands.

By winter's end, however, the unrest had spread across the country. A Scots army crossed to Ulster and engaged the rebels, rapidly gaining the upper hand; but in July 1642, the Spanish-educated Owen Roe O'Neill – nephew of Hugh O'Neill – landed at Sheephaven Bay in north Donegal to direct the rebels' efforts. The administration in Dublin began to dispatch punitive expeditions to quell the unrest: these targeted not only the Ulster rebels but Catholics across the Pale and into Munster. The events of the rising, however, are best remembered in Ulster, where events would escalate swiftly and get out of control: thirty years of plantation and dispossession exploded into violence, as Irish Catholics who had once been submissive tenants now turned on the Protestant settlers. The subsequent unravelling of Ulster society remains a defining moment in Irish history, marking as it does the onset of the province's first round of sectarian blood-letting.

As winter descended, Protestant planters were attacked across central Ulster and expelled from their homes. The attacks were at first focused on property, as the rebels descended on farmsteads and made off with whatever goods could be carried on their backs. Before long, though, the settlers themselves became targets and the attacks heavily ritualized attempts to sever – sometimes literally – the Protestant presence from the land: the planters, in a symbolic echoing of Catholic dispossession, were stripped of their garments and possessions before being driven from their properties. Tellingly, the precious documents giving planters leasehold to the land were frequently seized too and destroyed. Refugees straggling south towards Dublin told stories of corpses unearthed from Protestant graveyards; flesh sliced from the bodies of living animals in Protestant-owned flocks and herds; planters forced to convert at the point of a pike. This was a world turned on its head, violently and traumatically.

There was no over-arching plan to exterminate planter culture. Rather, the widespread chaos and anarchy took the leaders of the rising by surprise, and calls for discipline went unheard. Atrocity and massacre became commonplace as a host of local grudge matches, simmering personal bitterness and vendettas found expression: approximately four thousand settlers were killed, and another eight thousand refugees died from cold and starvation. The most notorious episode took place at the market town of Portadown in County Armagh, where in November 1641 a group of some hundred Protestant men, women and children who had previously been expelled from their lands were assembled at the crossing of the river Bann. Here they were stripped before being herded into the water; if they did not drown or die from exposure, they were shot or beaten to death with the oars of rowing boats. A survivor named Elizabeth Price saw her five children murdered; she testified later that 'those that could swym and come to the shore they either knockt them in the heade & soe after drowned them, or els shott them to death in the water'. Reprisals against Catholics followed: at Islandmagee in County Antrim, for example, dozens of Catholics – women and children included – were killed, many hacked to death; and this was not an isolated incident.

The events of 1641 have reverberated in the culture of Ulster Protestantism ever since. Long-term lessons were drawn from the examples of Portadown and other violent incidents: first, that the sense of embattlement that had from the outset characterized the Scots settlement of Ulster had been wise and prescient, foretelling as it had the shocking events to come; and second, that the native Catholic community in Ireland – inherently treacherous, disloyal and opportunistic – could simply never be trusted. The story of the rising acted, generation after generation, both as a warning and as a reminder to Protestants that they were indeed a chosen people, to be tested by God. It led to the creation of a specific persecution narrative; and it laid down a firm template for the course of history still to come.

The flames were further stoked by the actions of the Puritan-dominated English parliament which, from the end of 1641, began systematically amassing sworn evidence against 'these bloody Papists' guilty of 'cruelties and tortures exceeding all parallel, unheard of among Pagans, Turks, or

Barbarians'.[7] These depositions (many now held in the Library of Trinity College Dublin) were witness statements with a very political purpose: central planks in what became a major propaganda exercise in order to raise an army to reconquer Ireland. They provide – all thirty volumes of them – a window into the nature of contemporary life in Ireland in general and in Ulster in particular. Ordinary people told their stories of what had happened in the early months of the rebellion: these were narratives that consisted principally of an inventory of stolen possessions, cattle and household goods. Very quickly, however, the commission that was set up to take these depositions began specifically to seek evidence of massacres by the native Irish; at the end of the rebellion, such testimony could be used to demand the execution of the leaders.

The result was a series of accounts of various atrocities that had taken place – some related by eyewitnesses, others second- and third-hand accounts – published in pamphlets that received large print runs in England throughout the course of the 1640s. The evidence detailed in the depositions tended to be magnified: Protestant deaths, for example, were estimated to run to over 150,000 – greatly exceeding, in fact, the entire Protestant population of Ulster at the time. The violence against person and property that accompanied the rising was rendered even more lurid by further allegations: Protestant babies had been jammed on to the points of pikes; settlers roasted alive on spits like pigs; women in the act of childbirth driven through the fields to drown in the nearest river. Significantly, many of these dreadful images are stock stories, atrocity tales that abounded in Europe in the sixteenth and seventeenth centuries and were adapted here to a specifically Irish context. In the process, it becomes virtually impossible to ascertain the cold facts of these cases: the dividing line between historical detail and hysterical propaganda becomes too blurred. The depositions, then, were in part a seventeenth-century 'dodgy dossier' that would justify the horror soon to be visited on Ireland.

For the moment, however, the Parliamentarians had the monarch himself in their sights. In London Charles was under growing pressure, and he moved now to abandon his putative Irish allies. With highly coloured atrocity stories from Ireland on everyone's lips, and a growing clamour for action, Charles signed into law the Adventurers' Act of March 1642. Under its terms, 1 million hectares (2.5 million acres) of Irish land were confiscated – to be given in parcels to anybody willing to finance a war against the rebels. For a mere £200, an English adventurer could secure 400 hectares (1000 acres) of Irish land. One Parliamentarian who came forward with £600 was a man driven less by land hunger than by the imperative of bringing divine vengeance and English law to the barbarous Irish: Oliver Cromwell.

> We have seen the many tides that one time or another have joined the inhabitants of the western islands, and even in Ireland itself, offered a tolerable way of life to Protestants and Catholics alike. Upon all of these Cromwell's record was a lasting bane. By an uncompleted process of terror, by an iniquitous land settlement, by the virtual proscription of the Catholic religion, by the bloody deeds already described, he cut new gulfs between the nations and the creeds ... upon all of us there still lies the curse of Cromwell.[8]

Even in the fraught context of the relationship between Ireland and England, Oliver Cromwell is a uniquely polarizing figure. Against the image of the English Lord Protector, democrat and defender of religious liberty, is set that of a genocidal tyrant wading knee-deep in Irish blood. Yet Cromwell was more complex a character than allowed for in either of these versions. Born in Cambridgeshire in 1599 into a family of middling rank – 'by birth a gentleman, living neither in any considerable height, nor yet in obscurity'[9] – he rose to power in an age when religion, politics and ethnicity were fused to heady effect, and when the absolutist power structures of a feudal age were giving way to government guided by a new kind of moral identity, answerable to both God and parliament.

Cromwell's moral universe largely mirrored that of the Puritan faction of which he was a product. However, his opinions on the subjects of Catholicism in general and of Irish Catholicism in particular were relatively ambiguous. He held the Catholic clergy in profound contempt – a view that stemmed from his own fervent sense of a sacred and personal relationship with God. The idea that a priest must mediate that relationship revolted him; and in the same way, he regarded the Catholic emphasis on ritual to be little better than witchcraft. But his attitude towards lay Catholics was rather more liberal: so long as they kept themselves to themselves and resisted the temptation to evangelize among good Protestants, they were free to worship whom they chose – in private. At a very fundamental level, after all, Cromwell's belief that Catholics were damned to burn in hell enabled him to leave them well alone: if God had washed his hands of them, then in the normal course of events Cromwell should do likewise. (It was Royalists, rather than Catholics, that he hated with a passion.)

His ideas about specifically Irish Catholicism, however, had been fixed by the experience of the 1641 rising in Ulster – or, rather, by the manner in which the rising had been represented in England. He considered the Catholic Irish not merely a barbaric popish race destined for eternal damnation but also a people who were overdue a hefty repayment for their onslaught on the Protestant settlers of Ulster. Add to this the persistent vein of racial hatred of the Irish that ran through Puritan culture, and the Irish role in the savage civil war that scarred English society in the 1640s, and it is possible to grasp the unique combination of factors that moved Cromwell to action.

Both the 1641 rising in Ireland and the civil war in England were elements in a much larger political, military and ideological conflict that raged across Ireland and Britain throughout the whole decade. This 'War of the Three Kingdoms' was further complicated in Ireland by foreign interventions, notably by the papacy, which dispatched a representative, Giovanni Battista Rinuccini (complete with military supplies), to direct operations. Such additional elements confused yet further an already anarchic situation. On the one hand, both Owen Roe O'Neill and Rinuccini aspired to the creation of a Catholic government in Ireland. On the other, many Old English leaders of the Irish Confederacy were fundamentally Royalist, supportive of Charles I's efforts to keep his throne in England and hopeful of creating a status quo that would permit both self-government for Ireland and full and equal rights for Catholicism. It complicated matters significantly that Charles had signed the Adventurers' Act – but in spite of this fact, many members of the confederacy still held to the belief that the monarchy was their best defender against the Puritans. Other members of the confederacy, however, did not support the monarchy, placing their faith instead in the idea of European intervention. Indeed, the Spanish and French governments – now observing an ever-increasing influx of Irish Catholics, as soldiers and university students scattered across the continent – set about sending modest flows of aid to Ireland.

By 1648, a socially and politically chaotic Ireland hosted armies from a multitude of factions – Gaelic Irish, Old English, Royalist – which were (usually) opposed to the English parliament but cannot neatly be categorized by religion or ethnicity. Finally, and in the face of what seemed Cromwell's *fait accompli* in England at the end of the civil war, an uneasy and fractious alliance was made: the Earl of Ormond, Charles's representative in Ireland, agreed to respect Catholic rights and to grant legal recognition to the Church. This was a mere promise, but in the face of the gathering storm it was enough for some of the Catholic leadership; accordingly, they threw in their lot with Ormond on 17 January 1649. Whether or not the king would honour the agreements was never put to the test: on 30 January Charles was executed in London and the Puritan political ascendancy in England confirmed. A month later the papal nuncio – who had been holding out for complete recognition of Catholicism and a restitution of all confiscated lands, and who had, as a result, not been a success in Ireland – took ship at Galway, bound for Rome.

Ormond now moved hastily to consolidate his position. On paper, this was strong: Parliamentarian forces held only the immediate hinterland of Dublin and a small and rapidly shrinking enclave in Ulster. In early July Ormond captured Drogheda, a mere 50 kilometres (30 or so miles) north of Dublin, with the intention of using the port as a springboard for an assault on the capital itself. But the Dublin garrison could now call on the might of Puritan England, and at the end of July was duly strengthened by an infusion of English troops. In early August, Ormond's Royalist armies were defeated in an engagement just south of the city; and on 15 August, Cromwell himself landed unopposed outside Dublin at the head of an army of twelve thousand men, plus a consignment of modern artillery. As he set out for Ireland, John Milton, the greatest English poet of the time, had urged him to end the 'absurd and savage customs' of the Irish who had been made 'devils' by popery. This was language wholly in keeping with the spirit of the age, and Cromwell was not about to disappoint his poet friend. Another reconquest of Ireland had begun.

Cromwell's ferocious ideological clarity and moral zeal were coupled with a sense of urgent political necessity: he knew that resistance in both Ireland and Scotland must be crushed immediately if the new Puritan regime in England was to stand a chance of survival. There were also key economic motives underlying Cromwell's actions: many of his soldiers had received no pay for years, and the London merchants who had lent large sums of money to the English parliament were growing restless. Cromwell now prevailed upon parliament to begin channelling money towards the restive army; at the same time, he held out the prospect of fortunes available for the taking if only Ireland could be subdued at last. The country was portrayed as being in dire need of economic salvation, its population unable and unwilling to manage its own affairs profitably: 'For to what purpose was it to plow or sow, where there was little or no Prospect of reaping? – to improve where the Tenant had no Property? This universal Neglect of Husbandry covered the Face of the Kingdom with thickets of Woods and Briars; and with those Vast extended Boggs, which are not natural but only the Excrescences and Scabs of the Body, occasioned by Uncleanliness and Sloth.'[10] For the soldiers of Cromwell's army, many of whom thought of Ireland as a baleful sinkhole for English careers and lives, such comments made a cheering change. No wonder, then, that Cromwell 'came over and like a lightning passed through the land'.[11]

The New Model Army, handsomely fed and supplied and now with a chance of actually being paid to boot, was guided by a sense of coherence and discipline that its rivals in Ireland could not match; its cavalry was superb; and its leadership possessed the sort of focused strategic purpose lacking in the enemy. This was an army that knew what it was about; and now, anxious to secure his Dublin bridgehead, Cromwell made his way rapidly north along the coast to Royalist-occupied Drogheda, arriving below the walls of the town on 3 September. By 10 September, the town had been invested and Cromwell dispatched a note to the Royalist commander, Sir Henry Aston, ordering his immediate surrender: 'Sir, having brought the army of the Parliament of England before this place, to reduce it to obedience, I thought fit to summon you to deliver the same into my hands to their use. If this be refused, you will have no cause to blame me. I expect your answer and remain your servant, O. Cromwell.'[12]

The demand was rejected and Cromwell promptly brought his artillery to bear on Drogheda's medieval fortifications. The first assaults were beaten back, but on the following day the parliamentary army breached the defences and poured into the town. For knowledge of what followed, we are indebted to Cromwell himself: in subsequent reports to his parliamentary allies and friends in England he noted that, since the Royalist garrison at Drogheda had already been summoned to surrender and had refused to do so, no quarter could be expected. It was certainly not given, for some two and a half thousand members of the garrison were killed: 'Being in the heat of action,' as Cromwell remarked, 'I forbade them to spare any that were in arms in the town.'[13]

The sack of Drogheda is remembered principally, however, for the fate of the civilian population. A thousand or so townsfolk had sought refuge at St Peter's Church: in response, Cromwell ordered that the tower of the building be set alight; pews were piled up against its entrance and torched; those who had taken shelter within it died from suffocation or burning, or threw themselves from the tower to their deaths. Even to a society so accustomed to violence as that of seventeenth-century Ireland, these events were profoundly shocking. For Catholics, they came to represent what the massacres of 1641 had for Protestants: a dreadful and defining moment. Certainly the massacre at Drogheda, in its violence and brutality, was without question a clear and unparalleled violation of the military code of the day.

These events were, on one level, a manifestation of the righteous burning anger that Cromwell felt against anyone – be they Irish or English – who defied the judgement of God. He made no effort, for example, to explain the deaths at St Peter's in anything other than moral terms and in particular in language that reflected the memory of the rising of 1641: 'about one thousand Catholics,' he afterwards told parliament, 'were put to the sword, fleeing thither for safety .... I believe that this is a righteous judgement of God upon these barbarous wretches, who have dipped their hands in so much innocent blood. And it will help,' Cromwell added in what sounds like self-justification, 'to prevent more bloodshed in the future. It was God who gave your men courage. It is good that God has all the glory.'[14] Moreover, it is an indication of Cromwell's purpose that the English population at Drogheda was by no means spared. Indeed, it was sought out for execution: Aston was beaten to death with his own wooden leg; the heads of dead

English Royalist soldiers were set on spikes around the town; and survivors were transported to the sugar plantations of Barbados. The killings at Drogheda were bloody and indiscriminate, in other words, but they were not motivated solely or even principally by racial hatred.

While Cromwell connected events at Drogheda explicitly to the rising of 1641, there were also good strategic reasons for the attack on the town. Drogheda, after all, had remained in either Royalist or Parliamentarian hands throughout these years and had not at any time been under Catholic Irish control; and a mingled population of English and Irish, Protestant and Catholic made it a peculiarly inappropriate object of moral vengeance. It was much more likely, therefore, that Drogheda was deemed a suitable target and symbol for rather more practical reasons: it was convenient to Dublin; it opened up the road to Ulster; possession of another east-coast port would serve the campaign well; and the medieval walls, so easily breached by modern armaments, meant that Drogheda could be captured in a rapid, spectacular and morale-boosting curtain-raiser to the Irish campaign.

Parliament responded with approval to Cromwell's reports: 'the House doth approve of the execution done at Drogheda as an act both of justice to them and mercy to others who may be warned by it'. And in the short term Cromwell's tactics had the desired effect, for a number of towns in the vicinity of Drogheda surrendered hastily. Another massacre would follow a month later at Wexford, where it is clear that the army ran amok; here, another two thousand soldiers and civilians were killed; and again, in its aftermath, towns in the path of the army moved rapidly to open their gates to Cromwell. At Kilkenny, for example, financial penalties were exacted from the citizens, the churches were ransacked and the clergy expelled – but the city itself was spared. In the longer term, however, the bitterness generated by Drogheda and Wexford was shared by many and, as a result, resistance to the conquering army could not be so easily eliminated. By the onset of the winter of 1649–50, parliamentary forces were firmly in control of the entire eastern littoral of Ireland from Derry in the north to Cork in the south.

The hitherto divided Catholic hierarchy now turned belatedly to face the Cromwellian advance. In December 1649 it met in conclave in the old monastic site at Clonmacnoise and there, among the relics of an earlier Ireland, issued a sharp condemnation of Cromwell: government policies, the prelates claimed, would result in the enforced removal of Catholics from their land and, ultimately, the extinction of Catholic Ireland itself. The meeting was a clear attempt to resurrect the fractious and unwieldy confederate alliance in opposition to Cromwell – and it was viewed as such. The following month, wintering at Youghal, Cromwell replied in terms that left no room for doubt as to his opinion of the Irish bishops and their wicked ways: the document was entitled 'For the undeceiving of deluded and seduced people' and it accused the prelates of directing hypocrisy and false doctrine at their flock: 'You [the clergy] cannot feed them with the word of God but instead poison them with your false abominable and Antichristian doctrine and practices … you keep the word of God from them, and instead thereof you give them your senseless order and tradition.'[15] Cromwell concluded by asserting vigorously the English right both to intervene in and to rule Ireland; and to seek vengeance for the wrongs done to the settlers of Ulster in 1641.

He left Youghal to begin campaigning once more in January 1650; by the spring, the line of control had been extended further west, taking in most of the country's main centres of population. With a Scottish invasion of northern England threatening, however, Cromwell was forced home, taking ship in May 1650. He had been in Ireland for only a matter of months, and would return to a warm welcome:

And now the Irish are ashamed
To see themselves in one year tamed:

So much one man can do
That does both act and know.[16]

But such assessments, together with the image of Cromwell as a stable Lord Protector, disguise the difficulties he encountered in these years; from now on the affairs of Ireland would be but one of many problems he would face until his early death in September 1658. Nor were the Irish quite tamed: indeed, it was only with Cromwell's departure that the true war began. By the end of the summer, three-quarters of Ireland had been nominally occupied. Government forces crossed the Shannon into Connacht in the autumn, but Limerick and Galway, which had invested heavily in modern defences, held out until 1651 and 1652 respectively – by which point disease was afflicting both sides indiscriminately.

After the surrender of Galway, and in the face of overwhelming military superiority, the remaining Irish and Royalist forces resorted to guerrilla tactics. Thousands of irregulars were encamped in the bogs and forests, ready to attack the regular army as it moved around the countryside; and this fragmentation of the enemy made it impossible to strike a decisive blow. These renegade Irish came to be known disparagingly as 'tories', after the Irish word for a hunted man – the tory, the priest and the wolf, it was said, were the three principal enemies of the new regime, and all three were tracked across the fields. The guerrillas at least were able to rely on local support – unlike the Irish wolf, which was hunted to extinction at this time – and as a consequence they remained players on the Irish scene well into the future. These brigades retained the ability to cause havoc among the regular forces, destroying supply lines and food depots across the countryside.

The mopping-up of Ireland following Cromwell's departure was in fact a period of systematic violence and destruction. The response of the army to the guerrilla tactics of the enemy came inevitably in the form of savage reprisals – and the poor, the young and the old suffered disproportionately.

The conquered land was divided into protected areas and enemy zones – and woe betide any civilian who strayed into the latter: 'You may ride 20 miles and discern anything or fix your eye upon any object, but dead men hanging on trees and gibbets: A sad spectacle but there's no remedy; so perfidious are the people, that we are enforced thereunto for the safeguard of our own lives.'[17] Male civilians were routinely hanged for passing information or intelligence or otherwise giving succour to the guerrillas; females too were subject to hanging, though they were more frequently rounded up and shipped off to work the Caribbean sugar plantations – in all, fifteen thousand were deported. The infrastructure of the country was targeted and destroyed: villages lay empty, pockmarked by ruined mill houses and castles and roofless churches; homes were burned and great stretches of the countryside emptied; harvests were seized by troops for their own use and the surplus destroyed. By 1660 famine, fighting and disease had wiped out between a fifth and a quarter of the Irish population.

At the same time, the country began to undergo the greatest social change in its history. In 1652, the Act of Settlement was proclaimed by the English parliament. This was one of the most radical pieces of legislation ever enacted in the history of Britain and Ireland, and its preamble establishes its intentions vividly: 'Whereas the Parliament of England, after the expense of much blood and treasure for suppression of the horrid rebellion in Ireland, have by the good hand of God upon their undertakings, brought that affair to such an issue, as that a total reducement and settlement of that nation may, with God's blessing, be speedily effected….' This was a moment of unprecedented opportunity for the English administration. Ireland was, as Cromwell put it, 'a blank paper':[18] there was no need for treaty, for negotiation, for compromise of any sort; instead, a new society could now be brought into being. The Act was of course intended as retribution on the participants in the rising of 1641: its opening clauses picked out all those who had taken part and condemned them to death – by some estimations eighty thousand adult males, had the law been applied across the board. But in reality, the Act was focused on the seizure of Irish land: it constituted one of the largest transfers of property anywhere in western Europe in the early modern period.

The result, for the remaining Irish Catholic leaders, was calamitous. In an agricultural society – in Ireland as in all European societies in this era – land was the key indicator of wealth, the basis of status and power. The act of taking land from the Irish elite had the effect of decapitating native society; many remaining members of the country's Catholic aristocracy now emigrated to the continent to pursue their military careers and join the swelling Irish population in exile. In the short term society became largely demilitarized, denuded as it was of effective local military and political leadership. In the longer term, Irish society became increasingly open to outside influences. This is most notably the case in the language shift from Irish to English, which had begun in the first half of the seventeenth century and now gathered pace in Leinster and Ulster.

No landed Catholic family could possibly hope to escape the bill's attention: the percentage of Catholic land decreased from almost 70 per cent in 1641 to about 10 per cent by the end of the 1650s. Among those who lost their estates were many families who had succeeded in carving out a new status as part of the Plantation of Ulster. In all, some forty thousand members of the Catholic land-owning class had their lands seized and were presented with the unappetizing choice of being transplanted across the river Shannon on to new native reservations to be established across the western counties of Clare, Mayo, Galway and Roscommon, or execution: 'To hell', as the saying went, 'or Connaught'. Policy was being driven by a combination of urgent pragmatic need and ideology: the government had both soldiers and debtors to pay off; and vengeance could at last be visited on the persistently disloyal people of Ireland. Now, finally, they would be replaced by a loyal people.

The Act of Settlement could not, for practical reasons, be rolled out on the scale envisaged. Once again, colonists needed a ready labour supply that only the native Irish could fill; and for those further down the social scale, the new arrangements even opened up opportunities that had not hitherto existed. But the legislation was hugely significant. It was an attempt at social engineering on a vast and revolutionary scale, dispossessing landowners in order to hand their estates over to newcomers; and it was underpinned by the hope that, in the end, the Irish would depart for good. The effect was the creation of the Ascendancy in Ireland: a Protestant class of five thousand-odd families that would control the lion's share of the land – and this was the great shift that would dominate the country's affairs for the next 270 years. It was said that Cromwell himself was not enthusiastic about the Act, for practical reasons: he was frankly doubtful that so many people could be easily removed elsewhere.

In England, Crown and parliament would eventually reach an understanding. Charles II came to the throne in 1660, when Cromwell's body was uprooted from its grave and hung on a pole in London by the jubilant Royalists. In Ireland, the Catholic population once more began to sense that its lot might be improved. At first, such hopes were scotched firmly: the king did indeed restore a portion of the country's landed Catholics to their estates, but more than 80 per cent of Ireland's land remained in Protestant hands. By 1685, however, there was once again a Catholic monarch on the throne: James II, younger son of the executed Charles I, who had been drawn to the old faith while living in Royalist exile in France. His brother Charles II had disapproved of James's conversion and ordered that Mary and Anne, the two surviving children of his first marriage, be raised as Protestants; in 1673, however, James was permitted to marry a Catholic Italian noblewoman, Mary of Modena. So when he succeeded Charles, James II was bringing about what must have seemed a nightmare vision to English

Protestants. The new monarch wrote that: 'If occasion were, I hope God would give me his grace to suffer death for the true Catholic religion as well as banishment.' There was no doubting his allegiance to the old faith.

To watching Catholics, of course, James's accession to the throne represented dreams of renewed religious freedom. These sensations of Catholic excitement and Protestant horror only increased when James began instituting reforms: admitting Catholics to high government office, for example, and suspending the laws that had discriminated against them. In his Irish policies, to be sure, James proved to be as cautious as his brother had been before him, and equally mindful of the dangers of opening the floodgates of religious liberty. But stirrings could be felt nonetheless, in Ireland as in England, and Protestant unease spread across the country. At first, this discomfiture could be held in check: James and his consort were childless, and it was assumed that his Protestant daughter Mary would in due course inherit the throne, reintroducing reformed rule.

In 1688, however, Mary of Modena gave birth to a son. Now the work of Henry VIII, Elizabeth and Cromwell seemed set to be overturned by a new Catholic dynasty. For parliament, faith and liberty were indivisible – yet here was England about to be pulled back under popish rule. The Parliamentarians, therefore, began preparations for rebellion once again; and this time they looked abroad for a leader. They turned to Holland – to Prince William of Orange, who was both a leader of Protestant Europe and James's own son-in-law, having married his daughter Mary in 1677. William himself was pragmatic: his reputation as fervent champion of Protestantism is by no means deserved, because although Holland was ostensibly Calvinist in orientation, it was a remarkably diverse and liberal society, with large populations of Catholics and Jews.

This period in European history was dominated by a high degree of tension and frequent conflict involving France on the one hand and on the other a shifting Grand Alliance consisting of most of the other major powers of central and western Europe. The coming conflict in Ireland, indeed, was a sideshow, albeit an important one – a single component in a much larger continent-wide struggle for power that would continue into the eighteenth century. To be sure, it was partly religious in nature. By the middle of the seventeenth century the Counter-Reformation was in full flood and the boundaries of Protestant Europe had as a result been pushed back. The French revocation in 1685 of the Edict of Nantes, which since 1598 had granted civil and religious liberties to Protestants in that country, had caused several hundred thousand Huguenots to flee to England, Holland and Protestant parts of Germany and Switzerland. Yet in essence these were conflicts rooted not in religion – except in Britain and Ireland – but rather in political rivalry. At this time, William's Dutch lands were under constant threat from rampant French armies to his south; an alliance with England would bring the power of its army and navy to his aid – and William would, as a result, hold the destiny of Ireland and England in his hands.

So when the English parliament sought his aid against James, William seized the opportunity. When it came to the point, indeed, the so-called Glorious Revolution was effected without bloodshed and with remarkable rapidity. A Dutch army landed in southwest England in November 1688; by December, James had fled to France and his son-in-law William and daughter Mary were on the throne. At once the scene shifted dramatically to Ireland, where James's supporters, the Jacobites, would shortly face the Williamites in a bitter two-year struggle for supremacy. This would prove to be the last war of a violent century and the final stand of Catholic Ireland against a Protestant ascendancy. And it was a campaign shot through with irony: for the Catholics were defending the rights of the legitimate King of England, Scotland and Ireland, while the Protestants were fighting in the cause of a usurper.

The administration at Dublin Castle was in the hands of James's appointees – most of the rest of the undergraduates and Fellows of Trinity

College had fled Ireland in response to the new regime – and the Jacobites in addition controlled virtually the whole of Ireland, with the exception of pockets of resistance in Ulster. By any measure, therefore, the circumstances must have appeared bright for James when, in March 1689, he sailed from France and landed at Kinsale. He was in the company of the French ambassador and a force of French troops – and awaiting him was an Irish army of forty-two thousand men. He marched directly to Cork and from there to Dublin, cheered as he went by crowds who sensed an opportunity to win back the lands that had been confiscated almost forty years before. In Dublin, the Irish parliament declared that its English counterpart could no longer legislate for Ireland: James agreed to this measure but refused either to repeal the Act of Settlement or to establish the Catholic Church in Ireland. James's position was of course a difficult one: he was obliged to please his Irish hosts, but did not want to do so at the expense of provoking a watching English population. As a result of this balancing act, however, his welcome in Ireland cooled substantially.

By now the Jacobite hold over Ireland had been strengthened by further successes in Ulster, which had swept much of the province clean of resistance. Such as remained was holed up at Enniskillen and especially at Protestant Londonderry, which had proclaimed its loyalty to William and Mary and shut its gates to James's emissaries as early as December 1688. The crowded city had remained obdurately resistant ever since, but in April 1689 James himself resolved to travel north, confident that his presence would resolve matters and win over the leaders. Instead, he was fired on from the ramparts and forced to beat a mortifying retreat; and the siege of the city, which had been closing since December, now began in earnest.

Few held out much hope that the city could survive a siege of any duration: its fortifications had been built to withstand not modern weaponry but the raids of the surrounding Gaelic Irish; and while Derry was perched on a steep hill and surrounded almost entirely by easily defensible river and marsh, it was also encircled beyond that by even higher ground, from which the city was an easy target of enemy bombardment. Furthermore, it was by now chronically overcrowded. Hunger and disease soon became a serious issue for the population of some thirty thousand defenders and refugees; and it was doubtless of little comfort that the surrounding Jacobite army, at the end of its supply lines, had endured an uncomfortable winter and was now similarly ravaged.

The besiegers also lacked the paraphernalia of modern warfare: they possessed little ammunition and siege equipment, and it was clear that they hoped Derry would be taken as a result of starvation and weakness rather than by force. A boom had been laid downriver to prevent any Williamite supply ships from coming to the city's aid; and this measure worked well until 28 July, when, with conditions inside the walls now desperate, two ships did succeed in breaking through the barrier and sailing up to the quays of Derry to bring supplies to the defenders. Shortly afterwards, the 105-day siege was lifted and the disconsolate Jacobite army began to straggle away. At the same time the simultaneous siege of Enniskillen, which had pinned down Jacobite forces across much of the midlands, was raised.

The Siege of Derry marks the apotheosis of the Ulster Protestant tradition of defiance ('No Surrender') in the face of adversity. Quite apart from this profound symbolic resonance, however, the event was of some political significance too, for its duration and its ultimate failure had significantly weakened James's position in Ireland. This deterioration was further signalled a few weeks later, when the first Williamite forces sailed into Belfast Lough and took up quarters in Belfast. The winter to come consisted of stalemate, but many more thousands of Williamite soldiers arrived from England and Europe in the spring of 1690; and William himself arrived – reluctantly, for he had no wish to be diverted towards distant Ireland – in Belfast on 14 June with a force of fifteen thousand. On 30 June, the two kings met on the banks of the river Boyne in County Meath: William at the head of thirty-five thousand Danish, English, Huguenot and German soldiers, plus Ulster regiments; James leading twenty-five thousand Irish and French troops.

The Battle of the Boyne of the following day, though it was certainly not the great decisive engagement of Irish myth, has provided one enduring image: that of William on a white charger, his vast force wholly outnumbering, outgunning and outflanking the Jacobites. Afterwards James fled, first to Dublin and then back to Kinsale: he didn't stop, in fact, until he reached France. His reputation was damaged fatally in the process; and in addition, the Battle of the Boyne took on a practical significance that it would have lacked had James stayed to fight another day: it delivered Dublin and the province of Leinster to William. And yet the Boyne did not end Irish hopes of recovering religious liberty and lost landholdings: the Jacobites had been only scattered, not destroyed; and William would encounter a significant reverse just over a month later, as his attempt to take Limerick by storm was repelled by the city's defenders. Shortly afterwards he sailed from Ireland, leaving final victory to his lieutenants.

The war in Ireland ground on, in fact, for another year – and the decisive battle was the bloodiest in Irish history. On 12 July 1691, at Aughrim in County Galway, the Williamites faced another army of Irish and French troops; each side fielded approximately twenty thousand men. The Jacobites had previously retreated west across the Shannon out of weakness – but now at Aughrim their leaders felt renewed confidence. Their situation was strong, not least because the army was under the command of the French general Charles Chalmont, Marquis de St Ruth, a name associated with the crushing of the Protestants of France. The Jacobites also had the advantage of being positioned on high ground and dug in amid the ruins of Aughrim Castle; any Williamite advance would have to be made across flat fields that even in high summer consisted of little more than bog. For St Ruth, moreover, this was holy war. Addressing his army on the eve of battle, he declared that the Jacobites were engaged in a battle for souls: 'Stand to it therefore my dears, and bear no longer the reproaches of the heretics who brand you with cowardice, and you may be assured that King James will love and reward you, Louis the Great will protect you, all good Catholics will applaud you, I myself will command you, the church will pray for you, your posterity will bless you, God will make you all saints and his holy mother will lay you in her bosom.'[19] As if to underline this fact, a phalanx of priests moved through the ranks to offer Communion just before battle commenced.

And, at first, fortune favoured the Jacobites: their enemy advanced three times through waist-high waters, only to be repeatedly driven back and slaughtered; many Williamite soldiers drowned in the bog. It seemed to be a rout – yet at the crucial moment, the Jacobites were stymied by poor planning and incompetence. Running short of ammunition, they discovered that their reserve supply was of English design and incompatible with their French-made muskets, so the tide turned once again. The Williamites now advanced, and St Ruth – who still believed that victory was within his grasp – was decapitated by a flying cannon-ball. Now his men were thrown into confusion: their line broke, the enemy surged forward and the Jacobites were hunted across the marshy fields. At the close of battle, seven thousand had been killed: it was the biggest loss of life in any Irish battle, and the bulk of the remaining Catholic elite lay among the dead. It was at this point that the Catholic threat was extinguished for the next hundred years. Protestant control had at last been achieved: by the end of the Williamite wars, only some 20 per cent of Irish land remained in Catholic hands. Yet for all that, a sense of siege had not been wholly dissipated. It was necessary now to design a new political order – one that would eliminate the Catholic threat and secure once and for all a Protestant dominion in Ireland.

CHAPTER SIX

A DIVIDED NATION

By October 1691, Jacobite resistance in Ireland had ended. In that month the city of Limerick opened its gates to the Williamites, and a new era in Ireland began. Among Protestants, hopes were high that the postwar settlement would bring at last the sense of security they had long craved – but just as the Irish conflict had been but one element in a wider European conflict, so too was the final treaty heavily influenced by events overseas. William's essential pragmatism was once more in evidence: he and his officials judged it imperative to wind up operations in Ireland as rapidly as possible in order to see off a resurgent French threat closer to home. He understood clearly that this could best be achieved by giving certain limited favours to the Jacobites, including a measure of religious toleration and guarantees in relation to land ownership; and the Jacobites also knew that, their dire military situation notwithstanding, they were now in an unexpectedly strong bargaining position.

The result was the Treaty of Limerick of 3 October 1691, which formally ended the war in Ireland. Its terms provided, somewhat ambiguously, for Catholic freedoms 'consistent with the laws of Ireland or as they did enjoy in the reign of King Charles II'; other clauses ensured the continuation of the property and commercial rights of those who had surrendered at Limerick, provided they swore allegiance to William and Mary. Those who wished to leave Ireland for a new life in Catholic France would be permitted to do so – although they would be stripped of their property and privileges of citizenship. It is estimated that some twelve thousand individuals left for France at this time, swelling even further the Irish population in Europe; these exiles would later become known as the Wild Geese.

The Treaty of Limerick was condemned by elements from both parties. For many Jacobites its terms were punitive; their negotiators, it was felt, might have held out for a better deal. On the other side, many Protestants felt that the king and his officials had been duped into agreeing lenient terms:

Had fate that still attends our Irish war,
The conquerors lose, the conquered gainers are;
Their pen's the symbol of our sword's defeat,
We fight like heroes but like fools we treat.[1]

In response, the Protestant government in Dublin set about refashioning the treaty. The result was the design of a new political and cultural order in Ireland – one that was overtly punitive and anti-papist.

The first fruits of this decision appeared in 1697, when anti-clerical legislation – the first of the so-called penal laws and a signal breach of the Treaty of Limerick – was enacted. The legal and cultural phenomenon of such legislation was, of course, far from being unique to Ireland. Statutes designed to persecute various minorities had been a feature of Europe's cultural landscape for centuries; in Ireland itself, Catholics, Presbyterians, Jews and others had been the target of various statutes since the Reformation. The intention behind the penal legislation enacted progressively by the Irish parliament between 1691 and 1760, however, was specifically to crush what remained of Catholic power in the country.

If the penal laws were at first defensive in nature, they soon developed into a remarkably dense maze of legislation that encompassed every aspect of daily life. Catholic priests were outlawed; Catholics were prohibited from entering parliament; from voting; from owning firearms; from marrying Protestants or adopting children; from buying land; and from owning a house valued at more than £5. New inheritance laws stipulated that any land left by a Catholic must be broken up among all his children, the idea being to ensure that no large Catholic estates could possibly survive intact for more than a generation or two. Bars were set on Catholic education – 'no person of the Popish religion shall publicly or in public houses teach school, or instruct youth in learning within this realm' – leading to the establishment of discreet 'hedge schools' across Ireland.

The penal laws make for fascinating reading, being a heady combination of shrill paranoia and beady-eyed realism. Much of the legislation was informed by the notion of cunning papist plots and propaganda concocted in Rome to be exported wholesale to Ireland with the intention of defeating Protestantism by guile; at the same time, clear and cool attention was paid to the importance of property and land in the operation of power. Female sexuality was the subject of the usual hysterical attention, as the preamble to the law barring inter-religious marriage makes clear:

> *Whereas many protestant woman, heirs or heirs apparent to land or other great substances in goods or chattels, or having considerable estates for life, or guardianship of children intitled [sic] to such estates, by flattery and other crafty insinuations of popish persons, have been seduced to contract matrimony with and take to husband, papists, to the great ruin of their estates, to the great loss of many protestant women that they forsake their religion and become papists, to the great dishonour of Almighty God, the great prejudice of the protestant interest, and the heavy sorrow of all their protestant friends....*[2]

But, although the intention of the penal laws was to intimidate, the legislation taken in its entirety did not succeed. Indeed, it would have required unprecedented resolve for such a vast body of law to be enforced; and – as had been the case with the Statutes of Kilkenny three centuries previously – such a resolve was not always in evidence. Sometimes, this absence of will emanated from the Irish authorities themselves: the futility of attempting to enforce such laws must rapidly have been understood in government circles. Sometimes too, the English – and following the Union of Scotland and England of 1707, British – authorities had good political reasons for watering down much of the legislation that flooded their way from the Irish parliament. An eighteenth-century *entente* with Catholic Austria, for example, made aspects of the penal laws politically unpalatable. Passive resistance on the part of the population also had its effect: it would be next to impossible to pursue a renegade Catholic priest across the fields if the local community – Catholic but not infrequently supported tacitly by Ascendancy families – was determined to provide that priest with succour.

In Ireland itself, the web of penal legislation was subject to scathing criticism. Looking back at the era, the political commentator Edmund Burke (1728–97) – whose own family had Catholic antecedents – claimed that the code was 'a machine as well fitted for the oppression, impoverishment and degradation of a people, and the debasement in them of human nature itself, as ever proceeded from the perverted ingenuity of man'.[3] Burke also criticized its short-sightedness: in oppressing the great majority of the Irish population in such a way, he claimed, the penal code had had the effect of preventing them from tasting the delicious fruits of British civilization and orienting them instead towards the siren calls of the French Revolution.

Even if the penal laws were not everywhere enforced, they criminalized an entire culture and crucially helped to make the connection between faith and nation indivisible in the minds of its people. Faith as an expression of national identity had long been central to English culture; now, loss of land and of religious freedom became the defining marks of caste for the Irish. As for the wider purpose behind the formulation of the penal legislation, it remains an open question as to whether the Protestant administration of Ireland truly imagined it could reverse the Catholic tide in Ireland and evangelize to remake the country in an Anglican image. European models certainly existed, albeit in reverse: during the Reformation in Austrian Bohemia and Hungary, large sections of the population had embraced Protestantism, but this movement had been crushed by the Hapsburgs and these lands were now solidly Catholic once more. In parts of France where Protestants had formed the majority, the Huguenots had been expelled and their religion suppressed ruthlessly.

There were clear differences, though, between Ireland on the one hand and Austria and France on the other. The Counter-Reformation had had the aid both of the wider Catholic Church in Europe and of the overwhelming power of the Hapsburg and Bourbon states; such conditions did not exist in Ireland, where the State simply did not possess the same cultural or military resources, apparatus of government, modern bureaucracy or police service. Nor, in the British State to which Ireland was now intrinsically connected, was there any longer the political will to attempt anything on such a scale. The Protestant ruling class in Ireland realized rapidly that it would have to settle for a situation in which papism must be borne as a persistent presence in the land – always provided that Catholics conducted themselves quietly and deferentially; assertiveness would not be tolerated. At the same time, in the first decades of the eighteenth century the Catholic Church in Ireland continued to develop some of the characteristics of an underground organization, its structures existing outside of, and in a sense against, the State.

In practical terms, however, the primacy of the Ascendancy seemed assured. Within two generations the Cromwellian troopers and planters who had settled across Ireland had become an aristocracy, and their scattered country seats – the so-called 'big houses' – were features in every corner of the Irish landscape. Many of these houses were relatively modest;

others – in keeping with the spirit of the picturesque that typified the age – were grander and built in peerless locations across the country. The construction of many 'big houses' nearly bankrupted the families that lived in them – such mansions tended to be ruinously difficult to heat and maintain, and the walls of many an otherwise gracious drawing room ran with water in the course of an interminable Irish winter – but they were necessary and crucial statements of authority. They dominated the landscape as the Anglo-Norman keeps and castles of previous centuries had done.

At the same time, many parts of the country's cities were rebuilt in a manner fit for the aspirations of this ruling class, and Dublin in particular became an architectural showcase boasting all the elements of a national capital: in particular, the foundation of the city's glorious Parliament House in 1729 was symbolic of a new political energy. It was accompanied by a broader cultural dynamism, as befitted the eighteenth-century Age of Enlightenment. In philosophy and architecture, in economics, city planning and literature, Dublin now sparkled with energy. This vitality found expression in a host of ways: in a loud and boisterous theatrical life; in the great quadrangles of Trinity College, the Georgian set-pieces of Merrion and Mountjoy Squares, and the green copper domes of the Custom House and Four Courts reflected in the waters of the river Liffey; in the earnest salons and glittering balls of the city's winter season; in the first performance, in April 1742, of Handel's *Messiah* in the Music Hall. But such frenetic activity was viewed coldly by some observers, who regarded these Ascendancy families, for all their activity and influence, as mere *arrivistes*: the satirist Jonathan Swift, for example, scorned William Conolly (1662–1729) – owner of the splendid Palladian pile at Castletown in County Kildare, Speaker of the Commons and unrivalled dispenser of patronage – as a mere 'shoe boy'. Yet there existed hitherto unsuspected common ground between men such as Swift and many members of this ruling class. Once again, the notion of acculturation was complicating Anglo-Irish affairs, as those who lived in Ireland began to question their cultural identity and to look askance at the treatment of Ireland by the ostensible mother country.

The Woollen Act, passed in 1699, is frequently taken to epitomize Ireland's inferior status as a British dominion, its economic needs subjected to those of the mother country. The Act – it was a backbench measure, rather than one formulated by the government itself – expressly prohibited the export of Irish woollen materials, a measure designed to protect the British wool industry from Irish competition. The new law had the unexpected side effect of stimulating the infant linen industry in Ulster: in general, however, it led to considerable economic hardship in Ireland and helped to underscore the country's position as an entity subordinate to British interests. After all, Poynings' Law of 1494, which had made manifest the inferior status of the Irish parliament in relation to its English counterpart, had never been repealed; Ireland, since the reign of Henry VIII a kingdom in its own right, was being treated by the British government as a mere colony, a subservient appendage.

The political journey of Swift himself exemplifies the evolving nature of the Anglo-Irish relationship. He was born in Dublin in 1667, spent much his life travelling between Ireland and England, and was at all times ambivalent in his feelings towards the land of his birth. In 1714, however, he settled at Dublin, taking up an appointment as Dean of St Patrick's Cathedral. He returned reluctantly, disappointed and embittered that his Tory political connections in England had not sufficed to advance a metropolitan career. (Queen Anne was reputed to have taken a cordial dislike to both him and to his Tale of a Tub, and to have blocked his career at every turn.) Once established on the Dublin social scene, however, Swift had leisure to consider the society around him and its place in a wider empire – and his response was to move towards an ever closer identification with the city. Indeed, he could scarcely have avoided questioning his situation: St Patrick's lay in the middle of some of the city's most appalling slums; deprivation and poverty pressed all around. Dublin's social scene may have been glittering indeed, but only for the few: poverty, want and hunger remained facts of life for the great majority of the city's population.*

Swift became ever more critical of the imperfections of the British control of Ireland, and of its negative impact on Irish affairs. He could not fail to realize that the colonial model being mapped on to Ireland was simply not working; and many of his subsequent writings were informed by this realization. His *Drapier Letters*, for example, written in the guise of a Dublin shopkeeper in 1724 and 1725, savaged British economic and political policies in Ireland. In urging his fellow Irishmen to burn everything English except coal, Swift was giving voice to a version of Irish patriotism. The tracts consequently caused fury in government circles, though his identity as their author was never revealed.

He was equally scathing in his analysis of how the colonial relationship impacted on the poorest in society. A succession of failed harvests in the late 1720s created famine conditions, with Ulster being particularly stricken. Swift responded with *A Modest Proposal*, which suggested that the children of the Irish poor be sold off in order to bring in valuable income for Irish families reduced to desperation by British economic policies; the skins of Irish babies would make 'admirable *Gloves* for *Ladies*, and *Summer Boots* for fine Gentlemen'.[4] Alternatively, their flesh could be sold: 'A young, healthy child is … a most delicious, nourishing and wholesome food, whether stewed, roasted, baked or boiled.' The satire underlying Swift's proposal was not detected by all.

Irish nationalists in later times – including many cut from a very different cloth – spoke of him as a precursor, as someone who articulated this

---

* Not that this emotional relationship was ever permitted to tilt into sentimentality, for Swift remained sharp in his references to Ireland's many imperfections: in providing the money to found St Patrick's psychiatric hospital in Dublin, for example, he noted acidly that 'no Nation wanted it so much'.

separate cultural and political consciousness in his writings. He was a Janus-faced character: a conflicted loyalist, anguished by the mediocrity that characterized the English presence in Ireland and aware that it amounted to little more than profiteering; in the end, therefore, a kind of nationalist too. Ultimately, perhaps, Swift's writings were fuelled by the bitter realization that the gap of understanding between Ireland and England could not now be adequately bridged. His work was both a scathing diagnosis of past failure and a warning of events to come.

Swift's criticisms, then, accorded with the spirit of the times: more and more voices – not least among the mass of Irish parliamentarians – were calling for greater measures of autonomy and self-determination. And yet the Irish parliament, beautifully housed, vigorous and energized though it may have been, was in no way a national debating chamber. On the contrary, it remained an institution dominated by Ascendancy interests and absentee landlords; and the changes it wished to enact did not include extending representation to the country's Catholic and Presbyterian major-ity. Irish society remained profoundly divided: the question of reform was a pressing issue, but it seemed destined always to be viewed through the prism of a fraught and violent sectarian history.

Indeed, such reform as materialized came from an ostensibly unlikely quarter: faced with war after exhausting war and anxious to tap abundant Irish manpower for its overstretched military, the British government began to introduce measures of Catholic political freedom, repealing aspects of the penal laws. Such changes were proposed in the teeth of bitter opposition from the powerful conservative lobby in parliament, which wanted any reform solely on its own terms: 'We consider the Protestant ascendancy to consist of a Protestant king in Ireland, a Protestant parliament, a Protestant hierarchy, Protestant electors and government, the benches of justice, the army and revenue, through all their branches and details, Protestant. And this system supported by a connection with the Protestant realm of Britain.'[5] Catholics, however, could never be wholly excluded from the military: quite simply, they were numerically too important to be discarded. Recruiting parties for the army, therefore, began moving through overwhelmingly Catholic Munster, Leinster and Connacht; the British government offered to raise a column of three thousand Irish Catholics for its oldest ally, Portugal; and thousands of Catholic Irishmen were among the British troops who sailed for British North America in the course of the Seven Years War of 1756–63.

In the 1770s, British military might was stretched almost to breaking point by the American War of Independence – and now a 'patriot' faction in parliament, led by the charismatic lawyer Henry Grattan, saw its opportunity to carve out a version of political autonomy. It began agitating for legislative independence: for an Ireland that was able to make its own laws and that was linked to Britain by the monarchy alone. At the same time, a heavily armed Volunteer movement emerged across the country, its membership mainly but certainly not wholly Protestant. In theory, it existed to defend Ireland from a possible French or Spanish invasion; in practice, however, it provided the patriot faction with a good deal of public political muscle. In November 1779, for example, these armed Volunteers rallied at College Green in central Dublin – and an alarmed administration in Dublin Castle was quick to read the signs and to grant Ascendancy Ireland a degree of self-rule.

By 1782, therefore, the era of formal subordination to the British parliament had ended. London would in practice continue to control the political process in Ireland – but largely now by means of patronage, a cumbersome and expensive method. It was a signal moment in an evolving Irish patriotism – but when the dust of legislative independence settled, it revealed a parliament still deeply corrupt and governed by patronage and privilege; a Catholic and Presbyterian majority that still had no political rights; and a population that was now armed to the teeth. Once more the country was tinder-dry, only awaiting a spark to set it alight.

*

The storming of the Bastille in Paris, on 14 July 1789, provided that spark – and not only in Ireland. 'Like the dew of heaven,' the Belfast *Northern Star* later proclaimed, the French Revolution 'inspires all Europe, and will extend the blessing of liberty to all mankind as citizens of the world, the creatures of one Supreme Being'.[6] What was taking place in France – the bloody destruction of an imperium – was watched avidly in Britain and Ireland, and responses varied from horror at the prospect of classless anarchy to excitement at the cry of '*Liberté, égalité, fraternité!*' In 1782, legislative independence had conceived of two kingdoms linked by a common crown – but now the revolution enabled different ideas to begin to circulate in Ireland: separatism became imaginable; and for the first time, a movement began to evolve with the avowed aim of breaking the link both with Britain and with the monarchy and creating in its place a secular republic in Ireland.

This revolutionary sentiment sank its deepest roots into the Presbyterian bastion of Belfast. In one way, it was an unlikely location: the Protestant population of the city and its industrializing hinterland had been raised with a vivid collective memory of Catholic massacre and betrayal. But other facets of Presbyterian culture made this society highly receptive to the radical ideas now emanating from Paris. Presbyterianism was rooted firmly in the idea of religious freedom, private judgement and individual conscience against coercion in matters of faith. The very structure of its Church was a model of democracy in comparison with either Anglicanism or Catholicism: it spurned hierarchies of bishops and instead emphasized egalitarianism. And of course the Presbyterians of Ireland had been excluded from power throughout the century: they could not hold political office until 1780; they were forced to pay tithes to the established Church; and they had very little influence in parliament. This experience of powerlessness merely served to reinforce what was already an ingrained Presbyterian culture of anti-authoritarianism.

Not all of Ireland's Presbyterians had been prepared to remain in their homeland under such unpromising circumstances, preferring to seek religious and political liberty elsewhere. The eighteenth century witnessed the first mass emigration in Irish history: between 1717 and 1776, a quarter of a million Presbyterians sailed from Belfast, Derry and the smaller ports of Ulster for a new life in North America. Some made for Canada, leaving a lasting imprint on the culture and politics of Ontario in particular; the majority, however, chose to settle in the United States, where they came to be known as the Scots-Irish. Landing for the most part at Philadelphia, these migrants found the fertile lowlands already cultivated by English colonists: nothing daunted, they moved wave by wave into inland Pennsylvania and Virginia, fanning out in time across the Appalachians and into the South. And, when the American Revolution erupted in the 1770s, this same emigrant society gravitated towards the cherished cause of freedom and liberty. In October 1780, for example, Scots-Irish men played a pivotal role in the crucial revolutionary victory at Kings Mountain on the border of North and South Carolina.

In Ireland, meanwhile, their co-religionists had followed the progress of the American war with keen interest. They rejoiced in the formation of the United States – in the creation of a polity that was democratic and overtly republican, and that rejected the notion of a connection between Church and State; and when the American Declaration of Independence was printed in July 1776 (by John Dunlap, a Presbyterian emigrant from County Tyrone), the *Belfast News Letter* was the first foreign newspaper to publish it. Belfast, still a small city in the second half of the eighteenth century, was referred to repeatedly as the Boston of Ireland in recognition of its pro-Americanism; its deeply felt disloyalty to the Crown; and its status as a centre of political ferment, radical ideas, subversion and potential revolution.

Unlike Boston, however, Belfast was a Presbyterian island in a Catholic sea. It was for this reason that the French Revolution was so important:

France had traditionally been one of Europe's most prominent Catholic powers; it had supported the Jacobite cause in Ireland and Scotland; and it had brutally suppressed its own Huguenot minority. If Catholic France could become so radically enlightened – so the thinking went in certain circles in Presbyterian Belfast – then there was potential for Catholic Ireland to do likewise. Dour introspection might have been Belfast's special trademark, but now there was an unexpected energy in the air. In the early 1790s, for example, it was becoming tentatively fashionable for Catholics and Presbyterians to mix socially. Belfast was a city that could surprise, as would soon become apparent.

In September 1791, the young Dublin barrister called Theobald Wolfe Tone (1763–98) published a pamphlet entitled *Argument on Behalf of the Catholics of Ireland*. Articulate, vivacious, born into the Church of Ireland and educated at Trinity College, Tone had seemed a natural member of the Irish political elite. He was deeply attracted by the prospect of a military life – in his teens, he had watched enthusiastically as the Volunteers had drilled in central Dublin – and only his father's objections forced him to alter his plans and study instead for the law. But he remained fascinated by the prospects offered by the expanding world into which Ireland was increasingly connected: he had read James Cook's journals of his Pacific discoveries, for example, and as a result had petitioned the authorities to allow him to establish a British military colony in what are now the Hawaiian Islands.

But Tone was also sensitive to the political climate in which he lived: he was appalled by the thickets of aristocratic patronage through which he was required to pass in order to advance his career, and disgusted by the general corruption of the Irish system. He was also a committed atheist and convinced of the need – as a first step – for unity and equality between the principal religions of Ireland. Although his mother had converted from Catholicism when Tone was eight years old, he knew little about the mass of the Catholic poor; he knew enough about Dublin's ambitious and increasingly restless Catholic middle class, however, to understand that its members were not unlike him in outlook and ambition.*

English Catholics had begun petitioning for relief in 1788; three years later, their demands were met with a bill that removed many of the remaining restrictions on their activities. Tone's pamphlet, then, was in part a response to the new mood of the times: it called for emancipation for Ireland's Catholics and, while it was ostensibly directed at a Protestant audience, its target was principally the Dissenters – the Presbyterians of Ulster who were themselves oppressed but nonetheless hesitant at the notion of papist political liberty. 'No reform,' Tone argued, 'can ever be obtained which shall not comprehensively embrace Irishmen of all denominations.' Tone's argument hit its target: very soon he was invited by a group of young Presbyterian men to a meeting in Belfast. The result, in October 1791, was the formation of the Society of United Irishmen.

Its founding members were merchants, manufacturers and the sons of Presbyterian clergymen: in other words, the Belfast and Ulster merchant classes. A second chapter was founded in November in Dublin, and the *Northern Star* – the organization's dedicated organ – began printing in the same month. The ideology of the United Irishmen was heavily influenced by revolutionary rhetoric: while the stated aim of the movement was to unite the Protestant, Catholic and Dissenter populations of Ireland and to achieve parliamentary reform, its ultimate goal was the creation of a secular national republic wholly separate from Britain. 'We have no national government,' declared the manifesto of the Belfast Society of United Irishmen, 'we are ruled by Englishmen, and the servants of Englishmen, whose object is the interest of another country.'[7] Such comments were received in some quarters

---

* The law forbidding intermarriage between Catholics and Protestants was not repealed until 1778; the Tone marriage therefore indicates the extent to which penal legislation went unheeded in everyday life.

with horror: although members of the Ascendancy feared Catholics, they feared Ulster Presbyterians even more, understanding that the rise of such a middle class represented a potent threat to their own economic hegemony in Ireland. And now here was evidence of a coalition emerging between Dissenters and Catholics: the United Irishmen were bringing together these two great demons against a backdrop of revolution in Europe.

As part of its activities, the organization fostered links with other bodies in order to create a network of potential insurrection across the country. These other groups were notably diverse, with Masonic lodges, Presbyterian congregations and a variety of town meetings all utilized as vehicles of political agitation. The United Irishmen also made contact with the Defenders, a shadowy body of Catholic insurgents that had formed in the 1780s in south Ulster and north Leinster. This organization drew its strength not from the Catholic peasantry, but from a rural and semi-rural proletariat of weavers and other industrial workers; and its aim was the protection of Catholics from sectarian attacks. Its political beliefs, in other words, were hardly akin to those of revolutionary France; and such an alliance between a Catholic vigilante group and a collective of middle-class Belfast Presbyterians would have been unimaginable at other periods in Irish history. Its very existence helps to illustrate the fluidity and flexibility of these politically explosive years.

That the Defenders existed in the first place, of course, was also an indication that not all of Ulster was in a revolutionary ferment; that not all Ulster Protestants were convinced by events in France; and that older sectarian tensions continued in rude health. The subtle political and religious alterations that came with the passing years – in particular, the growing cultural and economic confidence of the papist population of the country – had had the effect of upsetting the delicate balance of power in areas of Ulster where Catholics and Protestants lived side by side. In densely populated districts of County Armagh – scene of the worst violence in 1641 – the sight of Catholics being given, for example, longer leaseholds on land was alarming to many; the sight of them routinely maintaining stores of arms gave rise to yet more consternation.

Such sensations were not purely or even mainly religious in nature: rather, they were grounded in more practical economic worries. Armagh was by this time heavily industrialized and an important centre of linen production; and its Protestant population, disturbed by the growing Catholic competition for both markets and land, became all the more determined to protect whatever privileges remained to them. The result was the emergence of such bodies as the Peep O'Day Boys – essentially a vigilante organization in the habit of raiding Catholic homes at dawn (hence the name) and seizing any arms kept there. The Peep O'Day Boys conceived of their activities in law-abiding terms: they were merely upholding the laws of the land, which until this moment had forbidden Catholics to own weapons. Naturally, there were others who did not share their view: the Defenders emerged in response, its members raiding the homes of the gentry in their turn.

In February 1793 war was declared between Britain and revolutionary France, and tensions in Ireland rose still further. Until this date, it had still seemed possible for radical Irish reformers to make political advances through constitutional means, and in particular to introduce the Catholic emancipation and parliamentary reform that were their declared aims. It appeared that the Irish system might truly be able to reform itself peacefully from within. As late as 1792–3, indeed, the prime minister, William Pitt, and his home secretary, Henry Dundas, had forced a Catholic relief bill through the Irish parliament, hand-in-hand with a militia bill ending the prohibition on Catholics bearing arms; within a few years, there were seven thousand Catholic armed militiamen in Ireland. Now, however, the declaration of war with France caused a change in the political climate. Suddenly, the conservative faction had no need to persuade and oppose: it and the

British administration were suddenly on the same side. The need to maintain political stability and guard against the spread of the revolutionary virus was now paramount, and the authorities were in no mood to grant further reform of any kind.

At a local level, the cooling of this climate of conciliation and revolutionary zeal had immediate ramifications. Clashes between Protestant and Catholic factions – the Peep O'Day Boys and the Defenders – in south Ulster, which had for a while almost died away, erupted again into violence. At one pitched battle at Loughgall in September 1795, a large party of Defenders came off much the worse; and the Peep O'Day Boys now coalesced under the more impressive name of the Orange Order. The Order's name came from the memory of William of Orange and his victory at the Boyne; and the organization itself was dedicated to stemming the expansion both of the non-denominational United Irishmen and of Catholic influence. Rapidly the situation in Armagh and other areas became deeply alarming, with the Volunteers, who provided the effective police in Armagh, absorbing former Peep O'Day Boys into their ranks. This dynamic was played out at higher levels in Ulster and across Ireland throughout the 1790s: the Orange Order was by no means trusted in government circles, but ultimately the authorities in Dublin and London would throw in their lot with those Protestants who would be their most reliable allies in an increasingly dangerous situation.

In the aftermath of this crackdown, the United Irishmen were banned: and with the possibility that the armed might of the State would be used against it, the organization went underground. By 1794, Tone was producing reports for French agents on the state of Ireland: 'The Government of Ireland is to be looked upon as a Government of Force; the moment a superior force appears it would tumble at once as being neither founded in the interests nor in the affections of the people.' In 1795 he passed through Belfast, climbed the promontory of Cave Hill overlooking the city and with other United Irish leaders swore an oath 'never to desist in our efforts, until we had subverted the authority of England over our country, and asserted her independence'.[8] And with this, Tone left for America on the first stage of a journey that would lead him to France by February of the following year.

In Paris, Tone immediately set about enlisting the help of the authorities. In his diaries, we hear the voice of a young man who is anything but a humourless ideologue: he notes wryly the attempts of French hoteliers to fleece him and of his landlady to seduce him, and (less wryly) the frustration and endless kicking of heels as he waits to press his case to the French government. At last, on 24 February 1796, Tone was called to meet the leaders of the Directory, the government that had succeeded the first republic. Making his way 'in a fright' into the splendour of the Palais de Luxembourg and rehearsing speeches all the while, he found a French leader waiting to meet him: none other than the great military tactician and founder of the revolutionary army, Lazare Carnot.

> *I began my discourse by saying, in horrible French, that I had been informed he spoke English ... I then told him I was an Irishman ... and that I wished to communicate with him on the actual state of Ireland ... I proceeded to state that the sentiments of all those people were unanimous in favour of France and eager to throw off the yoke of England. He asked me then, 'What they wanted'. I said, 'An armed force in the commencement' ... until they could organise themselves and undoubtedly a supply of arms and some money.*

Tone's opinions fell upon open and eager ears. The French government, though militarily dominant in Europe, had been infuriated by British efforts to foment internal agitation and instability. Now it was ready for vengeance, and in a restless Ireland it saw its opportunity. Carnot was after hard facts: he wanted details concerning Irish anchorages north and south, numbers and possibilities. 'I think,' Tone concluded with relief, 'I came off very clean.'[9] And in the end, his quest for aid was indeed successful: the French resolved now to send a force of fifteen thousand men, together with munitions and arms, in support of insurrection. The decision would result in one of the most dangerous moments for British authority in Ireland.

On 16 December 1796, a naval force of forty-three ships set sail from Brest. On board the *Indomptable* was citizen Wolfe Tone, now a *chef de brigade* in the French navy. The fleet, which had been brought together in conditions of intense secrecy, was an impressive sight – yet it was little short of miraculous that it had been assembled in the first place. French naval power had long been hobbled by shortages of hardware and personnel, a succession of humiliating defeats at the hand of the Royal Navy and British blockades of its most important bases. Until the very last minute, there had been doubt about whether the force should sail: even as it slipped anchor, messengers were on their way from Paris to cancel the entire operation. But too late: in the darkness, the fleet evaded the British blockade of the harbour and made for the open sea. This was a piece of good luck – but it was the last the fleet would encounter: for one ship foundered off the Brittany coast and storms separated the rest, with the flagship being driven out into the Atlantic.

By the time the snow-covered mountains of southwest Ireland were sighted on 21 December, however, thirty-six vessels of the fleet had come together; and on the following day sixteen of them anchored in Bantry Bay, with the remainder waiting outside the mouth of the inlet. The news reached Dublin on Christmas Eve, causing consternation and the dispatch of troops south along rutted winter roads. A landing, had it taken place at this point, would surely have been successful: at no point had the flotilla encountered a single enemy ship, which rather gave the lie to the notion of British mastery of their home waters. The British authorities, indeed, had been foiled by French secrecy, and later guilty of staggering complacency:

they simply did not believe that a French naval force would contemplate a midwinter expedition to Ireland. Even when news emerged that the fleet had slipped through the blockade of Brest, the British assumed that its final destination was Portugal, perhaps, or even the West Indies. And in Ireland, there was no great military presence in Munster: the French troops might have taken Cork and its great natural harbour without too much trouble.

But the wind, blowing gales and snow from the land, was against the French; and their spirits had been further lowered by the desolate winter scene and all too evident absence of any fraternal welcome from the Irish themselves. Eventually, after remaining in the area for a week – so close to land, as Tone said, that he might have thrown a biscuit ashore – the invasion force beat a retreat and reached France once more on New Year's Day, 1797. It was a bitter blow for Tone, who had watched as this glorious opportunity for French intervention had been swept away in an Irish snowstorm. But it was also a blow to French prestige: the authorities in Paris were humiliated by yet another naval fiasco, and angered that there had been no promised Irish uprising. Tone's stock was greatly reduced.

The threatened invasion – and information that the French government was preparing yet another expeditionary force – whipped up fear and anger in Irish government circles. The result was a two-year security crackdown of unprecedented scale and ruthlessness. By the end of 1797, the organization of the United Irishmen in Ulster had been broken up by means of house-burning, floggings and various forms of torture. One favourite method was 'pitch-capping': a piece of softened tar was applied to the victim's head and set alight; removing it usually resulted in the removal of a portion of the scalp too, while burning pitch flowed into the victim's eyes. By March 1797, these harsh methods were being applied to the remainder of the country and the national United Irishmen leadership was under arrest. The reform-minded Anglo-Irish nobleman Lord Moira spoke of 'the most disgusting tyranny that any nation groaned under. The most wanton insults, the most cowardly oppression…thirty houses are sometimes burned in a night.'[10] But the government's tactics were certainly successful: arms caches all over the country were exposed and seized, and mass arrests all but destroyed the network built up so painstakingly over the years. Indeed, the uprising against British rule, when it eventually materialized, was driven not by some notional United Irish central command but rather by a sense of fearful panic. After all, there was nothing like the sight of smoke from burning cottages rising on the horizon to impel people into protecting themselves – even against overwhelming odds.

The rebellion broke out first at Dublin on 23 May 1798, but the action there was over within a week. Only in Wexford did the rebels strike effectively: and here they were not primarily inspired by French revolutionary ideas. The actions in the county of government troops – especially those of the North Cork militia, led by Protestants but as usual consisting mainly of Catholics – had been especially violent; and as tales spread of excessive floggings of civilians, these same civilians acted to protect their interests. By the end of May, the rebels had taken the towns of Wexford and Enniscorthy, and government forces were scattered to isolated strongholds.

The decisive battle for the southeast took place at New Ross on 4 June. The rebels had attacked the town, but they were only lightly armed and were driven back with many killed: within twelve hours, fifteen hundred were dead. Corpses lay in the streets for days; one Protestant shopkeeper spoke of seeing straying pigs feasting on the dead. Later that day, rebels at Scullabogue burned to death a group of one hundred or so civilians – mainly, though not exclusively, Protestant – in a barn; those who tried to escape were hacked and bludgeoned to death. The failed rebel assault proved to be the turning point, ending hopes of breaking out of County Wexford in force. On 21 June, the rebel encampment at Vinegar Hill above Enniscorthy was surrounded and crushed with slaughter; many of the wounded were burned alive in their makeshift hospital.[11] A belated uprising in Ulster in June was quickly mopped up with the assistance of the Orange Order; by the end of the summer, thirty thousand people had died. A second French force landed on the Mayo coast in the autumn and even succeeded in winning an engagement at Castlebar before its inevitable defeat: the French soldiers were handled appropriately as prisoners of war, but some two thousand of their Irish allies were executed.

Tone himself was captured on a French ship on Lough Swilly – close to the harbour at Rathmullan, from which Hugh O'Neill had set sail almost two hundred years before. Tone was sent to prison in Dublin and on 10 November 1798 was brought before a military tribunal, clad in his cherished uniform of an adjutant general of the French Republic: 'a large and fiercely-cocked hat, with broad gold lace, and the tri-coloured cockade; a blue uniform coat, with gold embroidered collar, and two large gold epaulets; blue pantaloons, with gold-laced garters at the knees; and short boots, bound at the tops with gold lace'.[12] The trial was sensational – Tone was remembered affectionately by many Dubliners, regardless of their political views – and the defendant faced the judges as a proud revolutionary: 'I mean not to give you the trouble of bringing judicial proof to convict me legally of having acted in hostility to the government of his Britannic Majesty in Ireland. I admit the fact. From my earliest youth I have regarded the connection between Great Britain and Ireland as the curse of the Irish nation, and felt convinced that, whilst it lasted, this country could never be free nor happy....'[13]

That Tone would be sentenced to death was certain. But he wished fervently not to be hanged as a common criminal, rather to face a firing squad as a soldier. After all, he had defended himself as a soldier, citing the example of George Washington; and he had overtly rejected the sectarian lurch that the uprising had taken at Wexford, grieving that 'any tyranny of circumstances or policy should so pervert the natural dispositions of my countrymen ... for a fair and open war I was prepared; if that has degenerated into a system of assassination, massacre and plunder I do most sincerely lament it....'.[14] Tone's request was denied, but he cheated the hangman by taking a rusty razor and cutting his own throat. Not very efficiently: 'My dear Sir – ' wrote Chief Secretary Lord Castlereagh to the British spymaster William Wickham, 'Tone died this morning of his wound.'[15] He had lingered for two days.

Wolfe Tone's belief in the principle of Irish independence and self-determination, his links with revolutionary France and his hatred for the British connection have made him a compelling figure in the story of Irish nationalism and a potent symbol for generations of revolutionaries. Yet the totality of Tone's vision could not fit smoothly into any of the dominant traditions of later Irish history. Here was an atheist of Protestant birth, deeply influenced by middle-class Ulster Presbyterianism, and cherishing dreams of a united and secular republic. Meanwhile, the country he left behind was more bitterly divided than ever: the dream of a non-sectarian Irish republic was gone; and never again would there exist such an alliance between Presbyterians and Catholics. Instead, the events in Wexford had intervened to reveal the sectarianism that so often underlay Irish life. Events such as Scullabogue would lodge in the collective Protestant memory, with the result that 1798 was now inscribed as 1641 all over again. The secular experiment in political organization had failed and the country had been traumatized by the experience of violent revolution. A new leader would emerge in the century to come – one whose understanding of Ireland's destiny was quite distinct from that of Tone, and one who would accordingly mould Irish nationalism into an entirely different shape.

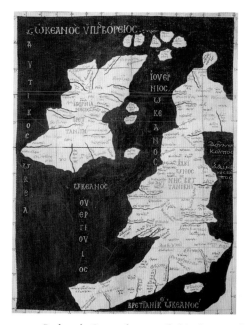

ABOVE: Ptolemy's *Geography*, compiled in the second century AD, charted the position of Ireland on the edge of the Roman world; this map is a thirteenth-century copy.

TOP RIGHT: The opening page of Matthew's Gospel in the *Book of Kells*. This famous illuminated manuscript is a dazzling example of early Irish art.

RIGHT: The national saint, captured in the stained glass of St Patrick's Cathedral, Dublin. Christianity had in fact taken root in the country well in advance of Patrick's mission to Ireland, and his exalted status in history owes much to politics and to later hagiography.

BELOW: Detail from the Ardagh Chalice, wrought in gold, bronze and silver. This treasure of early monastic Ireland was lost for centuries, before being rediscovered in 1868 in a County Limerick field.

ABOVE: The tomb of Columbanus at Bobbio, high in the Apennines of northern Italy. Columbanus founded monasteries across a swathe of western Europe; he died at Bobbio in November 615.

LEFT: Henry Warren's illustration of the death of the ageing Brian Boru at the sword of the Manx warrior Brodir during the Battle of Clontarf, April 1014.

BELOW: Giraldus Cambrensis – sharply observant, learned and untrustworthy – chronicled the first years of the Anglo-Norman presence in Ireland. His *Topographia Hibernica*, a page from which is shown here, was profoundly influential in medieval Europe.

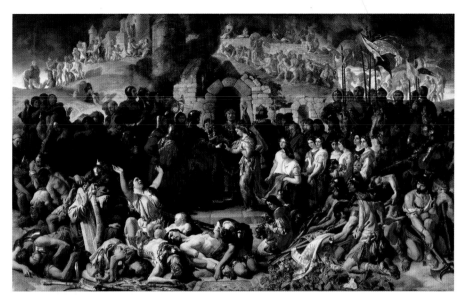

ABOVE: Daniel Maclise's *Marriage of Strongbow and Aoife* is a Victorian view of a pivotal moment in Irish history; the couple are wed amid piles of corpses, with divinities thronged around.

BELOW: The Battle of Kinsale – shown here in Franz Hogenberg's 1602 engraving – marked the eventual, hard-won and bloody Elizabethan victory in Ireland.

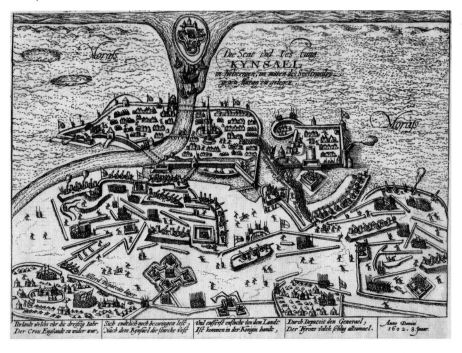

Conscientia nulle testes

Tyrones false Submission afterwards rebelling.

ABOVE: Hugh O'Neill morphed from ally to bitter enemy of the English state: this astringent image captures a contemporary Elizabethan view of the Earl of Tyrone surrendering to the English after the suppression of the rebellion in 1602.

BELOW: *The Buildings of the Company of Mercers*, from 'A Survey of the Estate of the Plantation of Londonderry'. The Company of Mercers was among the London guilds participating (reluctantly) in the Plantation of Ulster. The Mercers established estates in the valley of the 'fishy, fruitful' river Bann in the new county of Londonderry.

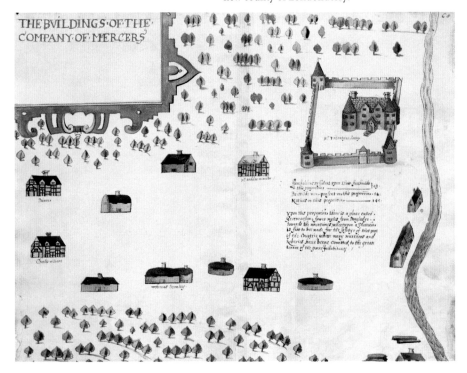

THE BVILDINGS OF THE
COMPANY OF MERCERS

ABOVE: Lough Swilly, County Donegal, looking north to the Atlantic. This fjord-like inlet witnessed both the Flight of the Earls and the capture of Wolfe Tone; and both Napoleon Bonaparte and Winston Churchill were alive to its strategic possibilities.

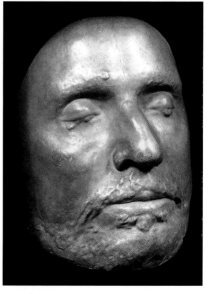

ABOVE: Two views of a figure celebrated in England as a democrat and vilified in Ireland as a genocidal maniac: Oliver Cromwell, at the notorious storming of Drogheda; and in death.

ABOVE: A popular image of the siege of Derry. With its images of defiant heroism in the face of adversity, the siege was a defining moment in the formation of an Ulster Protestant identity.

BELOW: The familiar image of the victorious King William on his white horse at the Battle of the Boyne, by Jan Wyck. King James – his defeated opponent and father-in-law – fled back to France; the conflict in Ireland continued for a further year.

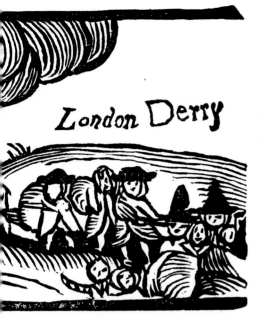

London Derry

ABOVE: The eighteenth-century elegance of College Green, Dublin, with a rebuilt and expanded Trinity College (right) and Ireland's new Parliament House, the first purpose-built bicameral parliament in the world.

ABOVE AND RIGHT: In *A Modest Proposal*, Jonathan Swift suggests sardonically that 'a young healthy child well nursed, is, at a year old, a most delicious nourishing and wholesome food, whether stewed, roasted, baked, or boiled'. Swift was a waspish observer of eighteenth-century Irish society – and a vital contributor to the country's cultural debate.

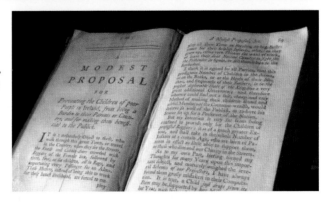

ABOVE: The Irish House of Commons in the eighteenth century, neither democratic nor representative of the Irish population, but nevertheless a crucible of energetic debate.

LEFT: Theobald Wolfe Tone eagerly embraced the principles of the French Revolution, and envisaged an Ireland in which religious division was set aside in the interests of a secular republic.

E. Scriven, sc.

ABOVE: Thomas Moore, creator of *Moore's Melodies*, was born over a grocer's shop in Dublin and died in rural Wiltshire, having established himself as a favourite of London society.

ABOVE: Arthur Wellesley, Duke of Wellington – Irish-born soldier, statesman and prime minister. His insights into the Irish political scene eased the passing of legislation enabling Catholic Emancipation.

ABOVE: Young, idealistic and a famous orator, Robert Emmet led a rebellion that in hindsight symbolized the end of French Revolutionary fervour in Ireland.

RIGHT: Lord Castlereagh's political career took him from Dublin in the aftermath of the 1798 Rising to the Congress of Vienna as British foreign secretary. He committed suicide by slitting his throat with a letter opener.

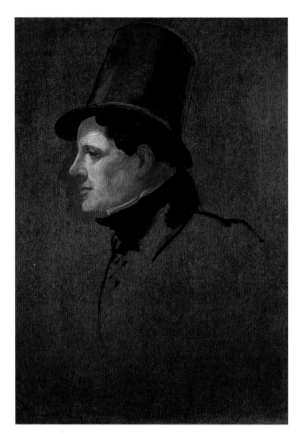

LEFT: Colourful, vigorous and politically daring, Daniel O'Connell was the 'Liberator' to his followers, whom he led in the cause of repeal of the Act of Union.

BELOW: This *Punch* cartoon captures the loathing felt for O'Connell in many quarters of British society. Here he is portrayed grown obscenely fat on the activity of his loyal supporters.

ABOVE: Ford Madox Brown's *Work* (1852–65) shows the increasing visibility of Irish emigrants – here 'a stoic from the Emerald Island, with hay stuffed in his hat to keep the draft out' – in British society.

BELOW: Many Irish migrants went further afield than England. In this engraving of the emigration office on the wharf at Queenstown (Cobh), passengers are preparing to set sail for America.

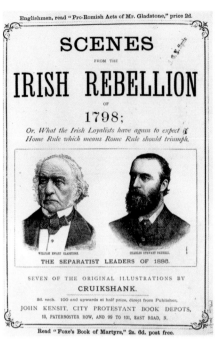

ABOVE: 'Ireland's Latest Martyrs' were executed at Manchester in 1867 for the murder of a policeman. The executions came amid a wave of anti-Irish feeling in Britain; in Ireland the events at Manchester bolstered the Fenian cause.

ABOVE: This pamphlet explicitly linked the agitation for Home Rule with the rebellions of 1641 and 1798.

ABOVE: William Ewart Gladstone's political mission 'was to pacify Ireland'. He became a passionate supporter of Irish Home Rule, and in the course of a long career, he brought two Home Rule bills to parliament.

ABOVE: Charles Stewart Parnell was the enigmatic, authoritarian and charismatic Protestant leader of the Irish Home Rule movement. Following his citation in a divorce case, the Catholic Church publicly condemned him, and his support ebbed away.

ABOVE: Scots-born James Connolly became a leading proponent of Irish socialism. He sustained a leg injury in the course of the Easter Rising so he had to sit rather than stand for his subsequent execution.

ABOVE: Women were present in virtually all theatres of the Easter Rising. Elizabeth O'Farrell accompanied Patrick Pearse in his formal surrender to British officials; in this photograph she is imperfectly edited out, with her disembodied feet still visible behind Pearse.

ABOVE: In the course of a long career, Arthur Griffith was by turns a journalist, political theorist, founder of Sinn Féin, treaty negotiator – and ultimately president of Dáil Éireann.

ABOVE: Maud Gonne is remembered for her passionate involvement – as actress, journalist and political agitator – in the cause of Irish nationalism.

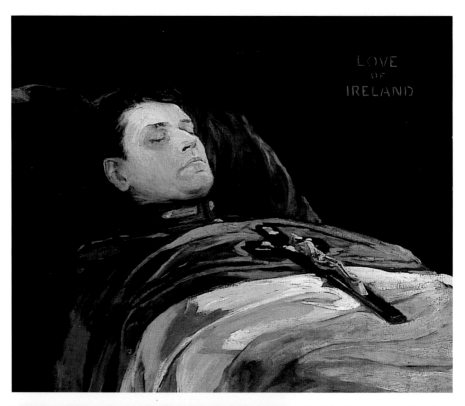

LOVE
OF
IRELAND

Sir John Lavery's portraits of Michael Collins and Éamon de Valera capture the differing destinies of the two men. Collins took the reins of power in the newly independent Irish Free State, but was killed months later at the age of thirty-one; de Valera lived for a further fifty-three years, in the process holding the offices of both taoiseach and president of Ireland.

Scenes from the Irish Troubles:
a mural of a civil rights march at
Derry; Bobby Sands was the first
man to die in the hunger strikes of
1981; the iconography of the Orange
'marching season' recalls scenes from
Ulster's tempestuous history.

LEFT AND BELOW: Ireland in the aftermath of the Troubles: Ian Paisley, now first minister of Northern Ireland, shakes hands with Taoiseach Bertie Ahern in Dublin (April 2007); Sinn Féin leaders welcome the Good Friday Agreement (April 1998).

BELOW: John Kelly, whose brother Michael was killed on Bloody Sunday, welcomes the findings of the Saville Inquiry at the Guildhall, Derry; the backdrop image is of a second victim, James McKinney (June 2010).

PART FOUR

THE GREAT CHANGE

CHAPTER SEVEN

UNION

In 1798, they [the Catholics of Ireland] were charged; in 1799, they were caressed; in 1800, they were cajoled; in 1801, they were discarded.[1]

In the momentous year of 1800 the Act of Union was passed by the parliaments at Dublin and London, abolishing the former and in the process ending Ireland's brief era of ostensible legislative independence that had been inaugurated in 1782. In the aftermath of the tumult of 1798, such a move had become inevitable: a mere two days after Tone's agonizing death, the chief secretary, Lord Castlereagh (1769–1822) had written to an ally: 'I take the earliest opportunity of intimating to you in the strictest confidence that the incorporation of the two countries by legislative union is seriously looked to.'[2] The authorities had become convinced now that the Anglo-Irish ruling caste could no longer be trusted to govern the country safely and efficiently.

This view had not simply emerged fully formed. The British prime minister William Pitt (1759–1806) had long been of the opinion that political union between Britain and Ireland was both inevitable and desirable. Since 1782, the nature of the relationship between the two kingdoms had become increasingly blurred: the British government was ever more reliant on an elaborate system of patronage to maintain control of Irish politics – but such methods were both inefficient and unacceptably expensive. Pitt had become convinced that union, combined with a judicious measure of Catholic emancipation, was the only means of bringing clarity to such an unsatisfactory situation. As early as 1792 he had raised the question with the Irish administration, noting that the two issues of union and emancipation went hand-in-hand.

Catholic emancipation was by no means desired as an end or a principle in itself. Pitt reasoned rather that it would be a potent tool if used in combination with political union: taken together, the two measures would solidify British authority and appease Catholic opinion in Ireland once and for all. Union would in fact limit the political impact of emancipation – for Catholic political freedoms would be granted within a political context in which they could pose no threat to the established order. In a note to Lord Westmorland, the anti-Catholic viceroy of the day, the prime minister had made his calculations explicit: 'The admission of Catholics to a share of the suffrage could not then be dangerous – the protestant interest in point of power, property and church establishment would be secure because the decided majority of the supreme legislature would necessarily be protestant.'[3] Emancipation, then, was an important symbolic and practical step to securing Irish Catholic loyalty to the Crown – while in return forfeiting little of substance.

By 1798, the Catholic sympathizer Lord Cornwallis was viceroy in Dublin; and although Pitt's fundamental calculations had not changed, the political shifts in the wider world had helped render the prime minister desperate for a measure of peace and stability in Ireland.* The international situation had become grave for Britain: hastily assembled coalitions of European powers – Austria, Britain, Prussia, Russia – were being defeated again and again by a rampant France; Britain itself was living once more in fear of a French invasion; and the European wars in general were proving to be

---

* Cornwallis already had a considerable military and political career behind him: he had been present in 1781 at the Siege of Yorktown, which effectively ended the American War of Independence; later, he was posted to India, where he was credited with instituting widespread reforms to British rule and in the process laying the foundations for the Raj. In 1798, he oversaw the defeat of the French.

cripplingly expensive. And now Ireland had erupted once more into bloody conflict, adding instability to Britain's western flank. As a result, it was now viewed as imperative to regularize the relationship between the two countries and, in the process, to end the system of patronage in Ireland. Pitt and Cornwallis were more than ever convinced that emancipation, combined with the removal of the Ascendancy's political power, would be instrumental in establishing this new *pax britannica* in Ireland. Working on the principle that it was better to keep your friends close and your enemies closer, Pitt planned to gather Britain and Ireland together into a new united state.

But the issue of Catholic emancipation would prove too sensitive to be attached explicitly to the Act of Union bill. Instead, the measure would be introduced quietly once political union itself had been achieved – a course of action much preferred by the Catholic religious hierarchy, with its horror of any whiff of potentially revolutionary public disorder. But lay Catholics were equally pragmatic in accepting the government's discreet promise: all sides understood clearly that a more public arrangement would be doomed to failure – not least at Westminster itself, where within the establishment a powerful current of anti-Catholic bias remained.

Union itself, of course, was never going to be simply waved through: indeed, in Ireland it spawned improbable coalitions in opposition. Elements within the Ascendancy understood that Union would mean the end of political control and patronage: as a result, they made common cause with Henry Grattan and his fellow proponents of Irish legislative independence, for whom the measure represented an act of absorption, rather than union. Others noted that the colonial framework that had characterized the relationship between Britain and Ireland would stay intact: a British representative would remain at Dublin Castle, answering to a distant parliament and government. A small group of educated Catholics, meanwhile, rejected on principle any diminution of Irish independence, emancipation or no emancipation.

But a body of opinion also existed in favour of Union: an influential constituency within Irish Catholicism perceived that emancipation was on balance more likely to be granted by a Westminster parliament than by one sitting at College Green; and while many Presbyterians found the idea of Catholic emancipation difficult to countenance, they certainly shed no tears over the prospective passing of an Anglican Ascendancy that had done so much to limit their political and religious freedoms. It was also the case, of course, that the great majority of the population was always more occupied with the matter of earning and growing enough to live on than with the devising of new constitutional arrangements: whether or not the Act of Union was passed, it would do little to help the crops. And the harvest of 1799 was indeed poor, diminishing even further the appetite of the mass of the Irish people for the minutiae of politics.

A first vote on Union failed in a hostile Irish parliament in January 1799. The measure's opponents argued, convincingly enough, that all dangers were now past: the state had crushed the 1798 rebellion, and nothing of its ilk was likely to occur again. In the light of this reversal Pitt, Cornwallis and Castlereagh understood that the government's pockets would have to be turned out: the stick that had been used to crush the rebellion must now be replaced by the carrot, and the good will of the Irish parliamentarians acquired – for the last time, perhaps – by the time-honoured methods of bribery, horse-trading and endless application of patronage. As a result, the remainder of the year was devoted to the assiduous buying up of parliamentary seats and promising of pensions to those whose administrative jobs would vanish with Union. The result was that when parliament met on College Green on 15 January 1800 a variety of crucial alliances had been locked into place and victory for Pitt and his ministers was all but assured. In the meantime, the prime minister had opined aloud – and a trifle optimistically – that a time was coming when 'a man can not speak as a true Englishman, unless he speaks as a true

Irishman; nor can he speak as a true Irishman, unless he speaks as a true Englishman.'[4]

Not that the opponents of Union were prepared to concede without a fight. The debate continued through the night; early the following morning Grattan, who had purchased the Wicklow parliamentary seat the previous evening, arrived on College Green clad dramatically in his old blue Volunteer uniform, in order to lambast the supporters of the Union. Having secured permission to speak from his seat – for he was too ill to stand – Grattan addressed a chamber packed with political allies and foes. Chief among the latter was Castlereagh, who had undertaken a remarkable political journey in his own right, moving from his Ulster Presbyterian roots towards Anglicanism and a place at the heart of the establishment; he would later carve out a substantial political career in Britain and become hated by many in the process.[5] For the moment, however, he was the object of Grattan's specific loathing: on this day in Dublin, the old parliamentarian pointed at his enemy and claimed that he and his cronies were striving 'to buy what cannot be sold – liberty.... Against such a proposition, were I expiring on the floor, I should beg to utter my last breath and record my dying testimony.'

Grattan's words, though impassioned, were too late, for the deal had already been done: an amendment designed to reject Union was defeated by a substantial majority and on 7 June – after more months of favours promised, compensation paid, bribes doled out and the government's own laws broken – the Irish parliament voted itself out of existence. An identical bill asserting that the two islands 'shall ... for ever be united into one kingdom' passed at Westminster; both bills received royal assent from George III; and the Act of Union came into effect on 1 January 1801. At Belfast, the *News Letter* hailed the Union: 'Yesterday Morning a union flag was hoisted at the Market House and at one o'clock a Royal salute was fired by the Royal Artillery in garrison ... it is now become an *interest* as well as a *duty* ... to bury, if possible, all political differences ... one people united in interest as in dominion.'[6] The first Irish members – there were one hundred of them in the Commons as part of the new deal – and peers took their seats at Westminster on 22 January. The glorious Parliament House on College Green, meanwhile, became an art gallery and then a barracks. In the summer of 1803, however, the building was sold to the Bank of Ireland on condition that it was remodelled internally to remove traces of its original function as a parliament; the Commons chamber was therefore broken up, although the House of Lords remained intact.

As for the promise of Catholic emancipation: this could not, in the end, be delivered. Pitt's credibility was now on the line – but he and his allies had failed to take into account the views of one crucial figure. George III – 'old, mad, blind, despised and dying'[7] – had been for over a decade drifting in and out of a state of insanity; at the idea of emancipation, however, he was outraged. For the monarch, emancipation was not simply a question of pragmatics and politics; it was a religious and personal bottom line, in that the admission of Catholics to public office would run counter to his sacred vow to defend and uphold the Anglican faith. So the monarch – 'considering the oath that the wisdom of our forefathers has enjoined the kings of this realm to take at their coronation' – refused his consent. In the face of royal displeasure Pitt had no option but to resign, which he did in February 1801.[8]

This failure to carry the emancipation measure had in a moment thrown away the nascent loyalty of Ireland's Catholic middle class. Had it come to pass – had tangible benefits begun to flow from the very act of Union – Catholic opinion might have committed decisively to the new status quo. Instead, the great majority of the Irish population was denied access to the benefits of membership of this new United Kingdom – and the promise that Union would bring in its wake full religious liberties and civil rights had proved to be hollow. Figures such as Cornwallis, dedicated to the stability and success of the new polity so recently brought into existence, recognized that the seeds had already been sown for years of future instability and that the course of future events had been altered. The Catholic lobby might have been neutralized and its power dispersed – instead, however, new life had been breathed into the notion that the English, in their dealings with Ireland, simply could not be trusted. 'What, then, have we done?' he wrote. 'We have united ourselves to a people whom we ought in policy to have destroyed.'[9]

Catholic Ireland, an entity that might have been quietened with kindness, would now have to navigate an alternative route towards a state of political, religious and commercial liberty; it would begin to assume an adversarial attitude that would require only a focus and a leader to spark it to life. The episode provides yet another 'what if' moment in Irish history: if Catholic emancipation had been coupled with the Union, it is possible that Irish identity would have evolved on Scottish lines, with a sturdy carapace of nationalist sentiment surviving alongside a unionist reality. The economic development of Scotland in the course of the eighteenth century had, after all, cemented that country into the Union, the failed uprisings of 1715 and 1745 notwithstanding: this expansion would continue in the course of the nineteenth century, in the shape of the booming shipyards and factories of Glasgow that exported to the world.

Indeed, in Ireland itself a similar model was already evolving: and the industrial growth witnessed in Ulster in the course of the eighteenth century continued into the new age. The populations of Belfast, Derry and a host of smaller market towns began to rise steadily; the textiles sector and the linen industry evolved; and as the century went on, Belfast developed a shipbuilding reputation to rival its Scottish counterpart on the Clyde. The province was being increasingly drawn into a larger British and imperial economy – and this was a sign to many that the Union could succeed in tangible and practical ways. Presbyterian culture in Ireland would continue to provide a home to both liberals and conservatives, to both progressive and reactionary wings – but those same middle-class political and cultural figures that had impelled the expansion of the United Irishmen would, in the course of the new century, move to accept the Union. This was in part a pragmatic decision: they could increasingly see no other course of action open to them, and the brutal suppression of the rising of 1798 had taught a lesson not readily forgotten. As the nineteenth century went on, however, it would also become evident that the Union was fulfilling Presbyterian commercial instincts and aspirations – and the consequences of this profound cultural change would in time ripple far beyond the bounds of Ulster itself.

With the Act of Union now a reality, the government's principal wish was to allow the new constitutional arrangements to settle down and become part of the fabric of life. A mere three years passed, however, before the new order was challenged in what proved to be the last flicker of revolutionary activity from the United Irishmen. Robert Emmet, born in Dublin into a prosperous Protestant family, had been twenty years old in 1798. He had imbibed revolutionary principles of liberty and freedom from his ostensibly respectable father; and his elder brother, Thomas Addis Emmet, had been a friend and ally of Wolfe Tone. Robert himself, though academically brilliant, was expelled from Trinity College as a result of his political sympathies, being condemned by the college as 'one of the most active and wicked members of the United Irishmen'.[10] After the failed uprising he had left the country for France, seeking assistance for a further rebellion against British rule. But it was to no avail: the French would fund no more Irish adventures. Nothing daunted, however, Emmet returned home in the autumn of 1802 and set about planning a revolt.

Although he was essentially an idealist, he did make considerable efforts at military preparedness: he organized, for example, the stockpiling of thousands of pikes (collapsible, the better to be safely stored), rockets and explosives in depots in central Dublin; and he planned an assault on Dublin Castle, with its store of arms and supplies and potent symbolic associations.

His blueprint for rebellion, however, came to naught, for ultimately it pivoted on factors that were incalculable: in capturing the castle complex, Emmet believed that he would tap into a vein of latent anger across Ireland and ignite a spontaneous uprising that could simply not be controlled. On the morning of 23 July 1803, the fragile foundations of his plan crumbled: the thousands of men whom Emmet had hoped to summon had dwindled to a mere eighty, some of whom were drunk; Emmet was jeered for his youth and idealistic rhetoric; and the fuses for the stockpiled rockets were mislaid. The castle was not stormed and the revolt degenerated into scenes of violence in central Dublin, in the course of which the lord chief justice, Lord Kilwarden, was pulled from a passing carriage and piked to death. It was all over in a matter of hours; Emmet himself became a fugitive, hunted through Dublin and the Wicklow mountains before being captured in September.

Before his execution, Emmet delivered the famous oration that, more than his deeds and or the events of the rebellion itself, earned him a place in Irish history: 'When my country takes her place among the nations of the earth, then, and not until then, let my epitaph be written. I have done.' His fame, built on idealism, enthusiasm, oratory and youthful energy, was thus secured; and it spread in the years to come. Set against this was the fact of his slender achievements: later, such figures as James Joyce mocked his developing cult; in *The Old Lady Says No!* Denis Johnston portrayed Emmet unflatteringly as deluded and violent, and the Dublin that had so conspicuously failed to succour him in his time of need as a 'wilful, wicked old city …. Strumpet city in the sunset.'[11]

The authorities, however, were alarmed by the fact that Emmet's abortive rising had – after a fashion – been carried through. Allegations soon circulated that the Catholic Archbishop of Dublin, John Thomas Troy, had known of Emmet's plans in advance but had neither alerted the authorities nor used his own influence to end the uprising. Given the social and political conservatism of the Catholic hierarchy, these claims were almost certainly incorrect:

Troy was anxious above all to maintain the strength and position of the Church in the aftermath of the period of the penal laws; neither he nor his colleagues could be accused of being secret revolutionaries. In the matter of public loyalty, indeed, Troy had considerable form: in 1789, on the (temporary) recovery of George III from ill health, he had brought together at Dublin the highest ranks in society, both Protestant and Catholic, in a *Te Deum* to give thanks for the monarch's deliverance; another service had been held following the failed French landings at Bantry Bay at Christmas 1796. Throughout his career, he had been consistent and loud in his abuse of events in France and of any form of civil unrest in Ireland itself. He and his colleagues in the Irish hierarchy were not about to jeopardize their institution's hard-won place in society for the sake of a doubtfully planned and poorly executed revolutionary plot. Granted, some Irish priests were certainly Jacobin sympathizers and a handful of them were indeed active in, for example, the events of 1798; to Troy, this minority was 'scum', but he could not alter what was a bald and uncomfortable truth.

In the years immediately following Union, the anti-papist sentiment at the centre of the British establishment was fully exposed by further attempts to return emancipation to the political agenda. Following the return of Pitt to power in 1804, meetings were held at Dublin to sound out the state of Catholic opinion; the result was a petition – an unwise petition, in the view of both Catholic pragmatists and the Pitt administration – for emancipation that was carried to Westminster in the spring of the following year. Pitt duly rejected the petition; the Whig opposition showed itself favourably inclined, but to no avail; and the measure was debated in the House of Commons and rejected, by a huge majority, in May 1805.

The measure had always been doomed to failure, and not merely by the opposition of the government. George III was still on the throne and would be until his death in 1820; and antipathy towards Catholicism and mistrust of its allegiance to Rome had by no means vanished from the British body politic. In purely political terms, meanwhile, it was understood in London as well as in Ireland that the desire for emancipation was merely one thread in a rather larger political tapestry involving Irish Catholic society, its Church and the eventual destiny of Ireland itself: tug just one of these threads, it was feared, and the picture in its entirety might begin to alter. The Catholic deputation, then, returned home empty-handed: the following years would see renewed petitions, occasional concessions from Westminster and a good deal of querulous debate on the status of Irish Catholicism – but little of substance; the question of emancipation became a running sore.

The wider issue of the relationship between Westminster and Ireland was also moulded by such events as the Napoleonic Wars that lay beyond the control of any of the interested parties. When the pendulum swung away from Britain and its continental allies (as it so frequently did during these tumultuous years), the government became anxious to allay Catholic fears, the better both to quieten Ireland and to enlist once again valuable Irish manpower in the British armed forces. As events began moving away from French control, however, the need to appease was much less pressing – and this became increasingly so following Napoleon's disastrous invasion of Russia in the winter of 1812–13 and the subsequent collapse of French military dominance in Europe.

Yet there was more to this period than a mere fractious relationship between the British State and its new subjects in Ireland; and the Napoleonic Wars – or, rather, their culmination on the battlefield at Waterloo in June 1815 – provide an excellent illustration of a more complex Irish stake in British affairs. For, as Irish troops had served in North America in the course of the Seven Years War in the previous century, so now did they, in ever-increasing numbers, serve a British State that in this new century was intent on rebuilding and expanding its empire. Military service had always held the prospect of adventure and a possible route out of poverty, isolation and economic stagnation, and in the early nineteenth century it was no different: in the first half of the century, Irish-born soldiers provided over 40 per cent of the manpower of the British army.

At Waterloo the 27th Inniskilling Regiment, having been instructed to hold its vital position on the field in the face of an enemy surge, was cut to ribbons by French cannon fire. By the end of the battle, some five hundred of the seven hundred Inniskillings had been killed. The regiment earned a glowing mention from the British commander, Arthur Wellesley, first Duke of Wellington, one of the foremost military figures of the day and a man normally sparing in his praises. By 1815 Wellington already had a glittering career behind him, with successful campaigns in India and against Napoleonic France in the Peninsular War, as a result of which he had been ennobled; he would later carve out a political career too, becoming prime minister in 1828. And, like his faithful Inniskillings, he was Irish, born into an Ascendancy family with estates in counties Kildare and Meath. Famously, he did not like to be reminded of the fact – though his insights into Irish culture and politics would prove useful later. The vital roles of such Irish figures as Wellington and the Inniskillings in what was an iconic *British* victory indicate the extent to which the destiny of the two countries was now intertwined. As a later rhyme had it:

> *There was a man named Wellington,*
> *Who fought at Waterloo.*
> *So never let yourself forget,*
> *That you are Irish too.*[12]

Nor was it only on the battlefield that an Irish presence could be found: while Wellington was performing on the European military stage, an Irish poet and singer named Thomas Moore was making himself at home in the most elegant salons of London society. Moore's Irish airs and ballads – his so-called *Melodies*, ten collections of songs that were published between 1808 and 1834 – charmed the city's aristocratic circles; and Moore himself became one of the most popular poets of the era. His success was all the more remarkable given that he held mildly nationalist views – although this did not stop him receiving the patronage of the Prince Regent – and that he was a Catholic, born over his father's grocery shop in the centre of Dublin. Moore attended Trinity College – one of the first Catholics to do so – as a contemporary of Robert Emmet; and although his travels took him to North America and Bermuda, he returned to Ireland frequently through-out his life. Yet much of that life was spent at the heart of the British establishment: Moore's portrait was painted for the Royal Institution by Sir Thomas Lawrence, and Moore himself died at his cottage in the depths of the Wiltshire countryside.

The *Melodies* tapped into a wave of growing interest in nostalgia and folk history that was rising across Europe in these years; and Moore's mingling of traditional Irish airs and lyrics with patriotic and nostalgic themes was popular not merely in rarified London social circles but in all classes. To the British, they represented an acceptably romantic view of the exotic other island – and yet it is clear that Moore intended to be disingen-uous in his *Melodies*, which if attended to carefully (rather than merely listened to now and again) might provide much to alarm. The Ireland in these songs was more than merely fey and a little wild: it was also heroic, grave, substantial and possessed of a golden age that was past but still potent. Nor was Moore above evoking contemporary events, as when he glanced at Emmet's pre-execution speech:

> *Oh breathe not his name, let it sleep in the shade,*
> *Where cold and unhonour'd his relics are laid;*
> *Sad, silent, and dark, be the tears that we shed,*
> *As the night-dew that falls on the grass o'er his head.*

But the night dew that falls, tho' in silence it weeps,

Shall brighten with verdure the grave where he sleeps,

And the tear that we shed, though in secret it rolls,

Shall long keep his memory green in our souls.[13]

Little wonder, then, that Moore's songs had their critics. 'Several of them,' grumbled the *Anti-Jacobin Review*, 'were composed with a view to their becoming popular in a very disordered state of society, if not in open rebellion .... The effect of such songs upon the distempered minds of infuriated bigots may easily be imagined.'[14]

These were years of steadily increasing political repression and social unrest, as the impact of the European conflicts, the requirements of a war economy and the economic depression that followed the final defeat of Napoleon marked the fabric of this new United Kingdom. Social distress, vagrancy and destitution became part and parcel of the lives of the poor; agrarian crime, want and hunger grew following a disastrous collapse in agricultural prices. The Anglo-Irish novelist Maria Edgeworth, who steadily recorded the Irish scene through the first half of the century, notes just such conditions close to her family lands in County Longford: in January 1816, she notes that Jane Austen has just sent her a copy of the newly published *Emma*; and that 'a man near Granard robbed a farmer of thirty guineas and hid them in a hole in the wall. He was hurried out of the country by some accident before he could take off the treasure, and wrote to the man he had robbed and told him where he had hid the money. "Since it can be of no use to me, you may as well have it…"' [15]

Not all such tales, though, ended so happily. In particular, tension between landlords and tenant farmers – never an easy relationship in the Irish context – became commonplace. It was generated by any number of factors, including rent disputes, reorganizations of the land and the application of tithe to families that could ill afford to pay it; and violence and intimidation became prominent features of rural life. These incidents were very frequently flavoured with sectarianism, directed sometimes by the Ribbonmen (yet another secret system of oath-bound Catholic conspirators) and sometimes by their Orange counterparts, especially in Ulster.* But on occasion these attacks were more class-based: assaults, for example, by poor Catholics on their wealthier co-religionists were far from uncommon.

The desperate human poverty that darkens these years in Europe was chronicled in Ireland too – and frequently with that same note of prurience that marked eighteenth-century accounts. Wretchedness abounds in such reports. The dispiriting account of a representative of the Fishmongers' Company of London, who was sent to assess the values of the guild's holdings – now two hundred years old – in the former Plantation county of Derry, is typical:

> In the course of the day we entered … many very wretched hovels, called cabins. The following picture will apply with variations to most of them. On entering the cabin by a door thro' which smoke is perhaps issuing at the time, you observed a bog-peat fire, around which is a group of boys and girls, as ragged as possible, and all without shoes and stockings, sometimes a large pig crosses the cabin without ceremony, or a small one is lying by the fire, with its nose close to the toes of the children. Perhaps an old man is seen or woman, the grandfather or grandmother of the family with a baby in her lap; two or three stout girls spinning flax, the spinning wheels making a whirring noise, like

---

* On occasion, this violence was extreme: gang-rape was a feature of the so-called Rockite uprising in Munster in the early 1820s, which led to the deaths of at least a thousand Protestants. See James S. Collins, *Captain Rock: The Irish Agrarian Rebellion of 1821–24* (Cork: Collins Press, 2010).

the humming of bees, a dog lying at his length in the chimney corner;
perhaps a goose hatching her eggs under the dresser; and all this in a
small cabin, full of smoke, an earth floor, a heap of potatoes in one
corner, and a heap of turf in another; sometimes a cow; sometimes a
horse occupies a corner.[16]

Such dispatches were circulated and reported in Britain, and they helped to feed a developing sense of Ireland in general (and rural Ireland in particular) as an unrelentingly primitive and backward society. They were also, of course, nothing if not consistent: Giraldus Cambrensis had written in an identical vein six centuries previously.

The full picture was a little more nuanced. For one thing, observers and proto-tourists not infrequently went specifically in search of such scenes of misery – and made certain they found them; and in general, the situation was in some ways a little less persistently grim than these reports suggest. The great bulk of the population certainly lived at subsistence level, in Ireland as in other European countries. But the Irish poor continued to have certain factors in their favour, in particular an abundance of dairy produce and miraculously nourishing potatoes to sustain them. Irish life expectancy at the beginning of the nineteenth century was on a par with that of England, and notably higher than it was in much of Europe.

Yet there were looming issues specific to Ireland, in particular an exploding population (which topped 8 million by the spring of 1845) subsisting on ever-smaller plots of land. As early as 1808, Maria Edgeworth was observing unsustainable conditions in the Longford countryside: 'My father and mother have gone to the Hills to settle a whole clan of tenants whose leases are out, and who expect that because they have all lived under his Honour, they and theirs these hundred years, that his Honour shall and will continue to divide the land that supported the people among their sons and sons' sons, to the number of a hundred....'[17] Teamed with this was the steadily increasing over-reliance on the potato, with calamitous results when the harvest failed. Its failure in 1822, for example, led to widespread hunger; famine conditions were averted only by State intervention and by the workings of private – and often English – charity.

The response of some commentators to this narrow escape, however, was less thankful than furious: 'English generosity has interposed and sent relief, and what relief is it? Some of the food that, in our poverty early this season, we were obliged to send away, even though we knew we would want it this spring'.[18] This, of course, was the beginning of an argument that would be given a thorough airing several decades later: the extent to which the market should be permitted to operate freely at times of social distress. By the third decade of the nineteenth century, the dangers of dependence on the potato crop had become fully evident. In the late spring and early summer of most years, when the winter store of potatoes was exhausted and the new crop was not yet ready, a period of hunger arrived for an ever-larger proportion of the population.

Nor did the agrarian distress in Ireland go unnoticed by the wider world. In 1825, Sir Walter Scott – whose appetite for things Irish had been whetted in the course of a long correspondence with Edgeworth – had received a rapturous welcome during a tour of the country. The experience, however, had also shocked him: of the Irish peasantry, he wrote that 'their poverty has not been exaggerated: it is on the extreme verge of human misery'; following his visit, Scott became a convert to the cause of emancipation.[19] A decade and more later, the French penal reformer and Catholic liberal social commentator Gustave de Beaumont visited Ireland and was shocked by what he witnessed. In his treatise *L'Irlande* (published in 1839 to instant acclaim in France and elsewhere), he professed his admiration for the British system of government in general – but was nevertheless forced to concede that in Ireland at least, this same system, characterized as it was by stark divisions between the very rich and very poor, was demonstrably not working. Arguing that the indigenous social structure was unsustainable, and observing the 'wretched hovel' with walls of mud that many a peasant family called home, Beaumont wrote:

> *I have seen the Indian in his forests, and the negro in his chains and thought, as I contemplated their pitiable condition, that I saw the very extreme of human wretchedness, but I did not then know the condition of unfortunate Ireland .... In all countries, more or less paupers may be discovered but an entire nation of paupers is what was never seen until it was shown in Ireland.* [20]

Ireland was indeed increasingly marked by sharp divisions between wealth and poverty, stagnation and energy. Nor was economic distress to be found only in the countryside: a profound agrarian depression was mirrored in, for example, the continuing economic decline of Galway; and the legislation of 1824 that created a United Kingdom-wide free trade area resulted in the abrupt failure of many of the country's industries. One answer that presented itself was emigration: to leave behind the privations of the Old World and strike out to embrace the possibilities of the New. Successive waves of Atlantic migrants had up to this point been predominantly Presbyterian: in the years 1769–74 alone, some forty thousand individuals had set sail from Ulster for a new life and a new experience of religious freedom on the other side of the Atlantic.* This flow of emigrants continued into the

---

* An exception was the localized emigration from Waterford and the southeast in order to work on the Newfoundland fishery. This migration had continued throughout the seventeenth and eighteenth centuries, with the result that a substantial Irish population had become established on the Newfoundland coast. By 1720, the British authorities were remarking 'the great numbers of Irish roman Catholick servants' (that is, fishery workers) settled on the coast south of St John's. (Quoted in Willeen Keough, 'Creating the "Irish Loop"', in *Canadian Journal of Irish Studies*, Vol. 34, No. 2 (Fall, 2008), 12–22, 12.

nineteenth century; and the newcomers would leave a deep cultural imprint on both the United States and Canada. This Presbyterian migration, however, became but one element in a much larger phenomenon: over a million Irish departed for North America in the period from the Act of Union to 1845. Such migrants tended now to be Catholic and unskilled; they tended too to leave on their own account, rather than as part of a move sponsored by either state or private agencies.

Many of these early nineteenth-century Catholic migrants – unlike later arrivals – tended not to settle principally in large communities on the eastern seaboard. Although the later Irish centres of Boston, New York and Philadelphia were inevitably among their first ports of call, many newcomers moved west and south as the United States itself expanded towards the Pacific; and as they did so, they assimilated into wider American society in a manner that became less common later in the century. Their swelling numbers began to bring political clout: Irish Catholics naturally gravitated towards the new Democratic Party; and the presidency in particular of Andrew Jackson (1829–37) – though he was himself of Ulster Presbyterian stock – was notable for its effective harnessing of Irish political energies. This contributed to the rise of anti-Irish and anti-Catholic sentiment in North America: newspapers and pamphlets, for example, alleging the existence of Catholic political conspiracies and secret societies now began to circulate . For these new waves of immigrants, such accusations proved difficult to counter: acclimatization to their new lives was indeed accompanied, in general terms, by a consistently strong emotional bond with the land they had left behind, the affairs of which they continued to follow closely – and this continuing attachment would leave them open to accusations of divided loyalties.

It was becoming evident in both America and Ireland that the growing Irish communities in the New World had increasing power and influence at their disposal; and that events in Ireland itself were being tracked now by an international audience. At the same time, a slowly developing Catholic middle class of traders and merchants in the home country was becoming increasingly dissatisfied with its lot: deprived of representation in parliament and barred still from many professions, its ambitions and aspiration remained consistently stymied. It was at this point that a new Irish leader stepped on to the stage – one who had long observed the intricacies of a complex and frequently festering society, and who understood both the importance of communication and the vast possibilities that were opening up in a shrinking modern world.

In January 1797, days after the French expedition had turned back from Bantry Bay, the twenty-one year-old Daniel O'Connell had enlisted in the Lawyers' Artillery Corps. The assorted yeomanry was dedicated to the maintenance of the state against the threat of revolutionaries; and O'Connell had little choice but to enlist: failure to do so would surely spell the end of his legal career before it had properly begun. Three years later, O'Connell was in principle opposing the Act of Union. 'My blood boiled,' he wrote, remembering the bells of St Patrick's pealing across Dublin in honour of the Union in 1800, 'and I vowed on that morning that the foul dishonour should not last, if *I* could put an end to it.'[21]

History has assigned to O'Connell the role of the hero, the natural leader. 'Three men,' wrote Balzac, 'have had in this century, an immense influence – Napoleon, Cuvier, O'Connell … the first lived on the blood of Europe; the second espoused the globe; the third became the incarnation of a people.'[22] O'Connell was educated, cosmopolitan and blessed with keen organizational and oratorical skills; he possessed colour and flair; and his eye for self-promotion ensured that he became a dominant figure in the politics of Ireland and Britain and influential on the global stage too. He charmed the young Queen Victoria – but only for a brief interval, before the monarch took fright at his political methods. He fought a fatal duel with a member of Dublin City Council; was prone to drunkenness and vulgarity; and was accused of all

manner of lechery and womanizing.* Not beyond using the courtroom itself
as a political stage, it mattered to him if his client received a harsher sentence
as a result.** He was a champion both of the abolition of the death penalty
at home, and of the anti-slavery cause in the United States in the 1830s and
1840s; and while he managed to tap the energies of the swelling Irish immi-
grant communities in the New World, he also provoked strong reactions.[23]
For every one of his supporters in the United States there was an opponent:
'Konno [O'Connell] was a knave', notes Herman Melville in his allegorical
Mardi (1849); and this bald declaration was shared by many.[24]

Although Catholic emancipation was ostensibly O'Connell's principal
goal, his ultimate desire was for the repeal of the Union – a result to be
achieved in a series of slow increments. The society that he wished to see in
the aftermath of repeal, however, was one thoroughly respectful of the rights
of propertied men (such as O'Connell himself) and at ease under a united
Crown. He was firmly opposed to the Ribbonmen and their kind: 'I would
not join in any violation of the law,' he wrote in 1833. 'I desire no social
revolution, no social change ... in short, salutary restoration without revolution, an Irish Parliament, British connection, one King, two legislatures.'[25]
And he had observed the fate of the United Irishmen, in the process becoming convinced that any vehicle for change in Ireland must be public and not
secret in nature, and that it must draw its strength openly from the mass of

---

* Patrick Geoghegan notes suspicions of a string of affairs, some of which can be given
credence. The most notorious scandal involved Ellen Courtenay, who accused O'Connell
of rape. It seems more likely that they had an affair, and a child may have been the result.
O'Connell's enemies may have been out to damage him, yet 'Courtenay's claims cannot be
discarded lightly'. There are indications of a string of other affairs too, including with his
daughter's governess. See Patrick Geoghegan, *King Dan: The Rise of Daniel O'Connell
1775–1829* (Dublin: Gill & Macmillan, 2008), 181.
** As in the case of John Magee, prosecuted for printing in his *Dublin Evening Post* a harsh
review of government policies. O'Connell, in his defence of Magee, grandstanded his own
opposition to the government, in the process earning Magee the harsh sentence of two
years' imprisonment and a £500 fine. Magee, unsurprisingly, later became estranged from
O'Connell.

the people rather than from cells planted discreetly here and there throughout the country.

A third conviction sprang – in part – from the experiences of his youth, when he had witnessed first-hand the bloodshed of revolutionary France and had resolved as a result that any campaign for change in Ireland must be peaceful and constitutional. He had, in addition, noted that violent action in Ireland had never worked in the past. But his attitude towards constitutionality also encompassed certain ambiguities: the fact that he sent his son Morgan to South America to join in Bolívar's uprising against Spanish colonial rule on the continent demonstrated that he was not always averse to the use of violence; and there was of course also the matter of the duel he himself had fought.

O'Connell understood the importance of continually probing the limits of constitutional politics. Having observed the failure of tried-and-tested methods to achieve reform – and in particular the repeated votes against change at Westminster – he knew well that the British ruling class could not be relied upon to resolve the issue of emancipation satisfactorily. It would have to be jostled into action – and, much as he had disliked the actions of the Paris mob in the eighteenth century, he perceived that the mass of the Irish people themselves must be employed to ensure that the issue was properly dealt with. But at first he had a difficult time convincing his colleagues that *any* action could be taken. Given the litter of failed promises and petitions that had followed the Act of Union, there was a widespread and reasonable belief that emancipation could not be achieved – at any rate, not by conventional political ends. As for Union itself, this was dormant as an issue, for its opponents in Ireland were of the view that, if emancipation could not be brought about, then separation from Britain was well-nigh a political impossibility.

It was in this unpromising climate that the Catholic Association was established at Dublin in May 1823, with the explicit aim of finally bringing about Catholic emancipation – specifically, the right of Catholics to sit in parliament without renouncing their faith. There was, of course, nothing in law to prevent Catholics from being members of parliament. The obstacle instead lay in the nature of the oath a new member was required to take, which stated 'that the sacrifice of the mass and the invocation of the blessed Virgin Mary and other saints as now practised in the Church of Rome, are impious and idolatrous' – a problem insurmountable for a pious Catholic. The Association was from the off an underwhelming affair, seemingly afflicted by the prevailing political lethargy: its members tended to come from the upper classes and bourgeoisie, and it seemed that this latest attempt to bring reform would go the way of all previous efforts.

In January of the following year, however, O'Connell introduced a new category of associate member – and the subscription fees for such members could be as little as a penny a month. At a stroke, the Catholic Association was transformed from a moribund talking shop into a mass movement. At the same time, other administrative innovations were put in place with the aim of maintaining a structure of local branches; and a good deal of effort went into ensuring that the Association's work was properly reported and disseminated throughout Irish society. O'Connell's own public appearances became important events, with crowds gathering to hear his fiery oratory. The Catholic Association had become a force to be reckoned with.

Daniel O'Connell had created one of the first popular democratic organizations in the modern world – and at a most auspicious moment too: the Catholic Association appeared and expanded at a time when news and gossip could travel farther and faster than ever before, when modern communications permitted the passing on of information in a way previously impossible. Literacy had also developed among the general population to a point where all manner of pamphlets and newspapers could be used to spread the word. While the Catholic Association was not always, perhaps, the well-oiled phenomenon of lore, it certainly did enough within a very short time to energize the communities within which it worked and to turn itself into a very potent political force.

Much depended, of course, on the willingness of the Catholic Church to work alongside the organization; and here too a change was quickly detected. While many priests and members of the hierarchy stuck to the old view that loyalty and obedience were the paths that the Catholic faithful must follow, others noted O'Connell's popularity and held their tongues; and still others demonstrated an overt willingness to work with this new political force in the land and to assist in the spread of its message by providing lists of clergy and parishioners. Bishop James Warren Doyle of Leighlin and Kildare went further still, commenting publicly that the British government could not expect the Irish Church to act as its handmaiden in matters of security:

> *The minister of England cannot look to the exertions of the Catholic priesthood ... the clergy, with few exceptions, are from the ranks of the people, they inherit their feelings, they are not, as formerly, brought up under despotic governments ... they know much more of the principles of the Constitution than they do of passive obedience. If a rebellion were raging from Carrickfergus to Cape Clear, no sentence of excommunication would ever be fulminated by a Catholic prelate.*[26]

But it was evident that not all Doyle's fellow bishops shared his opinions – and apparent too that some of the strategies of the Catholic Association were viewed as disturbing in other quarters. In particular, its conflation of the issue of emancipation with a broader range of Catholic grievances – especially the existence of remnants of penal legislation on the statute books – was a dangerous game, arousing as it did expectations that could not easily be satisfied. Penal laws, for example, had limited the extent to which the Catholic funeral rite could take place in Ireland: so it had become common practice to inter Catholics in Protestant graveyards, accompanied by a limited form of funeral. The Catholic Association moved to establish the country's first Catholic cemetery, at Goldenbridge outside Dublin, and this was consecrated in 1829 – the national cemetery at Glasnevin would follow several years later – thus fulfilling a specific Catholic need to bury the dead according to their own rites. But not all such grievances could be so readily answered: in particular, the hardship and privations of daily life could not be instantly eased by means of emancipation or legislative reform, as implied by the campaigns of the Catholic Association. And although O'Connell himself publicly rejected violence as a means of bringing about political change, he made it clear that violence would certainly ensue if his demands were not met.

As the 1820s went on, so the signals transmitted across the Irish Sea became ever more unmistakable and impossible to ignore. In the general election of 1826 a candidate sponsored by the Catholic Association challenged and broke the political mould in Waterford; further results elsewhere in the country demonstrated that the world was changing and the establishment could no longer pretend to hold fully the reins of power. At the same time, the context of a changing culture and a rapidly modernizing world meant that anti-Catholic sentiment in Britain – at its highest point in an era of nation-building – was now quickly losing its potency: O'Connell was pushing suddenly at an opening door.

His opportunity came in July 1828, in the form of a by-election that took place in County Clare. O'Connell himself stood as a candidate – and it rapidly became obvious that the Clare by-election would be the ultimate test of the government's resolve on the issue of emancipation. O'Connell won with ease: his supporters invaded the county town of Ennis, marching in step like a civilian army; their determination, potency and discipline demonstrated to the weakening anti-emancipation lobby that the game was up. O'Connell came to the silent Commons to claim his seat and, with due ceremony, read to himself the words of the oath. 'I cannot do it,' he told the watching House and he flung the papers away, in the process forfeiting his seat. Wellington was now prime minister and his understanding of Irish affairs proved decisive. He was privately sympathetic to the cause of emancipation; more pressingly, he and his home secretary, Sir Robert Peel, feared that a failure to amend the oath and to legislate for Catholic emancipation would lead inevitably to unrest in Ireland. 'We have also had the experience,' said Peel, 'of that other and greater calamity – civil discord and bloodshed. Surely it is no womanly fear that shudders at its recurrence' – in the eyes of some, an ungracious argument that conceded little to those larger notions of justice and fair play implicit in the idea of emancipation.[27] Catholic emancipation was voted through in the spring of 1829 and signed into law by George IV – though the additional clause that a man had to earn over £40 per annum in order to vote had the effect of raising the bar beyond the reach of nearly all of O'Connell's natural supporters. He himself stood for re-election, as he was required to do, and finally claimed his seat in the Commons – the first Catholic in parliament in over three hundred years – in November of that year. Irish Catholicism for the first time sensed its potential political power; the Catholic press hailed O'Connell as a new Brian Boru and acclaimed him as the Liberator.

Protestant factions reacted sharply to the emergence of this new force that was able to fuse religion and nationalism to such heady effect. Ulster's Protestant merchant class, absorbed in building their banking and textiles businesses, viewed such a disturbance of the status quo with much trepidation. Religious tension and incidents of sectarianism rose markedly, with the Orange Order becoming an increasingly prominent player throughout much of Ulster. Crucially, however, not all observers in the province had watched O'Connell's actions with dismay. Ulster Presbyterianism was no more monolithic than was Catholicism; and not all Presbyterians had forgotten the radical agenda embodied in the United Irishmen. Liberals naturally sympathized with O'Connell's pro-emancipation agitation: after all, this was another step along the road to removing all remaining religious-based discrimination from the British political system – discrimination that historically had targeted both the Catholic and Presbyterian churches. Liberals in Ulster could now, perhaps, anticipate a progressive political agenda that would embrace both Catholic and Protestant. After all – so the thinking went – it had happened before; and it might happen again, if only O'Connell could accept the Union as a done deed.

He could not: with emancipation now achieved, he set his sights immediately on the greater goal of repeal. At the beginning of 1830, his *Letter to the People of Ireland* laid out an ambitious reformist programme that encompassed repeal, a measure of parliamentary reform, and the abolition of the tithe system so deeply resented by both Catholics and Presbyterians. This last measure was of course crucial, for it would help to ensure that popular support would swing behind him once again. Ultimately, however, such a measure could not bridge the political gap that yawned between O'Connell and all shades of Presbyterianism: the abolition of the tithe was all well and good, but the two sides aspired to fundamentally different national conditions.

O'Connell also had to deal with changing political circumstances. From reliance upon Protestant opinion as its base of support in Ireland, successive British administrations now reacted to the success of the Catholic Association by attempting to draw majority opinion into the administration of Ireland. This task got underway with a gradual reform of the justice system and local government – aspects of life that impacted most immediately on the mass of the population. These efforts bore fruit in such legislation as the Municipal Corporations Act (1840), which ensured that the town corporations were a little less medieval in their organization and a little more representative of the people they were designed to serve. Moneyed and propertied Catholics would now be able to vote and sit on local government bodies; and in 1841 O'Connell himself became Dublin's first Catholic lord mayor in 150 years.

His own power base, however, was not wholly secure, for a grouping within his ostensibly united front began to grow restless. The leadership of the Young Ireland movement, passionate, articulate and non-sectarian, was devoted to a conception of national culture and the common good that owed much to classical philosophy: 'It is true wisdom to raise our thoughts and aspirations above what the mass of mankind calls good to regard truth, fortitude, honesty, purity, as the great objects of human effort, and *not* the supply of vulgar wants.'[28] The movement's newspaper, the *Nation*, was founded in 1842 in order to share and disseminate this vision of an inclusive society: it was imagined as carrying forward in print form the classical ideal of a citizens' forum. The Young Irelanders, under such leaders as the Protestant Thomas Davis, were inevitably far from enamoured of several of O'Connell's methods – in particular, his steady deployment of Catholicism as a political weapon and his overt links to Rome. To Davis and others, religion was a private matter, and an element that nationalism could manage without.

Yet O'Connell did manage to keep his movement together, not least because the political context continued for a period to be favourable for agitation. The power of the Irish lobby at Westminster was enhanced by the Reform Bill of 1832, which produced an altered and less monolithic Commons: it was clear that henceforth the Irish voting bloc might frequently hold the balance of power. The raising of the voting bar had of course produced a whole new grievance to be exploited; and ironically, the Reform Bill itself supplied another, in that it diminished the proportion of Irish seats in the Commons. But in 1841, with an insurmountably large Tory majority at Westminster and the avenues of political possibility closing down, O'Connell shifted his attention away from Westminster-based legislative reform. His prime objective remained repeal of the Union – and now the changing political scene in Ireland was working once more in his favour. The question of land reform was opening up a new front: in particular, the absence of security of tenure for tenant farmers was a bitter grievance. This was an issue that would suppurate for the next forty years – but for the moment, it provided a useful rallying tool.

O'Connell now opted to return to his former pattern of mass meetings and popular protest. He set about convening the Monster Meetings of 1843 – events that replicated in discipline and determination the congregations of the 1820s, but on a much larger scale. A crowd of over thirty thousand gathered at Limerick in April to hear the now ageing Liberator speak; much larger multitudes came together during the course of the summer at Mullingar, Lismore, Cork and Mallow; and the largest meeting of all took place on the hill of Tara in August.* 'Step by step,' O'Connell told his listeners, 'we are approaching the great goal of Repeal of the Union, but it is with the strides of a giant.' The government, unsurprisingly, took fright, and in the second half of 1843 a sharp security crackdown and the prospect of uncontrolled bloodshed forced O'Connell to cancel the last Monster Meeting of the year, which was to have taken place at Clontarf in October. The setting was of course no accident: just as Tara had been the seat of the high kings and the location of a notional unified Irish nation of yore, Clontarf was the scene of what, in an evolving nationalist historiography, had been a famous victory of the native Irish over the Vikings.

In cancelling the Clontarf rally, O'Connell had blinked first – and in the process had shot his political bolt. Arrested on grounds of sedition, in February 1844 he was convicted, fined and imprisoned. He was released after three months, when the House of Lords overturned the sentence – but on his release, it was apparent that the disparate energies that he had harnessed were now dissipated. During O'Connell's incarceration, moreover, the Tory

---

* Attendance numbers at the Monster Meerings were inevitably a matter of dispute: O'Connell's supporters claimed that 400,000 gathered at Lismore, Cork and Mallow, and almost a million at Tara; others disagreed.

government had granted additional reforms in Ireland, which – it was hoped – would have the effect of quietening Irish disaffection and at the same time sowing disunity in the Catholic ranks. Peel, now prime minister, complained to the Cabinet that 'I know not what remedy there can be for such an evil as this [Catholic unrest] but the detaching from the ranks of Repeal, agitation and disaffection of a considerable portion of the respectable and influential Roman Catholic population.'[29] And disunity did indeed arise: while the Church accepted the government's proposal to award an annual grant to the seminary at Maynooth, this arrangement was anathema to many Catholics; equally, the foundation of the secular ('godless') Queen's Colleges at Cork, Belfast and Galway was agreeable to many Catholics – including the Young Irelanders – but not to all members of the hierarchy and not to O'Connell either.

Daniel O'Connell died at Genoa in May 1847, in the course of a pilgrimage to Rome: his heart was sent on to the city, his body returned to Ireland for burial, witnessed by vast crowds, at Glasnevin. His presence in Irish history is substantial and vital: he had demonstrated that public opinion could be harnessed, shaped and directed towards a specific goal – and this was a lesson that was absorbed by a global audience. He had understood that modern technology could be utilized quickly and easily as a means of broadcasting a political message and achieving certain ends; and that the policies of the state, at certain times and in certain ways, could be rapidly altered and channelled in a particular direction. He had also understood that the message of Irish nationalism could be internationalized and transmitted to a watching world, in particular in the direction of a rising America; and he had tapped into a version of Irish history that linked contemporary events to a distant, misty and frequently mythical past. Wolfe Tone's vision of an independent Irish republic, however, had been succeeded by an entirely different model: O'Connell was at ease with the notion of an Ireland under the Crown; and he had, moreover, fused Irish nationalism and Catholicism in a manner that was new and altogether defining.

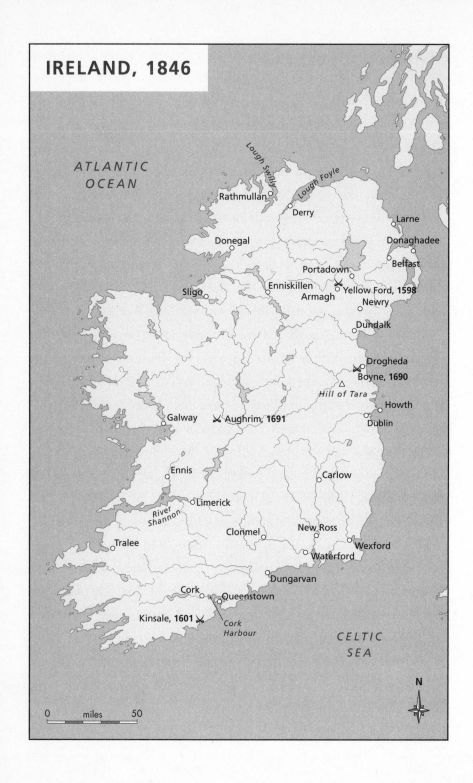

IRELAND, 1846

ATLANTIC
OCEAN

Lough Swilly

Rathmullan

Lough Foyle

Derry

Larne

Donegal

Donaghadee

Belfast

Portadown

Sligo

Enniskillen

Yellow Ford, **1598**

Armagh

Newry

Dundalk

Drogheda

Boyne, **1690**

△ *Hill of Tara*

Galway

Aughrim, **1691**

Howth

Dublin

Ennis

Carlow

Limerick

River Shannon

Clonmel

New Ross

Tralee

Wexford

Waterford

Dungarvan

Cork

Queenstown

Kinsale, **1601**

Cork Harbour

CELTIC SEA

N

0   miles   50

CHAPTER EIGHT

HUNGER

And if from one season's rottenness, rottenness they sow again, rotten-ness they must reap.[1]

In 1824, the ordnance survey of Ireland was inaugurated. Beginning with the flatlands on the shores of Lough Foyle, the country was mapped comprehensively, triangle by painstaking triangle; by 1846, the survey had been completed in County Kerry. With other economic surveys of the country being undertaken at the same time, Ireland could now be said to be more thoroughly known than at any point in its history: its social trends, its economic circumstances and potential were now fully charted, tabulated, calculated. This was a land where a line might have been drawn the length of the country, from Derry to Cork: east of that line, economic circumstances were in general more favourable; west of it, less favourable. But they were nowhere especially benign: there was still little work to be had in the towns; the wellbeing of much of the population was bound up alarmingly with that of the annual potato crop; and the fate of the country hung by a thread.

Early in September 1845, as the first potatoes were being harvested across Ireland, news began to filter through to the administration at Dublin Castle: the crop was coming out of the ground rotten and putrid. The news would not have been greeted with much surprise: already in Europe that summer similar reports had passed from town to town; the phenomenon was everywhere. The disease was the potato blight, *Phytophthora infestans,* a microscopic fungus spread by wind and rain. Although previously present in the Americas, it had been quite unknown in Europe before 1842, when it was likely brought by ship to one of the continent's Atlantic ports. Early in the summer of 1845, it was already destroying crops in Belgium and the Netherlands; by the year's end, it had swept to the borders of Russia, Scandinavia, Germany and on to Britain and Ireland. It was only in Ireland, however, that such a high proportion of the population was so utterly dependent on a single crop.

The effect of the blight was rapidly to turn the stalks black and reduce the tubers to a stinking pulp. At first, the response in government circles was measured: the loss appeared not to be so very great; and supplies could be augmented by the bumper oat harvest that year. As the autumn went on, however, it became clear that much of the crop had failed, though some districts suffered more than others; the western seaboard and much of Ulster at this time escaped with the least damage, while a great stretch of the midlands, east and southeast suffered the greatest. A massive wave of human tragedy had broken upon Irish society.

The authorities investigated means by which the good potatoes could be safely stored: if they were kept in cool, dry, ventilated conditions, the blight might not spread and infest the entire crop. But the potatoes continued to rot as before. It was then suggested that the dug tubers be stored suspended in bog water. Lastly, farmers were advised that any surviving potatoes could be used safely for seed the following year. In the meantime, a good deal of the much-vaunted oat crop and other Irish cereal crops were sent for export as usual; and the price of the remaining oats and sound potatoes went through the roof. Peel's administration now took steps to alleviate the developing crisis – though it did so reluctantly, as the orthodoxy of the time in British political circles dictated that the 'natural' workings of the economy and the market ought not to be meddled with.* The government's plan was

---

* The Free Trade Act signed between Britain and France in 1867 symbolized a wider acceptance of the principles of laissez-faire economics.

to import cornmeal into Ireland: this would be held by local committees wherever possible, and released only when prices in the open market climbed too high. These rations, however, were no free hand-out: they would be given in return for the recipients' participation in public works schemes, including road-building and stone-breaking.

The sulphur-yellow cornmeal – it was nicknamed 'Peel's brimstone' – had been largely unknown in Ireland until this point; and it was deeply unpopular among a population accustomed to the comforting ballast provided by the potato. By the late spring of 1846, however, demand for corn had exploded and the prospect of mass starvation forced the government to open the warehouses and offer the supplies for general sale. By this point, reports were reaching Dublin of widespread unrest and spiralling crime rates in many districts: crops and cattle were being stolen from the fields; carts filled with cash crops of wheat and oats on their way to market were being stopped and ransacked by the desperate and starving. It appeared that the Irish countryside was descending into chaos.

The story of the following three years is one of savagely bad luck combined with gross government inefficiency. The potato harvest of 1846 failed even more calamitously than that of the previous year; as early as July, the fields were ravaged and blackening, and the destroyed plants emitting the stench of blight. The blight struck across Ireland – though now with especial severity in the west – and with horrifying suddenness:

On the 27th of last month [July 1846] I passed from Cork to Dublin, and this doomed plant bloomed in all the luxuriance of an abundant harvest. Returning on the 3rd instant, I beheld with sorrow one wide waste of putrifying vegetation. In many places the wretched people were seated on the fences of their decaying gardens, wringing their hands and wailing bitterly [at] the destruction that had left them foodless.[2]

The situation facing the country was now immeasurably worse. After the 1845 crop failure, at least seed potatoes had remained available; in 1846, however, any remaining seed potatoes were eaten in order to stave off hunger. The Tory government – now headed by Lord Russell – refused to intervene to replenish stocks. The situation in 1847 was therefore destined to be equally bad, for there were scarcely any potatoes to plant and thus there would be no crop to reap. It is one of the ironies of the Famine that the blight was actually much reduced in 1847 so that such paltry crops as could be sown came up green and healthy and remained so. A desperate effort was then made to sow the fields again for the 1848 harvest – but a sodden summer brought blight once more and the crop was destroyed.

Prevailing economic doctrines continued largely to hold sway, so Irish cash crops continued to be exported rather than diverted to feed the population. At the same time, government strategies for dealing with the crisis were characterized by contradiction and reversal of policy. Late in 1846, the programme of public works began to wind down and it was decided that the shipments of cornmeal should also cease as soon as possible: the situation and the market in Ireland – and the two were firmly connected in the mind of the politicians – must be allowed to find their own level. In the real world, however, Ireland was lurching towards disaster: the destitute and the starving were besieging the country's workhouses. The relief projects could not be terminated under such circumstances, economic orthodoxies notwithstanding. But government action was invariably reluctant, with much emphasis placed on the duties of the private sector in dealing with the crisis.

There were, in fact, many private sources of succour: Quaker groups in Ireland and Britain ran soup kitchens; and as international attention was trained increasingly on Ireland, so other assistance arrived. (This assistance assumed a variety of forms: the French celebrity chef Alexis Soyer, for example, set up a soup kitchen to feed Dublin's hungry, delivering one hundred gallons of soup for a mere pound in cost and saving numerous lives. In a Bedlam-esque footnote, however, Soyer supplemented his efforts by charging the city's elite five shillings to observe proceedings; it cost only a shilling more to watch the animals eating in nearby Dublin Zoo.) A number of Ascendancy families were also prepared to do all they could for their tenants, some nearly bankrupting themselves in the process. The response of many others, however, was not so flexible: many families were evicted from their holdings and thrown upon the mercy of workhouses and of a Poor Law system that had not been designed with such a calamity in mind, and could not possibly cope with the numbers seeking aid.[3] 'The Irish landlords as a class,' observed the *Spectator*, 'have shown no capacity for the business of landlords' – and many agreed with such opinions.

The human toll in these years was stark, mounting inexorably into the tens and then into the hundreds of thousands. Epidemics of typhus, incubated in the overcrowded workhouses, swept through the population: as a result, the cities and the middle class began for the first time to feel the impact of what was taking place in the countryside. Famine victims were buried in mass graves; in the west, whole towns and villages began to empty. The British media devoted considerable resources to the disaster, with the *Illustrated London News*, for example, dispatching an illustrator to Skibbereen in County Kerry to record the event. Images of the Famine therefore spread rapidly, accompanied by reports of scenes of horror in Ireland. In response, the *Times* complained that the Irish were exaggerating, declaring that 'it is the old thing, the old malady breaking out. It is the national character, the national thoughtlessness, the national indolence.' In Cork, the *Examiner* retorted acidly that Victoria had sworn at her coronation a decade before to protect and defend her subjects without exception: 'How happens it then, while there is a shilling in the Treasury, or even a jewel in the Crown, that patient subjects are allowed to perish with hunger?'

On 3 October 1846, the *Vindicator* in Belfast printed a simple appeal: 'Give Us Food or We Perish'; and by the summer of 1847 the government, under pressure from events, had wound up its programme of useless and body-destroying public works and instituted soup kitchens in its place. For a brief period, rations were dispensed for free and without strings attached: soon, some 3 million people were receiving food aid. But before long, the government suspected that among these 3 million lurked the feckless and idle; and the soup kitchens were abruptly closed at the end of September of that year. The deaths continued to mount – but now the government had concluded its interventions, and soon it began to claim that the emergency in Ireland was ending. Balls and the usual round of social engagements carried on in Dublin; and in 1849, Victoria paid her first visit to the country. The failure of the potato crop that summer was as absolute as in earlier years; after this point, however, the Famine began slowly to peter out.

Famine years had been an intrinsic part of the fabric of Irish history. In 1740–1, for example, severe famine killed, proportionate to the then population of Ireland, as many people as did the crisis of 1845–9, but this earlier event holds no such well-defined place in the collective consciousness. This has much to do, of course, with the fact that a modern media and swift communications ensured widespread coverage of the nineteenth-century Famine. What makes it unique in Irish history, however, is the fact that it fused with issues of politics and national identity. As 1845 approached, the country had been in the midst of a debate on its destiny; the future of the Union itself was under discussion; and Daniel O'Connell had succeeded in forging, in the minds of the great majority of the population, a national consciousness that was distinctively Catholic and that questioned the British connection.

Moreover, the British response to the crisis fed this debate, for it undermined the central claim of the Act of Union: that the fates of Great Britain and Ireland were bound together now by sacred ties of mutuality. In the eyes of many, the government's willingness to countenance scenes of mass death and unparalleled misery in Ireland meant that it was abdicating its responsibility and demonstrating in the process that the philosophical foundations underpinning the Union were hollow. Such sensations led to, for example, the incoherent Young Ireland rebellion of 1848 – the year of revolutions in Europe – that began and ended most ignominiously in a County Tipperary cottage garden. Its leaders scattered to the winds: some were transported to Australia and Van Diemen's Land (Tasmania); others fled the country, carrying their potent version of national radicalism to France, the United States and beyond.

An estimated 1 million people died of hunger and disease in the course of the Famine, and more than a million emigrated, gathering in a host of Irish ports to take ship for Britain, North America and further afield. The conditions aboard these 'coffin ships' were frequently horrifying: disease and thirst claimed the lives of untold thousands; and more died within days of landing in such notorious quarantine camps as Grosse Isle in Quebec. The emigration statistics are startling: between 1851 and 1921 some 2.5 million people left Ireland, a proportion of the population that far outstrips the exodus from any other country. As many females left as males; the young inevitably in greater numbers than their elders. The crisis also had the effect of fraying the potent bonds of society, sometimes to breaking point: cherished norms and values were forgotten, so that aged parents were abandoned by their children and young children by their desperate parents; bodies were dumped in ditches for want of coffins and the strength to dig a grave; foodstuffs were stolen from equally desperate neighbours; crimes undreamt of were committed in the struggle to stay alive. In the light of such facts, it is little wonder that the Irish looked for guilt in the corridors of Whitehall. Young Irelander John Mitchel summed up this response in his famous claim that 'the Almighty sent the potato blight but the English created the Famine' – an attitude that formed a central plank of later historiography. It was perhaps inevitable that the collective trauma brought about by the years of hunger would be distilled and heaped, in grief and rage, on to the head of the British government.

British policies *did*, of course, exacerbate famine in Ireland. And other decisions were equally disastrous: the government's claim, for example, that property taxes levied solely in Ireland would suffice to cover relief work in the country was simply wrong: there never was the wealth base in Ireland to manage such a situation alone. Indeed, later government claims on private British charity to cover the shortfall implied as much – though they did not bespeak a concomitant change in heart: 'No assistance whatever will be given from national funds to those unions [workhouses] which, whether they have the will or no, undoubtedly have the power of maintaining their own poor and … the collection of the rates will be enforced so far as it can, even in those distressed western unions in which some assistance from some source or other must be given.'[4] British policy towards the calamity in Ireland, then, was short-sighted, counter-productive and characterized by ignorance, wilfulness and incomprehension. Famine followed: and politicians then failed, in a host of ways, to change or augment policy in time to head off further disaster. But these facts do not – as Mitchel suggested at the time – imply an *intention* to create famine in order to weaken and diminish Ireland.

Had the politicians cared to look about them in these years, they would have found no shortage of advice emanating from the voluble and quarrelsome British press: after all, the various political and cultural situations that manifested themselves in Ireland had always been a favourite topic of discussion. For some, government stupidity was manifest; other voices, however, complained bracingly that policy towards Ireland was in fact a good deal too indulgent: aid would be embezzled; the Irish were congenitally idle; and as a result the country should be left to its own devices and to the will of God. And there was a broad spectrum of opinion in Ireland too: in advance of the Famine, Young Ireland and the *Nation* had rejected the very notion of humanitarian aid, disgraceful and degrading as it would be to Irish society, and had called for the country to be given control of its own economic destiny: 'It is a blundering system of legislation which converts the whole population of the country into paupers, by taking away the produce of the labour and giving it to idlers, and then sets up a costly machinery for the purpose of relieving their distress.'[5] Later, in the teeth of the disaster, the movement would step back from such rigorously non-interventionist attitudes and condemn the British government for its failure to apply the laws of economics in a manner that took account of Ireland's specific situation and needs.

The Famine altered the nature of Irish society in manifold and far-reaching ways. The disaster had of course affected disproportionately the poorest layer of society; but a number of wealthier Catholic families did quite well out of the crisis, acquiring land quietly and in the process laying the foundation for future prosperity. The number of Irish speakers, which had long been on the decline, now went into freefall; by 1851, only 5 per cent of the population spoke Irish alone. And the population of the country would continue an inexorable decline for another century: it would become a demographic truism that Ireland could simply not hold on to its population.

The million and more emigrants and their descendants, meanwhile, would change for ever the relationship between Ireland and the rest of the world. The nature of British society, for example, was affected permanently by the massive Irish influx during and following the Famine. This swelling population soon made its presence felt: Irish itinerants and navvies, for example, slip into the fringes of novels and paintings of the period. In Elizabeth Gaskell's *Cranford* (1853), female Irish vagrants disturb the profound rural peace of Cheshire and attempt to force their way into spinsters' cottages. Ford Madox Brown's panoramic *Work* (1852–65) seeks to capture a representative moment of everyday life in mid-century London: the artist describes, among the throng of characters crowded on to the canvas, 'a stoic from the Emerald

Island, with hay stuffed in his hat to keep the draft [sic] out ... a young, shoe-less Irishman, with his wife, feeding their first-born with cold pap'.[6]

In the United States and Australia, and to a lesser degree in New Zealand and Canada, large and increasingly confident Irish Catholic communities grew in political and economic clout. These same communities would alter the face of Ireland itself: not only as a result of the remittances that at once began to flow, but also in the form of new ideas and new expectations that the emigrants fed back into the Irish social and political scene. They would also influence the attitude of their host countries towards Ireland and its politics. Even before the Famine had begun, Repeal meetings had been commonplace in American politics; and the language that featured at such rallies was striking, connecting as it did the plight of Ireland with specifically American imagery: 'Ireland has just toiled from out the Valley of the Shadow of Death. The sunshine is around her and about her. She is standing upon the top of the Delectable Mountains, and the shining city is in full view. That shining city is Repeal – the total repeal of the miscalled, tyrannical, and accursed union between Great Britain and Ireland.'[7] Moreover, the bitterness against the British that the emigrants carried with them on their long and foetid journeys to New York, Quebec and Sydney would form an important note in the new cultures they founded overseas – and provide an invaluable flow of ideas and resources to Irish nationalists in the years to come.

In 1863, one of these Irish emigrants stepped ashore into an America convulsed by civil war. He had arrived with a unique aim: to recruit angry and armed young men in the fight for Irish independence. James Stephens (1824–1901), County Kilkenny-born and Protestant, had been a Young Ireland activist before fleeing the country for France in the aftermath of 1848. While in Paris, Stephens had attended the Sorbonne and imbibed a radical political education; in 1856, however, he had returned to Ireland to assess the extent to which his native country was inclined towards revolution. The result was the evolution of the Irish Republican Brotherhood (IRB), yet another secret society created with the intention of severing the British connection. The organization was one aspect of a more general oppositional movement that came into being at this time, with roots deep in an array of varying traditions and contexts. Radical French politics, indigenous agrarian disaffection and Irish-American émigré emotion and money jostled together in this movement: it was truly international in scope, drawing strength not only from Ireland itself but also from Irish communities in Britain and the United States.

Across the Atlantic, a similar organization was founded in 1859 on a wave of sympathy and interest, and at once began building upon the already considerable Irish influence in the northeastern states – and in New York in particular. By this point, Irish interests had come to dominate the Democratic Party's so-called 'Tammany Hall' political machine that controlled the affairs of New York City. Tammany bought and sold votes, jobs and influence, operating on the basis of a nod and a wink – and these characteristics of a secret society inevitably appealed to Irish nationalist operatives. The American organization was named the Fenian Brotherhood – after the Fianna, the warriors of Irish mythology – and since it was permitted to operate legally and in the open, the name 'Fenians' came to be associated with the entire international movement.

The Fenian movement was a political and cultural response to the Famine: its membership had begun to absorb both the shock of the 1840s and the altered context of the Ireland that had emerged from the disaster. Moreover, with Irish culture now possessing a vastly increased international dimension, the Fenians understood that they could use this new state of affairs to broadcast their message abroad. Having learned the lessons of the past, meanwhile, Stephens and his supporters were determined to apply them to their new organization. As part of the dedication to the principle of secrecy, small membership cells were formed across the country: each of these was to be a closed circle, with no more than one member of each cell aware of the composition of any other.

This was in many ways an auspicious time for the creation of a new movement. Britain was in a position of unrivalled power, with an empire that encircled the globe and an industrial base that outpaced all rivals, but there were nevertheless signs of ill-preparedness and weakness. The bloody and costly Crimean War had ended in 1856 in a pyrrhic victory for the British, with many of their military leaders exposed as class-bound, incompetent fools. In India, the Mutiny had burst upon the Raj in the spring of 1857. Meanwhile, in Ireland itself there were a good many bored and disaffected young men scattered about the country's market towns: this was a constituency waiting to be tapped. Economic depression and persistent disaffection at the tenant–landlord relationship, moreover, could only add further to the movement's appeal, especially as Fenian publications were at pains to connect political independence to the prospect of a new land settlement. Now, surely, was a good time to move.

It was not long before the authorities, both civil and religious, were aware of the potential dangers posed by the Fenians. At Dublin Castle the administration began to use the term in its dispatches, though without having at this point a clear idea of the group's membership or strategies. More significantly, the Catholic Church, under the powerful and conservative Cardinal Paul Cullen ('little old Paul Cullen!' wrote James Joyce. 'Another apple of God's eye!') began to denounce the organization from the pulpit.[8] The Church knew a rival when it saw one. In this case, Cullen and his officials were increasingly angered at the note of rebellion and insubordination that emerged from the Fenian phenomenon; and alarmed too by Fenian secularism, by the sense that the movement was offering an alternative model of nationhood to that of the Church itself.

The Catholic Church had by this point begun to assert itself vigorously as a power in the land. Its religious orders were educating the Catholic youth of the country; and the seminary at Maynooth (underpinned by its state grant) was the largest in the world. The golden age of church-building that was underway, meanwhile, is best exemplified in the Pugin-designed St Colman's Cathedral that rises today above the port of Cobh. The foundation stone was laid (in what was then Queenstown) in 1868: and its soaring neo-Gothic architecture exemplifies the muscular confidence of a Church that conceived of itself now as a power in the land. Cullen's firm vision was of a Catholic Ireland devoted not to the political revolution imagined by the Fenians, but to a form of devotional revolution that would occupy the heart and souls of a Catholic people and would be led, controlled and directed by their priests.

In contrast to this vision, the cardinal felt, Fenian political agitation filled the people 'with impractical madness, so that they no longer think about education' – overall control of which was at all times his particular preoccupation – 'and the conditions of the poor and ... other necessary things'.[9] Cullen was particularly repelled by the Fenian cult of secrecy – the very quality that added inevitably to its allure across Ireland. Moreover, the movement also offered much in the way of ceremony, in the form of drills, marches and other theatrical events – and since the Church too was much given to ceremony, it rapidly perceived the danger of another power in the field.

Cullen was right to be alarmed: for if the Church could claim a devoted following, so too could the Fenians. Simultaneously, such parallel organizations as the National Brotherhood of St Patrick, founded in 1861, established dozens of chapters across Ireland and among the Irish communities in Britain, complete with libraries, reading rooms and social opportunities for its members. Stephens and other Fenian leaders naturally had rather more than library provision on their minds, but they were prepared to tolerate such loose fellow organizations because they provided a useful screen that sheltered from view the Fenian movement itself. The founding of the *Irish*

People newspaper in 1863, meanwhile, enabled the easy transmission of news and propaganda around the country, and by extension gave a sense of a new movement taking shape.

That movement received a further fillip in 1861 with the stage-managed funeral of Terence MacManus, a Young Irelander who had died in exile in California. The leadership conceived the notion of having MacManus brought home to Ireland for burial – and Stephens duly arranged a gala funeral that caught the public imagination. Some fifty thousand people followed the cortège through central Dublin for burial at Glasnevin – Cullen had refused permission for the funeral to take place in a church – and afterwards membership of the IRB soared: by 1864, there may have been sixty thousand Fenians in Ireland. None of which meant, of course, that any form of military insurrection was likely or even contemplated by the majority of the group's members; if anything, the note of gaiety, theatricality and excitement probably meant the reverse. Still, Stephens could now point to the successful establishment of a network of sympathizers on home ground. The next step was to cross the Atlantic to advance his vision of an Irish uprising underpinned and supported by a network of international – and specifically American – material support.

At this time, however, such potential support was flowing in other channels. In the course of the American Civil War (1861–5), many American Fenians enlisted in the opposing Union and Confederate armies; and Stephens knew that once the conflict ended he would have to strike before the throngs of soldiers were demobilized and absorbed back into civilian society.* Such a waiting game was naturally unsatisfactory, and it was for this reason that Stephens spent six months in 1864 on a coast-to-coast speaking tour, selling his notion of armed action as a means of gaining Irish

---

* The effects of the civil war manifested in other ways too: the Union government's introduction of the draft led to an immediate tapering off of Irish immigration into the United States; and competition for employment between the Irish and free black Americans led to increasing racial tension and occasional acts of extreme violence.

independence, visiting the camps of the Union soldiers and attempting to recruit battle-hardened men to his cause. It was a strategy not without hope: anti-British sentiment thrived among the Irish in America; more significantly still, tensions between Britain and the Union were rising too and war seemed a distinct possibility.

Stephens also never forgot the importance of the theatrical gesture, in America as at home. In particular, his printing of a form of Irish money – he called them 'Irish Republic' bonds – sold the notion of Ireland as an independent country and told his followers (by his own estimation, some eighty-five thousand of them in Ireland alone) that their day had come. But he was guilty of over-egging his pudding by exaggerating the possibility of an imminent uprising in Ireland behind which his new American allies could throw their weight. No such uprising was in the offing, and Stephens was encouraging the sort of keyed-up expectations that could not possibly be satisfied.

Still, his strategy at least paid short-term dividends: interest grew and membership lists expanded in America. Such activity inevitably attracted state attention: in Ireland, government intervention came in September 1865 in the form of raids on the offices of the *Irish People.* Stephens himself was arrested, only to escape from jail, slip out of the country and make his way back to the United States – in the process gaining considerable notoriety. On arrival in America, he attempted to unite the local Fenian organization, which had become riven with dissent. The organization sponsored small invasions of Canadian territory in April and May 1866 as a means of boosting morale: one, on the disputed border island of Campo Bello in the Bay of Fundy, was foiled by United States forces; the second was launched on Niagara and repelled by the Canadians themselves. So Stephens's efforts were to no avail. The raids accomplished nothing, serving only to antagonize Irish–Canadians – who feared, reasonably enough, becoming the target of reprisals in their new home – and to lower Fenian morale still further.* The two incidents marked but the beginning of twenty years of repeated Fenian skirmishes and raids along the United States–Canada frontier – both in the east and in British Columbia – which soured the relationship between the two countries.

By the spring of 1867, however, a rising at last seemed possible. On 5 March, the Fenians transmitted a goading proclamation to the *Times*, which remained notoriously anti-Irish. 'Our War,' ran the statement, 'is against the aristocratic locusts, whether English or Irish …. Republicans of the entire world, our cause is your cause, avenge yourselves. Herewith we proclaim the Irish Republic.' The Fenians had by this point already attempted an English-based raid, on an arms depot at Chester in February; and now a further uprising began in Ireland itself. It was doomed from the beginning: in spite of the the organization's emphasis on secrecy, it had been infiltrated thoroughly by informers, who had kept the government very well abreast of plans. The rising ended rapidly and in disarray.

There were postscripts to this event: in April, a large contingent of soldiers set sail from New York in a ship renamed for the occasion *Erin's Hope*. The ship was finally tracked down and boarded off the Waterford coast; in the hold officials found five thousand modern rifles, three artillery pieces and a million and a half rounds of ammunition. The overseas connection, then, came to nothing – but Stephens had demonstrated that he understood its potential. He was the first to tap into the United States as a vast pot of material resources, both men and money. He saw that the New World could provide many opportunities for the Irish in Ireland – and hundreds of other organizations since have echoed Stephens's approach and come to depend on Irish–American support and funds. And in Ireland itself, the Fenian movement had proved to be capable of engaging the support and enthusiasm of a

---

* Fenian incursions into Canadian territory have been credited with helping to mend the testy relationship between the original Canadian provinces and to nudge them towards Confederation – this came about in July 1867.

swathe (if not a very broad one) of the population. In London, the *Spectator* was impressed against its will: 'The mass of the Fenians are, no doubt, dupes, and ridiculous as it may seem that 103 linendraper's (sic) assistants should have quitted Dublin to declare war on the British Empire, still, there must be in men who risk life and liberty for an idea an element of nobleness.'[10] Nobody could be blind to the significance of this failed rising.

It was not in Ireland, however, or even in the United States, that its consequences were first felt – but in Manchester, the population of which had been swollen by thousands of Irish emigrants escaping the Famine. Tom Kelly, who in 1866 had replaced Stephens as formal Fenian leader, was by the following year on the run in England; he was finally arrested in Manchester in mid-September. Fellow Fenians hatched an audacious escape plan: thirty of them ambushed Kelly's prison van on the way to court, and in the resulting mêlée a policeman was shot and killed. Their plan had succeeded – for Kelly escaped and was never recaptured – but there were far-reaching implications. The British government might have avoided deaths in Ireland during the Fenian uprising, but it felt it must make an example of those operating in England. Those involved in the Manchester ambush were rounded up and put on trial: three of them were found guilty of the policeman's murder and sentenced to death on 23 November 1867.

At last the Fenians had acquired what previous insurrections had lacked – martyrs to the cause. As their sentences were pronounced, all three men had cried out in chorus: 'God Save Ireland'. The song that was inspired by this slogan would become one of the most celebrated nationalist anthems, and the case of the Manchester Martyrs became another example of how the British authorities, having managed one crisis with cool efficiency, could go on to create a worse one. Moreover, the Fenians had tapped into the influence that the media could exert on public opinion. The failed Fenian rebellion, which by now was being ridiculed in Ireland itself, was saved on the streets of northern England by British political short-sightedness.

CHAPTER NINE

THE IRISH QUESTION

Fenian activity in Ireland and England introduced a note of urgency to the Irish Question: in British political circles, there could be no more dismissal of the fact that a large proportion of the Irish population was chafing under rule from London and that something – even if nobody yet knew quite what – would have to be done to address the situation. In London, the pacification of Ireland was a crucial policy objective of Sir William Ewart Gladstone, whose Liberal Party in 1868 was currently in opposition to Benjamin Disraeli's Tories but was eyeing power. In Belfast, meanwhile, Ulster's Protestant political establishment began to monitor with increasing dismay a political landscape that was being refashioned around them.

This was an age of ever-broader parliamentary representation: in 1867, the minority Tory government's reform bill had extended the franchise to the majority of householders – and in the process had revolutionized the political landscape. So while Gladstone saw the Irish Question as a moral issue to be settled once and for all, he could also perceive the political dividends that might flow from including Ireland's Catholics in a Liberal-led political movement: in the upcoming election, the fragile Tory administration might be swept away by Irish votes. As a result, his public pronouncements now began to imply that Ireland could henceforth expect much in the way of political attention: if the Liberals were elected to office, he promised, the country's various issues would be addressed. This was a carefully vague commitment:

it remained to be seen what it might actually mean in practice, and whether his words would amount to much more than lip service. Besides, fundamental change in Ireland was not a gift that only the British could bestow; Irish MPs might also have a crucial role to play in fighting for it.

Whatever his motives and intentions, Gladstone understood that Catholic approval might be purchased in one relatively easy step. He had voted against the disestablishment of the Church of Ireland as recently as 1865, considering that the time was not right for such action – but now he promised this very measure if he came to power. The privileged status of the established Church had long irked Catholic opinion, and it was a wise move in other ways too: a month after the executions in Manchester, a Fenian bomb had exploded at Clerkenwell in London's East End, killing twelve and injuring over a hundred. Karl Marx, living in exile in London, was exasperated: the bombing, he said, was 'a very stupid thing. The London masses, who have shown great sympathy for Ireland, will be made wild by it .... One can not expect the London proletarians to allow themselves to be blown up in honour of the Fenian emissaries.'[1] And indeed, the event led to reprisals, such as attacks on Irish neighbourhoods. In cold political terms, however, it paid a certain dividend, giving rise to fears that the Fenian threat could never be wholly contained in Britain itself; and as a result, it focused attention on the state of Ireland and how it might be improved so as to quieten its mutinous inhabitants. Gladstone could now point authoritatively to the disestablishment of the Church of Ireland as a necessary move that would eliminate the Fenian threat while not in fact interfering much with the status quo.* 'So long as that establishment lives,' he said, 'painful and bitter memories of Ascendancy can never be effaced.'[2]

---

* These fears of Fenian activity were not wholly unjustified, and Gladstone's implied solution did not work as planned: in the course of the 1880s Fenian bombers targeted Scotland Yard, the Palace of Westminster, London Bridge, the Tower, the city's fledgling Underground and Greenwich Observatory.

The canny Gladstone also knew that the proposed legislation in Ireland would appeal greatly to his own natural nonconformist constituency in Britain, which would see disestablishment as one in the eye for the Church of England. And so it proved to be. In the general election of November 1868, a grand coalition of Liberals and nonconformists in Britain and Catholics and Presbyterians in Ireland propelled Gladstone into office for the first time, with a majority of 110 over his opponents. 'The Almighty,' Gladstone wrote in his diary, 'seems to sustain and spare me for some purpose of His own, deeply unworthy as I know myself to be.'[3] The disestablishment bill came before the Commons in March 1869 and was passed by the summer. Its effect was not only to sever the connections between the Church of Ireland and the state, but also to remove both the annual subsidy that the Presbyterians had enjoyed and the annual grant awarded to the Catholic seminary at Maynooth – though all three Churches received compensation to cushion these financial blows.*

Other measures introduced by Gladstone included the release under amnesty of a number of Fenian prisoners – a symbolically important move, though not nearly enough to satisfy many in Ireland. A movement led by the Protestant barrister Isaac Butt set out ostensibly to make a political issue of the amnesty situation. Butt, a former Orangeman, was intellectual, respectful, careful, uncharismatic, dour and unexciting – in short, lacking in many of the qualities that appealed in Irish political circles. He could not, however, be accused of being ineffective. He was instrumental, for example, in the organization of mass political rallies in support of extended Fenian amnesties; the largest of these, at Dublin in October 1869, was attended by over a hundred thousand people. Naturally, Gladstone could not be seen to bow to opinion in this way; and Butt's movement seemed to

---

* The disestablishment bill also relieved the Church of Ireland of the expense of maintaining many ruinous and ageing buildings; as a result, it emerged from the settlement financially rather better off.

have steered itself into a dead end. In reality, however, he and his supporters had rather larger issues on their agenda: their engagement with the amnesty issue had more to do with introducing a new presence in the Irish political landscape, and in the most public way possible. Butt's ultimate aim was to create a new politics: eighty years after the passing of the Act of Union, he wanted to raise the prospect of Home Rule in Ireland: legislative independence under the Crown.

Butt had a delicate balancing act to perform if his movement was to achieve anything at all. The most pressing political and social issue continued to be not constitutional change, but land reform and tenants' rights. In spite of the steep demographic decline which had accompanied the Famine, the small tenant farmer (usually with a large family to feed) remained a significant presence on the Irish social scene; the potato remained the crop of choice; and a poor harvest could still spell misery for the Irish peasantry. There was, to be sure, a little less pressure now on the land's ability to feed the people; and a run of good harvests had eased matters further. Moreover, a new *de facto* deal involving the ownership of the land had evolved since 1849: tenants could now pass their lands on to their nominated heirs as if they actually held title. Yet the fact remained that they did not: a tiny elite continued to own the vast majority of the land in Ireland, and brutal evictions were commonplace if a tenant farmer fell into arrears. Before he took power in 1868, Gladstone had been well aware of this state of affairs: he had already floated the possibility of land reform in Ireland – and the natural result was that the tenant class fully expected action on this matter to follow the disestablishment legislation.

Butt himself was doubtful as to the political consequences of land reform: he wished, for one thing, to see Ireland's farmers on his side and not on that of Gladstone, as they assuredly would be if the prime minister delivered on reform. He wanted the landlord class on his side too, as part of a national coalition seeking Home Rule; and he feared the prospect of an embittered rump of angry former landowners well disposed neither to him nor to anyone else. Yet political realities ensured that he could not possibly come out against the prospect of reform: as a result, he was a founding member of the Irish Tenant League, which met for the first time in County Tipperary in September 1869. Gladstone's land reform bill came to the Commons in February of the following year, but in Ireland it was perceived to be too modest in content. The *de facto* inheritance situation was now given force of law, but there was no measure compelling landowners to sell their land to their tenants, as had been demanded; nor were there measures to deal with that over-riding grievance, the absence of security of tenure. It satisfied nobody, in other words, although it did serve to underscore the sense that a measure of agitation in Ireland could produce a measure of reform at Westminster.

Butt now set about his greater agenda. He published *Home Government for Ireland: Irish Federalism, Its Meaning, Its Objects and Its Hopes*, which portrayed a federal United Kingdom, with Ireland governing itself under a common Crown. Butt's argument was partly – and cannily – couched in language designed to appeal to British sentiment: the Reform Bill of 1832, he suggested, had peeled British and Irish interests apart; there was no longer a united establishment that straddled the two countries. Instead, Ireland was now sending to Westminster a large body of members who were proving to be a deeply disruptive and distorting presence in the House of Commons: they were disturbing the balance of power at Westminster and it would be better, therefore, to remove them from the political equation and let them go their own way into a newly constituted parliament at Dublin.

In Ireland itself, meanwhile, Butt's desire to forge a national movement resulted in the formation of the Home Government Association at Dublin in May 1870. He succeeded in luring to the inaugural meeting a series of establishment figures, including landowners, dons from nearby Trinity

College and a number of newspaper owners – all Protestant and all vexed with Gladstone and his reforms. Butt's idea of a big tent, however, was inherently unstable: he was asking for these disaffected figures to make a vast leap – from irritation with the new status quo directly into the uncharted waters of Home Rule. For many of them, recent events implied that a self-governing Ireland would be a cold house for Protestants of whatever hue. Moreover, these gentlemen were fully aware of the surge of popular Protestant disaffection now ongoing in Ulster, and in Belfast and its environs in particular: Orange activity remained high, evangelism was fervently active, and sectarianism in general – that particular hallmark of life in Ulster for over two hundred years – was alive and well. In such a context, Butt's notion of a national force with room for all faiths began to seem fantastical.

The Home Rule faction in Ireland, then, rapidly took on a Catholic hue, and disaffection with the government led in March 1873 to the defection of those Liberal members of parliament who had been elected to Irish constituencies on the Gladstone ticket in 1868. A powerful electoral alliance was now disintegrating and the Liberal government was hobbled, limping on until the next general election a year later. In 1872 the secret ballot (another Gladstone innovation) had been introduced for all elections in the United Kingdom, meaning that for the first time votes in Ireland (for example) could be cast by tenant farmers without fear of reprisals from their landlords. The results of the 1874 election were a crushing blow for Gladstone's Liberals, who lost fifty-nine of their Irish seats to Butt's Home Rulers. (The exception was in Ulster, where the Liberals scored some modest successes.) The Home Rule faction could do little in the short term – the composition of the House of Commons and the majority now held by Disraeli's Tories meant that the Irish members could exert no leverage at this time. A year later, however, an electoral vacancy in County Meath would provide an opportunity to bring new energy to the task at hand.

*

Charles Stewart Parnell (1846–91) was a Protestant landowner with some thousands of acres at Avondale in County Wicklow and a positively heady mix in his ancestry. His paternal grandfather had been of the firm opinion that the Ascendancy, of which he was of course himself a member, was doomed unless it engaged fully with the great mass of the people of Ireland; the family tradition was thus to champion the country's ability to govern its own destiny. Parnell's mother was American: her father, Commodore Charles Stewart (or 'Old Ironsides') had engaged the British and captured two of their ships in a naval battle during the war of 1812. Parnell's schooling, however, had been impeccably English – although he had been suspended from Cambridge for brawling and had never completed his degree – and he adhered to a mild Anglicanism. He possessed the rare ability to be all things to all people, a gift that would be put to the test when he took up his seat in the Commons in 1875: for his task was to walk that most tensely strung of tightropes, charming the militants without actually offering any commitment while at the same time unifying Irish constitutional politics behind the common cause of Home Rule. He was a truly formidable character; not since the era of Daniel O'Connell had such an iconic figure entered Irish politics.

Parnell's maiden speech in the Commons was notable. 'Why,' he asked, 'should Ireland be treated as a geographical fragment of England? Ireland was not a geographical fragment but a nation.'[4] In spite of this rousing beginning, however, his initial impact on the stagnant political scene at Westminster was negligible. Disraeli's government had fine-tuned its tactic of employing parliamentary rules and procedure as a means to run unwelcome Irish bills into the sand. Measure after measure was killed off in this way; and, in combination with Butt's uncharismatic leadership, the sense was growing rapidly that the Home Rule Party could not hope to achieve much if anything at Westminster. But in the following year Parnell once more began to attract the attention of the media with a powerful intervention in defence of the Manchester Martyrs, who had been referred to in the chamber by the Chief Secretary for Ireland, Sir Michael Beach, as murderers. Soon, Parnell and his allies recognized that a creative deployment of Commons procedures was not a Tory monopoly but could be used by all sides – and they set to their task with a will.

In the course of the parliamentary session of 1877, this element within the Home Rule faction began to obstruct the work of the House, by introducing amendment after amendment, by talking out bills crucial to the government and by turning their collective backs to the established Westminster procedures. Such tactics may not have been original, but Parnell's faction now began to apply them to parliamentary business in general, as opposed to that part of it concerning Ireland alone – and the work of the House was paralysed. This campaign of obstruction began in July and August with the South African Confederation Bill – a moment that marked the beginning of an unlikely relationship between the politics of Ireland and southern Africa that would later have profound implications. Not everyone in the party was at this time pleased with such a strategy – Butt certainly was not – but the obstructionist faction forged ahead regardless. Before too long, Parnell was being considered the real leader of the Irish group in the Commons – and inevitably his increasing stature, powerful public performances and confrontational style led to growing tension with Butt. As anger mounted in the Commons chamber and out of it, Butt continued to cling grimly to the gentlemen's model of politics that esteemed civility above all else. The inevitable result was a split between the two factions. Butt would die in 1879: although his own political journey had been considerable, his legacy would be overshadowed thoroughly by the story of Parnell.

For now, however, Parnell and his allies had to deal with a range of political dangers: a split party, in which their majority could not yet be assured; the still-bubbling land issue, which offered both political dangers and opportunities; and a renewed attempt by Gladstone's Liberals to connect with Irish voters as a means of re-creating the potent electoral alliance that had brought the party to power in 1868. Gladstone himself – now in opposition and restive – had visited Ireland in the cool, damp summer of 1877 in order to reconnoitre the country and his own political prospects there. He had sailed for Holyhead again in the autumn, carrying with him a sense that Ireland was relatively prosperous and settled, even if the potato yield of that year was poor; certainly the country would be able to weather a single bad year.

But the disappointing harvest of 1877 was only the beginning of a run of bad years, and agricultural prices continued to fall as vast reaches of the American and Canadian prairies continued to be opened to intensive cereal cultivation, adding to the plight of those hard-pressed small Irish farmers who relied on their cash crops. A vast charitable effort swung into action in order to head off widespread famine: a lecture tour of the United States undertaken by Parnell early in 1880 ensured publicity for the plight of Ireland and generated substantial relief funds; the US government dispatched a supply ship, which docked at Queenstown in the spring of 1880; and ships of the Royal Navy landed relief supplies along the west coast. Significantly, a flood of remittances from Irish-Americans also poured into the country, underscoring again the significant alteration in the relationship between Ireland and the world in the years since the Famine of the 1840s.

The issue of land regulation now became a crisis, for the situation in the fields had left many tenant farmers in rent arrears and liable as a result to be evicted from their homes. The response was a sharp increase in agrarian disturbance in the west, where social distress was greatest. Fenian activists assessed the situation, to see if the makings of a further revolt were present; Parnell also travelled west to address mutinous tenants at Westport in County Mayo. Gradually militancy – the beginning of what would become known as the Land War – spread across the remainder of Connacht and further afield. The National Land League of Mayo was established in August 1879, forerunner of the National Land League, founded in October and backed by a range of respectable figures, including clerics and wealthy farmers. Parnell was one such, participating on the understanding that he would act only within the law. For many other members of the new league, however, this structure was promising: it was a constitutional carapace that sheltered a Fenian presence, and it represented the beginning of a potential national revolution.

Central to the foundation of the organization was Michael Davitt, who like Parnell cut a compelling figure on the contemporary national stage. The social backgrounds of the two men could hardly have been more different: while Parnell had grown up in comfortable and wealthy surroundings, Davitt had been born in Mayo in 1846 to parents who were poor, though with a degree of education. As a small child the consequences of the Famine had driven the family to contemplate entering the local workhouse before instead choosing migration to northern England. The result was a new life in the midst of a tightly knit Irish community in the industrial heart of Lancashire; it was here that Davitt acquired the accent that remained with him throughout his life. Here too he became steeped in working-class politics at a time when the condition of this class was having an ever-greater impact on the wider public consciousness. Elizabeth Gaskell's *Mary Barton* (1848) and *North and South* (1855), Charlotte Brontë's *Shirley* (1849), George Eliot's *Silas Marner* (1861) and many other such literary portrayals appeared in these years to testify to this growing attention.

A novel might have been written about the travails of Davitt's life too. As a child he was employed in the cotton industry, working in the local mills that resounded to the din of vast and deafening spinning machines that regularly nipped off workers' limbs and scalps; in 1857, Davitt himself lost an arm to one of these machines and was dismissed from the works without compensation. In his teens, he managed to acquire an education courtesy of a local Methodist schoolteacher – a formative experience that left him free of sectarian animosity – before going on to acquire a position in the postal service. Later still, a developing fascination with his Irish roots led him to become involved in Fenian activity: he participated in the abortive raid at Chester, and in 1870 was imprisoned in England for gun-running. His writings, detailing the harsh conditions in which prisoners were kept and the degrading work they were forced to undertake, began to find their mark in these years: Parnell and others read extracts from them in parliament so that they would be entered in the official Commons record.

When he emerged from prison in 1877, however, Davitt understood that he was living in a changing world, one in which direct but peaceful activism might bring about the changes he sought. His vision was revolutionary, encompassing an alliance of the working classes of Ireland and Britain in a struggle to overthrow the power of the propertied, sever the bond with the Crown and establish a republic. Davitt, then, was committed to a struggle that was concerned fundamentally with class rather than religion or nationality; this focus would later find expression in tours and essays exploring, for example, the more egalitarian cultures of New Zealand and Australia. And, with his intimate understanding both of agrarian conditions in the west of Ireland and of the industrial proletariat of northern England, he was also well placed to formulate a political view that connected and reconciled these ostensibly different worlds. Ironically, then, it was Davitt who persuaded a reluctant Parnell to become president of the Land League, noting that the latter was 'an Englishman of that strongest sort moulded for an Irish purpose'. Yet Parnell the landlord's son and Davitt the tenant's son were hardly a unified force. For the latter, the burning issue was to enable the lower classes to own their own land. Parnell, on the other hand, was a good deal more cautious, and land reform was a means of achieving the greater goal of Home Rule.

While the Land League officially opposed violence, the organization's leaders knew as well as had O'Connell before them the need to keep the potential for mass action, even violent action, in play – both as a means of maintaining alliances with more radical political forces and as a way of demonstrating the grassroots power of the Home Rule movement. Matters, indeed, had come to just such a head in November 1879 when the farmer and Fenian activist Anthony Dempsey was threatened with eviction from his cottage at Loonmore in Mayo. Parnell led some eight thousand men in concerted resistance to the move in which they surrounded the house and barred access to Crown forces. At the eleventh hour Parnell placed himself between his men and the authorities, thus averting a violent encounter. The authorities were obliged to withdraw; in response, Parnell declared that the massed crowd had 'broken the back of landlordism'. Yet the story did not end there. The authorities returned a month later to carry out the eviction as planned, and the Land League was compelled to pay Dempsey's rent to avoid leaving him homeless days before Christmas. But Parnell had set out explicitly his constitutional vision: 'Our country is a great country, worth fighting for. We have opportunities denied to our forefathers. Remain within the law and the constitution. Let us stand, even though we have to stand on the last plank of the constitution; let us stand, until that last plank is taken from under our feet.'[5]

When the general election of 1880 returned Gladstone's Liberals to power at Westminster with a healthy majority, Parnell had an opportunity to take control of the Home Rule Party once and for all. He was now obliged to add his voice – for he had no choice in the matter – to a new national campaign by the Land League. The movement was bankrolled by American funds and driven by men such as Davitt himself – politically engaged individuals who were prepared to be consumed by the cause; and the league's activities now reached into most of Ireland. The notable exception was the northeast, where the Orange Order was bitterly opposed to an organization such as the league, in which – and in spite of Davitt's larger purpose – nationalism and Catholicism were for now inescapably intertwined.

The Land League's new campaign was national only in the sense that agitation against landlords was widespread across the country, except in those areas where the local landlords had already taken public steps to ease the plight of their tenants; Parnell's own estate at Avondale was one example. The nature of this agitation, however, was not consistent: in one district, tenants might refuse to pay any rent whatever to their landlord; in another, a portion of the rent would be paid, but no more. Certain methods, however, proved to be so successful that they began to be adopted universally – in particular, Davitt's formulation of passive resistance, which had the joint merits of being perfectly legal and next to impossible to counter. Evictions of recalcitrant or destitute tenants could in this way be opposed effectively: neighbours could block the entry of the bailiffs; tenants could immediately and peacefully resume occupancy of the property, or take steps to ensure that nobody else moved in; and the league itself might take a landlord to court – a time-consuming and expensive process that would be avoided by the latter wherever possible.

The league had two especially potent weapons at its disposal. It now had the financial means to support its members in distress: in effect, the ultimate guarantee that gave many a tenant the will to resist. Davitt had also honed the idea of social ostracism of those individuals and businesses deemed to have acted against the league's members: the so-called boycott, named after the eponymous land agent who had refused to reduce the rent paid by the tenants on Lord Erne's lands in Mayo. Boycott's experience illustrated the impact of a successful campaign of ostracism: local shops would not trade with him or sell him goods, his postal deliveries were stopped, and he was shunned by the entire local community. His crops could be harvested only by a contingent of Orangemen sent down from Ulster for the purpose – a ruinously expensive exercise that that had to be policed by seven thousand soldiers – and Boycott himself was eventually forced to retreat to England. But such campaigns of ostracism could not always be properly policed: on occasion, they were turned against those who had 'grabbed' the land of others, or failed to observe the league's local rules; and – inevitably – they could be abused by some individuals for personal reasons, or to gain a measure of advantage over a commercial rival.

After the first shock of the land campaign, Gladstone's new government began to put together strategies of its own: Davitt and others were arrested; and *habeas corpus* in Ireland was suspended, leaving the government free to round up suspected dissidents and imprison them indefinitely. But the administration remained on the defensive: in the Commons, Parnell's Irish members were continuing with a policy of obstruction that undermined the government's legislative programme; and in Ireland, the league campaign of civil disobedience made the smooth running of the country all but impossible. Finally, in April 1881, Gladstone introduced his second land bill to parliament: by the summer, it had passed into law; and a third followed in 1882. Taken together, this new legislation transformed the fortunes of many hard-pressed tenants: rents could be appealed and, when this happened, were invariably fixed much lower than before; furthermore, tenants who paid their rent could never be evicted; and tenants were now permitted to sell their lease on the open market. These acts removed the sting from the land issue: for most Irish farmers, the matter was at an end.

In October 1881, shortly after the passing of the second land bill, Parnell was locked up in Dublin's Kilmainham Gaol, the government claiming that he had done nothing substantial to compel the Land Leaguers to keep the peace. In London, Gladstone told an audience at Guildhall that Parnell 'has made himself beyond all others prominent in the attempt to destroy the authority of the law'; both Parnell and Davitt were held until May 1882.[6] Parnell's imprisonment – he was held in comfortable conditions, although his health deteriorated during his incarceration – did his career nothing but good; furthermore, the proscription of the league itself, which soon followed, freed him from having to attend to an organization that had begun to limit his room to manoeuvre. Davitt, meanwhile, had used his time in prison to recalibrate his political vision; he concluded that Irish land must all be nationalized as a means of changing the power structure once and for all. It was a radical vision that diverged fundamentally from any mainstream views, and marked the next phase of Davitt's own political journey. But he was a pragmatist too: in a meeting at Avondale he agreed to Parnell's request to set aside for the moment his plans for land nationalization, which in any case had little or no popular support.

As for Parnell's political journey, the most dramatic scenes were still to come. The immediate future seemed inauspicious, for in the same week as he and Davitt had been released from prison the Chief Secretary of Ireland, Frederick Cavendish, and his permanent under-secretary, Thomas Henry Burke, were assassinated in Dublin's Phoenix Park – just beyond the palings of the Viceregal Lodge itself. The killings were carried out by members of yet another secret society, the Invincibles. This act had immediate political repercussions: Gladstone – who was related to Cavendish – was obliged to delay his future legislative plans for Ireland; Parnell also moderated his rhetoric as he planned his next move.

The history of these years can seem dominated by the results of United Kingdom general elections as Tory and Liberal governments chased each other in and out of power at Westminster as political fortunes shifted in Ireland and Britain, and as Home Rule bills were tabled periodically in the House of Commons. Yet Parnell and others were steadily tracing their separate paths through this morass. The Irish Home Rule Party appeared to be in the ascendant after the general election of 1885. It was a triumph for the party, which won 85 out of 103 Irish seats and even captured constituencies across Ulster; a further seat was won, spectacularly, at Liverpool. Because the Conservatives and the Liberals were relatively evenly matched, Parnell could in effect act as kingmaker. And, although Gladstone at first refused to declare publicly in favour of Home Rule, there could be no doubt that elements within the Liberal Party were moving – albeit slowly and in some quarters reluctantly – in this direction. A Liberal government – Gladstone's third – was duly elected with Irish support in February 1886, and a Home Rule bill was brought to the Commons shortly afterwards.

Gladstone's public pronouncements throughout that electric political spring were listened to with fervent attention in both Britain and Ireland. He had shifted his ground markedly, from a position of reluctance to outright acceptance of the notion of Home Rule, for reasons that were both pragmatic and philosophical. And, having made this shift, he embraced his new cause fully, announcing explicitly a preference that Belfast's Protestants embrace the Irish identity that had so marked the city's character in the eighteenth century. To the Ulster political establishment such a plain state-ment came as a profound shock – and in response a series of pro-Union demonstrations gathered pace, culminating in February 1886 in a 'monster meeting' at Belfast's Ulster Hall. The Tory politician Randolph Churchill had been enlisted as the rally's chief speaker: his career was now on the wane, but at Belfast he gave a speech of masterful subtlety. He had watched the careers of O'Connell and Parnell: and as they before him had done, so now Churchill verged on – but did not quite touch – illegality, conjuring the spectre of widespread civil unrest and disorder if Protestant demands for exclusion from any Home Rule settlement were not met. Resolving that the 'Orange card' was the one to play, he urged the Protestant population of Ulster to prepare so that Home Rule did not come upon them 'like a thief in the night'. The response was deafening.

The Ulster Hall meeting would emerge as a key turning point in Irish history: the moment in which Ulster unionism coalesced as a political force. Later, Churchill would coin the phrase 'Ulster will fight and Ulster will be right' that dominated politics in the northeast of Ireland for generations to come. It was all a far cry from the scene in Belfast less than a century earlier, when the Presbyterian middle class had listened with approval and excitement to Wolfe Tone's calls for revolution in Ireland. Now Presbyterian culture in general had in a matter of decades become staunchly unionist and monarchist, the exhortations of *'Liberté, égalité, fraternité'* abruptly and startlingly replaced by 'God Save the Queen'.

There were many reasons for this conversion. In part, such fervent opposition to Home Rule pivoted on urgent economic imperatives. Belfast in the closing years of the nineteenth century had become a boom town, home to a proliferation of businesses from tobacco to ship-building: and Ulster Protestants wanted to remain an intrinsic element in the world's superpower. Belfast had also become a centre of scientific inquiry, hosting visits from eminent figures such as Charles Darwin; the Queen's College in the south of the city was rapidly establishing a reputation for progressive thinking in the natural sciences – a state of affairs that scandalized elements of Catholic Ireland. The development of a scientific base in Belfast – the thinking went – would be placed in jeopardy if Home Rule led to a parliament in Dublin in thrall to a host of clerics.

At the heart of the debate, however, lay religion and sectarian fears. Belfast was more than ever now a city run by and for Protestants: sectarianism was increasingly fundamental to the city's character, with members of the Catholic minority edged out of lucrative jobs in factories and shipyards. At the same time, the uneven development of Irish capitalism had created an ever-widening economic and cultural division between the northeast of Ireland and the remainder of the country. Ulster's commercial prowess appeared all the greater when viewed relative to the economy of the rest of Ireland – and this, in the minds of an Ulster Presbyterian establishment contemptuous of the apparent backwardness they saw further south and west, was no coincidence. Gladstone's response to this gathering debate, however, was not comforting: he argued that he could no longer stand up to the will of the Irish majority – and Protestant opinion in Ulster began its shift from bursting confidence into a state of siege.

As it turned out, that first Home Rule bill of April 1886 failed to pass. The period had seen British imperial hegemony threatened on a number of fronts, with rising nationalist sentiment in Egypt, continued strife on the northwestern frontier of the Raj and the unsatisfactory result of the First Boer War (1880–1) all contributing to a sense that the might of the Empire was under threat. Autonomy for Ireland could not be countenanced by many – including ninety-three members of Gladstone's own Liberal Party: Gladstone's three-and-a-half-hour speech in support of the bill could not win them over, and in June 1886 they joined the Tories in voting it out. Gladstone's infant government fell as a result: another general election in July resulted in a crushing defeat for the Liberals, who were replaced by a Tory administration unsympathetic, as always, to the very notion of Irish self-government. Yet for Parnell this was only a temporary reversal of fortune: he spent the next few years consolidating his position in Ireland, calculating the political arithmetic at Westminster and consulting with Gladstone on the best way of resurrecting the issue of Home Rule. There seemed every possibility that, after the next election, Parnell would once again assume the role of political kingmaker. Instead, however, Parnell's world was about to come crashing down around him.

On Christmas Eve 1889, Parnell was publicly served with papers naming him in a divorce case. Since 1880, he had been having a relationship with Katharine O'Shea, the well-connected English wife of one of his own MPs: when in England, Parnell had lived with O'Shea and in the course of these nine years had fathered three children with her. Throughout this period the O'Sheas had lived separate lives; it is evident that Captain William O'Shea had used his wife's circumstances to further his own political career; and clear too that, in political circles, the Parnell–O'Shea relationship was common knowledge. Now that the facts were public knowledge, however, the situation became a scandal with the potential to rock politics to its core. Gladstone had himself used Katharine O'Shea as an intermediary in the past – but now he let it be known that he would resign the leadership of the Liberal Party if Parnell was not removed from his post. Gladstone, indeed, had little option in this matter: his own political base would melt beneath him if he did not take a moral stand on the issue. Thus the Irish party faced a stark choice: to support Parnell and abandon the imminent prospect of Home Rule – or abandon Parnell himself, their 'uncrowned King'.

The matter was to be decided in a series of meetings in Committee Room 15 in the Palace of Westminster, beginning on 1 December 1890. At stake was whether Parnell could pull off the biggest coup of his career. For six days he defended himself: 'My position,' he told his critics, 'has been granted to me, not because I am the mere leader of the parliamentary party, but because I am the leader of the Irish nation.'[7] Yet Parnell could not now depend on the support of his party. This was in part as a result of his own temperament: he had always held himself aloof from his supporters; and had instead run the organization as he saw fit. In his dealings with colleagues, he tended to be dictatorial and not infrequently arrogant; and party candidates – selection processes notwithstanding – tended to be hand-picked by Parnell himself.

In the course of that long year, moreover, the details of Parnell's relationship with Katharine O'Shea had been raked over and his political enemies had taken the opportunity to smear his reputation. Socially conservative Ireland had watched in shock and dismay as the drama unfolded – and it was evident that Parnell's political fate was sealed, not least because on 3 December the country's Catholic bishops issued a statement condemning him. The long series of meetings ended in an apparent lack of conclusion: the anti-Parnell faction – the majority – withdrew from proceedings, an act that spelled the end of his leadership of the party.

Parnell himself refused to accept this conclusion, and in the first months of 1891 toured Ireland relentlessly in an attempt to rebuild support. At this time, too, he and Katharine O'Shea were married, the ceremony taking place in June at a registry office near Brighton: 'I and my wife are perfectly happy,' he said. 'As for myself I can truly say I am now enjoying greater happiness than I have ever experienced in the whole of my previous life.'[8] The marriage was deeply offensive to mainstream Catholic opinion ('Charles Stewart Parnell has divorced himself from holy Ireland').[9] In Ireland, Parnell's speeches were met with vituperation or icy silence, and his new wife was condemned as 'debased and shameless'.[10] A series of by-elections in counties Kilkenny, Sligo and Carlow were won by the anti-Parnell faction; but the approaching general election would perhaps give Parnell the chance to demonstrate that his following in Dublin had held strong in the face of the scandal, thereby providing the opportunity to reunite the entire party under his leadership. In fact his position was wholly lost, and Parnell would not survive to see the election: the frantic pace of his life had taken its toll, and his vitality had been steadily undermined by kidney disease and other health problems. He died of heart failure at Brighton on 6 October 1891.

Could Parnell have brought about Home Rule? It is, in truth, difficult to imagine how this could have been achieved: irrespective of the arithmetic in the House of Commons, the forces ranged against the measure would always have been daunting. The House of Lords was firmly in opposition, and at this time there was no parliamentary mechanism to neutralize its veto. Large sections of the Liberal Party remained hostile to the very notion of Home Rule; so too were the Tories and the unionists of Ulster. Following Parnell's downfall, however, the Belfast political establishment breathed a sigh of relief at what appeared to be a lucky escape; nationalists had, by contrast, been given a glimpse of a promised land only to have the prospect whisked away. For the poet William Butler Yeats, the loss of such a man was a calamity: he came to represent the nobility, integrity, reserve and self-control of a leader overcome by a horrid barbarism; a noble stag, as he later implied in 'Parnell's Funeral', pulled down to his death by the 'hysterical passion' of the Irish hounds.[11] In *A Portrait of the Artist as a Young Man*, James Joyce too displayed a sort of acute Parnellite melancholia: the lost leader was again a victim of the Irish, who were 'an unfortunate priestridden race and always were and always will be till the end of the chapter'.[12]

The delicately calibrated movement Parnell had built with such care was now rent asunder; and, although this rupture would in time be patched over, the party would never capture hearts and minds as it had done under his leadership. A weary Gladstone, who had become prime minister for the last time in 1892, did indeed introduce another Home Rule bill in the following summer, but in the full and certain knowledge that it would be thrown out once more. He retired at last in 1894; and his successor as Liberal leader, Lord Rosebery, showed himself to be wholly uninterested in dealing with the now shattered Irish party. The Conservatives, under Lord Salisbury, took power once more in 1895: their attitude to Irish agitation remained chilly, although they were pragmatic enough to attempt to alleviate discontent through a policy of 'constructive unionism'. Home Rule would be killed by kindness, by which was meant 'killing it with money': additional land reform measures were passed; and money was invested in the depressed west of Ireland in the form of new railways, harbours and other infrastructural projects.[13] And in the meantime, the ghost of another idea was beginning to circulate: that of dividing Ireland in some as yet undetermined fashion, and allowing the unionist-dominated northeast of the island to secede.

As a long century drew to its close, hopes of Home Rule had been dashed – and yet the question of Ireland's future had certainly not been laid to rest. This future, for many in Ireland, was rather more nuanced than had ever been allowed for by either Parnell or Butt or indeed O'Connell, each of whom had been impelled by a vision of self-government and political autonomy that paid scant attention to the broader state of Irish culture. Some, of course, could take pride in the solid range of national cultural institutions now established in central Dublin: these included the National Library, which moved into its new Kildare Street premises in 1890; and the National Gallery, an imposing fixture on Merrion Square since 1864. The Royal Irish Academy and Royal Dublin Society, meanwhile, had been steadily amassing a collection of priceless objects in gold and silver that had been lost for centuries and these, together with booty gathered abroad by Irish soldiers and collectors, formed the core of a new Museum of Science and Art (later the National Museum). Some of the objects contained in such collections – the Tara Brooch, for example, and the Ardagh Chalice, redis-covered in 1850 and 1868 respectively – certainly fed into the notion of an ancient Irish nation. For the most part, however, this activity was cool, orderly and rational, lending weight to the notion of the city as a national capital, and of the Irish nation as being in peaceful and eternal commun-ion with Britain.

The monument to Daniel O'Connell unveiled on Dublin's Sackville Street in 1882, however, told a rather different story: the Liberator himself was accompanied by representations of Hibernia, Patriotism, Fidelity, Eloquence and Courage. These were distinctly arresting ideas, and they appealed to a restive element in Irish society: that evolving constituency of educated middle-class Catholics – schoolteachers, small farmers and civil and public servants – who were conscious of their Irish identity and anxious to do something to conserve and energize it. The Irish language was contin-uing its slow – many felt, terminal – decline, and many nationalists believed that Ireland as a whole was in danger of losing its cultural identity. To these observers, the parliamentary process in general and post-Parnell Irish party in particular held no allure; instead, they sought a cultural revolution.

One result was the foundation in 1884 of the Gaelic Athletic Association (GAA) with the intention of promoting interest in such specifically Irish sports as Gaelic football and hurling and in the process countering British cultural dominance. The organization frowned on such 'British' sports as cricket, tennis and rugby; and it banned policemen and soldiers from membership. The Gaelic League, meanwhile, was founded by Douglas Hyde in 1893 to foster the Irish language and Irish culture in general: Hyde was a Protestant and his vision was of a national language owned by all of the population, regardless of their denomination. Religion, indeed, was replaced in Hyde's vision by race: a common Gaelic Ireland that could take its place alongside the modern nations of the world. Joyce, in 'The Dead', would capture the popularity of such language-based cultural politics among a certain Irish middle-class constituency: his sharp-tongued Miss Ivors castigates those who prefer to study foreign cultures and languages, who cannot feel her fervent affinity with the 'national' language. But the league soon assumed both an explicitly Catholic and a sharper political edge.

Ancient history and myth were additional tools in this gathering discourse. The Fenian movement had looked to the legendary Fianna of ancient mythology, using a notional version of the past as a means of influencing the contemporary world, and now others would rework history in a similar fashion in order to create heroes and villains, winners and losers. The writing of Standish James O'Grady well exemplifies this move, his work of the 1870s and 1880s acting as a midwife to the Irish cultural revival and his self-imposed task of revivifying the myths and legends of Irish history for a modern audience. His version of the history of Ireland was, by his own admission, very largely a work of fiction: an act of reaching back in order to resolve how best to move forward; of creating a glorious and distant past as a means of counteracting the recent bad times of the Famine.

O'Grady's *History of Ireland*, indeed, was a book that directly inspired the greats of what became known as the Irish Literary Revival: Yeats, who was already publishing poems in English based on a mythical Irish past, declared that his readings set him directly to work on his 'Wanderings of Oisin', noting that 'the only person who while belonging to the head class has the central fire of the old people is O'Grady. Everything he does is a new creation, a new miracle.'[14] Yeats, his aristocratic confidante Augusta Gregory, the young Protestant playwright John Millington Synge and others combed the rugged western littoral in search of a culture in contact with its past, unadulterated by the contamination and grubbiness of the modern world. The past was being mined and refashioned to suit contemporary needs; and in particular to satisfy the present desire for self-government. Yet Yeats' notion of a 'head class' also indicated the character of his national vision. For one thing, his language was English – and his new national literature was explicitly an English-language project. For another, he – like Gregory and Synge – were Protestants: they were alert to Ireland's Protestant heritage and they believed in the importance of a Protestant stake in the country's new future. Yeats was prepared to treat with the Catholic middle-class interests who were driving much of the nationalist debate – but it remained to see whether such a philosophical gap could be bridged.

In these closing years of the nineteenth century, then, the various elements of Irish nationalist culture had so very much to say for themselves that each struggled to be heard; and it was unclear whether, in the midst of such a national debate, a consensus could ever be reached on any future national shape or direction. In the face of this ongoing tumult – and with the clash of unionism and nationalism continuing all the while – it was perhaps easy for the authorities to become complacent. Yet change was on the way – although it would take an event thousands of miles away on the southern tip of Africa to galvanize matters fully: to direct once more the disparate currents of cultural nationalism into explicitly political channels.

PART FIVE

TWO IRELANDS

CHAPTER TEN

SCHISMS

On 21 June 1897 the aged Queen Victoria celebrated her Diamond Jubilee. Around 3 million people gathered in London to witness the events of Jubilee Day, which included a three-hour-long royal procession through the streets of the city, followed by a service of thanksgiving at St Paul's Cathedral. Victoria herself had made it clear that the Jubilee must be connected explicitly with a celebration of the British Empire, so the colonial secretary, Joseph Chamberlain, ensured that representatives were brought together in London from each British possession, protectorate and colony, with an accompanying march-past of some fifty thousand imperial troops. Chamberlain's own views on the empire were perfectly clear: 'I believe,' he said, 'that the British race is the greatest of the governing races that the world has ever seen …. It is not enough to occupy great spaces of the world's surface unless you make the best of them. It is the duty of a landlord to develop his estate.'

Chamberlain had every reason to be complacent about the future: the empire was at its zenith, and Britain remained the hub of world commerce. And yet discordant voices could be heard. The Scottish labour activist Keir Hardie, for example, baldly condemned Victoria and her large family as parasites. In Ireland, a gathering in Dublin of the disaffected resulted in a march by torchlight from the castle through the centre of the city: at the heart of the throng was an empty coffin, symbolizing the death of the empire. The march was dispersed by the police; the coffin tipped into the river Liffey. Even in this jubilee year, then, the British imperial project faced opposition. Looming events in Ireland and in Africa would soon make this fact abundantly clear.

The situation at the southern tip of Africa was at this time highly unstable and marked by political and commercial tension between the British (in the colonies of Natal and the Cape) and the Boers, the Calvinist descendants of the original Dutch-speaking colonists. For the British government the region had long been of the utmost geopolitical importance, since the Cape controlled the vital sea lanes between Europe and India; as a result Britain had formally acquired the Cape Colony in the aftermath of the Napoleonic wars. Many Boers then migrated northwards to assert a measure of independence from the British; in time they established the twin republics of the Transvaal and the Orange Free State, in the process asserting control over the African majority population. These republics were autonomous entities that nevertheless existed in a state of permanent friction with the British authorities, in whose eyes they were anomalies in the context of a now almost wholly colonized continent. Furthermore, they stood in the way of the desired continuous belt of British occupation from the Cape north to Cairo.

The discovery first of diamond deposits in the Orange Free State and later of gold in the Transvaal had transformed this already tense situation. The *uitlanders* or foreign workers who began to migrate to the region were for the most part British, and their increasing presence would ultimately provide an opportunity for British intervention. The result was the annexation in 1877 of the Transvaal and the attempt to create a Union of South Africa (as seen in Chapter Nine, a process hampered in the Commons by Parnell and his supporters) that would be controlled by British interests. The resulting First Boer War of 1880–1 produced a series of defeats for the British, confirmed the autonomy of the two Boer states and led to the resumption of a fitful peace in the region. Yet migrant workers continued to flood into the Boer republics to work in their burgeoning mining industries: eventually, the *uitlander* population of the Transvaal outnumbered that of the Boers.

In 1895, a British attempt to incite an *uitlander* rising against Boer rule in the Transvaal – the so-called Jameson Raid – failed: in its aftermath, the two Boer states drew together in a tighter alliance and to prepare for war. The jingoism of the British press on this issue, however, ignored the stark fact that the empire's military strength at the Cape was weak: Britain was simply not in a position to easily win a war against the Boers on their home ground. Tensions came to a head in September 1899, when Chamberlain demanded the extension of voting rights to all *uitlanders* living and working in the Transvaal; the Boer authorities refused and in their turn demanded the removal of the British troops clustered on the borders of the Republic. On 11 October the Boer governments took the initiative: their forces crossed into Natal and the Cape Colony and the Second Boer War began.

Events in southern Africa had long been of great interest to Irish nationalists. It was not difficult to see the Boers as the put-upon victims of monstrous imperialist aggression – an independent-minded pastoral culture that wanted only to be free of the predatory British. Moreover, connections with the region were relatively strong: great floods of Irish emigrants might not have washed up on the shores of southern Africa as they had in Australia and North America, but a small core of Irish had gone to the Transvaal in the hope of making their fortune in the goldfields. They included John ('Foxy Jack') MacBride, a shopkeeper's son from County Mayo, who had emigrated in 1896; and the Irish-language enthusiast and Gaelic League founder member Arthur Griffith, who had come to Johannesburg in 1897 for a two-year stint with a gold company. Griffith found the atmosphere on the high veldt much to his liking: Boer society, he said, demonstrated that 'God Almighty had not made the earth for the sole use of the Anglo-Saxon race'.[1]

This thousand-strong community was more than ample, in those days of improving communications, to spread the word quickly and efficiently of Boer suffering at the hands of the British; and its political complexion was demonstrated in the form of the boisterous celebrations that took place at Johannesburg to mark the centenary of the 1798 rising. With the outbreak of war, the sight of another small, white Christian nation struggling for freedom electrified Irish nationalism. Constitutional politicians had already patched up their bitter post-Parnell factionalism, with the result that a united Irish Party now re-established itself under the leadership of John Redmond. The movement had been only mildly invigorated: its performance – lacking the heady energy of the Parnell era – was frequently anaemic. Yet it remained the dominant force in nationalist politics for years to come.

Other nationalists, meanwhile, continued to reject the parliamentary route. Shortly after his return from Africa, for example, Griffith established the *United Irishman* newspaper, which would provide a vital media platform in the succeeding years. It first appeared in March 1899, and enabled further airing of the plethora of fiery debates and disputes that at this time characterized Irish cultural life. The *United Irishman* was kept afloat financially with the assistance of Maud Gonne, the wealthy daughter of an English army officer who is best known for her long association with the poet W. B. Yeats. Early in her life Gonne had come to identify fiercely with the world of nationalist Ireland, and she penned many campaigning pieces for the paper.

These were exciting times – so exciting, indeed, that there was neither time nor inclination to reflect on certain problematic aspects of the African situation. The deeply ingrained anti-Catholic nature of Boer society was widely recognized: it was for this reason that England's Catholic bishops lent their support to the British government's policies in Southern Africa. In Irish nationalist circles, by contrast, this question of religion tended to be dismissed: national liberation was what mattered, and other factors were regarded as essentially immaterial. As to the marginal place allotted to black Africans in Boer society, the prevailing lack of attention given to this question reflected much broader European racist attitudes – to which Irish nationalism was certainly not immune.

So Irish nationalism threw its weight behind the Boer cause: the *vierkleur* flag of the Transvaal became a familiar sight on the streets of Dublin as the southern African war rapidly developed into a *cause célèbre*, while the pages of the *United Irishman* filled with articles calling for resistance and fellowship with the Boers and urging those who might enlist in the British army for pressing economic reasons to reconsider. 'Think on this, Irish mothers,' Gonne proclaimed in a piece anatomizing the plight of British soldiers left maimed and disabled in the course of a variety of imperial campaigns, 'even when there is hunger in your cabins and things look dark and hopeless for the land we love.'[2] In October 1899, Griffith, Gonne and James Connolly were instrumental in the foundation of the Irish Transvaal Committee: in the same month a crowd of twenty thousand gathered in front of Custom House in Dublin to show solidarity for the Boer cause; and Michael Davitt – who had been elected to represent South Mayo in 1895 but who thoroughly disliked Westminster and its atmosphere – resigned his seat in the Commons, telling his fellow members: 'When I go I shall tell my boys, "I have been some five years in this House, and the conclusion with which I leave it is that no cause, however just, will find support, no wrong, however pressing or apparent, will find redress here, unless backed up by force."'[3]

In southern Africa itself, figures within the Irish community had come together in September that year to organize a fighting force, to be placed at the disposal of the authorities in the Transvaal; President Kruger gave his assent a few weeks later. The resulting Irish Brigade, commanded by MacBride, was composed of Irish, Irish–Americans and other nationalities: it was but one of several such overseas brigades (Dutch, Italian, German and Russian; and there might have been more, had Kruger permitted it) that turned out for the Boers. Each member of the Irish Brigade – never more than five hundred strong – swore an oath 'to the people of the South African Republic … that I will work for nothing but the prosperity, the welfare, and the independence of the land and people of the Republic, so truly help me, God Almighty'.

The existence of such a fighting force, comprised as it was of United Kingdom citizens fighting a war against their own country, was in legal terms an act of treason; and it was to avoid the likelihood that they would be shot as traitors if captured that the members of the brigade were granted Boer nationality just before the outbreak of war. Yet the brigade was but one facet of a highly diverse Irish community: some of its members were repelled by the actions of the brigade; others sympathized in secret; still others fought as members of the regular Boer army. And yet, although the numbers of Irishmen enlisting in the British forces had been in steep decline since the Famine – down to a mere 13 per cent of the total in arms by 1900 – the fact remained that far greater numbers of Irishmen would serve on the British side than would support the Boers – in spite of all the passionate urgings of Gonne. In the coming war, Irishman would be pitted against Irishman on the southern tip of Africa.

Members of the Irish Brigade were in the vanguard of the Boer forces that crossed into Natal, and on 20 October British and Boers came face to face at Talana Hill, near the town of Ladysmith. Accounts of the encounter are confused and tainted by propaganda: assertions that regular Irish troops were pleased to be captured by their fellow countrymen and pleased too to defect to the Boer side jostle against other claims that Brigade members showed hostility to captured imperial soldiers. Animosity grew in the subsequent four-month siege of Ladysmith, when the Brigade engaged in regular skirmishes with members of the Dublin Fusiliers, Royal Irish Rifles and Royal Artillery holed up in the town. Later, a British counter-offensive proved disastrously ineffective: during 'Black Week' the Boers repulsed British attacks at Stormberg on 10 December and the following day at Magersfontein. At Colenso, in the early hours of 15 December, the Boers (accompanied by members of the Irish Brigade) inflicted a third heavy defeat on the British: the Irish regiments present, and especially the 'Dublins', bore the brunt of the onslaught, with four hundred soldiers killed in less than an hour at the crossings of the Tugela river.

The news of the British defeat at Colenso rapidly reached Ireland: the newspapers, regardless of political complexion, could thrill at the news of Irish heroism and martyrdom; while the nationalist press could further revel in the presence of MacBride and his men at the front line. A few days later, Chamberlain arrived in Dublin to receive an honorary doctorate from Trinity College ('He is coming! his hand dyed with freeman's best blood / His heart black and false as Lucifer's own'[4]); and Griffith, Gonne and Davitt were part of another large, noisy crowd that gathered – in spite of a ban – to protest against the ceremony; the demonstration ended in riot and arrests. (Yeats sent a supportive note.) Gonne had organized the dispatch to the Transvaal of a new flag for the Brigade, and a few days before Christmas it was raised above the Irish camp. It was a cheering gesture of solidarity; at the same time, the Irish Transvaal Committee redoubled its efforts to prevent enlistment in the British army.

Yet Colenso, humiliating and destructive as it had been to British morale, also proved to be the high-water mark of the Boer campaign. On 23 February 1900, Irish troops were in the vanguard of a British assault on Hart's Hill in an attempt to relieve Ladysmith. The Irish Brigade and Irish regulars exchanged fire, but four days later the Boers had been broken and began retreating towards their own borders, with MacBride's men now defending the rearguard. On 3 March, the British entered Ladysmith. The Brigade remained active for some months, harrying the British across the veldt of the Orange Free State, but by September the game was up and

MacBride and his men slipped across the border into the Portuguese colony of Mozambique. There they were briefly interned before being deported; most of them made for America, though MacBride himself made for Paris and the waiting Gonne. The couple would marry – briefly and disastrously – in 1903.

Thirty-one members of the Irish Brigade were killed in the course of the war – a figure that pales in comparison to the four thousand regular Irish troops that died. Yet it was 'MacBride's Brigade' that created waves in Ireland. Branches of the Gaelic League increased fourfold during the course of the Boer War; and Davitt travelled to the Transvaal later in 1900 in order to observe events for himself. In the first few months of the year, Gonne busied herself with a startling plan to sink Royal Navy vessels on the high seas by disguising explosives as pieces of coal, which would explode when loaded into the ships' boilers. The execution of the plan depended upon the raising of a very great deal of money and the support of the Boers: lacking both, it failed – but the fact that it was proposed at all illuminates the lengths to which Gonne was prepared to go to achieve her political objectives.

The visit of Queen Victoria to Ireland in April 1900 – her fourth in all, and her first in thirty-nine years – further galvanized the nationalist cause in general. *The Times* piously urged 'the better class of nationalist' to welcome her – but such exhortations fell mostly on deaf ears. The royal visit was correctly perceived by nationalists as part of a drive to enlist young Irishmen: Griffith observed that the monarch had come 'to seek recruits for her battered army'; and Gonne condemned her in vituperative terms in an article for the *United Irishman* entitled 'The Famine Queen'.[5] Although the royal visit proceeded smoothly – not least because Dublin was positively bristling with police and soldiers for the duration of her stay – it also exposed the divisions within Irish nationalism. For many members of the public were frankly proud of the actions of the 'Dublins' and other Irish regiments in the South African war; and pleased too with Victoria's decision that these Irish regiments should be permitted henceforth to sport the shamrock on St Patrick's Day. The Irish Party leader Redmond was among their number – and was castigated for his decision by many nationalists. He also, however, criticized the royal visit to Ireland: indeed, such a balancing act between imperial and national interests would become a hallmark of his career in general.

Victoria's presence in Ireland – and the warmth of the welcome she received in many quarters – provided ample evidence of the fundamental ambivalence that marked the Irish relationship to Britain, and highlighted too the many opinions that continued to circulate as to the future of the British and imperial connection. The queen had after all visited Catholic convent schools; loyal toasts had been received from Dublin's nationalist city councillors; and (amid complaints at having to fraternize with Church of Ireland officials) Catholic clerics had attended royal functions. The erection in 1907 of the Fusiliers' Arch at St Stephen's Green in Dublin – a memorial to the South African war and identical in its dimensions to the Arch of Titus in Rome – seemed to seal this ambivalence in stone: it was denounced as a 'traitors' gate' by some, but certainly not by all.

The lengthy defeat of the Boers – the war would drag on until 1902 – and the news coming from southern Africa of burned farms and of women and children held in concentration camps continued to resonate in Ireland. Its impact was magnified by the return of Davitt in July 1900, bringing tidings of plucky Boer resistance in the face of overwhelming odds.* Nevertheless the political focus moved rapidly on in a wide range of ways. With the death of Victoria in January 1901 came what would inevitably appear as a fresh start, nineteenth-century ceremony and pomp easing into an era

---

* Davitt viewed the conflict in terms of a clash between the Boers and British. He had little or nothing to say about the denial of political rights to the majority African population. This attitude contrasts sharply with his sharp observations on the situation of the New Zealand Maori and Australian Aboriginal populations during his 1889–90 tour of the region.

of reduced formality. But the South African war was perceived by the government as a warning too: victory, though sweet, was infused with relief; and George Wyndham – who had become Chief Secretary for Ireland in 1900 – now took steps to underpin the peace in Ireland by continuing the government's policy of constructive unionism.

The result was that the final pieces were now inserted into the jigsaw of land reform. The Wyndham Land Acts proposed that the British government finance the full-scale buyout of the landlords by the tenants, and by 1903 Ireland had completed the process of agrarian reform: the tenant class had become a caste of owner-occupiers. Such reform, however, was significant not merely legally and socially but also psychologically – and the Conservative government was in some ways a victim of its own success. Once enough people controlled their land, the next rational step would be to seek to control their local affairs too – and then their country. Reform breathed new life into the question of Ireland's political status and made formal independence an outcome that was now seen by some – though not by a majority of public opinion – as perfectly possible.

Elements within Irish nationalism were equally occupied with planning for the future. Griffith and Gonne had established new organizations – Cumann na nGaedheal (Confederation of the Gaels) and Inghinidhe na hÉireann (Daughters of Erin) respectively – with the intention of bringing a larger national focus to the energy unleashed by the South African war. Griffith continued to use the pages of the *United Irishman* to amplify his political vision, and in the first half of 1904, a series of articles appeared advocating the idea of Ireland and Britain becoming a dual monarchy. This would be an arrangement similar to the one that had tentatively resolved the fractious relationship between Austria and Hungary and appeared to guarantee the future of the Hapsburg Empire through the *Ausgleich* – the Compromise – of 1867; Griffith's articles would later appear in book form as *The Resurrection of Hungary*. In addition, in 1905 he founded the

National Council: originally intended to resemble a pressure group, it morphed into a modest political movement and in 1907 amalgamated with other similar groups to form a small – and at this point far from radical – party known as Sinn Féin.

The debate as to the future of the country continued to involve a large number of participants. In 1900, the polemicist D. P. Moran had founded the *Leader,* a publication dedicated to the dissemination of a purist vision of an 'Irish Ireland' that was Catholic, economically self-sufficient and Irish-speaking. In his writing Moran disparaged a host of enemies, living and dead, from Wolfe Tone and Daniel O'Connell to Redmond and his party, and from Home Rule to Protestants in general and Orangemen in particular. Later, he would come to accept the notion of partition: if Ulster could not be brought around to the national ideal by argument and debate, he reasoned, then it would be better to excise it entirely from the Irish body politic.

Nor did Moran have any patience with the cultural vision of Yeats and his circle, which at this time was also continuing to evolve. In 1899 the Irish Literary Theatre was founded by Yeats, Edward Martyn and the aristocrat Augusta Gregory: it would become the Abbey Theatre in 1904, having secured sufficient funding (courtesy of an English tea heiress) to establish itself in the centre of Dublin. At once, the new institution set about offering its own contributions to the ongoing debate, probing in its productions the ambivalent nature of Irish culture and the form of the country's identity. In April 1902, in a further demonstration of the range of her interests, Gonne appeared in a production of *Cathleen Ní Houlihan.* Her eponymous role was the embodiment of an Ireland that called for a sacrifice in blood from her sons; one critic commented that 'I went home asking myself if such plays should be produced unless one was prepared for people to go out to shoot and be shot'.[6] But Yeats and Gregory experimented and adventured too with the European *avant garde,* and disturbed their audiences' complacencies by staging such works as J. M. Synge's *The Playboy of the*

Western World (1907) with its lurid representations of degeneracy, coarseness and brutality in the west of Ireland. Elements in the audience rose in outrage at the sight of the fresh-tongued, sexualized women and their feeble menfolk inhabiting the stage, police had to be stationed in the auditorium, and Moran condemned the theatre as the 'shabby'.

At the same time, the widespread deprivation and social distress of the period helped to animate the Irish labour movement. The Irish Trades' Union Congress had been founded in 1894, but only to represent skilled workers; so-called unskilled and casual labourers remained without union support. Their cause was animated, however, by events in Britain, and in particular by the bitter strike that began in London's West India Dock in the summer of 1889. The docks were paralysed and the strike soon spread to involve other trades – so after three weeks the employers gave way, offering improved pay and conditions. Dockers and other workers in Ireland absorbed the lessons of the London strikes, and one consequence was the eventual attempt, in 1907, to bring Belfast's dockers together in order to win a similar deal. The organizer of this attempt was James Larkin, Liverpool-born of Irish parents: but while his efforts had some limited success, they ultimately failed to bridge the sectarian divide between working-class Catholics and Protestants in the city. The following year Larkin left Belfast for Dublin, where in 1909 he founded the Irish Transport and General Workers' Union (ITGWU).

James Connolly was the second notable labour organizer to arrive in Ireland at this time, and his career in particular highlights the many different threads running through the history of the period. Connolly, like Larkin, was British-born (in Edinburgh in 1868) of Irish stock: his father had worked as a carter with the city corporation and the family could, as a result, count on a steady, if slender, wage – enough to scrape a basic education and protect them from the worst ravages of poverty. Connolly enlisted in the British army at the age of fourteen: he discharged himself in 1889, shortly after meeting Lillie Reynolds – a servant and Protestant – at a Dublin tram stop. The couple married a year later, by which time Connolly had renounced his Catholicism in favour of pursuing a socialist dream: by 1888, Keir Hardie had represented local miners at a by-election in central Scotland; the British labour movement founded its own political party five years later; and a socialist world seemed there for the taking.

By 1896, Connolly had moved to Dublin with his expanding family in order to pursue this agenda. A socialist republic was his aim, but Ireland presented very different challenges: the rising tide of cultural nationalism and the clamour for Home Rule inevitably absorbed much of the available political energy. Nevertheless, Connolly began the process of disseminating his class-based message in the city via a series of pamphlets and publications and in street-based demonstrations. He was loud in his dismissal of Home Rule as a political solution: 'England would still rule you,' he wrote. 'She would rule you through her capitalists, through her landlords, through her financiers, through her usurers, through the whole array of commercial and individualistic institutions she has planted in this country and watered with the tears of our mothers and blood of our martyrs. England would rule you to your ruin…'[7]

An agent sent by the authorities at Dublin Castle to listen to one of Connolly's public speeches dismissed it as 'the usual twaddle' – although the fact that the authorities considered him worth listening to in the first place indicates that he had managed to carve out something of a niche for himself.[8] He was a nationalist in the sense that his socialist republic would be founded on the Irish nation; indeed, he had always been prepared to ally himself with explicitly nationalist causes. He was arrested, for example, at the demonstration against Chamberlain's honorary doctorate from Trinity College Dublin in December 1899, and was in general active in the cause of the Boers. Socialism, however, remained key to his political message – and the limitations of this message in an Irish context were all too evident. In general terms

Connolly addressed himself neither to cultural nationalists, nor to the mass of the rural poor, nor to the country's Catholic middling classes. In the process, he ended any prospect of widespread popular backing.

From 1903 he spent seven years in the United States, organizing, lecturing and observing the labour movement at first hand; three more were passed in Belfast, where class politics still struggled to be heard amid the city's prevailing bitter sectarianism. In the summer of 1913, however, industrial unrest in Dublin brought Connolly south once more. Confrontation between workers and employers had become a dominant feature of economic life: the ITGWU had rapidly increased in membership and influence and had gradually won concessions from a variety of employers. Larkin now felt secure enough to challenge Dublin's most powerful employer: William Martin Murphy, a former nationalist MP and the present owner of the *Irish Independent* and *Irish Catholic* newspapers, Clery's department store in central Dublin and much of the city's tram network. On 15 August Murphy had 'locked out' union members from their jobs in the *Irish Independent* building; Larkin called a strike, Murphy extended the lock-out – and by early September, matters had escalated into an all-out confrontation.

The lockout was marked by a good deal of violence: the workers were threatened by attack from both the police and a series of employer-backed vigilante groups, and in response Connolly organized a protective group, the Irish Citizen Army (ICA). Ultimately, some twenty-five thousand workers were locked out and deprived of a regular wage: this in turn, because they had families, meant that close to one hundred thousand people were threatened with penury and hunger. A relief fund brought a degree of respite, but by the end of January 1914 the ITGWU was forced to admit defeat. The union members gradually returned to work, on terms drawn up by the employers, shortly after the end of the lock-out. Meanwhile, the Catholic bishops condemned socialism, thus leaving no room for doubt as to the attitude of the Church.

Connolly's speeches to the workers during the lock-out had led to his arrest and imprisonment, and he had briefly gone on hunger strike. Now, with the defeat of the workers in the spring of 1914, he was forced into a reassessment of his political views. The events of the lock-out reinforced his sense that labour needed more than ever to organize, the better to withstand its capitalist enemies; in addition, he devoted much energy to expanding and training the ICA as a front line of defence. At the same time, however, the failure of the lock-out undermined his class-based vision of Ireland's future, while the notion of a united socialist Ireland seemed as remote as ever. It was clear to him that the war now approaching in Europe might present a golden opportunity – and clear too that nationalist and not socialist politics might prove the best vehicle for bringing about change.

Amid this plethora of activism, constitutional politics had certainly not become irrelevant. By 1910, for example, parliamentary reform had once again brought the possibility of a form of Irish political autonomy, the old goal of Home Rule, within reach. In that year, the delicately reunited Irish Party at Westminster supported the formation of a new Liberal government under Herbert Asquith – on the clear understanding that a Parliament Act would be passed, enabling the veto of the Conservative-dominated Lords to be overridden for the first time by the Commons. This was reform fundamental to the very institution of parliament itself – and it was indeed passed, with a third Home Rule bill swiftly proposed in the spring of 1912.

In truth this was a modest enough measure, repatriating to Dublin authority many domestic issues but retaining at Westminster control over Irish foreign policy, taxation and military affairs. Yet it was a bill that this time stood a very good chance of passing both the Commons and the Lords and becoming law. In Belfast the Ulster Unionists mustered in opposition, the fault lines in Ireland opening now into chasms. In September 1912 Sir Edward Carson led 250,000 Ulstermen in signing the Covenant,

ULSTER, 1910

ATLANTIC
OCEAN

DONEGAL

DERRY   ANTRIM

TYRONE

FERMANAGH

MONAGHAN

ARMAGH

DOWN

CAVAN

IRISH
SEA

The 1910 Elections
Winners of parliamentary seats

	Unionist
	Nationalist
	Independent Nationalist
	Liberal

0   miles   25

N

a declaration of intent to use 'all means which may be found necessary' to resist Irish self-government. Ulsterwomen had another, rather less martial Declaration, that noted 'our desire to associate ourselves with the men of Ulster' in their opposition to Home Rule. And in London, the Conservative opposition declared its support for the Unionists: 'I can imagine no length of resistance to which Ulster will go,' noted their leader Andrew Bonar Law, 'in which they will not be supported by the overwhelming majority of the British people.'[9]

Ulster Unionism was an articulate and daunting political force. It was unified by fear – and yet it was essentially no more homogeneous an entity than was Irish nationalism. For there was more to the Protestant population of Ulster than the prosperous mercantile elite of Belfast and its hinterland: it also embraced a class of small farmers scattered throughout the province, the remnants of the Anglican Ascendancy, and the tens of thousands of employees of Belfast's shipyards and factories. The harsh by-products of Belfast's industrial class, meanwhile, were evident for all to see in the forms of heavy reliance upon child labour, minimal levels of welfare, widespread poverty and general social distress. Class, in other words, was as intrinsic an aspect of life in Ulster as it was in other developed societies. Yet – as Connolly had discovered – such divisions and internal tensions could be papered over in the face of Home Rule, to be replaced by the imperatives of religion and race.

In these years leading up to World War I, Unionist political leaders engaged in the slow process of securing the extrication of Ulster, or a section of the province, from any new constitutional arrangement. The partition of the country, which had first emerged as an issue in the aftermath of the first Home Rule bill two decades previously, was now live and pressing; however, nobody could as yet determine whether partition would in fact happen, much less what final shape it might take. It was also an issue riddled with contradiction: the Home Rule that Unionists had rallied to prevent in the closing decades of the nineteenth century was now acceptable to them – if only Ulster could be removed from the equation.

Underlying these political calculations was a cold numbers game. According to the 1911 census, the Protestant population of the province of Ulster was just under 900,000, the Catholic population just under 700,000. This was too slender a demographic majority for comfort, especially when a generally higher Catholic birth rate was taken into account. Unionist leaders envisaged an Ulster in which Protestants would form a permanent political elite: one consisting of counties Antrim and Down (with hefty Protestant majorities), and Derry and Armagh (with small Protestant majorities); Fermanagh and Tyrone (with no Protestant majorities at all, although Protestants held the greater part of the land) would be added to bring a sense of critical mass to the new order. The three remaining Ulster counties with their substantial Catholic majorities, however, would not be included. Unionist leaders were thus open to the charge that they were on the one hand deploying the argument of democratic imperatives, while simultaneously denying the justice of that same argument. They could also be accused of abandoning their Unionist brethren in Cavan, Monaghan and Donegal to their fate, in the interests of *realpolitik*.

The Home Rule bill passed a third reading in the Commons in January 1913. In the same month, the Ulster Volunteers were created as a resistance militia; rapidly, its membership climbed to over ninety thousand. The force was daunting and professional: it included many highly trained former members of the British army, and soon it had diversified into women's auxiliary units and the paraphernalia of a regular army. Its creation led inevitably to the formation of a rival force: the Irish Volunteers, the inaugural meeting of which took place in November 1913 amid the bourgeois surroundings of Wynn's Hotel in central Dublin, a few doors along from the Abbey. Redmond's Irish Party had a stake in this new organization – figures in the party sat on its council – but so too did the

Irish Republican Brotherhood (IRB), reconstituted from the Fenian period and consisting of individuals who had nothing but disdain for the forces of constitutional nationalism as embodied in Redmond and his Westminster colleagues. Soon, the IRB membership was working discreetly to radicalize the politics of the new movement.

These IRB members consisted of older Fenian figures – for example, Tom Clarke, who had spent years in prison for his involvement in bomb attacks in England – together with younger, highly educated and energetically committed activists. Among these were Joseph Plunkett, a well-travelled scholar of Irish and Esperanto; Thomas MacDonagh, also an Irish scholar and a trade unionist; and Patrick Pearse, a poet, intellectual, barrister and founder of a school in Dublin dedicated to the revival of the Irish language. Pearse's cultural nationalism was influenced in part by the romantic mythology of Gaelic Ireland – yet he was a pragmatist too: of the rising Unionist military organization in Ulster he noted bluntly that 'an Orangeman with a rifle [is] a much less ridiculous figure than the nationalist without a rifle'.[10] A key aspect of Pearse's political ideology was 'blood sacrifice', the Christian-inflected concept prevalent in Europe at this time that war might help to cleanse and renew a nation. 'When war comes to Ireland,' he wrote during World War I, 'she must welcome it as she would the angel of God. And she will.'[11]

The sense of a rising threat to public order was reflected in the government's tentative proposal, in March 1914, to send army divisions to Ulster in order to face down any potential threat. This plan came to nothing, however, in the face of a proto-mutiny at the Curragh barracks, west of Dublin, in which scores of cavalry officers threatened to resign if ordered north. The episode amply demonstrated the range of Ulster Unionist support – and now tension was ratcheted up yet further as each of the rival militias armed itself, beginning in the small hours of 25 April when members of the Ulster Volunteers unloaded several hundred tonnes of German-manufactured guns and munitions at Bangor, Larne and Donaghadee harbours and distributed them with smooth efficiency across the province.

In response – and with the assistance of Sir Roger Casement, an Irish-born former British diplomat who had gravitated towards the Irish nationalist cause – the Irish Volunteers too procured weapons from Germany: in July, the yacht *Asgard* sailed into the harbour at Howth, north of Dublin, and unloaded its (rather smaller) cargo of munitions in broad daylight.* The arms were taken into the city for distribution; an army detachment belatedly sent out to intervene fired into a crowd of jeering Dubliners later that day, killing four; the event was captured by the painter Jack B. Yeats in *Batchelor's Walk, In Memory* (1915), which portrays a woman laying flowers at the scene of the killings. Ireland appeared indeed to be on the edge of widespread civil unrest – and for the British authorities, a kaleidoscope of other problems was already looming: imprisoned suffragettes were on hunger strike; a general strike was threatened; and Archduke Franz Ferdinand, the heir to the Austrian throne, had been assassinated at Sarajevo in June. It seemed clear that, by summer's end, Europe would be on fire.

It was in this context of both national and international danger that the government invoked the authority of King George V and convened a summit on Ireland at Buckingham Palace. Here, for four days in the middle of July 1914 – a few days before the Howth gun-running operation – the two sides thrashed about in stalemate. In his opening address, the monarch sought the middle ground: 'Today the cry of civil war is on the lips of the most responsible and sober-minded of my people ... to me, it is unthinkable that

---

* Casement was born outside Dublin to a family with Ulster antecedents. He was sent by the Foreign Office as consul to postings in Africa and South America. His reports on the widespread human rights abuses in the Belgian Congo led to changes in the political governance of the territory. He was knighted in 1905.

we should be brought to the brink of fratricidal strife upon issues so capable of adjustment – if handled in a spirit of generous compromise.'[12] The last word was of course key – but it did not at first appear as if any form of compromise could be achieved; certainly, the issue of Ulster's possible exclusion from Home Rule represented a vast divide between the two sides. Eventually, Redmond implied that he would not see Home Rule forced on to any county in Ireland against the will of its population: a sign, perhaps, that the divide could after all be bridged; and while the Home Rule bill did indeed become law in September, it was immediately suspended.

For World War I had now begun in Europe, and the constitutional affairs of Ireland would as a result have to wait. Redmond consented to such a suspension in the expectation that a united Irish effort against Germany and Austria–Hungary would lead in turn to a measure of national reconciliation in Ireland itself – and to a form of postwar Home Rule that would prove acceptable to all. He could not know that his plans would be wholly outstripped by events.

CHAPTER ELEVEN

REVOLUTION

For the moment, Redmond and his constitutional approach remained ostensibly in the ascendant in nationalist Ireland. In Ulster, Sir Edward Carson had offered the Ulster Volunteers for service in the British armed forces; and in a speech at Woodenbridge in County Wicklow in September 1914 Redmond matched the Unionist offer, with the result that a surge of Volunteers signed on to fight; in the first two years of war alone, it is estimated that a hundred thousand Irishmen enlisted in the services. Redmond was operating on the understanding that this would be a short, sharp European war that would be concluded victoriously by Christmas – a fatal miscalculation that would eat into his support in the months and years of war to come. But the prospect of the sacrifice of Irish lives in the course of any British war – irrespective of its duration – was wholly unacceptable to some: at the same time as Redmond was making his Woodenbridge speech, a meeting of the IRB in Dublin had rejected both his suppositions and his leadership of the nationalist cause, seeing the war in Europe as a potential opportunity for Ireland to throw off British rule once and for all.

The result was a split in the Volunteer movement: the great majority followed Redmond and became the National Volunteers; and it can be fairly estimated that in the war years some 260,000 Irish served the Crown in one capacity or another. Their reasons for enlisting were many and varied. Doubtless some now did so out of a sense of duty and conviction, but it is equally evident that many, as in years past, enlisted for simple economic and social reasons: in order to draw a wage, to have a job, to be fed and clothed. The experiences of these Irish soldiers both signify the tangled and shifting loyalties of these years and illuminate the harsh material reality of life for many Irish communities.*

Meanwhile, a small minority – ten thousand or thereabouts – refused to participate in the war effort and continued to march under the banner of the Irish Volunteers. The Volunteers were headed by Eoin MacNeill, but unbeknownst to him, the movement was being subtly infiltrated by the IRB, with the latter's leadership occupying positions of authority within the Volunteer organization: among these leaders was Pearse, who held the title of director of military organization. The Irish Volunteers were supported by a substantial body of anti-war sentiment in Ireland, stemming from principles of pacifism as well as of nationalist and anti-British feeling; in addition, Pearse and others could see positive virtues in the creation of a relatively small but tightly knit fighting force. Equally, the Volunteer movement was nothing if not diverse: MacNeill's measured pragmatism did not, for example, suit the more passionate politics of Pearse, Plunkett and MacDonagh.

The formation in 1914 of Cumann na mBan, the female association affiliated to the Irish Volunteers, added to this sense of breadth. Its composition was equally varied in background and outlook: while it was not a feminist organization *per se*, for example, it existed and operated against a backdrop of fierce cultural debate as to the role of women in wider society. In the small world of radical nationalist politics, moreover, overlap was inevitable: figures such as the Anglo–Irish aristocrat-turned-political agitator Constance Markiewicz, for example, had close connections to both the suffrage and the labour movements, and had been active during the

---

* 'A typical volunteer', writes Diarmaid Ferriter, 'was James English, a 38-year-old labourer from County Waterford, married with five children. By enlisting, he instantly increased his family's earnings by 154 per cent, and if anything was to happen to him, his wife was guaranteed a pension.' (Quoted in Ferriter, *The Transformation of Ireland, 1900–2000* [London: Profile, 2004], 133.)

lock-out. Cumann na mBan brought distinctive sensibilities to the debate – even if its membership was frequently marginalized and ignored.

Soon, the rising death toll on the western front impacted upon public opinion, and the popularity of Redmond's party began to dwindle. Yet for radical nationalism these remained unpromising times, for the majority of the population was inclined firmly away from insurrection. The on-going conflict in Europe and the demands of the war effort were leading to a gradual rise in agricultural prices and thus to a measure of prosperity for many; in addition, army pay was adding to the modest incomes of families up and down the land; and for some, Ireland's future was simply and indissolubly bound up with Britain and the empire. Yeats, meanwhile, could look icily on a Catholic commercial middle class that, content to 'fumble in a greasy till / And add the halfpence to the pence / And prayer to shivering prayer', was much too busy making money to throw in its lot with a rebel of any complexion.[1]

World War I was almost two years old before trouble erupted in Ireland. The potential revolutionaries remained far from united: Connolly, for example, still maintained a separate militia in the form of the small Irish Citizen Army – although figures such as Markiewicz moved easily between it and the Irish Volunteers. Connolly's interests and those of elements within the IRB would not mesh definitively until January 1916, when the former was brought to a secret meeting of the IRB leadership and formally involved in the slowly developing plans for an uprising of the Irish Volunteers that Easter. The revolutionaries' plans, moreover, were muddled by divergences of views within their ranks: even the small core of IRB leaders was at cross purposes as to the merits of a rising. Initial proposals for a revolt against British rule had envisaged a national uprising, abetted by German military landings on the west coast. This plan had then been gradually altered, with the final scheme – as with Emmet a century before – anticipating a rising in Dublin that would then fan general unrest across the country; and a second theatre of operations in the west triggered by the arrival of German arms shipments on the Atlantic seaboard.

Ironically, this evident lack of clarity also hampered the response of the British authorities to the developing situation. While it was clear that trouble was brewing in Ireland, it was also true that military drills and parades were a familiar sight on the streets of Dublin. In October 1915, for example, Connolly and Markiewicz had led the ICA militia in a mock assault on Dublin Castle. It was therefore no easy matter in these times to distinguish a mere drill from something more dangerous. The chief secretary, Augustine Birrell, mourned that 'the misery of the situation is this – you had armed bodies of Volunteers all over the place'.[2] At the same time, British calculations tended naturally to discount the perils of home-grown insurrection in favour of time-honoured fears: in this case, the possibility of an invasion of Ireland by Germany, as a back-door means of attacking Britain itself. So, even though the authorities were in receipt of a good deal of intelligence, when trouble did flare in central Dublin on Easter Monday, 24 April 1916, they were still caught unprepared.

For the rebels, Easter approached in a miasma of confusion and ill fortune. Early in April, Pearse had flatly denied to MacNeill that any rising was planned for the Easter weekend; several days later, Pearse again met his commander – but now to tell him that a rising was indeed imminent and that the Volunteer movement had in fact long been secretly controlled by the IRB. On 20 April, Volunteers in County Kerry failed to make contact as planned with the German vessel *Libau*, which, following negotiations by Casement, had been dispatched to Ireland with twenty thousand guns and a million rounds of ammunition on board.* When news of this reverse reached Dublin, the administration in the Castle relaxed still further – if trouble had in fact

---

* In the course of the voyage, the *Libau* was disguised as a Norwegian cargo vessel (complete with a consignment of kitchen equipment) and renamed the *Aud*. The ship was eventually captured by British naval vessels on 22 April and escorted into Cork harbour, where she was scuttled by her captain. Casement was captured at the same time on the Kerry coast.

been planned, it would surely not now go ahead – and began looking forward to the upcoming horse-racing festival at nearby Fairyhouse.

At the same time, MacNeill stood down the Volunteers – and it was now that the fragmentation and competing agendas of the leaders of the rising came starkly to the surface. On Easter Sunday, the IRB leadership voted to ignore MacNeill's instructions and to summon the Volunteers on to the streets; but on the following day, the abiding confusion meant that a mere fifteen hundred Volunteers – including some two hundred women – turned out, supported by a handful of members of the ICA who took up their positions on St Stephen's Green. Their intention was to occupy and hold a medley of buildings and positions in Dublin, the general idea being to control both the city centre and, eventually, communications across the country. And indeed, the General Post Office was taken by Connolly and Pearse as planned, the latter reading the Proclamation of the Irish Republic from the front of the building. But the strategic importance of some of the other targets was questionable; and to make matters worse, the lines of communication between the various positions could not be secured.

The rebels failed to capture the castle, even though it was occupied that holiday Monday by only a skeleton staff. A constable at the gates of the compound was shot dead, after which the gates were hastily shut and the rebels forced to retreat into the adjoining City Hall. This failure was repeated across the city: in taking up their positions, the rebels were hampered consistently by a lack of numbers and a sense of confusion, and many other strongpoints thus remained unoccupied. Beggar's Bush Barracks to the southeast of the city centre lay essentially undefended and might have been smoothly taken by the Third Battalion under Éamon de Valera: no attempt, however, was made to occupy the compound. The rebels also made no attempt to occupy the easily defensible grounds of Trinity College, in the heart of the city; and, fatally, the railway stations at Amiens Street and Kingsbridge continued to function. Some of the rebels, meanwhile, displayed a glaring lack of understanding of the nature of urban warfare: those members of the ICA who had occupied St Stephen's Green, for example, busied themselves with the digging of trenches across the park, evidently heedless of the ranges of tall buildings overlooking the area. Before long, sniper fire from the roof of the Shelbourne Hotel forced them to take refuge inside the College of Surgeons building on the west side of the square.

By the end of that first day, order was breaking down across the city centre: public transport had stopped running and shops were being looted. By the following morning, government forces were pouring into the city by train and ship and were beginning to tighten the noose around the rebel positions. Trinity College had become both a barracks – with some four thousand soldiers and their horses stationed in its quadrangles – and a field hospital catering to ever larger numbers of military and civilian casualties. Food began to run short, and over the next few days the various rebel battalions across the city surrendered one by one. By Friday night, much of central Dublin had been devastated: Pearse and Connolly were forced to abandon a GPO in flames; and on Saturday, 29 April the final, formal surrender was announced. Some 450 people had died in the course of the week: of these, one hundred or so were British military personnel and 64 were rebels. The rest were civilians.

The Easter Rising was always doomed to failure. The mood in the country, buoyed by the modest prosperity of wartime, was not in its favour; and in practical terms, the numbers and resources at its leaders' disposal were nowhere near sufficient to ensure a victory against the power of the state. For some of those leaders, of course, the rising's failure was beside the point: for Pearse, for example, the sacrifice of a short-term defeat contained the promise of a larger and more substantial victory in the longer term, even if he would not live to see it. For others less moved by such emotion, a good and sturdy battle was an end in itself and might succeed in lighting a fire of resistance among the people; and Connolly, at any rate, must have carried with him the bitter knowledge that the strategy for holding Dublin city centre, flawed though it was, might have worked a little better had sufficient numbers cut through the fog of order and counter-order and turned out in support.

Women had been present in all theatres of activity, with the exception of the Third Battalion: de Valera refused to have females in his ranks. Although the Proclamation read by Pearse claimed 'the allegiance of every Irishman and Irishwoman', the substantial female part in the rising was downplayed in subsequent histories of the period. Later events, as we will see, had a crucial role to play in this; in addition, the death of men such as Connolly, for example, removed from the scene important proponents of egalitarian policies. This airbrushing is best – indeed, literally – encapsulated in the fate of Elizabeth O'Farrell, a member of Cumann na mBan and one of three women among the last group of rebels to leave the GPO. Farrell was later given surrender orders to be distributed across the city, and was with Pearse when he was photographed formally surrendering on 29 April. Later, however, her image was excised from the photographic record, albeit in a most clumsy manner: her disembodied feet remain in evidence behind Pearse.

The reactions of the public to the rising were inevitably various and fragmented. For the relatives of those serving in the war the rising was an evident betrayal, the work of stay-at-home cowards who would not go and join in the fight overseas; and the so-called 'separation women' – those separated from their men fighting on the western front and as a result in receipt of government funds – were involved in a number of confrontations with the rebels. For the socially conservative Catholic 'shopocracy',[3] the presence of such figures as Connolly in the body of the rebels added a fearful socialist taint to the events in Dublin: the *Irish Independent* condemned the rising as 'insane and criminal' and pressed for Connolly's execution;[4] and Redmond, speaking in the Commons at the end of April, voiced what he considered to be the revulsion of the Irish public. While many Dubliners were enraged by the destruction of much of the city centre and the widespread civilian deaths, there was also a degree of support in some quarters for the rebels: 'We tried hard to get the women and children to leave North King Street area,' wrote Sir John Maxwell, the British commander in the city. 'They would not go. Their sympathies were with the rebels....'[5] In the end, the response of the government was decisive in bringing together many of these disparate elements and in proving the events of Easter week to be, in hindsight, a pivotal moment.

In the aftermath of the rising, over three thousand men and just under a hundred women were shipped off and interned in Britain. Approximately a third of these internees, once it became evident that they had had no involvement in the events of the rising, were within a fortnight sent back to Ireland. Those who remained quickly developed networks and close bonds of solidarity in such a claustrophobic environment, as well as a new understanding of the necessity of taut and well-oiled organization, if nationalist objectives were ever to be realized. The prisoners were returned to Ireland later in the year – the authorities reasoning that it did more harm than good to keep a large number of prisoners in conditions that fostered such a degree of resistance and resentment – more convinced than ever of the justice of their cause.

Furthermore, they came back to a country whose mood had changed fundamentally: for by mid-May, fifteen of the leaders of the rising – including Pearse, Connolly, Clarke, MacDonagh, Plunkett and John MacBride – had been brought into the stonebreakers' yard at Kilmainham Gaol and executed by firing squad. Connolly, who had shattered his ankle during the rising itself, was bound to a chair to be shot. Casement was executed in London in August.* Many of these figures died with Catholic prayers on their lips and crucifixes about their persons – on the edge of death, Casement had converted to Catholicism, while Connolly had returned to his

---

* Several leading players in the rising escaped death, including Markiewicz (officially by reason of her gender). It is often supposed that de Valera, who was American by birth, was spared in order not to give offence to the United States government, now a crucial ally in the war with Germany; de Valera himself, however, claimed that he avoided execution only because his court-martial and sentence came very late in the day, after most of the other executions had already taken place. See Diarmaid Ferriter, *Judging Dev: A Reassessment of the Life and Legacy of Éamon de Valera* (Dublin: Royal Irish Academy, 2007), 28–9.

Catholic faith – and their all-too-evident martyrdom at the hands of the British authorities now struck the clearest of chords with the public.

There had been no shortage of voices counselling moderation: the Irish playwright and political activist George Bernard Shaw wrote that 'the shot Irishmen will now take their places beside Emmet and the Manchester Martyrs in Ireland and beside the heroes of Poland and Serbia and Belgium in Europe … the military authorities and the British Government must have known that they were canonising their prisoners';[6] and even Herbert Asquith, now in his final months as prime minister, had been clear in his own mind that too harsh a reaction would only engender further trouble.

By mid-May, Redmond was condemning the executions at Kilmainham – but now his party's hold over public opinion was even more tenuous. In Belfast in June, a congress of his party consented reluctantly to a government plan that would exclude the six northeastern counties from the provision of Home Rule, on the understanding that such a partition would be strictly temporary: the majority of delegates at the conference (though certainly not all of them) felt this a price worth paying for the early implementation of Home Rule. But events were sweeping away all such fine calculations: the mounting death toll on the western front continued to gnaw away at Redmond's support, and in July the Ulster Division sustained horrifying losses in the battle of the Somme, with the result that Ulster Unionism gained a new traction, respectability and sympathy in British political circles. 'I am not an Ulsterman,' gasped a correspondent in the British press, 'but yesterday, as I followed their amazing attack, I felt I would rather be an Ulsterman than anything else in the world.'[7]

Furthermore, the government's proposals were already being interpreted in a host of ways. Unionism already viewed this new Irish border as being decidedly permanent in nature: its leaders extracted a promise that the partition of Ireland would end only with the consent of the people of this six-county Ulster – consent that, in a new Unionist-dominated entity, would never be forthcoming. Redmond's party was condemned for agreeing to the principle of partition in exchange for nothing: it was now eclipsed by a surging Sinn Féin, the cause of which had been unwittingly aided by the government's practice of referring to all rebels and malcontents as Sinn Féiners, regardless of whether they had been associated with that decidedly marginal party; most, of course, had not.

Throughout 1917, this new Sinn Féin scored a number of by-election victories – including that of de Valera in County Clare in July, a result that saw him replace Arthur Griffith as leader of the movement – and in the process began to occupy the space on the political spectrum previously held by Redmond's party. In carving out a position as a broadly anti-British political force, however, Sinn Féin was also creating problems for itself: many of those who gravitated towards the movement had little in common except the wish to be free of British rule; internal tensions were inevitable. While loudly critical of the Irish Party's apparent willingness to stomach partition, for example, Sinn Féin itself held no coherent stance on the issue. Yet this fact did little to halt its political success, and the Irish Party reaped this particular whirlwind instead: when Redmond died in March 1918, his party's support had crumbled. Sinn Féin was able to exploit opposition to the threat of conscription being imposed on Ireland in order to build on a heavy-handed British response that saw many party members arrested and jailed; and to voice an abstentionist policy towards representation at Westminster. In the general election of December 1918 (held as the country was being ravaged by the postwar global influenza epidemic) the party won seventy-three seats to the Irish Party's six.

In January 1919, the first Dáil met at the Mansion House in Dublin. A mere twenty-seven members took their seats in this phantom parliament: although invitations had been extended to all members returned in the December election, the Unionists and a handful of constitutionalists had unsurprisingly failed to turn up; while most of the Sinn Féin representatives were in prison. The session was short: within a few hours a brief constitution had been adopted, providing for a unicameral parliamentary system in what was ostensibly a new Irish republic; and a statement of social intent, focused squarely on issues of welfare and education, had been tabled and passed. A parallel administration now gradually took shape: de Valera, who had spectacularly escaped from Lincoln prison, convened a cabinet in April; and Michael Collins was appointed minister for finance. Collins organized the finances of this new government so rapidly and efficiently that it was able quickly to assume the status of a parallel administration within the country.

Collins was an excellent candidate for such a role. Born in County Cork in October 1890, he was a widely read workaholic steeped in nationalist politics, with administrative and financial abilities to match. Described as 'one of the few Irish revolutionary leaders to be at ease with a card index system',[8] he had worked as a bank clerk in London before returning to Ireland in advance of the rising. Collins had spent much of Easter week inside the GPO, as an aide to Joseph Plunkett. Interned afterwards at Frongoch camp in north Wales, he had demonstrated a talent for administration that would later stand him in good stead; since then he had developed a network of friends and supporters that encompassed the world of nationalist Ireland.

This communications web Collins could now put to excellent use, for he was also appointed director of this new administration's intelligence operations. At once he drew upon his many contacts now embedded within the British administration, and at the same time paralysed British spy operations with a campaign of assassinations carried out by a hand-picked 'squad'. De Valera was absent from Ireland for most of this period: the eighteen months from June 1919 he spent in the United States raising cash, political support and awareness of the Irish situation. De Valera's safe passage was ensured by the presence of Collins's operatives at the seaports; in the former's absence the latter's stock continued to rise, much to de Valera's chagrin.

This shadow government also established its own parallel legal system in Ireland: by the summer of 1920, the 'Dáil courts' were a widespread phenomenon and made the effective wielding of power by the British authorities even less possible. They dealt mainly with minor social issues and were recognized as prompt and often useful arbiters of justice – but they also, perhaps inevitably, brought in their wake a degree of confusion and chaos that mirrored the situation in Ireland as a whole. The new government was also equipped with an army: the Volunteers became increasingly known as the Irish Republican Army (IRA); and its members began an armed campaign against Crown forces in Ireland which escalated after the government's suppression of the Dáil later in the year.

The definition of Crown forces would come to include civilians: individuals suspected of assisting the state 'whether by accusation, supposition, employment or sentiment' were regarded by the IRA as legitimate targets.[9] This campaign is generally considered to have begun in January 1919 with an ambush at Soloheadbeg in County Tipperary, in which two Royal Irish Constabulary (RIC) policemen were killed. This operation had gone ahead without the authorization of the republican leadership – an indication of the degree of confusion between civilian and military authority that characterized this period. Soloheadbeg also highlighted other kinds of moral and political blurring: the dead policemen were part of the local community and – as was the case with the National Volunteers who had joined the British army – much of the general membership of the constabulary had enlisted for simple economic reasons.

But the forces of the State itself came to be increasingly feared at this time, especially as new players entered the arena. The British government sent a further forty thousand soldiers into the country; gradually, however, its efforts to maintain a degree of order in Ireland began to depend less on these regular forces and more on irregular militias. Some twelve thousand Black and Tans – named after their distinctive initial uniforms – and Auxiliaries were drafted into the country, ostensibly as support for the RIC. The Auxiliaries in particular were characterized by violence: the membership of the force for the most part consisted of men who had seen action in World War I and who were unable or unwilling to be reassimilated into civilian life. They rapidly built a reputation for excess: Austin Clarke writes in his poem 'Black and Tans' that no man could drink quietly in a pub for fear of the door being broken in by 'these roarers' looking for trouble.[10]

Cycles of violence became the norm. The war became a struggle of ambush, assassination and retaliation. On the morning of Sunday 20 November 1920, for example, an IRA squad acting under the order of Collins killed fourteen suspected British intelligence agents, including twelve former army officers, in various locations across Dublin. Later that day at Croke Park, Black and Tans fired into a crowd of spectators at a Gaelic football match: twelve were killed, and another two crushed in the resulting stampede. A week later, a troop of eighteen Auxiliaries was ambushed and killed at Kilmichael in County Cork; a fortnight after that, the centre of Cork city was torched by the Black and Tans. Such ceaseless violence was extensively covered in the British press and had its effect on public opinion; it also inevitably took its toll on Britain's image abroad. But there were also indications that the British were beginning to gain the upper hand in this conflict. Collins's intelligence machine had been thoroughly infiltrated by British agents, and in May 1921 an IRA attack on Dublin's Custom House, which destroyed the building and its precious store of archives, also resulted in the deaths of five IRA members and the capture of a hundred or so more.

In the political realm, the situation in Ireland had already resulted in the Government of Ireland Act of December 1920, which regularized what had already become the *de facto* division of the island and established separate parliaments at Belfast and Dublin. Government negotiators had proposed the extraction of the province of Ulster in its entirety from the rest of the country – but the Unionist leadership was wholly committed now to its six-county rump Ulster, with its in-built Protestant majority. Sinn Féin abstention at Westminster essentially amounted to tacit acceptance of the principle of partition, and the legislation was as a result passed without any political opposition. In June 1921 George V formally inaugurated the new

Northern Ireland parliament, as sectarian violence mounted steadily across the new province. This was the situation on 11 July, when a formal truce (in part negotiated by Jan Smuts, prime minister of the new Union of South Africa) was declared in Ireland. De Valera now travelled to London for a formal meeting with the prime minister, Lloyd George; following this event, a long exchange of letters attempted to set out the terms by which an agreement might be reached. For the British, an Irish Republic was never on offer; while de Valera sought a form of autonomy that would establish a connection between Ireland and the Empire, though not one between Ireland and the Crown – the concept of 'external association'.

In September, de Valera chose to exclude himself from the proceedings in London, claiming that as a symbol of the Republic he could do more good at home, and sending Collins and Griffith instead. From the beginning of the negotiations, it was clear that British opposition to the prospect of the Republic remained unwavering: a tough British negotiating team (including Lloyd George and the then colonial secretary, Winston Churchill) offered the prospect of a new Irish Free State, with Dominion status inside the empire; Ireland would thus occupy a constitutional position similar to that of New Zealand, Canada, Newfoundland, Australia and South Africa. The monarch would remain head of this new state; all Irish parliamentarians would be required to swear an oath of allegiance to the Crown; and the British would retain substantial military rights in Ireland, in the form of naval bases – the so-called Treaty Ports – in counties Donegal and Cork. And the division of Ireland would be fully ratified, with the new Northern Ireland free, if it so wished, to opt out of the Treaty.

This last clause, of course, was a certainty – but the Irish delegation gained what appeared to be a concession: the establishment of a boundary commission that would in time fix a fair and sensible border between the two parts of Ireland. In fact, the issue of partition barely arose in the course of negotiations: the Irish team was focused principally not on the notional issue of national unity but on the emergence, once and for all, of some form of Irish state –

albeit one that did not cover the entire island of Ireland. Crucially, the British delegation opted to play a stark game in the closing stages of the talks: it insisted on completion of the negotiations within three days, and in particular made the retention of the new Irish state within the empire a deal-breaker; the alternative would be a return to full-scale war. The Irish delegation, headed by Collins, agreed. The Treaty was signed on 6 December 1921, and the delegation returned to Ireland and to bitter criticism.

Having declined to be present at the negotiations, de Valera now rejected the Treaty: he would not accept Dominion status, holding out instead for the concept of 'external association'. This idea was encapsulated in his own alternative 'Document No. 2', which envisaged a sovereignty that derived from the people rather than the Crown. He further objected to the fact that the Irish negotiators had signed the Treaty without first relaying its final terms back to Dublin, as they had been bound to do. Moreover, it was clear that de Valera was going to bring a large proportion of the Dáil with him. In the course of an acrimonious debate, Collins and his supporters were condemned and harangued as 'oath breakers and cowards', who had been foolishly deceived by high London living and by the perfidious English. Yet on 7 January 1922, the measure was passed by 64 votes to 57: de Valera resigned as president, then offered himself for re-election, but was defeated and replaced by Arthur Griffith – so, with his supporters, he walked out of the Dáil. ('Deserters all!' shouted Collins.) The Treaty had been accepted by the Dáil: on 22 January, Dublin Castle was handed over to Collins and a massive evacuation of British soldiers and military equipment was speedily completed. The Irish Free State was now indeed free to order its own affairs.

The narrowness of the Dáil vote did not reflect the mood of the majority of the people, who were by and large less exercised by the constitutional niceties embedded in the Treaty. In general, the more prosperous were more likely to welcome the new order: the middle classes of various stripe and profession, as well as shopkeepers, farmers, the press and the Catholic

Church, were all anxious to see the measure take effect smoothly. Cumann na mBan came out in opposition, echoing the opinion of the female deputies in the Dáil, all six of whom had walked out in protest; the labour movement was divided; and a host of garrison towns, accustomed to the trade and prosperity brought by the British army, soon learned what an impact an overnight evacuation would have on their commercial activities. As for the IRA, it is a measure of Collins's influence that enough members of the organization fell in with his wishes to keep a lid on dissent – at least in the short term.

Politics was marked now by a general fluidity. Both pro- and anti-Treaty sides were divided between moderates and extremists; and both Collins and de Valera grappled with the need to retain their existing supporters and at the same time to build up their power bases. The two men agreed to postpone the looming general election for several months; and in the meantime, Collins focused on building up his army's strength. De Valera, meanwhile, moved between the politics of conciliation and extremism: he and Collins agreed, for example, to field common panels of candidates in the coming election, for it suited them both to fend off conflict if at all possible. But simultaneously, de Valera made a series of speeches that could be read as incitement to civil war: the IRA, he proclaimed in a speech at Thurles, would have to 'wade through the blood of the soldiers of the Irish government ... to get their freedom'.

In the early days of 1922 Collins also had talks with the new leader of Northern Ireland, James Craig. The aim was to arrive at a degree of inter-island diplomatic understanding: the outline of an all-Ireland council and a revised boundary commission were pencilled in; and Craig agreed to take measures to bolster Catholic interests in Northern Ireland – especially in the sectarian cauldron of Belfast, where killings had become a dreadful commonplace. Collins for his part undertook to end the boycott of Northern Ireland businesses that had been gathering pace south of the border: it was understood that both sides would do what was necessary to protect the minorities – southern Protestants and northern Catholics – in each jurisdiction.

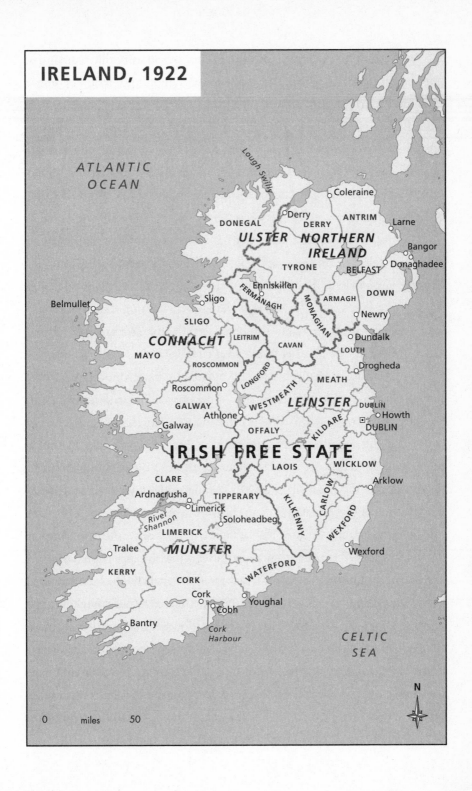

IRELAND, 1922

ATLANTIC
OCEAN

Lough Swilly

Coleraine

Derry
DONEGAL
DERRY
ANTRIM
Larne

ULSTER
NORTHERN
IRELAND
Bangor
TYRONE
BELFAST
Donaghadee

Enniskillen
FERMANAGH
ARMAGH
DOWN

Belmullet
Sligo
MONAGHAN
Newry

SLIGO
LEITRIM
Dundalk

CONNACHT
CAVAN
LOUTH

MAYO
ROSCOMMON
Drogheda

Roscommon
LONGFORD
MEATH

GALWAY
WESTMEATH
LEINSTER
DUBLIN

Athlone
Howth

Galway
OFFALY
KILDARE
DUBLIN

IRISH FREE STATE

CLARE
LAOIS
WICKLOW

Ardnacrusha
TIPPERARY
Arklow

River
Shannon
Limerick
CARLOW

Soloheadbeg
KILKENNY
WEXFORD

LIMERICK

Tralee
MUNSTER
Wexford

KERRY
WATERFORD

CORK

Cork

Bantry
Cobh
Youghal

Cork
Harbour

CELTIC
SEA

N

0   miles   50

By February of that year, however, Collins was assuring the nationalist population of Northern Ireland that the new Dublin government would insist on the transfer of large swathes of Northern territory into the Free State, thus rendering the former economically unviable. Raids and kidnappings across the border had begun to escalate; Collins facilitated the transfer of arms via anti-Treaty forces to IRA units operating in the North; and by June, Southern forces had crossed the border and briefly occupied districts of County Fermanagh. War between the two parts of Ireland appeared as likely as not; at the same time, sectarian violence was flaring up anew in Northern Ireland – 'on a per capita basis, Protestants were scoring four kills to every one by Catholics' – while violence against Protestants escalated in parts of the Free State.[11] But now a change was coming that would shift attention away from the relationship between the two parts of Ireland, and usher in the Free State's brief but vicious civil war.

In March, an IRA convention had opened up barely hidden divisions: members voted to reject the authority of the provisional Irish government; and after this point, it was evident that neither Collins nor anyone else controlled the organization in its entirety. On 14 April, IRA members opposed to the Treaty occupied the Four Courts in central Dublin, home to the country's Public Record Office. On 28 June, under intense pressure from the British to resolve the situation, the pro-Treaty government began shelling the building; like the Custom House before it, the Four Courts went up in flames. Shortly before the surrender, however, a massive explosion destroyed one side of the building: the anti-Treaty forces had packed the Public Record Office with gelignite – which had now been detonated, obliterating centuries of Irish history. By the end of this period of bloodletting, pro-Treaty forces were in control of Dublin; by mid-July, anti-Treaty forces had been driven from Limerick, Cork and Waterford; and within months, government forces controlled most of the Free State. Emergency powers were introduced and between November 1922 and May 1923 seventy-seven executions took place, some of them, with fine historical irony, at Kilmainham Gaol.

Collins himself was killed in August 1922, in an ambush in his native County Cork. He had continued to show a steely resolve throughout the civil conflict: the army of the Free State, for example, was equipped with British arms and munitions, and this military advantage was used ruthlessly. To his enemies (not least the British he had sought to undermine), Collins had been no more than a terrorist and a begetter of assassination squads – though ultimately these same enemies had to negotiate with him. To his admirers, however, Collins was truly charismatic – and a military and administrative genius. His dominance of the Irish political scene helped to establish a myth and cult that would stand the test of time; his stature in Irish history, however, also owes much to the fact of his death at the age of thirty-one, before he could prove or disprove himself as a peacetime political leader.

There are no firm tallies of deaths in the course of the Free State's civil war, though estimates of over a thousand seem realistic. Its psychological effects, as with all civil conflicts, were profound, lasting and poisonous to the politics of the new Irish state; and a veil of silence settled over many communities. Northern Ireland, meanwhile, had become a 'Protestant land for a Protestant people', a process accompanied by further paroxysms of ferocious sectarian rioting and completed formally in December 1922, when the new Northern administration opted not to unite with the Free State. The violence that had accompanied the creation of this new entity was also not easily forgotten, in addition to which its large nationalist minority felt itself abandoned and isolated. The future, for both parts of the island of Ireland, was daunting.

CHAPTER TWELVE

DIVISION

In 1925, work began on an enormous hydroelectric scheme at Ardnacrusha in County Clare. The aim was to harness the power of the river Shannon – for years, the dream of a host of engineers – in the service of the new Irish Free State. The contract was awarded to the German firm Siemens, for Ireland could not itself supply such engineering expertise. The construction period, however, supplied both thousands of jobs and a substantial lift to the local economy – although Siemens, backed by the government, refused to pay workers at the going industrial rate. The vast sluice gates opened for the first time in 1929, and by the mid-1930s the works were supplying most of the country's (modest) electricity needs.* They displayed to the world the confidence and ambition of the new Ireland: a fact that was made explicit both in the unabashed concrete modernity of the design and in the muscular realist-style paintings – such as Seán Keating's *Night's Candles Are Burnt Out* – commissioned by the State to chronicle the event.

This scheme was nevertheless hardly representative of the reality of life in the Free State. By the time the vast works at Ardnacrusha were completed, the cautious and conservative character of the new Cumann na nGaedheal government – which had emerged in 1923 from the pro-Treaty ranks of Sinn Féin – had become evident. Ardnacrusha was not, for example, teamed with much else by way of industrialization: the government was rather more

---

* By 1939, most towns in the Free State had been connected to the national grid – at which point the outbreak of war slowed the process considerably. The last districts in *rural* Ireland, however, were not electrified until 1973; and some of the islands were connected later still.

concerned with facilitating stability, order and a modest degree of tax collection than with fostering innovation or economic dynamism. This attitude was best exemplified in the shape of the institutions established to administer the state, which were scarcely distinguishable from their British predecessors. The civil service was retained essentially intact; many members of the RIC enlisted in a new (unarmed) civil guard, An Garda Síochána; while the Dáil courts were dismantled with all speed and replaced with a legal system that was identical in virtually all respects to that of England. The country's new leader, W. T. Cosgrave, was solidly uncharismatic – the *Irish Times* opined that 'he looks rather like the general manager of a railway company' – but he exemplified the dour character of a new order.[1]

Cumann na nGaedheal was also deeply authoritarian. This was an attitude that had been displayed as early as the autumn of 1922, when restive postal workers had been stripped of their right to strike and forced back to work by calling the army on to the streets; one striker was even shot to set an example to her colleagues. (Happily, the bullet was deflected by a garter buckle.) The Cumann na nGaedheal government was able to run the new state as it saw fit, and without having to seek much in the way of popularity or support from the people. The prospect of swearing the repugnant oath of allegiance kept de Valera out of parliament for four years, and Cosgrave had only to deal with opposition from the small Labour Party. De Valera at length broke with anti-Treaty Sinn Féin: in 1926 he founded the Fianna Fáil Party, and in the general election of the following year entered the Dáil for the first time. He now took the oath with the aid of mental reservation: he covered the text of the oath as he signed it, had the accompanying Bible placed in the furthest corner of the room, and declared the entire exercise to be an 'empty formula'. Cosgrave would remain in power until 1932.

His focus on the virtues of stability can, of course, be put down to the trauma of civil war that the country had recently experienced; it was vital, in psychological terms, that this phase in history be sealed tightly and locked to the past. This helps to illuminate the otherwise curious lack of attention paid to economic matters – and the resulting low level of economic activity in turn explains why the numbers of those emigrating rose considerably in the years following independence: there was little work to be had, few signs of this situation being addressed in any meaningful way, and thus every incentive to leave Ireland for good. It also explains why the issue of partition was seldom addressed in practical terms: leaving aside the public hand-wringing that developed over the issue, the practical course was inevitably to accept the situation as it existed and begin work on building a new state.

It was a guiding tenet of this new state that a return to a Gaelic Ireland was both desirable and achievable. This in turn meant the fostering of the Irish language, but the methods chosen to incubate and revive it were distinctly odd. An Irish-language test was rapidly introduced to the civil service, but its usage was not extended to the government at large. Instead of becoming the chosen language of state – of the Dáil or of ministerial business – Irish became instead the language of the country's primary schools. Here, its teaching became compulsory: teachers, in other words, were entrusted with the delivery in time of an Irish-language Ireland, and with the resolution of a problem that nobody else much wanted to face:

> Today the people leave the problem to the Government, the Government leaves it to the Department of Education, the Department of Education to the teachers and the teachers to the school-children. Only the very young are unable to shift the burden to someone else's shoulders, so perhaps they will learn to carry it, and save our faces. After all, infants before the age of reason can do marvels with language, so they may not notice the weight.[2]

But this was an experiment that failed, for the number of Irish speakers in the Free State continued inexorably to decline – and yet it was a policy that would not be substantially revised or re-imagined in the years to come. The fees levied for secondary education, meanwhile, ensured that it remained a luxury beyond the reach of all but the well-off; at the end of the 1920s, a massive 93 per cent of children were in receipt of no secondary education at all.* And there were other indications that nationalist rhetoric lacked a certain substance: the population of Ireland's western islands – predominantly Irish-speaking and with precious cultural traditions that were increasingly fragile – declined drastically in the years after independence; the populations of some of them were evacuated with government assistance; and it was painfully evident to all that there was no state policy directed at conserving this facet of Irish culture.

These years were characterized by much cultural self-absorption and preoccupation with issues of public morality. The writer and trades unionist Peadar O'Donnell, who had sympathized with the losing side in the civil war, described the behaviour of the new government as a 'hatching hen fussiness', concerned to an overwhelming extent with incessantly arranging and controlling its environment – so very concerned, indeed, that it had little time or energy left to attend to the wider world that surrounded it.[3] The result was a state marked by a degree of insularity that can seem remarkable today. The culture of censorship, for example, very quickly became a hallmark of Irish life. As early as 1923, the Dáil had passed the first Censorship of Films Act: this would be followed by successively amended legislation designed to keep track of evolving cinematic technology and to close any legislative loopholes. A Committee on Evil Literature was formed in 1926 in order to advise the government on the protection of public morality; and in 1929 the first Censorship of Publications Act was passed, designed to net any book or publication that tended towards the

---

* Joe Lee notes that 'teaching infants through Irish provided one further bulwark for the existing social structure in that it inevitably discriminated against already deprived children, and ensured that when they were despatched from the country as emigrants they would be equipped to serve their new masters only as hewers of wood and drawers of water' (in *Ireland, 1912–1985: Politics and Society* (Cambridge: Cambridge University Press, 1989), 134.

indecent or obscene. Such legislation was not unique to Ireland: amid the social trauma that followed World War I, similar laws appeared on the statute books of many European countries and of the United States. In the specific context of Ireland, however, such laws helped to unify a society deeply divided by the consequences of a recent civil war. They bolstered the notion of resurrecting and protecting a pure and unsullied new nation – in particular protecting it from contamination in the form of smutty British newspapers and books that would otherwise flood west across the Irish Sea.

A wide spectrum of opinion could be relied upon to support such legislation: the republican organ *An Phoblacht*, for example, was pleased to praise the work of the Committee on Evil Literature in seeking to 'check the tide of filth from Britain into this country', and later would mourn the sight of those artists and writers who showed an unhealthy interest in foreign matter. 'These writers,' it tutted, 'cannot have healthy brains, cannot have brains at all but a slack mass of matter like frog-spawn where grim, filthy ideas crawl and breed like so many vermin.'[4] Clearly, the boat to Holyhead was the best place for such individuals if they could not come to an accord with the ways of the Free State. And for the hierarchy of the Catholic Church, which had moved rapidly to assert itself following the years of political chaos, such strictures were simply good lawmaking – in addition to which, the bishops could be assured of many willing listeners in the ranks of government. Censorship would be a prominent feature of life in Ireland for decades to come, and many of the country's most prominent writers – Joyce, Beckett, Shaw, O'Casey, the novelist Kate O'Brien and short story writer Frank O'Connor among them – would join a host of foreign names among the legions of the banned.

One consequence of this prevailing censorious and conservative climate was the steady eclipse of a female presence in Irish public life. The roles of the suffrage movement in Ireland and of women in the politics of 1916–22 are thrown into sharp relief by the nature of the public sphere thereafter, as female room for manoeuvre gradually became more circumscribed. This backlash can be ascribed in part to the voluble anti-Treaty reaction of the membership of Cumann na mBan, which was viewed with horror in many quarters. ('It is women who were largely responsible for the bitterness and the ferocity of the civil war. In the whole period of war, both the "Tan" war and the civil war, the women were the implacable and irrational upholders of death and destruction.'[5]) The stream of legislation that followed seemed designed to keep them in their place: after 1925, women could not automatically sit for all entrance examinations to the civil service, restricting their presence in its highest ranks; from 1927, they had formally to opt *into* jury service; and in the 1930s the 'marriage bar' was introduced, obliging female teachers and civil servants to resign their posts when they married. Market forces naturally ensured that a female workforce existed in factories and shops, in midwifery and on farms. The views of the state, however, were captured in a remark to the Dáil by the minister for justice, Kevin O'Higgins, noting that through biological reproduction women performed 'the normal functions of womanhood in the state's economy'.[6] The Criminal Law Amendment Act of 1935 then took steps to police this area of biological reproduction by banning the importation or sale of contraceptives.[7]

The view of the Church, meanwhile, were summed up as early as 1922 when the Rev. J. S. Sheehy asked the ladies attending a meeting of the Catholic Truth Society: 'Will you be the bane or blessing of man: a ministering angel or wily temptress?'[8] And there were few options for women who fell foul of such rules: a large proportion of single mothers were among those who boarded the emigrant boat; and of those who remained in Ireland, many became inmates of the Magdalen laundries that had evolved since the late nineteenth century. Such foundations ostensibly offered a refuge to 'fallen' women; but they were also extremely lucrative commercial operations, enriching the religious orders that managed them. Many such women would become wholly institutionalized, spending their entire lives in the laundries.

Their offspring, meanwhile, tended to be placed in one of Ireland's fifty-odd industrial schools, also run and administered by a variety of religious orders on behalf of the state. These schools, like the Magdalen laundries, had existed in Ireland for decades: but whereas the system was phased out in the United Kingdom from early in the twentieth century, a decision was taken in the Free State to rely on these schools as a means of dealing with the marginal elements in society. For the schools' inmates tended to be 'needy' – that is, they came from troubled or otherwise deprived families who required additional economic or other assistance; the persistent notion that the schools principally took in orphans or young delinquents is quite incorrect. These industrial schools were state-funded to provide a functional education for the children on their books: in some girls' schools, the inmates were regarded as future domestic servants; while boys were frequently hired out to farmers to work in the fields. The full story of conditions in these industrial schools would not be revealed until the end of the century, but 2009, the Ryan Report noted that the authorities had long been aware that a culture of abuse was part and parcel of life in the industrial school system. A series of letters written in 1946 by a former inmate of Artane school in Dublin, for example, set out in some detail the regime of physical abuse that he and his peers experienced; the Department of Education was 'dismissive. No attempt was made to establish the veracity of the complaints.'[9]

There was, of course, more to the culture of the Free State in these years than harshness and moral censure. In particular, popular culture was in rude health and able to compete with the Church for influence over hearts and minds. While many films were banned, for example, the picture houses of the country (and there were well over a hundred of these by the 1930s) enjoyed a boom, with punters flocking to see the latest American romances and westerns – in spite of the criticism of such films that was voiced from the pulpit each Sunday. At the same time certain grassroots organizations were evolving, with the objective of providing support and advocacy services: the Irish Countrywomen's Association, for example, had begun its expansion from modest (and at first predominantly Protestant) origins in Wexford into something that spanned the whole country; it was strongly influenced by the self-help ethos of the cooperative movement and provided a precious social outlet in the lives of many otherwise isolated rural women.

Novels such as Edith Somerville's *The Big House at Inver* (1925) and Elizabeth Bowen's *The Last September* (1929) used the image of the Anglo–Irish big house to explore the plight of the Protestant community – rapidly shrinking and frequently socially isolated – in the new order. This community had an advocate in the poet Yeats, now a senator. 'We are no petty people,' he observed in the course of a 1925 Senate debate on divorce. 'We are one of the great stocks of Europe. We are the people of Burke, we are the people of Swift, the people of Emmet, the people of Parnell. We have created most of the modern literature of this country…' At the same time, voices could be heard questioning the Catholic moralizing and censorship that was coming to dominate the Free State. The reception given to the Abbey Theatre's first production of O'Casey's *The Plough and the Stars* in 1926 demonstrated that criticism was alive and well. The play portrayed the bleak reality of Dublin tenement life at Easter 1916, complete with drinkers, prostitutes, looters and death by tuberculosis – and offended nationalist complacencies by failing to glorify the leaders of the rising. The result was serious disturbances in the auditorium and a threat by the government to withdraw its annual grant. Yeats and Gregory, however, had clearly anticipated the reaction the play would provoke: 'if we have to choose between the subsidy and our freedom,' wrote Gregory, 'it is freedom we choose.' The production carried on, and the government did not withdraw the subsidy. It was a victory of freedom of expression – but a rare victory in a state that set a rather higher value on internal stability and security.

In these same post-Treaty years, a process of state-building was also on-going in the infant Northern Ireland. Stability and security were the main preoccupations of the new province too, although the definitions of these terms differed in the unusual Northern context. While taxation powers remained centralized in London, issues of law and order had been devolved to Belfast – and the new government wasted no time in securing its authority: internment without trial and other special security laws were introduced; and the IRA threat to the very existence of the state was countered by the expansion of the police force. Such measures worked, though at the price of diminishing still further the position of Northern nationalists in the new Northern Ireland: the 'B Special' force of reserve police in particular rapidly gained a reputation for violence and brutality against the minority community.

With the IRA threat in decline and the boundary commission report consigned safely to history, the Unionist majority could focus on moulding the institutions of government in such a way as to perpetuate the status quo. By 1929, the original electoral system of proportional representation had been replaced by one of single-member constituencies that would favour larger parties (that is, the Ulster Unionist Party, the party of the state itself) and disadvantage potentially troublesome smaller ones, including fringe Unionist groupings. Indeed, single-member *elections* became more common as time went on, with some two-thirds of constituencies in the 1932 general election, for example, uncontested by any save the Ulster Unionist candidate.*

At the same time, the essentially sectarian nature of Northern society grew still more stark. As early as 1923 an attempt was made by the province's first education secretary, Lord Londonderry, to create an integrated, secular and greatly expanded system of schooling. His proposals ran rapidly into the sand, faced as they were by insurmountable opposition from the Catholic and Protestant establishments that balked at – among other ideas – proposals to remove religious instruction from the school timetable. Education in Northern Ireland continued its evolution into two separate

---

* In the general election of 1933 Unionist candidates accounted for thirty-nine seats, nationalist candidates a third of that number.

and parallel systems, and a disillusioned Londonderry resigned from the Northern Ireland cabinet in 1926.*

Profoundly insular though it was, the Northern state could not keep the outside world entirely at bay. The global depression that began in 1929, for example, devastated the province's industrial base and brought buried class-based tensions within Unionism to the fore. The swelling numbers of unemployed in and around Belfast had little in the way of welfare provision on which to fall back; and it took a certain fleetness of foot on the part of the government – including the expansion of relief measures and improved conditions for the police – to put a lid on growing social disturbances in Protestant areas of the city. As the economy of the province continued its decline, meanwhile, the Northern state became ever more dependent on British government subvention – much to the disappointment of London, which had envisaged an economically healthy Northern Ireland being in a position to make modest contributions to the imperial exchequer. In the course of the 1930s this economic dependence would become explicit, with the Unionist establishment increasingly anxious to have an ostensibly autonomous Northern Ireland included in the gradual unrolling of greater welfare provision across the United Kingdom as a whole.

The result was that all sectors of society were able to share in the bounty of gradually expanding welfare payments, more generous pensions and improved healthcare – but such measures were not accompanied by political change. Northern Catholics were systematically discriminated against in the areas of employment and housing; local government was gerrymandered to ensure Protestant domination even in Catholic areas – most notoriously in the case of Derry, where a 1936 reorganization of the city corporation ensured Unionist control of a predominantly nationalist city.

---

* Londonderry – a descendant of Lord Castlereagh, who had been instrumental in the passing of the Act of Union – went on to follow his ancestor in carving out a political career at Westminster. His highly visible attempts in the 1930s to forge alliances with Germany would lead to his condemnation as a Nazi appeaser.

The inevitable consequence of such policies was to undermine any tacit nationalist acceptance of the constitutional status quo.

In the Free State, the accession of de Valera's Fianna Fáil to government in the spring of 1932 was a highly significant political moment. The transfer of power from Cumann na nGaedheal – in contrast to the situation in many other European countries in this fraught period – was accomplished smoothly and without any threat to the state's democratic institutions. Throughout the election campaign de Valera had emphasized his new party's social, economic and welfare credentials, in particular pledging to reduce the scourge of unemployment. His enemies had claimed that Fianna Fáil would bring only instability and factionalism to Irish politics: yet in the event, the new government proved to be just as keen as its predecessor on stability and continuity. There was little in the way of revolutionary fervour about its policies: rather, from its first months in power it displayed the pragmatism that soon became the party's hallmark, with rhetorical calls for pure, traditional nationalism jostling with actual – if modest – increases in the provision of welfare, housing and medical services.

De Valera's devotion to the principle of economic self-sufficiency, meanwhile, soon saw the erection of tariff walls around Ireland and a range of policies designed to keep foreign capital out and Irish money and investment in. In the traumatic years after the Depression, policies such as these were popular across the developed world. But Ireland had been losing its population since the time of the Famine nearly a hundred years earlier, and the countryside was rapidly depopulating, regardless of de Valera's belief that it was in the fields and lanes of Ireland that the true, authentic spirit of the nation was to be found. Neither political independence nor claims to self-sufficiency could alter the facts of economic decline and failure – nor disguise the tales of human tragedy that lay behind the statistics.

Fianna Fáil now faced a new parliamentary opposition. The new Fine Gael party consisted mainly of former Cumann na Gaedheal members; it

also, however, numbered in its ranks the so-called Blueshirts, an organization that traded on the distinctive straight-armed salute of the Italian and
German fascists. The Blueshirt ideology was a heady mixture of Catholic
conservatism and anti-Semitism; the movement was headed by Eoin
O'Duffy, a former Garda commissioner sacked by de Valera in 1933, and
was spiced with a loathing of de Valera that sprang from the ashes of the
civil war. The visually arresting aplomb of the organization and its various
activities (some of its members fought on the side of Franco in the Spanish civil war) have certainly earned it a place in the history of the period,
especially when seen in the context of the rise of European fascism. But
there was no appetite in Ireland for fascism – and, in truth, the Irish
Blueshirts were no more than a rag-bag movement that faded rapidly,
damaged and divided Fine Gael and left little or nothing behind by way of
a political legacy. If anything, its existence served only to bolster Fianna Fáil:
in taking steps to curb and finally eliminate the Blueshirt threat (such as it
was), de Valera's party was able to assume the mantle of the party of law
and order – in the process facilitating its own transition into the realm of
constitutional politics.

A decade after the Treaty, de Valera remained eager to return to the issue
of the constitutional arrangements between Ireland and the Empire. The
measures he took to alter these arrangements were highly effective: the existing governor general was boycotted; in time, de Valera nominated a new
appointment to the post, who was instructed to do nothing and remain invisible; the office itself, having been softened up in this way, was eventually
abolished in 1936. At the same time, annuities paid to the British government by Irish farmers (the price they were obliged to pay as a result of the
Land Acts in order to gain title over their land) were diverted to the Irish
exchequer. This was in direct contravention of the terms of the Treaty, and
the British government responded by imposing heavy taxes on a wide range
of Irish exports to Britain: the Irish government then responded in kind – but
this was an economic war in which Ireland came off much the worse.

Despite this, the episode ended well for de Valera: in April 1938 the British government agreed to give up its rights to the land annuities in return for a one-off payment of £10 million. Furthermore, it relinquished control of the Treaty ports in Cork and Donegal: a British assessment had concluded that, in the event of war, it would not be worthwhile retaining the ports against the explicit wishes of a restive and unhappy host country; furthermore, the British could rest assured that the Free State would now have no excuse to open its territory to German arms. De Valera, of course, had no intention of allowing any such situation to develop if it could possibly be avoided – so the return of the ports and the removal of this British presence from the Free State thus represented pure victory. Fianna Fáil, then, might not have declared a republic overnight: but the ground was being laid for such a step in the fullness of time – and the drawing up of a new constitution was another piece in this jigsaw.

The constitution of 1937 was a carefully poised document and one that sought, by means of a combination of clear assertion, allusion and implication, the allegiance and loyalty of all. On the one hand, the constitution reflected the overwhelmingly Catholic nature of the state by means of a clause enshrining the special position of the Catholic Church in Irish life, and through others banning divorce and blasphemy. At the same time, however, the constitution defended the position of the Protestant denominations and (not insignificantly, given the state of affairs in 1930s' Europe when the document was formulated) the country's small Jewish community. The Catholic Church may have been 'special', therefore, but it was certainly not the established Church – a situation quite unlike that of many of Ireland's European neighbours – and there was therefore no compulsion for certain office-holders to be Catholic.

This elusive quality was further reflected in other passages. The constitution adhered to the ambitions and aspirations of an independent republic – but it did not actually declare the country to be a republic. It re-established a bicameral legislature and founded the office of president –

but neither this new Senate nor the head of state would have much to offer by way of powers or authority. It called on the loyalty of Irish nationalism by declaring Irish to be the principal national language and by laying claim overtly to the entire island of Ireland and its surrounding seas – but at the same time it acknowledged the reality of partition by conceding that Dublin's legal writ ran, for the time being, only to the territory of the Free State. And while the document referred frequently to 'the Nation' – Article 9 stated that 'fidelity to the Nation and loyalty to the State are fundamental political duties of all citizens' – at no point did it offer a definition of this term. This was a crucial issue in a constitution so wholly shadowed by the fact and existence of partition and of a sizeable Northern population that had rejected rule from Dublin in the recent past – and that would do so again, given the opportunity.*

In July 1937, the constitution was passed by referendum: on a turn-out of a little over 50 per cent, there were some 685,000 votes in favour and 527,000 against. The people had accepted the constitution, thus lending it weight and authority – but such a vote did not indicate a resounding affirmation of the document; and in the general election held on the same day Fianna Fáil lost its absolute majority in parliament. Yet the state was now on a new footing and a republic in all but name. Soon too de Valera's suppression of his former IRA allies, by means of the Offences against the State Act of 1939, would underscore his authority. Threats to the state could no

---

* See Lee, *Ireland 1912–1985*, 206. The constitution's attitude to women too was founded in unreality. It was clear in its view that the correct position of women was within the home; and it envisaged a situation in which no woman would be obliged by economic necessity to go out to work. But no attempt was made either to pay the menfolk of Ireland enough to enable their women to stay at home, even if they so wished; or to ensure that the majority of the mothers of Ireland could raise their children in tolerable comfort; or to create the economic circumstances that would enable thousands of women to remain in Ireland and start a family, rather than board an emigrant boat to Britain or America. This gap between constitutional rhetoric and cold political reality was best exemplified in the aspiration to direct the energies and finances of the state towards the welfare and betterment of the people while at the same time explicitly ruling out recourse to the courts as a means of ensuring that these principles were actually applied.

longer be tolerated, and the deaths of nine IRA men – through execution and on hunger strike – in the years that followed underlined the government's determination on this point.

War was declared in Europe in September 1939 – and Ireland, in common with many other European nations, at once announced its neutrality in the face of what the government termed the 'Emergency'. That the country would choose this status had long been apparent: there was neither public nor political appetite to enter any conflict on the side of Britain, and the memories of the civil war were still too vivid. The country was, in any case, entirely unprepared. Defence spending had steadily declined in the 1930s, and did not begin to increase until after the war. The size of the army grew only after the German capture of Paris in June 1940, at which point the potential dangers for the country had become glaringly evident. Throughout the war, army training was hampered by faulty, obsolete or non-existent equipment; and the country had only the most slender naval and air defences.

Neutrality, then, was de Valera's only possible option – but this did not prevent the British making several overtures to the Irish government. In June 1940 – with Germany in the ascendant across Europe – a firm offer was tabled: the British authorities would publicly announce a preference for Irish unity in return for an Irish declaration of war against Germany. De Valera rejected the offer: at this moment, Germany looked likely to win the war; and quite apart from the internal resistance he would certainly face, he could not contemplate Ireland joining the British side at such a very inauspicious moment. Eighteen months later another offer was made, and now the timing was rather less hopeless: the United States had entered the war, and its eventual outcome seemed rather clearer. From the British point of view, of course, an Allied Ireland was greatly to be wished for: it would secure the flow of foodstuffs across the Irish Sea; it would enable the placing of a military presence in Ireland to see off any possible German landings; and it would open Irish seaports – so useful in aiding the vital

Atlantic convoys – to British ships. De Valera, however, again rejected the offer: he knew that internal opposition would be no less ferocious than it had been a year before, and that the government and Unionist population of Northern Ireland were unlikely to go along meekly with any such plan, regardless of how much British pressure was heaped upon them.

Irish neutrality, however, was another shadowy affair shot through with ambiguity. Ireland was both living and not living in a world of war. The Luftwaffe dropped bombs on the capital in January and May 1941, killing thirty Dubliners; a sea mine washed up on a Donegal beach in 1943 and exploded, killing nineteen men and boys who had gone to investigate; and dead bodies from torpedoed shipping – the exploding bombs themselves sometimes clearly audible from the shore – became a common sight along the coasts for the duration of the war.

Censorship – as was the case across Europe in these years – became more ubiquitous, with the daily newspapers presenting their copy to the censor in advance of publication and newsreels filleted of any disturbing content. Irish audiences saw and heard little from Stalingrad, for example; there were few details made available of the fall of France, or of the various bloody engagements that characterized the war in the Pacific; and the gradually accumulating knowledge of Nazi atrocities in Europe was also kept from Irish readers. Irish immigration policies were highly illiberal: the country was essentially closed to Jews and other refugees fleeing Nazi persecution. In May 1945, indeed, de Valera himself visited Dublin's German legation to offer his government's commiserations on the death of Hitler: it was a diplomatic move that caused consternation both among the staff at the legation and abroad – though de Valera claimed that not to have paid such a visit 'would have been an act of unpardonable discourtesy to the German nation'.[10]

At the same time, while German prisoners of war were hastily herded into camps for the duration of the war, British and Allied equivalents were just as hastily bundled across the border into the North; the government permitted Allied planes to overfly its territory to land at Northern air and seaplane bases; precious Irish intelligence flowed towards the Allies through-out the war years; and troops based in the North caught trains south to Dublin and promenaded around the streets of the city, studiously ignored all the while by the authorities. 'They are tolerated,' noted the novelist Elizabeth Bowen, who provided intelligence reports to the British government, 'as having money to spend ... they frequent the cheaper hotels, crowd the shop-ping streets and cafés and restaurants. Dublin is undoubtedly flattered to find herself in the role of a pleasure city.'[11] Everyone from Winston Churchill to the US government to the Northern poet Louis MacNeice ('to the west off your own shores the mackerel / are fat – on the flesh of your kin') railed at the stance of 'that neutral island'.* And yet it is indisputable that this osten-sible neutrality was tilted decisively and in favour of Britain and the Allies – particularly following the entry into the war of the United States.

The war brought with it special challenges for Ireland. Although self-sufficiency had been hailed as the supreme national goal, successive governments had in fact done little to achieve this end: Ireland had, for example, few merchant ships, relying instead on foreign-registered vessels to conduct its trade; and by habitually importing raw materials in order to fuel its economy, the country had in fact become more and more depend-ent on the outside world. Now, at the onset of the Emergency, the merits and challenges of actual self-sufficiency would be put rather more to the test. The result was a more straitened society during the war years. Coal ran short, forcing the population to rely on turf; city parks were turned into allotments in order to supplement an increasingly monotonous diet; compulsory tillage measures led to the sowing of more wheat; and although the country was more or less self-sufficient in bread and potatoes, food shortages and their associated maladies, such as rickets, were certainly not unknown. Smuggling

---

* Louis MacNeice, 'Neutrality', in *Selected Poems*, ed. W. H. Auden (London: Faber, 1964), 77. In one excellent illustration of Irish cooperation with the Allies, the meteorological station at Belmullet in County Mayo fed the Allied naval authorities with weather reports that were crucial to the timing of the Normandy landings.

along the border was a popular pursuit: it was not difficult to slip from Donegal or Louth into Derry or Newry with packs of butter and sugar, and many took this opportunity to make some regular extra cash.

In addition, emigration continued unhindered throughout the war years, with some hundred thousand Irish citizens (representing a full one-sixth of the working population of the state) leaving the country for employment in Britain – in the fields and factories, and not least in the armed forces. While there was an understanding in the government that this exodus undermined Irish claims to strict neutrality, there was equally the tacit knowledge that it would have to continue, war or no war: the alternative would be the presence in Ireland of a large and ever-growing body of discontented and unemployed citizens who could cause no end of trouble for a state that did not want and could not cope with them. It was an indication of the importance of emigration to Irish social stability that the government did not merely permit the passage of these thousands of its citizens, but actively oiled the process administratively and bureaucratically.

The war in Northern Ireland, in stark contrast to the situation south of the border, was a visible part of life – down to the rigidly enforced blackout sustained for the duration of the conflict. In many ways the province was cushioned from the worst effects of the war, not least because conscription was never applied there. The Unionist government had pressed for the measure but the British government declined the offer, understanding that, as a result of certain nationalist unrest, it would not be worth the trouble. The British evacuation of the Treaty Ports in 1938, however, had rendered the harbours of Northern Ireland even more strategically vital: Derry was the United Kingdom's westernmost port and as such played a pivotal role in the battle of the Atlantic; and the city in particular and province in general hosted tens of thousands of British, Commonwealth and – following the attack on Pearl Harbor in December 1941 – American troops. In the run-up to the Normandy landings, as many as three hundred thousand troops were stationed in Northern Ireland; chronic unemployment gave way to a jobs bonanza; and the dour Ulster air was charged with colour and a note of heady glamour.

There was a price to be paid for these prosperous times: in April and May 1941, massive German air raids resulted in the deaths of over a thousand people in Belfast, together with widespread destruction of property. Behind the scenes, meanwhile, British eyebrows were raised at the province's sluggish contribution to the war effort. In military and economic terms, this was indeed negligible: numbers choosing to enlist in the forces remained notably low throughout the war, dwindling to a mere six hundred per month by Christmas 1940; and the factories and shipyards of Belfast were reluctant to move to a war footing, continuing to charge prices above the odds and to cling to outmoded and slow-footed working practices. Yet for all these awkward facts, the fundamental strategic importance of Northern Ireland for the duration of the war continued to guarantee much public praise: 'If it had not been for the loyalty and friendship of Northern Ireland,' as Churchill commented on the airwaves just after VE Day, 'we should have been forced to come to close quarters with Mr de Valera, or perish for ever from the earth.'[12]

It seemed as though Northern Ireland's political and cultural deep freeze might conceivably come to an end as the excitement and relative prosperity of the war years gave way to the radical health and social welfare reforms of Clement Attlee's postwar Labour government – applied once again to the province as to Britain. The impact of such changes was felt immediately, but the potency of simultaneous education reforms – in particular the 1947 Education Act, which opened up access to free secondary and higher education – would be noticed only gradually.* Their result was the inevitable expansion of Northern Ireland's Catholic middle class and the

---

* The Northern Ireland Education Act of 1947 mirrored the provisions of the 1944 Education Act (the 'Butler Act') in Britain.

creation of a new generation of educated nationalists. These were potentially revolutionary reforms – but it remained to be seen how the Unionist establishment would respond.

Yet at first it appeared that this establishment had comparatively little to worry about. Unionist opinion was cheered when the Irish government's declaration of the Irish Republic in 1949 prompted a swift response in London: the Government of Ireland Act cemented the position of Northern Ireland as a constituent part of the United Kingdom and caused much discomfiture in Dublin. Yet not everything emanating from London in the postwar years seemed so palatable. Unionist leaders may have broadly welcomed Attlee's welfare reforms, but there were grumbles at what were felt to be its excesses. These opinions were genuine and deeply felt: in this conservative society, many could not appreciate measures that smacked of socialism or excessive state interference. But they were also politically motivated: some feared that too generous a welfare state might encourage Northern Ireland's Catholics to have more and yet more children, a state of affairs that might eventually threaten Unionist political dominance. In 1956, for example, the Northern Ireland government prepared changes to a Family Allowances Bill that would see payments cease after the third child: this was a measure aimed at large (and therefore mainly Catholic) families; and only pressure from Unionist MPs at Westminster caused these proposals to be dropped.[13]

More significant still was the political unease generated by government measures designed to address the North's chronic housing shortage. In a political culture founded on a demographic numbers game and the gerrymandering of political boundaries, seats could be won and lost – and political dominance threatened – by a mere handful of new arrivals, complete with voting rights, in this or that neighbourhood. The result was that in certain socially sensitive areas of Northern Ireland Catholic families could remain unhoused for long periods: in the course of twenty-four years in gerrymandered Dungannon in County Tyrone, for example, not a single Catholic family was housed by the local authority.

The social changes now being applied in Northern Ireland were not, in other words, about to be accompanied by similarly profound political changes. Instead, the maintenance of a Unionist hegemony remained the alpha and the omega of politics. Some Unionist figures did indeed perceive that the world was changing around them, but Northern Ireland's profoundly abnormal political system appeared wholly impervious to reform. There were ample indications of what might happen should the Unionist establishment ever attempt such a thing: the early 1950s, for example, saw the arrival on the scene of a young Protestant firebrand preacher named Ian Paisley, who specialized in the delivery of politico-religious fire-and-brimstone sermons. Here was evidence enough that any attempt to move with the times would lead to a split within Unionism – and perhaps to a loss of power.

Northern Ireland was therefore at once both developing and not developing: in social, economic and cultural terms, the province was witnessing profound change; and the growth of the Northern Ireland Labour Party in the course of the 1960s, for example, was evidence enough that the first generation of Catholics to benefit from the educational reforms was now both politically mature and politically dissatisfied. In 1963, the secretive and socially awkward Terence O'Neill became the province's prime minister: he envisaged that a policy of economic prosperity would eventually reconcile the province's Catholic minority to a British future. And a measure of economic growth was indeed attained: American firms such as DuPont established large plants in the province; the 'new town' of Craigavon was founded in County Armagh; a new university was established (albeit in predominantly Protestant Coleraine, rather than in Derry, where a university college already existed) and the motorway network was expanded.

But O'Neill was unwilling and unable to change the fundamental structures of Northern Ireland politics: for example, he could not or would not address the housing crisis; and even the modest reforms that he did enact led to a ferocious Unionist backlash. At the same time, Catholic political agitation rose throughout the 1960s: central welfare reform had certainly not eliminated poverty: social deprivation in parts of Belfast and Derry, for example, was acute.

The Civil Rights Association (NICRA) was formed in April 1967: a diverse organization, including in its ranks both political radicals and moderates, it consciously took aspects of its aims and identity from the United States civil rights movement. NICRA captured the attention of the media when a march in October 1968 in Derry led to widespread rioting and confrontation with an RUC force that seemed rapidly to lose any sense of discipline – a violent scene played out in front of the world's journalists. In Belfast, students and lecturers at Queen's University established People's Democracy (PD), a body affiliated to NICRA, though a good deal more radical in its outlook. Rapidly, PD settled on a way of making its mark: it organized a march between Belfast and Derry, modelled on the 'Long March' that Martin Luther King and his supporters had undertaken between Selma and Montgomery, Alabama. The demonstration set off from Belfast's City Hall on 1 January 1969; on 4 January it was passing Burntollet, east of Derry, when it was attacked by a loyalist crowd, including associates of Paisley and a number of off-duty B Specials who were occupying nearby high ground; RUC forces in the vicinity failed to intervene to end the violence. Terence O'Neill resigned as prime minister in April; as the summer approached, sectarian unrest spread across many parts of Northern Ireland – and now, in the face of violent and seemingly unstoppable disturbances in Belfast in July and Derry in August, the government made the decision, fateful and unavoidable, to put British troops on to the streets.

The postwar period would also slowly introduce change to the South. The end of the war in Europe had brought with it wider horizons: travel across Europe was now possible for some; and the proximity of a larger world contrasted sharply with Ireland's more muted colours. 'We emerge,' wrote Seán O'Faoláin in the summer of 1945, 'a little dulled, bewildered, deflated.

There is a great leeway to make up, many lessons to be learned, problems to be solved which, in those six years of silence, we did not even allow ourselves to state.'[14] The policy of neutrality had resulted in growing diplomatic isolation: relations with the United States, for example, remained cool long after the end of the war. Neutrality would nevertheless become a key component both of government policy and of national identity: it was understood to be good in itself, although its definition and form continued to morph and blur according to the political needs of the day.

Nor was Ireland wholly adrift from the cultural changes of the period: no country so closely wedded to a much larger neighbour, as Ireland was to Britain, could cut itself off completely from the world, either culturally or in any other way: the establishment by O'Faoláin and Peadar O'Donnell of *The Bell* periodical in 1940, for example, gives the lie to a sense of utter cultural stagnation. But the proportion of the population speaking 'our own poor, dear Gaelic' continued to decline, and rural Ireland to wither.[15] De Valera, in his (in)famous St Patrick's Day speech of 1943, had conjured a dream of his rustic homeland alive with 'cosy homesteads … the contests of athletic youths and the laughter of comely maidens'. Patrick Kavanagh, however, was on rather more realistic ground with 'The Great Hunger', which damned any such romanticizing tendency by emphasizing the suffocating loneliness, sexual and social frustration and absence of hope for many of its remaining inhabitants: 'The hungry fiend / Screams the apocalypse of clay / In every corner of this land'.[16]

In economic terms, the sense that the country had survived the war unscathed – that the political and cultural rupture witnessed in other European countries had *not* been experienced in Ireland – ensured that the policies and rhetoric of the 1930s continued to be applied to the postwar economy. Prewar economic dogma persisted, emigration continued unabated – and the result was that after 1945 Ireland's economic performance fell rapidly and decisively behind that of its European neighbours. While there were elements in government willing to recognize the inadequacies of the current economic regime, they remained few and commanded little attention; the drift was permitted to continue.

One change, however, did take place – and it must have proved startling to some: in the general election of January 1948 de Valera and Fianna Fáil lost power, to be replaced by a fractious coalition of opposition parties. Fine Gael was the largest element in this new government; but it also included ministers from a political party called Clann na Poblachta, which had been formed as recently as 1946. The leader of this new entity was Seán MacBride, the offspring of the short and unhappy marriage of Maud Gonne and John MacBride: the party itself was philosophically unwieldy, being composed of left-wing social reformers, Catholic intellectuals and activists who took a dim view of parliamentary politics in general. This new party would at length disintegrate under the weight of factionalism and bitter internal disagreements: the incoming government itself survived only three years, the first in a series of weak and unstable administrations.

This postwar government is best remembered for a struggle that took place between the zealous Clann na Poblachta minister for health, Noel Browne, and the Catholic Church. Browne had previously taken successful steps to cut dramatically the high rates of tuberculosis in Irish society, and in 1950 he turned his attention to other aspects of the country's health system. The wartime Fianna Fáil government had already begun to implement health reforms: sweeping change, however, had been stymied partly as a result of active lobbying on the part of the Irish Medical Association (IMA), which saw socialized medicine as a threat to its members' activities in the lucrative private health sector; and party because of private lobbying from the Church, which noted that the idea of the state educating 'women in regard to health [was] directly and entirely contrary to Catholic social teaching'.[17] Browne anticipated few such issues, however, with his so-called Mother and Child Scheme, which proposed free healthcare for expectant and nursing mothers: it was a useful measure, but seemed relatively uncontroversial.

But the Church – embodied in this instance in the figure of John Charles McQuaid, who since 1940 had served as Archbishop of Dublin – begged to differ, for again it sniffed in the air the stench of State interference in family life. But this was rather more than a mere struggle for power between Church and State: Browne was, for example, not wholly backed by his own party, elements in which would be happy to see him brought low; and McQuaid was essentially speaking on behalf of the IMA, the members of which wanted 'to remain gentlemen and not let officials near them or their tax returns'.[18] The scheme, in other words, was regarded as a threat to class interests and as a result was duly quashed; Browne resigned in 1951. Ironically, the essentials of the scheme were quietly passed by the subsequent government.

This episode, complicated though it was, does point to the tremendous temporal influence of the Catholic Church at this period – and to the authority of McQuaid not least. The archbishop was a commanding presence on the national stage, fiercely intelligent and deeply interested in matters of education and health. He was in his own terms a reformer and willing to respond to the changing times: in, for example, setting in motion a renewed programme of church-building in Dublin to cater to the city's rapidly increasing population; and in publicly opposing de Valera by supporting the cause of striking teachers during a six-month dispute in 1946. Yet it is his commitment to power and authority that reverberate down the years – and in particular his attempts to exert control over myriad Church and secular organizations, as well as over the lives of his flock. McQuaid monitored academic appointments to University College Dublin; his agents attended public meetings throughout the archdiocese and brought news of what transpired to the Archbishop's House in north Dublin; he had direct access to government ministers and civil servants, to administrators, legislators and medical consultants; and he sought to control the administration of charities and hospitals and to keep the Protestant influence of Trinity College Dublin from leaching into wider society.

McQuaid monitored cultural activities too – and sometimes his reputation preceded him, as in the notorious case of Tennessee Williams's *The Rose Tattoo*, staged at Dublin's tiny Pike Theatre in 1957 as part of the city's theatre festival. The script mentioned a condom; such an article being illegal in Ireland, an envelope was substituted – but to no avail: the production was closed down and its producer, Alan Simpson, arrested on a charge of lewdness and profanity. A year later, the case was thrown out by the Supreme Court, but the damage had been done: the theatre was bankrupted and Simpson's marriage to Carolyn Swift (with whom he ran the Pike) broke down as a result of a range of associated pressures, including widespread social ostracism. It was later claimed that the state itself – reacting to McQuaid's unrelenting moral activity – had engineered the entire episode in order to underscore its moral vigilance and support of censorship.[19]

That the Pike had existed in the first place – in its short life, the theatre had staged the works of, among others, Eugène Ionesco and Jean-Paul Sartre, and produced the Irish premiere of Samuel Beckett's *Waiting for Godot* –revealed an appetite for European art in Ireland that certainly gainsays the sense that the country was a cultural blasted heath. Yet the theatre's destruction by a combination of Church and State intervention indicates that the forces of orthodoxy were immeasurably stronger. The Church's temporal and spiritual power was further emphasized by the cancellation of the entire theatre festival in 1957 following clerical dissatisfaction with several productions. Three years later, in another equally notorious episode, Edna O'Brien's debut novel *The Country Girls* – already banned – was burned in the grounds of what had been her home chapel in County Clare. 'It was called a smear on Irish womanhood. A priest in our parish asked from the altar if anyone who had bought copies would bring them to the chapel grounds. That evening there was a little burning.'[20]

And yet the power and authority of the Catholic Church were certainly not absolute. For one thing, de Valera was not in the habit of taking orders from anyone: McQuaid could divine a silent distancing on the part of the

Fianna Fáil government of 1951–4; and by the end of the decade, politicians were able to disagree openly with McQuaid and his fellow clerics, to plough their own legislative furrow, to ignore the archbishop's incessant letters on a variety of matters. There were signs too that the middle classes were prepared to peel away from Church teaching and to give voice to a simmering resentment at such attempted control over the minutiae of daily life. Censorship or no censorship, Edna O'Brien's books – and a host of others – were readily available in Ireland, for the Irish border could be porous on these matters, and goods of all kinds could also be brought in on the ferries from Britain; and Catholics had been studying at Trinity College years before the Church ban on their attendance was at last lifted in 1970.

These years, characterized though they were by population decline and continued economic malaise, seemed to mark the tentative beginnings of a new order in Ireland – one upon which McQuaid found it increasingly difficult to stamp his authority. In 1956, marking the fortieth anniversary of the Easter Rising, the *Irish Times* editorialized that 'if the present trend disclosed continues unchecked … Ireland will die – not in the remote unpredictable future, but quite soon'.[21] It was indeed apparent now to even the most hidebound traditionalist that the country's economic situation was so dire that things simply could not go on as they were: from the mid-1950s the country was opened to direct foreign investment, and in 1955 the Republic became an enthusiastic member of the United Nations, its isolationism now definitively a policy of the past. UN membership in turn allowed the country to make its presence felt on the world stage: under Frank Aiken, who served as minister for external affairs from 1951 to 1954 and again from 1957 to 1969, the Irish at the UN and in other international bodies carved out a role as advocates for the rights of small countries elsewhere, from Tibet to eastern Europe; and as vigorous proponents of the policy of nuclear non-proliferation. The Republic also became a participant in many of the UN peacekeeping missions: its first mission was to the Congo in 1960, where nine men died in an ambush at Niemba in November of that year.

In 1959 de Valera at last stepped down as taoiseach, to be replaced by the energetic Seán Lemass, who had been a key proponent of more innovative economic policies in successive de Valera governments. That same year, the population of the state fell below the 3 million mark – and yet it was evident that a corner had now been turned. This sense was given symbolic expression in 1961, when the Lemass government applied for membership of what was then known as the European Economic Community (now the European Union). This application and subsequent ones failed – largely because the United Kingdom's applications were vetoed by France, rather than for any particular reason to do with Ireland. The Republic would eventually join the union on 1 January 1973, following a referendum in which a majority of 83 per cent approved entry. EEC membership would change the face of Ireland – yet at the same moment, Northern Ireland had become ensnared in the Troubles. It seemed that while the future could be willingly embraced, the past could not so easily be left behind.

CHAPTER THIRTEEN

BETWEEN HERE
AND THERE

On the afternoon of 15 June 2010, a crowd of thousands gathered in the Guildhall Square in the centre of Derry. Inside, in the central hall of the Guildhall itself – lit by long stained-glass windows chronicling the story of the seventeenth-century plantation of the city and the history of the British army and empire – the final report of the Bloody Sunday Inquiry had been made available to the families of the fourteen men killed in central Derry on 30 January 1972 in the course of a civil rights march.* The report's findings, though the subject of a good deal of speculation, had not been substantially leaked; and there was an air of palpable tension in the square outside.

Bloody Sunday was but one day in the thirty years of the Troubles – nor was it the bloodiest. It had, however, assumed a unique position: the fourteen men had been killed by members of the British armed forces – in other words, by the state itself – which lent a ghastly distinction to the events of the day. The official investigation, completed by April 1972, had backed the stance of the army: that its soldiers had only responded to attacks by members of the IRA operating within the crowd. The city's coroner, on the other hand, described the killings as 'sheer, unadulterated murder' – but the findings of the official investigation stood; and the events of Bloody Sunday became an open sore, a grievance visited and revisited in the following years.

---

* Thirteen men had died on the day itself; a fourteenth died later from his injuries.

In January 1998 the British government set up the Bloody Sunday Inquiry to address this grievance and unpick the events of the day. This was in its turn part of a greater political move: the British, Irish and United States governments were now investing vast amounts of political energy into securing a deal in Northern Ireland that would establish peace and a power-sharing local government; a new investigation into the events of Bloody Sunday was recognized as a necessary part of this manoeuvre.

On that afternoon in Derry, large screens had been set up in the Guildhall Square. At the moment of the report's release, television cut to the House of Commons, where the new British prime minister, David Cameron, was due to comment on the findings. Cameron announced to a silent House that British soldiers had fired the first shots on Bloody Sunday, that they had lost control, had killed civilians who had posed no threat to their safety, and had subsequently lied in order to cover up these acts. The crowd gathered in the Guildhall Square greeted his words with applause.

The Troubles that erupted in the summer of 1969 eventually claimed over three thousand lives. To the fourteen who died as a result of Bloody Sunday can be added the fifteen killed in a Belfast pub bombing in December 1971; nine killed in the Claudy bombings of July 1972; twelve killed in the M62 coach bombing in West Yorkshire in February 1973; thirty-three killed in Dublin and Monaghan in May 1974; twenty-six killed in the Birmingham and Guildford pub bombings in the autumn of 1974; twelve killed at the La Mon restaurant near Belfast in February 1978; twenty-two killed in separate incidents on the same day at Warrenpoint and in County Sligo in August 1979; eleven killed in London in July 1982 and seventeen at Ballykelly in December of the same year; twelve killed at Enniskillen in November 1988; nine killed at Greysteel in October 1993; twenty-nine killed at Omagh in August 1998 – and this a list that is far from exhaustive.

The roots of the conflict, as we have seen, were sunk deeply into the past: into centuries marked in Ulster by persistent ethnic and sectarian tension, territorial and economic rivalry, and occasional but horrifying surges of bloody violence. The folk memories of such past violence remained alive and well: and the carnage that had accompanied the birth of Northern Ireland, of course, had taken place a mere fifty years before the outbreak of the latest Troubles – still recent enough to be vividly recalled in some quarters. Meanwhile, the sorry history of Northern Ireland in the years since its birth, characterized as it was by injustice and ultimately by political immobility, stoked the fires of grievance still further. As for the character of the Troubles, this would shift continually over the course of three decades – now rising into spikes of brutal violence, now subsiding into periods of relative calm; in the early years in particular its nature sometimes approached that of civil strife, with civilians consistently figuring among the dead and injured.

This was on one level a clash between the Provisional IRA and a variety of representatives of the British State, including the army, police and part-time reservists. However, many other participants – including rogue elements within the security services, republican splinter groups and an array of loyalist paramilitary organizations with an eye on turf wars and the lucrative profits flowing from the sale of drugs – swirled together around the edges of the conflict.* Constitutional politics nevertheless continued for the duration of the Troubles, although this term must be qualified: in 1971, for example, Ian Paisley followed the constitutional route by establishing his Democratic Unionist Party (DUP); but he also continued to maintain close contacts with a range of extremist loyalist groups that drew support from the increasingly disaffected Protestant working-class population of the province. The politics of Northern Ireland, then, might

---

* The Provisional IRA emerged in 1969 from an ideological split with the ranks of the Irish Republican Army. The Provisional wing of the IRA embraced the use of force in the context of rising disorder in Northern Ireland; the 'Official IRA' embraced Marxist, class-based politics.

have seemed both impossibly poisoned and utterly deadlocked – yet conversation, negotiation and exploration continued throughout, usually under the most unprepossessing circumstances imaginable.

Many elements within the Catholic community were certainly not predisposed towards political violence: Northern society, indeed, was typified by an abiding conservatism that transcended sectarian boundaries. Many middle-class nationalists aspired rather towards a society founded on equality of opportunity – one far removed, that is, from the Unionist hegemony that had marked the first fifty years of Northern history. The failure of the British State to intervene in these decades in order to address such substantial issues of disadvantage had bred an inevitable sense of grievance and resentment. Indeed, there were echoes of the situation in 1800, when the Act of Union had not been accompanied by Catholic emancipation; it was in part the failure to bring the nationalist community fully into the governance and economic mainstream of Northern Ireland that had created the present political situation.

The foundation in 1970 of the Social Democratic and Labour Party (SDLP) answered the need within this community for a modern political party influenced by the ideology of constitutional Irish nationalism and of civil rights: led first by Gerry Fitt and then by John Hume, the party would for the next three decades play a pivotal role in the politics of the province. However, the responses of the state – in the form of internment without trial, curfews and such events as Bloody Sunday – to the worsening security situation also took many Catholics away from mainstream politics and pointed them in the direction of the IRA and its political wing, Sinn Féin. Conversely, the working-class Protestant population, from which loyalist terrorism drew its strength, was driven by fear of an inevitable loss of political, economic and social status should nationalists be accorded equality in what was traditionally a Protestant Northern

Ireland. It was tacitly understood on all sides that the British state had essentially lost any strategic or ideological interest in maintaining its presence in Northern Ireland. The high days of empire were long gone; the economic maintenance of the province was an ever-increasing drain on a stretched British exchequer; and the sense of an increasingly loveless attitude on the part of Britain towards Northern Ireland fuelled continuing Unionist and loyalist fears of what the future might bring.

The final main player was the Irish state: throughout the Troubles, the rhetoric of successive Irish governments continued to espouse the ideal of national unity, while at the same time political energy was principally channelled towards the preservation of stability in the Republic itself. The Irish state was obliged to bolster the position of Northern nationalists: the upsurge of violence in the late 1960s, for example, had been followed extensively in the Southern media; the presence of refugees from this violence in the Republic led to expressions of solidarity and material support in the form of money and accommodation; and the matter was raised at international level – for example, at the UN Security Council. The Irish state was also obliged to maintain its independence of action in this matter – in particular, by resisting overt British attempts to extract support for its security policies. The result was a disconcerting oscillation between periods of close cooperation between the two governments and spectacular quarrels, of which a series of bitter conflicts over the question of extradition of terrorist suspects were the most public.

This was a conflict, then, bound up with a tortured history – but one that was also fed by the strains inherent in a series of contemporary relationships: between the communities in Northern Ireland itself; between the two constituent parts of the island of Ireland; and between the British and Irish states. Any solution would be obliged to address all of these strands: it was perhaps little wonder that such a solution took time to present itself.

*

The troops that appeared on the streets of Northern Ireland in 1969 were greeted initially with a certain relief in working-class Catholic districts of Belfast and Derry: better to deal with British soldiers, it was widely felt, than with those elements in the police – the Royal Ulster Constabulary (RUC) – who had long since forfeited the trust of Northern nationalists. The IRA was obliged to accept such a state of affairs – but only temporarily: within months the relationship between the army and the Catholic community had frayed as a result of the imposition of curfews and by vigorous and often violent sweeps through these districts in search of hidden IRA arms. The Northern Ireland government was pressing for an end to those nationalist 'no-go' areas of Derry and Belfast where a police presence was not tolerated; and all remaining trust was torn away in the shocked aftermath of Bloody Sunday. In the face of mounting disorder and amid fears of actual civil war, the Northern Ireland government was first suspended and then dissolved; and direct rule from London was applied to the province.

The first serious attempt to create a new settlement in Northern Ireland (as opposed merely to managing the crisis) came as early as December 1973. In that month, the Sunningdale Agreement – named after the well-heeled Berkshire commuter town where the deal, rather incongruously, was thrashed out – provided for a new power-sharing executive in the province, together with a Council of Ireland that would allow Southern observations on the governance of the North. The agreement encompassed the Ulster Unionist Party together with the SDLP and the small, middle-class and non-sectarian Alliance Party. The architects of the accord, however, had not allowed for the bitterness felt by many mainstream unionists who were not yet reconciled to their loss of power in the province. They had also not counted on the absolute opposition expressed both by extreme loyalist factions who could not stomach the notion of Southern interference in the affairs of the North and by the IRA, for which Sunningdale was simply not enough. In May 1974, a widely observed strike managed by loyalist groups brought large areas of Northern Ireland to a standstill; by the end of the month, the power-sharing executive had collapsed.

Nothing on the lines of Sunningdale would be attempted for years to come: instead, Northern Ireland continued to be governed directly from London. Violence persisted: although its scale gradually decreased, loyalist terrorists continued their sectarian killings of Catholics, while the IRA and smaller republican groups carried on their campaigns against members of the RUC and part-time police reserve. The political tension was ratcheted up once more in March 1981, when IRA inmates of the Maze prison outside Belfast renewed a hunger strike in order to assert that they were political prisoners rather than mere convicts.* The demands that their status be recognized – political prisoners were entitled to wear their own clothes, for example – were denied by the new British government led by Margaret Thatcher. Bobby Sands was the first prisoner to go on hunger strike; in April, he won a Westminster by-election in the delicately balanced rural constituency of Fermanagh and South Tyrone. But Thatcher refused to budge: in May, Sands died inside the Maze; and by October, nine more prisoners had followed him.

The hunger strikes were accompanied by widespread and severe civil unrest and deaths. But while Thatcher's firm response certainly won her allies in some quarters, the episode did little to enhance British prestige abroad; and, indeed, the prisoners' demands were later quietly conceded. The episode handed a substantial propaganda boost to the IRA; paradoxically, it also indicated to elements in the organization's political wing, Sinn Féin, the possible advantages of participation in electoral politics. From this time, therefore, the party opted to contest all elections in Northern Ireland, though it abstained from taking its seats at Westminster. This, of course,

---

* This was the second hunger strike to take place at the Maze; the first had lasted from October to December 1980.

was a policy of considerable symbolic vintage: it could be traced back to Arthur Griffith's original Sinn Féin, which had in its turn taken a cue from those Hungarian nationalists who had declined to attend the imperial Austrian parliament in Vienna. Sinn Féin's new direction would slowly bear fruit: the party developed a highly effective grassroots structure and daunting fundraising abilities; and in time it eclipsed the SDLP as the pre-eminent voice of Northern nationalism.

In the aftermath of the hunger strikes, it appeared on the surface as though nothing much had changed in Northern Ireland. The economy puttered along sluggishly: this, however, was a society now kept afloat by British subsidies and one in which the state sector was wholly dominant, providing jobs and thus a high degree of financial stability. Indeed, it was a fact – though one seldom remarked on – that the prevailing political uncertainty and civic abnormality kept house prices low and living conditions high. Northern Ireland never experienced much in the way of economic boom conditions, but neither was it exposed to severe recession; and life – at least for the province's socially conservative middle class – progressed reasonably smoothly. For the Protestant working class, by contrast, economic conditions became progressively worse: as Belfast had shared the boom of the industrial revolution with Glasgow and the cities of northern England, so it shared too in the decline of the United Kingdom's manufacturing base; the guaranteed jobs provided by the city's cherished shipyards, for example, were now a thing of the past.

The political situation continued along sectarian and profoundly dysfunctional lines: while the violence had declined to what one British minister called 'acceptable' levels, the situation appeared frozen without hope of a breakthrough. Many Unionist politicians actually preferred it that way: full integration of the province into the United Kingdom was politically impossible; any move in the opposite direction, however, would present the disagreeable prospect of a renewed Irish government stake in

Northern affairs. And yet, despite this abiding air of political stasis, change was on the horizon. As early as the spring of 1980, Thatcher had met the new taoiseach, Charles Haughey, in Dublin – and the meeting had paid dividends: both for Thatcher, who was given a silver eighteenth-century Irish teapot; and for the Anglo-Irish relationship as a whole, in the form of an agreement to explore the 'totality of relationships between these islands'. Joint studies were commissioned to explore matters of common interest, including security and economic cooperation.

The hunger strikes had followed on the heels of this initiative; but in 1983 the Irish government (now headed by Garret FitzGerald) convened the New Ireland Forum, consisting of the three largest parties in the Republic and the SDLP in the North. In May 1984 the forum concluded that a united Ireland was the best basis for a stable and lasting peace, although there were alternatives: either a federal state in Ireland, or joint British-Irish authority over Northern Ireland. But in November of that year (a matter of weeks after the IRA had attempted to kill her and her cabinet at the Conservative Party conference in Brighton), Thatcher had declared at a press conference that all three alternatives were 'out...out...out'. It was a deeply humiliating moment for FitzGerald – and for Hume, whose party held a considerable stake in the forum deliberations.

FitzGerald nevertheless persevered with his efforts to find a way forward; in addition – and perhaps decisively – the Reagan administration in Washington, which had followed sympathetically the work of the forum, put pressure on Thatcher to move on the Northern Ireland issue. The result was the Anglo-Irish Agreement, signed at Hillsborough Castle in November 1985. This accord enshrined the right of the Irish government to be consulted on Northern issues. It guaranteed too the principle of consent: that the people of Northern Ireland itself would have the final say on their constitutional status. For the British authorities, the accord brought the prospect of increased Irish government cooperation in security issues; for the Irish government, it addressed the sense of isolation felt by Northern nationalists, for there was now an explicitly pan-Irish dimension to the governance of the North; and it also promised to bring stability to an unruly corner of the island – and thus to Ireland as a whole.

In Northern Ireland itself Sinn Féin, having been barred from the deliberations of the forum, now rejected the Agreement too. The leadership of the SDLP, on the other hand, could justly feel pleased with the new arrangement: the party's long-standing political philosophy was branded on the fabric of the Agreement. But for Unionists, the Agreement was wholly unacceptable. Their supporters were once more urged on to the streets – and several days later, a crowd some two hundred thousand strong gathered in central Belfast. This time, however, to no avail: just as Thatcher had declined to bend in the face of pressure from the hunger strikers, so now she refused to concede to Unionist demands. The Treaty remained in force, and there was a surge in loyalist killings. The attitudes of such groups towards the RUC now underwent a fundamental shift: tasked as it was with maintaining the peace in a changing province, the force and its members became the target of loyalist attacks, and many police families were forced to leave their homes as a result of loyalist intimidation. Paisley's DUP showed its willingness to probe the limits of constitutionality by consorting with the loyalist fringe; the party's deputy leader, Peter Robinson, even staged an 'invasion' of the Republic, which led to his spending a night in a County Monaghan police cell.

By the early 1990s, however, it was evident to all observers of the Northern Ireland scene that the cycles of violence, revenge killings, bombings and destruction of property held no prospect of ultimate victory for any side; this was a war that was ultimately unwinnable. As early as 1988 Hume and his Sinn Féin counterpart, Gerry Adams, were engaged in secret exploratory talks in a west Belfast monastery. Hume, whose courage and political vision formed a consistent thread running through the years of the Troubles, understood that without the presence of Sinn Féin, any negotiation process on the future of Northern Ireland would be ultimately pointless. There was a great deal at stake for both men: Hume knew that, by drawing Sinn Féin into the constitutional mainstream, he risked the sidelining of the SDLP itself (as indeed subsequently happened); Adams, though eager to pursue a constitutional path – his party had, for example, already abandoned its policy of abstention in the Dáil – also understood the peril that might come from a split in the ranks of Sinn Féin. The talks continued in fits and starts, in the face of scathing criticism and against a background of continuing violence; and at length they bore fruit, with Adams conceding that the principle of consent must underpin the future shape of Ireland.

Late in 1993 the British prime minister, John Major, declared explicitly what everyone already knew to be the case: that Britain had no 'selfish strategic or economic interest in Northern Ireland'. The Irish government signalled a willingness to look again at its long-standing territorial claim on Northern Ireland; while American pressure, in the form of direct contact with the new president, Bill Clinton, also played its part in thawing the province's long political freeze. In August 1994, the IRA declared a ceasefire: it was broken in spectacular style in February 1996 with a deadly bomb attack on London's financial district; but resumed in July 1997, in the face of a fresh political climate in both London and Dublin. New and stable governments were in place in both capitals; in the White House, Clinton remained engaged in this new political push to secure peace in the province; and a process of intense and often deeply fraught negotiations began.

The result was the Belfast (or Good Friday) Agreement, concluded in April 1998, and hailed by many as signifying the end of the Troubles. The principal Northern architects of the accord were the Ulster Unionists and the SDLP; and the result of their talks envisaged a new power-sharing executive in Northern Ireland, together with an assembly and a number of new cross-border bodies to regulate everything from transport to internal waterways.

Certain clauses provided for the release of paramilitary prisoners and the decommissioning of paramilitary weapons – but these were left deliberately vague, a reflection of the fact that on some issues common ground could simply not yet be found. The Republic agreed to relinquish its territorial claim to the North: and the following month, the accord was ratified in referenda north and south of the Irish border – in the former by 71 per cent of the electorate, with the Unionist vote split; in the latter by a full 94 per cent of those who voted, though on a turn-out of a mere 55 per cent. The Republic had now given up definitively its constitutional aspirations to Irish unity.

The Agreement was an immensely complicated document, locked and interlocked so as to provide balance and parity of esteem between the two communities in the North. It was also an imperfect document: for one thing, the province's sectarian divide – to many commentators, its abiding curse – became the very keystone of the proposed new dispensation; the executive and assembly were predicated on the notion of two camps bound into a working relationship. For another, those manifold issues 'parked' for the time being would eventually have to be addressed – and in the years that followed they were addressed, not always successfully. The IRA, for example, insisted on decommissioning its arms at its own pace – regardless of the political difficulties this created for the Ulster Unionists. For example, the assembly was suspended – 'our weak-kneed parliament / which, unlike Rome, we gained in a day / And then lost, spectacularly, several days later' – and suspended again; and as election followed election, the Ulster Unionists and SDLP were elbowed into the political shadows by Sinn Féin and Ian Paisley's Democratic Unionist Party.[1] The SDLP had, over a period of years, allowed itself to be outflanked and outspent by its younger and more nimble nationalist rivals, who could boast a host of activists at grassroots level; Unionist opinion, meanwhile, had never in any case been solidly behind the Good Friday Agreement; and the question of arms decommissioning, combined with the replacement of the RUC in 2001 by a new Police

Service of Northern Ireland, proved to be pills too bitter for many Unionists to swallow.

Ian Paisley had bitterly opposed the Agreement from its inception – but in the slow unfolding of history he ended by embracing its terms, and a long and vitriolic public career culminated in May 2007 with his appointment as the province's First Minister. The DUP may have specialized in appealing for decades to the margins of Unionism, but it possessed a pragmatic wing too: now that the Ulster Unionists had been vanquished, the DUP could focus on winning over the moderate, middle-class 'garden centre' Unionists, who had in the past disdained the party. In addition, Paisley unexpectedly revealed his own pragmatic side: he was now nearly eighty-one years old; his health was delicate; and he very much wished to crown his career by climbing to the summit of Northern Ireland politics. Sinn Féin's Martin McGuinness – who had formerly held a central position in the IRA – was his deputy: the duo became known as the 'Chuckle Brothers', their improbably cordial relationship observed unsmilingly by many in Northern Ireland. Shortly after his appointment to the top job, Paisley travelled south for a symbolically significant conducted tour of the site of the Battle of the Boyne: this had recently been remodelled as a lavish visitor attraction, complete with a formal walled garden, a ha-ha and an interpretative centre; the vista from the battle site was completed with a distant glimpse of the iconic modern bridge carrying the new Belfast to Dublin motorway over the river valley.

By 2010, Northern Ireland had reached a tentative equilibrium. The findings of the Bloody Sunday Inquiry were recognized as profoundly significant, though also inevitably imperfect. It was tacitly understood, for example, that the notion of the prosecution of British soldiers was highly fanciful; rather, the inquiry had been an element in that greater arrangement of checks, compromises and balances that had come to define political progress in the province. Dissident terrorist activity – carried on, for example, by the Real

IRA, which consisted of members who had broken away from the IRA following the pre-Good Friday ceasefire – remains a persistent feature of life. And there are other issues: the continuing segregation of education and to a large degree of housing too; and the abiding disaffection of a large Protestant underclass that perceives itself to be abandoned by mainstream politicians. Northern Ireland continues to be a profoundly unusual society, and one poised between a disturbing history and a future as yet uncharted.

The outbreak of the Troubles in Northern Ireland had immediate political consequences in the Republic. As violence erupted north of the border in 1968, the Southern government had briefly contemplated sending troops to the aid of the nationalist population; in 1970 two Fianna Fáil cabinet members, Neil Blaney and Charles Haughey (who of course would later become taoiseach), were arrested on suspicion of arranging funds for the importation of arms into the North and sacked from the government. (Charges against Blaney were later dropped, while Haughey was acquitted.) Yet notwithstanding such sensational facts, the Northern violence was only fitfully on top of the political agenda in the Republic. Events in Northern Ireland sometimes spilled south – as in the case of the 1974 loyalist bombings of Dublin and Monaghan.* And yet the situation in Northern Ireland increasingly became background noise, for the Irish state had a range of other issues with which to contend.

The accession of the Republic to the EEC in 1973 had been greeted enthusiastically, but at first it appeared to have little perceptible effect: the

---

* A 1993 British television documentary alleged that the Dublin and Monaghan bombers had had the assistance of elements in the British security services. The subsequent Barron Report commissioned by the Irish government found that these allegations, though they could not be proven, were 'neither fanciful nor absurd', and drew attention to the lack of cooperation offered to investigators by the British government. A later report added that the actions of the Irish police after the bombings had 'failed to meet an adequate and proper standard'.

public finances remained an intractable disaster, the economy stayed firmly in the doldrums, and high-spending economic policies pursued in the late 1970s merely exacerbated the country's problems. Governments came and went in rapid succession, unemployment spiralled, inflation rose spectacularly and emigration remained the stark reality for many citizens. These persistent economic issues were finally addressed from 1987, when a programme of cuts in public spending and tax – backed by both Fianna Fáil and Fine Gael – helped to bring a sense of stability to the public finances.

Starting in the late 1960s, the Republic began to undergo a slow process of social change. The introduction in 1967 of free secondary education, combined with increasing links to Europe and to modern media and the growth of the women's movement, all contributed to the development of a more progressive and liberal civil society – and led inevitably too to a medley of challenges to the Catholic-inflected assumptions that had formed the basis of social policy in earlier decades. In 1968, for example, the Church had restated its firm opposition to artificial contraception, which remained formally banned in Ireland; in 1971, however, opponents of this legal ban took the 'contraceptive train' to Belfast to buy these forbidden articles and carry them openly back to Dublin, in the process underscoring the absurdity of the existing law.

In 1978 Charles Haughey – now back in the government as minister for health – enabled a change in the regulations on birth control: married couples were finally permitted access to contraceptives, though only with the permission of a doctor; it was an 'Irish solution to an Irish problem'. In the eyes of many critics, of course, it was no solution at all; but by the mid-1980s the conditions relating to availability of contraceptives had been further liberalized. Lobbying on the issue of gay rights, meanwhile, had been ongoing since the 1970s: and in 1993, following a key decision on the issue by the European Court of Human Rights – it ruled that Ireland's criminalization of homosexual relations breached the European Convention –

the government moved to decriminalize homosexuality.* In addition, new laws permitting divorce were narrowly passed, after a good deal of public handwringing, in a referendum held in 1995.

This altering social climate was encapsulated in the election of Mary Robinson to the presidency in the autumn of 1990. In 1969 Robinson had been elected to the Senate for the Trinity College constituency; and in the intervening years she had become visible in challenging, among other issues, the bans on contraception and homosexual relations, and the legality of the 'bar' placed on married women in the civil service. In political terms, such activities had certainly done Robinson no favours – she had consistently failed, for example, to be elected to the Dáil – and so her elevation to the presidency following a long and closely argued campaign was regarded as a significant moment in Irish politics. Robinson commented that the women of Ireland – 'mná na hÉireann' – had propelled her into office, and her words had a certain resonance: for when during the campaign a senior figure in Fianna Fáil had questioned her commitment to her family and children, it (together with political scandals involving Fianna Fáil itself) led to a swell of support for Robinson that helped to carry her across the finishing line. Robinson went on to carve out a highly successful term as president, and in the process to breathe new life and relevance into what had become a moribund public office.

The renewal of the Irish presidency in these years threw into sharp relief the declining standards of probity in other areas of Irish public life. The career of Haughey, taoiseach at various times from 1979 to 1992, epitomizes this decline. An energetic administrator and notable patron of the

---

* The legislation in question had been passed by the Westminster parliament in 1885, and had remained on the statute books following independence. The most notorious prosecution stemming from this law was of course that of an Irishman, Oscar Wilde, in 1895. Interestingly, two future presidents of Ireland – first Mary McAleese and then Mary Robinson – acted as legal advisers to the Campaign for Homosexual Law Reform established in Ireland in the 1970s.

arts, Haughey lived the life of a country squire, complete with a large estate in north County Dublin, a private island off the Kerry coast, a yacht and expensive tastes in wine, restaurants and bespoke Parisian shirts – and all ostensibly paid for from the relatively modest salary of a public servant. It was evident, of course, that Haughey had additional sources of income: later investigations would make clear that his income in these years in fact ran into the millions, for the most part donated by a number of individuals, including prominent businessmen. Haughey was also found to have deposited assets in undeclared bank accounts, and to have appropriated for his personal use €250,000 from a fund that had been raised to enable a party colleague to undergo a liver transplant in the United States. Haughey's corruption was echoed in a tangle of other episodes involving members of the country's elite: for example, assistance in tax evasion was offered as a standard service by the main banks; and a number of public officials, including the former minister for foreign affairs, were jailed on corruption charges.

Added to this trend of decline in public life was the loss of moral authority by the Catholic Church, a process that gathered pace markedly in the 1990s. Details began to emerge of systemic sexual, physical and psychological abuse inflicted on minors by priests, nuns and members of the religious orders: gradually, more and more victims came forward with stories of regimes of abuse in residential homes and industrial schools and on the part of priests who were shifted from parish to parish, abusing as they went in the full knowledge of their superiors – all part of a complex pattern enacted and repeated over decades. Neither the state, guided as it was by a culture of deference towards the clerical authorities, nor the Church itself was willing to investigate these matters. As a result, the facts were wrung out with excruciating slowness: the Ryan Report, which set out in extensive detail the sexual, physical and emotional abuse endured by generations of children in government-funded and Church-administered institutions, was regarded as a definitive account – yet it emerged only in 2009, decades after the first allegations began to circulate. The Catholic Church had been at the very centre of Irish cultural life for centuries: it had formed a central plank in the country's sense of identity, and for many people its moral and spiritual authority had been unquestionable. Accordingly, its fall from grace was profoundly shocking.

These stories of corruption, criminal behaviour and moral decline ran as a kind of gruesome counterpoint to the dominant theme of life in Ireland at the turn of the new century. The economic reforms of the late 1980s and the billions invested in the country by the European Union together provided the basis for the consistent economic growth witnessed from the mid-1990s onward. The presence of a Celtic Tiger padding through Ireland's economic landscape was first detected in 1994: this beast remained much in evidence in the ensuing decade, bringing years of virtually full employment, economic growth rates of close to 10 per cent a year, overflowing state coffers and levels of investment in the infrastructure of the state that were undreamed of in previous decades.

Widespread immigration into Ireland replaced the systematic emigration of previous decades: young Irish citizens could now anticipate having a job in Ireland if they wanted one, with emigration now a choice rather than an obligation. Years of steady state investment in education began to pay rich dividends in the form of multinational companies rushing to locate in a country that boasted well-qualified, English-speaking graduates and good communication links to Europe and North America – not to mention extremely low levels of corporation tax. But there was a price to pay too: for example, poorly regulated development across great swathes of the Irish countryside and the startling growth of a culture of materialism.

The end of these good times was no less sudden than it was shocking. Although its onset was partly the result of the global financial crisis that struck in 2007, the subsequent turmoil witnessed by the Irish economy was largely due to home-grown factors. A real estate bubble had been permitted to expand unchecked throughout the boom years until property in certain districts in Dublin was, absurdly, among the most expensive in the world. In addition, the banks had engaged in an extravaganza of unregulated and unwise lending. The result of such activity was seen in September 2008, when a near-collapse of Ireland's banking system was only averted by a government promise to guarantee all deposits and bonds and by sharp reductions in state spending: these measures appeared in the short term to have headed off national financial disaster, and Ireland, indeed, briefly became a model for austere financial probity.

Yet the bank guarantee scheme was itself unsound: the state was not, for one thing, in a position to offer such an open-ended financial guarantee – and the markets knew it. More urgently, it became evident that the weakest link in this financial chain – Anglo-Irish Bank, which unlike the main banking institutions had little or no branch presence in Ireland's towns and cities but specialized as a property developers' agency – had been concealing a black hole at the centre of its finances. The bank was nationalized and the state moved to establish a new agency tasked with buying up and ring-fencing the toxic debts accumulated by the banking sector, in order to release a renewed flow of funds and credit. The taxpayer now owned the toxic debts; and while the authorities claimed that they could be paid off in the fullness of time, it was evident that nobody knew when this time might come – or, indeed, if it would ever come at all. The scale of the country's indebtedness was formidable, with the cost of bailing out Anglo–Irish alone amounting to some €30 billion, with the government as a result running a budget deficit equivalent to over 30 per cent of GDP.

There are certain specific cultural reasons why such a situation evolved. The history of Ireland had propagated a sense of failure and of inferiority, encapsulated in the forced emigration of generation after generation of young people in search of opportunities that their homeland simply could not provide. The economic boom seemed to put this traumatic history firmly in the past: it belonged in another era – virtually in another country. The ongoing moves towards resolving what had seemed an intractable conflict in Northern Ireland, moreover, served to copper-fasten this sensation that Ireland had indeed left its scarred past behind. The result was exuberance and genuine optimism on a widespread scale.

Ironically, however, the political and administrative structures of the country remained rooted firmly in this ostensibly banished past. The state continued to run along lines that were comfortable, reassuring, tried and tested: in particular, the power of patronage and of local connections ruled supreme; and a small political and economic elite, with guaranteed access to bank officials and ministers, ran the country in its own interests. There were other disturbing aspects to this situation: the long-standing Irish emphasis upon the ownership of property and the acquisition of more of it wherever possible, for example, ensured that – although the collapse of the property bubble was certainly foretold by many – enforced regulation of the market seemed unthinkable. And the emphasis traditionally placed in Ireland upon the importance of community was increasingly undermined by the understanding that this apparent boom had certainly not led to a more equal or just society: rather, as the elite became wealthier, so a growing number of people were living in poverty.

These economic difficulties led ultimately to the humiliating spectacle of international intervention, in the form of a massive financial bailout – approaching €100 billion – from the European Central Bank and the International Monetary Fund. Deep cuts to government spending have been immediately felt in the health and education sectors; and large-scale emigration has again become a central plank of Irish life. As the crisis continues, so it has become very clear that the structures of the state have responded ineffectively to these ongoing social and economic challenges. That the Republic requires thorough renewal is now manifest: the present crisis has underscored the need to create a sturdier civic culture, a stronger sense of social solidarity and a more accountable and responsive state; and it is evident that the country's long-standing culture of short-term, patronage-based and clientist politics has demonstrably failed its people. In the years of austerity that lie ahead, it may be that this painful lesson will indeed be learned, and that a new public mood will bring about the kind of radical political and structural change that Ireland urgently requires.

Ireland has always been open to the world, its population from the very beginning bolstered, its towns shaped and its gene pool widened by newcomers. It has been a target of invaders and the pawn of foreign policy-makers; its harbours have been seized and fortified and its fields planted by new hands. The results of such actions have very often been traumatic – as the briefest glimpse into Irish history makes clear – yet they have also been instrumental in weaving the country's complex identity. Ireland has donned the garb of many cultures over the years: its Gaelic kingdoms cheek by jowl with Norse city states and later with an English colony slowly taking root in the land; its post-Cromwellian Ascendancy estates living with a growing Catholic middle class. And for almost a century, two states in Ireland have been divided by a border that was once heavily policed but has now essentially vanished. Ireland has always been 'incorrigibly plural' – and, as part of a wider European culture, it remains so today.[2]

The consequences of such a history naturally take years – perhaps generations – to be fully explored. In Northern Ireland, for example, the 'great sea change on the far side of revenge' has not – or not yet – come to be: yet it is possible now to anticipate the development of the sort of pluralist society that has been so glaringly absent in the past.[3] Across Ireland, indeed, the old pieties, myths and habits of deference are dissolving; so too are the certainties that have underpinned the past. As for what will grow to replace them, these decisions are in the hands of the people themselves.

AFTERWORD

On 1 February 2011, the Irish parliament was dissolved and an early general election called. This development was not at all surprising, for in the preceding months taoiseach Brian Cowen's coalition government had lurched from one crisis to another. It held only the most slender of majorities in the Dáil, with horse-trading an essential element in the transaction of parliamentary business; the relationship between the two government parties – Fianna Fáil and the Greens – had become increasingly fractious.

Ireland's cycle of economic calamity was spinning remorselessly. It seemed evident that the humiliating intervention of the International Monetary Fund and the European Central Bank into the country's economic affairs, at punitive rates of interest, had sealed the fate of the Cowen administration – particularly as the bail-out failed to improve the situation in any significant way. The real cost to the taxpayer of the state's open-ended bank guarantee scheme continued to spiral upward; and spending cuts were felt ever more keenly in the areas of health, education and social welfare. Public anger rose against those bankers, ineffectual state regulators and politicians who had helped to spawn the country's economic crisis.

Several massive street demonstrations had taken place in the aftermath of the IMF/ECB intervention; but there appeared to be – in sharp contrast to the situation in Greece, Portugal and elsewhere – little appetite for public disorder. It seemed that voters were prepared to stomach the prescribed diet of economic austerity: the results of the 25 February election indicated that they had opted instead to express their unhappiness by taking revenge on

Fianna Fáil and on the cronyism, corruption and economic mismanagement it had come to represent. The party was swept from office, a once dominant Irish political movement reduced to a rump. The Greens lost all of their seats in the Dáil; and the incoming government – a Fine Gael–Labour coalition – held a super-majority in the new parliament. For Fine Gael leader and new taoiseach Enda Kenny – who had faced a challenge to his leadership only a few months before, and whose party had faced political extinction less than a decade previously – it was a sweet moment.

Such startling swings in electoral fortune, however, could not hide the fact that the choices offered to the Irish people in the course of the general election campaign had been distinctly limited. After all, one centre-right government had simply been replaced by another centre-right government – and by one, moreover, that had little room for economic and social manoeuvre. The new administration, aware of this unpromising situation, quickly implemented a series of essentially symbolic but important changes: these included (modest) reductions in ministerial salaries and the removal (for the most part) of the fleets of chauffeur-driven black ministerial cars and other perks that stood out shamelessly against a prevailing backdrop of economic gloom.

The new administration has in one specific way already set itself apart from the actions of all previous Irish governments. June 2011 saw the publication of a report into how allegations of child abuse in the Roman Catholic diocese of Cloyne had been handled by Church and state authorities. It might have been imagined that such documents no longer possessed an ability to shock: after all, investigation had followed investigation in recent years, each one uncovering multiple instances of the physical, sexual and psychological abuse of children. The Cloyne Report, however, detailed child abuse that had taken place as recently as 2009 – and concluded, moreover, that both the local bishop and the Vatican itself had by their actions enabled certain priests to disregard child protection rules.

The response of the Irish government was unprecedented: the actions of the Holy See were condemned repeatedly by senior ministers and by the taoiseach himself, who referred in the Dáil to the 'disconnected, dysfunctional, elitist and narcissistic' nature of Vatican culture. In response, the Vatican publicly recalled its representative in Ireland: ostensibly for 'consultations', but also to signal its displeasure at an 'excessive' response by the Irish state. Viewed in an historical context – the records, after all, are thronged with images of Irish government ministers kneeling before bishops and cardinals and declaring that their nationality at all times came second to their Catholicism – this very public divergence of opinion was truly startling.

There were other indicators too of a changing culture and society. In particular, the four-day state visit of Queen Elizabeth II in May 2011 was charged with significance. The event had been envisaged for years: with the signing of the Belfast (or Good Friday) Agreement in 1997, it had entered the realm of the possible; and with the conclusions of the Saville Report into the events of Bloody Sunday accepted in full by the British government, it became inevitable. Nor was anything left to chance, least of all the monarch's security: from the moment she landed in Ireland and stepped, emerald-clad, from the plane, Dublin was in virtual lockdown, with the capital's roads and bridges closed, its skies patrolled by plane and helicopter; television viewers looked upon a capital city that seemed to have been deserted by its inhabitants.

The royal visit – it was generally agreed – passed flawlessly. In its aftermath, commentators and political leaders suggested that a line had been drawn under the past: that the disharmony that had characterized the Anglo–Irish relationship over the course of centuries was now ended, once and for all; and that a new partnership of equal sovereign nations had been forged. These are understandable wishes and sentiments, particularly given both the historic nature of the connection between Ireland and the neighbouring island, and the inevitable wish to focus attention on the country's own present economic and social difficulties. Yet history can never be wished to a conclusion: rather, its legacies must be acknowledged before they can be set aside. Queen Elizabeth's visit, indeed, demonstrated this simple lesson in actions, symbols and a handful of words: the mere action of squaring up to a troubled past brought with it a sense of release.

Such acknowledgements, however, are not always to be had. Days after the state visit ended, the British foreign secretary, William Hague, announced that government files relating to the Dublin and Monaghan bombings of 1974 could not for legal reasons be opened for inspection. The full story of these atrocities – in which thirty-three people were killed – remains to be told, and without the co-operation of the British government it is highly unlikely that it ever will.

In Northern Ireland too, the consequences of history continue to unfold – most brutally, perhaps, in the murder in April 2011 of a police constable in County Tyrone. Ronan Kerr died at Omagh when a bomb, planted by dissident republicans, exploded under his car: the impact of his death was felt more keenly, maybe, because Kerr was young, a Catholic and a member of the Gaelic Athletic Association – a powerful emblem, in other words, of the new order evolving in Northern Ireland. His death was an indication of the limits of the success of this new order – and conversely, his funeral was accompanied by a proliferation of symbols which highlighted the changes that had already taken root. Members both of the GAA and of the police service flanked Kerr's funeral cortege; prominent Unionist politicians and members of the Orange Order participated in the funeral Mass – in some cases, for the first time in their lives. In the still abnormal society of Northern Ireland these were remarkable sights, and indicators of progress towards the creation of a new society.

There have also been warnings, however, of a developing disillusionment with politics as it exists in the province. In the local elections and election to the Northern Ireland Assembly held on 5 May 2011, turnout fell to a historically low level – this in a society which had traditionally boasted extremely high levels of voter participation. It could be argued that this was a good thing: that normal politics were bedding down; that voters were accordingly switching off; that the Northern Ireland public, in failing to vote, was simply following habits established across the mature democracies of the Western world. Yet there is a rather more disturbing lesson to be taken from such trends.

The systems of government and administration established by the Belfast Agreement do not allow for the concept of parliamentary opposition as it exists in other democracies: instead, the governance of Northern Ireland is by enforced consensus, embodied in the province's five-party Executive or cabinet. While such structures were certainly necessary to break the political freeze that had existed during the Troubles, they have by no means led to nimble or responsive government in the longer term: indeed, the Executive has been not so much sure-footed as lumbering, discordant and procrastinating in the matter of everyday politics. It cannot be positive or healthy if voters are turning their backs on politics, preferring to linger (as local wits put it) in the garden centre rather than the polling booth; and it is an indication that the structures of government established by the Belfast Agreement will in the longer term require adjustment.

Set against this are signs of a wider vision of cultural and political plurality. The splendidly rebuilt Lyric Theatre – the province's *de facto* national theatre – was inaugurated at Belfast in 2011, its twin stages and modern facilities providing the shared spaces that such a divided society urgently requires. Similarly, the sinuous new footbridge across the river Foyle in Derry has provided both a striking symbolic connection between the two halves of an often fractured city; and an excellent backdrop to Derry's year as inaugural UK City of Culture in 2013. In fact, it is evident that the city's bid was successful in part because it undertook to confront and explore the fraught issues of identity that pass like geological fault lines across the terrain of Northern Ireland society.

The identity of Ireland as a whole, indeed, appears malleable as never before. This island's exposure to the influence and currents of the wider world has in recent decades been emphasized consistently, and in a variety of (not always straightforward) ways: from the stake taken by the White House in the Northern Ireland peace negotiations of the 1990s to the enthusiastic openness of the Republic to the European single currency at the turn of the millennium – and now, to the country's problematic bail-out by European and international institutions. This internationalism is not likely to diminish in the foreseeable future, particularly while Ireland as a whole grows increasingly dependent on foreign investment and the export trade.

Yet the local texture and rhythms of Irish life have by no means disappeared. Former Irish President Mary Robinson has spoken in moving terms of the Irish tradition of *meitheal*: the acknowledgement of the essential interdependence of Irish communities, and of a willingness to work together in order to achieve common goals; a value system that has proved its worth in times of economic and social difficulty. It is to be hoped that balance and harmony can be found between Ireland's necessary internationalism and these potent local ties that bind its people together. And one must also hope – perhaps with an even greater sense of urgency – that the political institutions and the leaders that serve this island will not, in the future, be found wanting.

TIMELINE

BC

*c.*10,000   Ice sheets retreat from Ireland

*c.*8000   First human presence in Ireland

*c.*5500   Neolithic farmers work the Céide Fields

*c.*3000   Construction of Newgrange

AD

43   Roman legions occupy southern Britain

*c.*77   Agricola studies a possible Roman invasion of Ireland

*c.*370   Irish settlement of western Britain begins

*c.*400   First Christian communities in southeastern Ireland

*c.*430   Palladius sent from Rome to minister to the Christian Irish; Patrick begins his ministry

563   Foundation of Iona by Colum Cille

575   Kingdom of Dál Ríata reaches its height

590   Columbanus departs for France

612   Foundation of Bobbio by Columbanus

615   Death of Columbanus at Bobbio

635   Foundation of Lindisfarne by Irish monks

*c.*650   Compilation of *Antiphonary of Bangor*

*c.*700   Completion of *Lindisfarne Gospels*; Tírechán and Muirchú produce hagiographical works on Patrick

*c.*750   Compilation of the *Book of Kells*, probably on Iona

793   Beginning of the Viking age: Lindisfarne raided

795   First Viking raids on Ireland: monastery on Rathlin Island destroyed

802	Iona burned by the Vikings
837	Vikings settle at Dublin
c.840	Iona is abandoned
902	Viking leaders expelled from Dublin
917	Vikings return to Dublin
976	Dalcassians under Brian Boru capture Limerick
1002	Brian Boru rules as high king
1014	Battle of Clontarf; death of Brian Boru
1035	Foundation of Christ Church Cathedral in Dublin
1066	Battle of Hastings – Norman conquest of England
1132	Malachy appointed Archbishop of Armagh; papacy asserts its control over Irish Church
1152	Henry Plantagenet marries Eleanor of Aquitaine
1154	Henry II crowned at Westminster Abbey
1155	*Laudabiliter*
1166	Rory O'Connor appointed high king in Dublin. Dermot MacMurrough flees overseas
1169	Anglo–Norman capture of Wexford
1170	Anglo–Norman capture of Waterford and Dublin; Thomas Becket assassinated in Canterbury Cathedral
1171	Death of MacMurrough; Henry II comes to Ireland
1176	Death of Strongbow
1177	Anglo–Norman conquest of eastern Ulster begins
1185	King John in Ireland
1189	Giraldus Cambrensis's *Expugnatio Hibernica*
1204	Foundation of Dublin Castle; French conquest of Normandy
1210	King John campaigns in Ireland and subdues Anglo–Norman rebels
1215	*Magna Carta*
1216	Death of King John

1284	Formal English subjugation of Wales
1314	Battle of Bannockburn
1315	Edward Bruce lands in Ireland with a Scottish army
1316	Robert Bruce in Ireland
1317	Dublin repels a Scottish army; much of the city burned
1318	Edward Bruce killed at Dundalk; Scots leave Ireland; *Remonstrance of the Princes*
1337–1453	Hundred Years War
1348	Black Death
1351	Statute of Labourers in England
1367	Statutes of Kilkenny
1399	Richard II visits Ireland; in his absence, his throne is usurped by Henry Bolingbroke (Henry IV)
1455–85	Wars of the Roses
1485	Henry VII becomes first Tudor monarch
1487	Lambert Simnel claims Irish throne; battle of Stoke Field
1494	Poynings' Laws
1509	Accession of Henry VIII
1517	Martin Luther's *Ninety-Five Theses*; beginning of the Reformation
1533	Marriage of Henry VIII and Anne Boleyn
1534	Rebellion of 'Silken Thomas' is defeated
1537	'Silken' Thomas Fitzgerald executed
1539	Dissolution of the Irish monasteries
1541	Henry VIII proclaimed King of Ireland; 'Surrender and Regrant' policy begins
1547	Accession of Edward VI
1553	Accession of Mary I
1557	Plantation of King's and Queen's Counties
1558	Accession of Elizabeth I

1569–73	First Munster Rebellion; Catholic uprising in England defeated
1570	Elizabeth I excommunicated
1572	St Bartholomew's Day Massacre
1575	English massacre of Scots settlers on Rathlin Island
1578	Irish collegiate mission – forerunner of the Irish College – established in Paris
1579–83	Second Munster Rebellion; unrest spreads across Ireland
1585	Plantation of Munster
1587	Execution of Mary Stuart
1588	Defeat of Spanish Armada; many ships run aground off the Irish coast
1592	Foundation of Trinity College Dublin
1595	Hugh O'Neill rebels against the Crown
1596	Edmund Spenser's *A View of the Present State of Ireland*
1598	Battle of the Yellow Ford; rebellion extends to Munster
1600	An English garrison lands at Derry
1601	Battle of Kinsale
1603	Surrender of O'Neill; death of Elizabeth and accession of James I
1606	Private plantation of Antrim and Down begins; foundation of Irish College at Louvain
1607	Flight of the Earls; foundation of Jamestown colony in Virginia
1608	Plantation of Ulster begins
1613	Foundation of Londonderry
1620	*Mayflower* anchors off Cape Cod
1625	Accession of Charles I
1628	'Graces' agreed between Charles and the Old English in Ireland

1641	Outbreak of rebellion in Ulster; English government begins assembling 'depositions'
1642	English Civil War begins; Charles signs Adventurers' Act
1649	Execution of Charles; Oliver Cromwell lands in Ireland; sack of Drogheda and Wexford
1650	Cromwell leaves Ireland
1652	Cromwellian Settlement
1658	Death of Cromwell
1660	Restoration of monarchy; accession of Charles II
1685	Accession of James II; revocation of Edict of Nantes
1688	Birth of a son to James II and Mary of Modena; William of Orange lands in England and James flees to France; Londonderry closes its gates to James's supporters
1689	James lands at Kinsale and travels north; siege of Derry ends
1690	Battle of the Boyne; James returns to France
1691	Battle of Aughrim; Treaty of Limerick
1697	First penal legislation enacted
1699	Woollen Act
1707	Union of Scotland and England
1713	Jonathan Swift settles in Dublin
1724	Swift's *Drapier Letters*
1729	Foundation of Parliament House in Dublin
1740–1	Severe famine in Ireland
1742	First performance of Handel's *Messiah* in Dublin
1745	The 'Forty-Five': Jacobite uprising in Scotland
1746	Battle of Culloden
1756–63	Seven Years War
1776	American Declaration of Independence
1781	Battle of Yorktown ends American War of Independence
1782	Legislative independence accorded to Irish parliament

1789	Fall of Bastille; beginning of French Revolution
1791	Wolfe Tone's *Argument in Behalf of the Catholics of Ireland*; Catholic relief bill passed in Britain; foundation of United Irishmen
1795	Foundation of Orange Order; foundation of Catholic seminary at Maynooth
1796	French expedition enters Bantry Bay but fails to land
1798	United Irish rebellion crushed; death of Tone
1799	Act of Union rejected in Irish parliament
1800	Passing of Act of Union; Maria Edgeworth's *Castle Rackrent*
1801	Union of Great Britain and Ireland
1803	Robert Emmet's rebellion
1808	Thomas Moore's first collection of *Melodies*
1815	Battle of Waterloo
1823	Foundation of Catholic Association
1824	Beginning of the Ordnance Survey of Ireland; establishment of free trade area in Britain and Ireland
1828	Daniel O'Connell wins Clare by-election
1829	Catholic emancipation passed at Westminster
1832	Great Reform Bill
1837	Accession of Victoria
1839	Gustave de Beaumont's *L'Irlande*
1841	O'Connell becomes Lord Mayor of Dublin
1842	Potato blight detected in Europe; first publication of the *Nation*
1843	Monster Meetings across Ireland
1845	Beginning of Great Famine
1847	Death of O'Connell at Genoa
1848	Young Ireland rebellion
1849	Famine begins to peter out; first visit of Victoria to Ireland
1852	Paul Cullen appointed Archbishop of Dublin

1858	Foundation of Irish Republican Brotherhood (IRB)
1859	Fenian Brotherhood established in New York
1864	Establishment of National Gallery of Ireland
1867	Fenian Rebellion; execution of 'Manchester Martyrs'; Clerkenwell bombing
1868	William Gladstone becomes prime minister for first time
1869	Disestablishment of Church of Ireland; foundation of Irish Tenant League
1870	Isaac Butt establishes Home Government Association
1875	Charles Stewart Parnell takes his seat in House of Commons
1877	Irish obstructionism in parliament; passing of South African Confederation bill is delayed
1878	Standish O'Grady's *History of Ireland*
1879	National Land League founded; Loonmore eviction halted
1880	Michael Davitt's ostracism campaign targets Charles Boycott; Parnell begins relationship with Katharine O'Shea
1880–1	First Boer War
1881–2	Gladstone's land reform bills become law; Parnell imprisoned in Kilmainham Gaol; Phoenix Park assassinations
1884	Foundation of Gaelic Athletic Association
1886	First Home Rule bill; Ulster Unionists rally in opposition; bill thrown out by parliament
1890	Majority of Parnell's party withdraws support from him; party splits
1891	Death of Parnell in Brighton
1893	Foundation of Gaelic League
1895	Oscar Wilde's *The Importance of Being Earnest*
1899	Outbreak of Second Boer War and formation of Irish Brigade in support of Boers; foundation of Irish Literary Theatre; first publication of *United Irishman*
1900	Victoria's visit to Ireland sparks protests

1901	Death of Victoria and accession of Edward VII
1902	W. B. Yeats and Augusta Gregory's *Cathleen Ni Houlihan*
1904	Irish Literary Theatre becomes Abbey Theatre
1907	Formation of Sinn Féin; J. M. Synge's *The Playboy of the Western World* staged at Abbey, provoking public unrest
1912	Third Home Rule bill; Ulster Covenant signed
1913	'Dublin Lock-out'; formation of Ulster Volunteers and Irish Volunteers
1914	Ulster and Irish Volunteers execute gun-running operations; Curragh 'mutiny'; Buckingham Palace Conference; Home Rule passed by parliament and suspended; outbreak of World War I; James Joyce's *Dubliners*
1916	Easter Rising at Dublin; its leaders executed; battle of the Somme
1917	Éamon de Valera wins Clare by-election for Sinn Féin
1918	End of World War I; global influenza epidemic kills millions; Sinn Féin victory in general election
1919	Meeting of first Dáil; Soloheadbeg ambush
1920	Proposed partition of Ireland; sectarian violence in Ulster; Croke Park killings in Dublin; burning of central Cork
1921	Burning of Dublin's Custom House; first elections in post-partition Ireland – inaugural meeting of Northern Ireland parliament; Anglo–Irish Treaty
1922	Treaty ratified by Dáil; Michael Collins heads new provisional government; civil war; destruction of Four Courts and Irish national archives; death of Collins; special powers in operation in Northern Ireland; Joyce's *Ulysses*
1923	Civil war ends; formation of Cumann na nGaedheal government; Yeats awarded Nobel Prize for Literature; Censorship of Films Act passed
1925	George Bernard Shaw awarded Nobel Prize for Literature; works begin at Ardnacrusha hydroelectric works

1926	Seán O'Casey's *The Plough and the Stars* sparks disturbances at Abbey
1927	Fianna Fáil, led by de Valera, enters Dáil
1929	Elizabeth Bowen's *The Last September*; beginning of Great Depression
1932	Fianna Fáil forms its first government
1933	Formation of Fine Gael
1935	Sale and importation of contraceptives banned in Free State
1937	Constitution ratified by referendum
1938	Treaty Ports returned to Irish control
1939	World War II begins; de Valera declares Irish neutrality
1941	Belfast extensively bombed by German aircraft; air attacks on Dublin
1942	Patrick Kavanagh's *The Great Hunger*
1943	Sea mine explosion in Donegal kills 19 men and boys
1945	De Valera visits German legation at Dublin to commiserate on death of Hitler
1947	Education Act enables free secondary education in Northern Ireland
1948	Establishment of National Health Service in Northern Ireland
1949	Declaration of Irish Republic; Government of Ireland Act cements Northern Ireland's position in United Kingdom
1951	'Mother and Child' scheme fails to be enacted
1955	Republic enters United Nations
1957	*The Rose Tattoo* staged by Pike Theatre, Dublin
1960	Edna O'Brien's *The Country Girls*
1961	Republic applies to join EEC; its application rejected
1967	Formation of Northern Ireland Civil Rights Association (NICRA); second EEC application rejected; free secondary education introduced in republic
1968	Civil rights march in Derry ends in violence

1969	Burntollet attack; British troops sent to Northern Ireland
1970	Arms trial in Republic – Charles Haughey sacked from cabinet; formation of SDLP
1971	Ian Paisley establishes DUP; 'contraceptive train' travels between Belfast and Dublin
1972	Bloody Sunday in Derry
1973	Republic and UK join EEC; Sunningdale Agreement
1974	Sunningdale collapses; Dublin and Monaghan bombings; Birmingham and Guildford pub bombings
1976	Seamus Heaney's *North*
1979	Charles Haughey becomes taoiseach for first time
1980	Brian Friel's *Translations*
1981	Hunger strikes at Maze prison
1984	Report of New Ireland Forum
1985	Anglo–Irish Agreement
1988	John Hume and Gerry Adams begin secret talks; Remembrance Day bombing at Enniskillen
1990	Mary Robinson elected president of Ireland
1993	Homosexuality decriminalized in Republic
1995	Divorce laws passed in Republic; Heaney wins Nobel Prize for Literature
1998	Bloody Sunday Inquiry established; Omagh bombing; Hume and David Trimble awarded Nobel Peace Prize
2001	Dissolution of RUC; formation of Police Service of Northern Ireland
2008	Bank guarantee scheme in Republic
2009	Publication of Ryan Report into child abuse in Republic
2010	Bloody Sunday Inquiry report published; international financial 'bailout' of Irish economy

NOTES

Introduction
1. Louis MacNeice, *Autumn Journal*, Faber and Faber, 1940.

Prologue
1. Seamus Heaney, 'The Biretta', in *Seeing Things* (London: Faber, 1991), 27.
2. Tacitus, *Agricola* and *Germania* (Harmondsworth: Penguin, 1992), 74–5.
3. Ibid., 75.

PART 1
Chapter 1 – Children of God
1. Patrick, *Confession*, in Philip Freeman, *St Patrick of Ireland: A Biography* (New York: Simon & Schuster, 2004), 188.
2. Cited in Dáibhí Ó Cróinín, *Early Medieval Ireland, 400–1200* (London and New York: Longman, 1995), 14.
3. Patrick, *Confession*, 176.
4. bid., 180.
5. Austin Clarke, 'Pilgrimage', in W. J. McCormack (ed.), *Selected Poems* (Harmondsworth: Penguin, 1992), 38.
6. Bernadette Cunningham and Raymond Gillespie, "The most adaptable of saints: the cult of St Patrick in the seventeenth century', in *Archivum Hibernicum*, Vol. 49 (1995), 82–104.
7. Quoted in Thomas Cahill, *How the Irish Saved Civilization* (London: Sceptre, 1995), 183.
8. *Acta SS*, Feb. I, 141 (viii, 39), quoted by Donnchadh Ó'Corráin, 'Ireland *c*.800: aspects of society', in Dáibhí Ó'Cróinín (ed.), *New History of Ireland I: Prehistoric and Early Ireland* (Oxford: Oxford University Press, 2005), 598.
9. Paul Durcan, 'Fat Molly', in *A Snail in My Prime: New and Selected Poems* (London: Harvill, 1993), 38.
10. 1 Samuel 2: 10.
11. Adamnán, *Vita Columbae* in Seamus Deane (ed.), *Field Day Anthology of Irish Writing*, Vol. I (Derry: Field Day, 1991), 83.

12. Genesis 12:1.
13. Bede, *A History of the English Church and People*, trans. and ed. Leo Sherley-Price (Harmondsworth: Penguin, 1955), 195.
14. *Sermons of Columbanus*, Sermon VII: 2, in *CELT: Corpus of Electronic Texts*, University College, Cork (ucc.ie/celt).
15. Bede, *A History of the English Church and People*, 199.
16. *Letters of Columbanus*, Letter II: 1, in *CELT: Corpus of Electronic Texts*, University College, Cork (ucc.ie/celt).
17. Ibid,, Letter II, 7.
18. Quoted in T. M. Charles-Edwards, *Early Christian Ireland* (Cambridge: Cambridge University Press, 2000), 357.

Chapter 2 – Landfall

1. G. N. Garmonsway (trans. and ed.), *The Anglo-Saxon Chronicle* (London: J. M. Dent, 1953), 55–6.
2. Seán MacAirt and Gearoid MacNiocaill (eds), *Annals of Ulster* (Dublin: Institute of Advanced Studies, 1983), 251.
3. Anonymous (ninth-century Ireland).
4. James H. Todd, *The War of the Gaedhil with the Gaill or The Invasions of Ireland by the Danes and other Norsemen* (London, 1867), quoted in Ó. Cróinín, *Early Medieval Ireland*, 262.
5. John O'Donovan (trans. and ed.), *Annals of the Kingdom of Ireland, by the Four Masters, From the Earliest period to the Year 1616* (Vol. II), (Dublin: Hodges, Swift and Co., 1854), 741.
6. *Njál's Saga*, trans. Magnus Magnusson and Hermann Pálsson (Harmondsworth: Penguin, 1960), 157.

PART 2

Chapter 3 – The Lordship of Ireland

1. Giraldus Cambrensis (Gerald of Wales), *Expugnatio Hibernica: The Conquest of Ireland*, A. B. Scott and F. X. Martin (eds), (Dublin: Royal Irish Academy, 1978), 37.
2. Peter J. Conradi, *At the Bright Hem of God: Radnorshire Pastoral* (Bridgend: Seren, 2009), 50.
3. Giraldus, *Expugnatio*, 41–2.
4. *The Song of Dermot and the Earl*, trans. and ed. G. H. Orpen (Oxford, 1892), 3.
5. Ibid, 5.

6. St Bernard of Clairvaux, *The Life of St Malachy of Armagh*, trans. and ed. H. J. Lawlor (London, [1149] 1920), 37.

7. Seán MacAirt (ed.), *Annals of Innisfallen* (Dublin: Institute of Advanced Studies, 1951), 303.

8. William Hennessy (trans. and ed.), *Annals of Loch Cé* (London: Longman, 1871), 143.

9. *Annals of Loch Cé*, 145.

10. Giraldus, *Expugnatio*, 77.

11. Ibid., 95–7.

12. See Jessica McMorrow, 'Women in Medieval Dublin', in *Medieval Dublin*, ed. Seán Duffy (Dublin: Four Courts Press, 2001), esp. 205.

13. Giraldus, *Expugnatio*, 237.

14. M. P. Sheehy (ed.), *Pontificia Hibernica: medieval papal chancery documents concerning Ireland, 640–1261* (Dublin, 1962–5), cited in F. X. Martin, 'John, lord of Ireland 1185–1216', in Art Cosgrove (ed.), *A New History of Ireland II: Medieval Ireland, 1169–1534* (Oxford: Clarendon, 1987), 153.

15. *Chronique de la traison et mort de Richart [sic] Deux Dengleterre*, ed. and trans. Benjamin Williams (English Historical Society, 1846), 171; cited in Seán Duffy, 'King John's Expedition to Ireland, 1210: The Evidence Reconsidered', *Historical Society Studies*, Vol. 30, No. 117 (May 1996), 1–24.

16. For a longer discussion, see Robin Frame, *Colonial Ireland, 1169–1369* (Dublin: Helicon, 1981), esp. 109.

17. Giraldus, *Expugnatio*, 195, cited in Frame, *Colonial Ireland*, 73.

Chapter 4 – Wasted and Consumed

1. James Lydon, 'A land of war', in *A New History of Ireland II*, 243.

2. Friar Clyn, *The Annals of Ireland by Friar John Clyn*, ed. Richard Butler (Dublin, 1907), 210.

3. This figure for the population of Dublin is very approximate. Estimates vary considerably and it is impossible to guess the population of Ireland as a whole at this time. For a fuller discussion, see Maria Kelly, *The Great Dying: The Black Death in Dublin* (Stroud: Tempus, 1993).

4. *Statutes and ordinances, and acts of the parliament of Ireland, King John to Henry V*, ed. H. F. Berry (Dublin, 1907), 210.

5. Adam of Usk, *Chronicon*, ed. E. M. Thompson (London: 1994), 151.

6. *State Papers of Henry VIII* (11 vols, London, 1830–52), Vol. II, 141, quoted in G. A. Hayes-McCoy, 'The royal supremacy and ecclesiastical revolution, 1534–47',

in T. W. Moody, F. X. Martin and F. J. Byrne (eds), *A New History of Ireland II: Early Modern Ireland, 1534–1691* (Oxford: Oxford University Press, 1976), 66.

7. 'The vocation of John Bale', in *Harleian Miscellany*, vi (1745), 416–17, in Moody et al. (eds) *A New History of* Ireland *III*, 75.

8. National Archives of the United Kingdom: SP 63.29.

9. Anthony M. McCormack, *The Earldom of Desmond, 1463–1583: The Decline and Crisis of a Feudal Lordship* (Dublin: Four Courts Press, 2005), 119.

10. Edmund Spenser, *A View of the Present State of Ireland* (1633), in Seamus Deane (ed.), *Field Day Anthology of Irish Writing*, Vol. I (Derry: Field Day, 1991), 178.

11. Ibid., 192.

12. *Calendar of State Papers 1600–01*, quoted in R. A. Butlin, 'Land and people, *c*.1600', in Moody et al. (eds), *A New History of Ireland III: Early Modern Ireland*, 160.

13. Quoted in S. J. Connolly, *Contested Island: Ireland 1460–1630* (Oxford: Oxford University Press, 2007), 244.

PART 3

Chapter 5 – A Rude and Remote Kingdom

1. David Trimble, Nobel Peace Prize acceptance speech, Oslo, 1998, quoted in Conor Gearty, 'An Escalation of Reasonableness', in *London Review of Books*, Vol. 23, No. 17, 6 September 2001, 19.

2. *Calendar of State Papers 1600–01* quoted in Butlin, 'Land and people, *c*.1600', in Moody et al. (eds), *A New History of Ireland III*, 160.

3. Already, in the previous century, Edmund Spenser had noted the possibilities of the 'fishy, fruitfull Ban' in *The Faerie Queene*, Book IV, Canto XI, xli (Baltimore: Johns Hopkins University Press, 1935), 147.

4. *Motives and reasons to induce the city of London to undertake the Plantation in the North of Ireland* (May 1609), reproduced on http://www.bbc.co.uk/ northernireland/yourplaceandmine/londonderry

5. Cited in S. J. Connolly, *Contested Island*, 302.

6. Quoted in Marianne Elliott, *The Catholics of Ulster: A History* (London: Allen Lane, 2000), 88.

7. James Cranford, *The Tears of Ireland. Wherein is lively presented as in a map, a list of the unheard of cruelties and perfidious treacheries of blood-thirsty Jesuits and the Popish faction*, quoted in Micheál Ó'Siochrú, 'Oliver Cromwell and the massacre at Drogheda', in David Edwards, Pádraig Lenihan and Clodagh Tait

(eds), *Age of Atrocity: Violence and Political Conflict in Early Modern Ireland* (Dublin: Four Courts Press, 2007), 268.

8. Winston Churchill, *A History of the English-Speaking Peoples Vol. II: The New World* (London: Cassell, 1956), 232.

9. Parliamentary speech, 12 September 1654, quoted in Micheál Ó'Siochrú, *God's Executioner: Oliver Cromwell and the Conquest of Ireland* (London: Faber, 2008), 5.

10. 'Britanno-Hibernus', *An appeal to the people of Ireland* (Dublin, 1749), quoted in Ian McBride, *Eighteenth-Century Ireland: The Isle of Slaves* (Dublin, Gill & Macmillan, 2009), 7.

11. Nicholas French, *The unkinde deserter of loyall men and true frinds* (1846 edn.), 13, cited in Patrick J. Corish, 'The Cromwellian Conquest, 1649–55', in Moody et al. (eds.), *A New History of Ireland III*, 336.

12. Quoted in D. Murphy, *Cromwell in Ireland* (Dublin, 1885), cited in Pádraig Lenihan, *Consolidating Conquest: Ireland, 1603–1727* (Harlow: Pearson, 2008), 128.

13. Cromwell to John Bradshaw, 16 September 1649, quoted in Ó'Siochrú, *God's Executioner*, 5.

14. Cromwell to Bradshaw, ibid., 82.

15. Quoted in John Morrill, 'The Drogheda Massacre in Cromwellian Context', in Edwards et al. (eds), *Age of Atrocity*, 249.

16. Andrew Marvell, 'An Horatian Ode on Cromwell's Return from Ireland', in *Andrew Marvell: The Complete English Poems*, ed. Elizabeth Story Donno (London: Allen Lane, 1972), 56–7.

17. 'A bloody Fight in Ireland between the Parliaments Forces and the Kings Forces' (London, 1652), 8, quoted in Ó'Siochrú, *God's Executioner*, 212.

18. Cromwell to Edmund Ludlow, in C. H. Firen (ed.), *Memoirs of Edmund Ludlow* (1894), Vol I, 246–7, quoted in Christopher Hill, *God's Englishman: Oliver Cromwell and the English Revolution* (Harmondsworth: Penguin, 1970), 118.

19. Quoted in Piers Wauchope, *Patrick Sarsfield and the Williamite War* (Dublin: Irish Academic Press, 1992), 220.

Chapter 6 – A Divided Nation

1. *The British Muse* (London, 1700), cited in J. G. Simms, 'The war of the two kings, 1685–91', in Moody et al. (eds), *A New History of Ireland* III, 507.

2. 'An Act to prevent Protestants intermarrying with Papists' (Section One), 1697.

3. 'Letter to Sir Henry Langrishe, Bart M.P., on the subject of the Roman Catholics of Ireland, and the propriety of Admitting them to the Elective

Franchise, Consistent with the principles of the Constitution, as established at the Revolution', in *The Works of Edmund Burke* (Boston: Little, Brown, 1839), 530.

4. Jonathan Swift, *A Modest Proposal* (Amherst: Prometheus Books, [1729] 1995), 291.

5. National Library of Ireland, Pos 3142.

6. *Northern Star*, 7 November 1792.

7. 'Declaration and Resolutions of the Society of United Irishmen of Belfast', quoted in Thomas Bartlett (ed.), *Life of Theobald Wolfe Tone* (Dublin: Lilliput, 1998), 298–9.

8. Ibid., 107–8.

9. Ibid., 480–1.

10. *Hansard*, House of Lords debate, 19 February 1798.

11. 'Terraced thousands died,' writes Seamus Heaney, 'shaking scythes at cannon. / The hillside blushed, soaked in our broken wave.' From 'Requiem for the Crop-pies', in *Selected Poems, 1965–75* (London: Faber, 1980), 33.

12. *Proceedings of a Military Court held in Dublin Barracks on Saturday the Tenth of November, for the Trial of Theobald Wolfe Tone* (Dublin, 1798), 7.

13. Quoted in Bartlett, *Life of Theobald Wolfe Tone*, 876.

14. Quoted in Marianne Elliott, *Wolfe Tone: Prophet of Irish Independence* (London and New Haven: Yale University Press, 1989), 393.

15. *Memoirs and Correspondence of Lord Castlereagh, Second Marquis of London-derry, edited by his Brother, Charles Vane, Marquis of Londonderry*, Vol. II: *Arrangements for a Union* (London, 1843), 7; quoted in Paul Bew, *Ireland: The Politics of Enmity, 1789–2006* (Oxford: Oxford University Press, 2007), 1.

PART 4

Chapter 7 – Union

1. Jonah Barrington, *Historical Memoirs* (1833), Vol. II, 332.

2. National Library of Ireland, MS 2007, Castlereagh to the Knight of Kerry, 21 November 1798, quoted in Paul Bew, *Ireland: The Politics of Enmity*, 46.

3. Pitt to Westmorland, 8 November 1792, quoted in G. C. Bolton, *The Passing of the Irish Act of Union* (London, 1966), 12, quoted in Patrick M. Geoghegan, 'The Catholics and the Union', in *Transactions of the Royal Historical Society* Vol. 10 (2000), 244.

4. *The Speech of the Rt Hon. William Pitt in the British House of Commons on Thursday, 31 January 1799* (Dublin, 1799), 127, quoted in Bew, *Ireland*, 54.

5. 'I met Murder on the way – he had a mask like Castlereagh', noted Percy Bysshe Shelley in 'The Mask of Anarchy', written in the aftermath of the Peterloo Massacre of 1819, when the military put down a peaceful demonstration near Manchester. In 1822, Castlereagh committed suicide by cutting his throat.

6. *Belfast News Letter*, 2 January 1801, quoted in Bew: *Ireland*, 61–2.

7. Percy Bysshe Shelley, 'England in 1819', in *Norton Anthology of English Literature* (London and New York: Norton, 1986), 694.

8. Quoted in G. C. Bolton, *The Passing of the Irish Act of Union* (Oxford: Oxford University Press, 1966), 212.

9. Cornwallis to Portland, 1 December 1800, in *The Correspondence of Charles, 1st Marquess Cornwallis*, ed. Charles Ross, 3 vols (1859), Vol. III, 307, quoted in Geoghegan, 'The Catholics and the Union', 243.

10. Trinity College Library, Dublin, MS 1203.

11. Denis Johnston, '*The Old Lady Says No!' and Other Plays* (Boston and Toronto: Little, Brown, 1960), 83.

12. In Keith Jeffrey, 'The Irish military tradition and the British Empire', in *An Irish Empire? Aspects of Ireland and the British Empire*, ed. Keith Jeffrey (Manchester and New York: Manchester University Press, 1996), 107.

13. Quoted in Ronan Kelly, *Bard of Erin: The Life of Thomas Moore* (Dublin: Penguin Ireland, 2008), 160.

14. *Anti-Jacobin Review*, 28 (1820), quoted in Kelly, *Bard of Erin*, 164.

15. Maria Edgeworth to Margaret Ruxton, 10 January 1816, in Augustus J. C. Hare (ed.), *Life and Letters of Maria Edgeworth*, Vol. I (London: Edward Arnold, 1894), 235.

16. 'Mr Twogood's Irish Journal', 1 April 1820 (PRO Northern Ireland/Fishmongers' Company, Mic 9b/17, quoted in Cormac Ó'Gráda, 'Poverty, population and agriculture, 1801–45', in W. Vaughan (ed.), *A New History of Ireland V: Ireland Under the Union*, 1801–70, (Oxford: Clarendon, 1989), 109–10.

17. Maria Edgeworth to Sophy Ruxton, 9 June 1808, in Hare (ed.), *Life and Letters of Maria Edgeworth*, 156.

18. 'To my Darling Boys', 10 July 1822, in James L. Pethica and James C. Roy (eds), *'To the Land of the Free from the Land of Slaves': Henry Stratford Persse's Letters from Galway to America, 1831–32* (Cork, 1999), 95, quoted in Bew, *Ireland*, 105.

19. 20 November 1825, quoted in *Journal of Sir Walter Scott*, ed. W. E. K. Anderson (Oxford: Clarendon, 1972), 1.

20. Gustave de Beaumont, *L'Irlande: sociale, politique et religieuse*, trans. and ed. W. C. Taylor (London and Cambridge: Belknap Press, [1839] 2006), 130.

21. W. J. O'N. Daunt, *Personal Recollections of the late Daniel O'Connell*, Vol. I (London, 1848), 203, quoted in Oliver MacDonagh, *The Hereditary Bondsman: Daniel O'Connell 1775–1829* (London: Weidenfeld & Nicolson, 1988), 94.

22. Quoted in Leon Edel (ed.), *Henry James. Literary Criticism: French Writers, Other European Writers* (New York: Library of America, 1984), 58.

23. See Angela F. Murphy, 'Daniel O'Connell and the "American Eagle" in 1845: Slavery, Diplomacy, Nativism and the Collapse of America's First Irish Nationalist Movement', in *Journal of American Ethnic History* (Winter, 2007).

24. Herman Melville, *Mardi* (New York: Library of America, [1849] 1982), 1151.

25. Gearóid Ó'Tuathaigh, *Ireland Before the Famine* (Dublin: Gill & Macmillan, 1972), 162

26. J. W. Doyle, 'Letter to Robertson esq. M.P. on a union of Catholic and Protestant churches' (Dublin, 1824), in Stewart J. Brown and David W. Miller (eds), *Piety and Power in Ireland, 1760–1960* (Notre Dame: University of Notre Dame Press, 2000), 24.

27. *Hansard*, 5 March 1829, quoted in Bew, *Ireland*, 121.

28. John Mitchel, *Jail Journal; or, Five Years in British Prisons* (Glasgow, 1876), 42, quoted in David Dwan, *The Great Community: Culture and Nationalism in Ireland* (Dublin: Field Day, 2008), 10.

29. Donal Kerr, *Peel, Priests and Politics* (Oxford: Oxford University Press, 1982), 108.

Chapter 8 – Hunger

1. Melville, *Mardi*, 1151.

2. Father Theobald Mathew, in *Correspondence from July 1846 to January 1847 relating to the measures adopted for the relief of distress in Ireland and Scotland*, in Historical Manuscripts Commission, 1847, li, 26; quoted in James S. Donnelly, Jr, 'Production, prices and exports, 1846–51', in W. E. Vaughan (ed.), *A New History of Ireland* VI, 286.

3. *Spectator*, 30 January 1847, quoted in Bew, *Ireland*, 195.

4. Charles Trevelyan, *The Times*, 12 October 1847, quoted in Bew, *Ireland*, 198.

5. *Nation*, 26 November 1842, quoted in Dwan, *The Great Community*, 44.

6. Cited in Jeremy Paxman, *The Victorians: Britain through the Paintings of the Age* (London: BBC Books, 2009), 84.

7. Gansevoort Melville, 20 September 1843, quoted in Hershel Parker, *Herman Melville, A Biography*, Vol. I (Baltimore and London: Johns Hopkins University Press, 1996), 319.

8. James Joyce, *A Portrait of the Artist as a Young Man* (London: Flamingo, 1994), 234.

9. Paul Cullen to Alessandro Barnabò, 16 November 1861, quoted in Donal Kerr, 'Priests, Pikes and Patriots: The Irish Catholic Church and Political Violence from the Whiteboys to the Fenians', in Brown and Miller (eds), *Piety and Power in Ireland*, 34.

10. *Spectator*, 9 March 1867.

Chapter 9 – The Irish Question

1. Karl Marx to Frederick Engels, 14 December 1867, quoted in Marx and Engels, *On Ireland* (London, 1971), 149.

2. *Hansard*, 1 March 1869.

3. Quoted in E. J. Feuchtwanger, *Gladstone* (London: Macmillan, 1975), 147.

4. *Hansard* (House of Commons) 3S ccxxiii, 26 April 1875; quoted in F. S. L. Lyons, *Charles Stewart Parnell* (Dublin: Gill & Macmillan, 1977), 40.

5. Quoted in Lyons, *Charles Stewart Parnell*, 95.

6. Ibid., 167.

7. Ibid., 543

8. *National Press*, 26 June 1891, quoted in Frank Callanan, *The Parnell Split, 1890–91* (Cork: Cork University Press, 1992), 126.

9. *Clonmel Nationalist*, 4 July 1891, quoted in Callanan, *The Parnell Split*, 127

10. *National Press*, 27 June 1891, quoted in Callanan, *The Parnell Split*, 129.

11. W. B. Yeats, 'Parnell's Funeral', in A. Norman Jeffars (ed.), *Poems* (London: Macmillan, 1989), 395.

12. Joyce, *Portrait*, 233.

13. See D. George Boyce, *Nineteenth-Century Ireland: The Search for Stability* (Dublin: Gill & Macmillan, 1990), 229.

14. W. B. Yeats to Katharine Tynan Hinkson, 15 January 1895, in John Kelly (ed.), *Collected Letters of W. B. Yeats* (Oxford: Clarendon, 1986), 425.

PART 5
Chapter 10 – Schisms

1. Quoted in Keith Jeffrey, 'The Irish military tradition and the British Empire', in Keith Jeffrey (ed.), *An Irish Empire? Aspects of Ireland and the British Empire*, (Manchester and New York: Manchester University Press, 1996), 95.

2. *United Irishman*, 21 October 1899, quoted in Karen Steele, '"Raising her Voice

for Justice": Maud Gonne and the *United Irishman*', in *New Hibernia Review*, Vol. 3, No. 2 (Summer 1999), 93.

3. 25 October 1899, quoted in Laurence Marley, *Michael Davitt: Freelance Radical and Frondeur* (Dublin: Four Courts Press, 2007), 240.

4. *Irish People*, 16 December 1899, quoted in Donal P. McCracken, *Ireland and the Anglo–Boer War* (Belfast: Ulster Historical Foundation, 2003), 54.

5. Quoted in F. S. L. Lyons, *Ireland since the Famine* (London: Weidenfeld & Nicolson, 1971), 246.

6. The play was long ascribed to Yeats's pen; it now seems 'absolutely clear', however, that it was largely written by Gregory. See Colm Tóibín, *Lady Gregory's Toothbrush* (Dublin: Lilliput, 2002), 45, 47–8.

7. *Shan Van Vocht*, January 1897. Alice Milligan and Anna Johnston, the paper's editors, provided Connolly with his first publishing opportunity, even though they disapproved of his socialist aims.

8. State Papers CSO RP 14068/S, quoted in Austen Morgan, *James Connolly: A Political Biography* (Manchester: Manchester University Press, 1988), 29.

9. Quoted in F. S. L. Lyons, 'The Developing Crisis, 1907–14', in Vaughan (ed.), *A New History of Ireland VI*, 133.

10. Quoted in J. J. Lee, *Ireland 1912–1985: Politics and Society* (Cambridge: Cambridge University Press, 1989), 18.

11. Quoted in F. S. L. Lyons, 'The revolution in train, 1914–1916', in Vaughan (ed.), *A New History of Ireland VI*, 196.

12. *Burke's Peerage* online, *Archive*: fifteenth edn. (1937).

Chapter 11 – Revolution

1. W. B. Yeats, 'September 1913', in *Norton Anthology of English Literature* (New York: Norton, 1979), 1967.

2. Quoted in Shane Hegarty and Fintan O'Toole, *Irish Times Book of the 1916 Rising* (Dublin: Gill & Macmillan, 2006), 16.

3. Joe Lee writes: 'The shopocracy of Galway condemned the rebels equally as stooges of Prussia and of Larkin' in *Ireland, 1912–1985: Politics and Society* (Cambridge: Cambridge University Press, 1989), 33.

4. *Irish Independent*, 4 May 1916, cited in Lee, *Ireland, 1912–1985*, 31.

5. Quoted in Lee, *Ireland*, 31.

6. Quoted in Hegarty and O'Toole, *Irish Times Book of the 1916 Rising*, 162.

7. This 'anonymous' correspondent was Captain Wilfrid Spender, quoted in Bew, *Ireland: The Politics of Enmity*, 382.

8. Peter Hart, *Mick: The Real Michael Collins* (London: Macmillan, 2005), 69; also M. A. Hopkinson, 'Michael Collins', in *Dictionary of Irish Biography*, Vol. 2 (Dublin and Cambridge: Royal Irish Academy and Cambridge University Press, 2009), 679.

9. Diarmaid Ferriter, *The Transformation of Ireland, 1900–2000* (London: Profile, 2004), 228.

10. Austin Clarke, 'Six Sentences: Black and Tans', in Hugh Maxton (ed.), *Selected Poems* (Dublin: Lilliput, 1991), 29.

11. Lee, *Ireland*, 60.

Chapter 12 – Division

1. Stephen Collins, *The Cosgrave Legacy* (Dublin: Blackwater Press, 1996), 297; quoted in Ferriter, *Transformation of Ireland*, 297.

2. Osborn Bergin, 'The Revival of the Irish Language', in *Studies*, Vol. XVI, No. 61 (March 1927), 19–20, quoted in Terence Brown: *Ireland, A Social and Cultural History, 1922–1985* (London: Fontana, 1985), 52.

3. Quoted in Peter Hegarty, *Peadar O'Donnell* (Cork: Mercier, 1999), 203.

4. *An Phoblacht*, 11 June 1926; quoted in Hegarty, *Peadar O'Donnell*, 185.

5. P. S. O'Hegarty, *The Victory of Sinn Féin: how it won it and how it used it* (Dublin: UCD Press, [1924] 1998), 74.

6. Quoted in Maryann Valiulis, 'Engendering Citizenship: Women's Relations to the State in Ireland and the US in the Post-Suffrage Period', in Valiulis and Mary O'Dowd (eds), *Women in Irish History* (Dublin: Wolfhound Press, 1997), 159–72, 164.

7. See Molly O'Duffy, *Devout or Deviant? Irish Women, Nationalism and the Criminal Law Amendment Act, 1935* (Thesis: NUI Galway, 2009).

8. Quoted in Louise Ryan, *Gender, Identity and the Irish Press, 1922–1937: Embodying the Nation* (New York: Edwin Mellen, 2002), 258.

9. Commission to Inquire into Child Abuse, Chapter Seven: 'St Joseph's Industrial School, Artane', 7.82, 115; www.childabusecommission.ie

10. Quoted in Clair Wills, *That Neutral Island: A Cultural History of Ireland during the Second World War* (London: Faber, 2007) 389.

11. Elizabeth Bowen, *Notes on Éire* (Aubane: Aubane Historical Society, 1999), 8.

12. Quoted in Wills, *That Neutral Island*, 391.

13. See Bew, *Ireland*, esp. 480.

14. Seán O'Faoláin, 'The Price of Peace', in *The Bell*, Vol. 10, No. 4 (July 1945), 288, quoted in Brown, *Ireland*, 211.

15. Samuel Beckett, *All That Fall*, in *Samuel Beckett: The Complete Dramatic Works* (London: Faber, 1986), 194.

16. Patrick Kavanagh, 'The Great Hunger', in *Selected Poems*, ed. Antoinette Quinn (London: Penguin, 2005), 89.

17. Quoted in Lee, *Ireland*, 314.

18. UCD Papers of Michael Hayes, 18 June 1951, quoted in Ferriter, *The Transformation of Ireland*, 503.

19. See Gerard Whelan with Carolyn Swift, *Spiked: Church–State Intrigue and 'The Rose Tattoo'* (Dublin: New Island, 2002).

20. Quoted in Salon.com, 2 December 1995.

21. Quoted in Bew, *Ireland: The Politics of Enmity*, 476.

Chapter 13 – Between Here and There

1. Sinéad Morrissey, 'Tourism', in *Between Here and There* (Manchester: Carcanet, 2002), 14.

2. Louis MacNeice, 'Snow', in *Selected Poems* (London: Faber,1964), 27.

3. Seamus Heaney, *The Cure at Troy* (New York: Farrar, Straus & Giroux, 1991), 77.

FURTHER READING

Bartlett, Thomas. *The Life of Theobald Wolfe Tone* (Dublin: Lilliput, 1998).

Bartlett, Thomas. *Ireland: A History* (Cambridge: Cambridge University Press, 2010).

Bew, Paul. *Ireland: The Politics of Enmity, 1789-2006* (Oxford: Oxford University Press, 2007).

Brown, Stewart J. and David W. Miller (eds). *Piety and Power in Ireland, 1760–1960* (Notre Dame: University of Notre Dame Press, 2000).

Brown, Terence. *Ireland, A Social and Cultural History, 1922–1985* (London: Fontana, 1985).

Boyce, D. George. *Nineteenth-Century Ireland: The Search for Stability* (Dublin: Gill & Macmillan, 2005).

Callanan, Frank. *The Parnell Split, 1890–91* (Cork: Cork University Press, 1992).

Charles-Edwards, T. M. *Early Christian Ireland* (Cambridge: Cambridge University Press, 2000).

Collins, James S. *Captain Rock: The Irish Agrarian Rebellion of 1821–24* (Cork: Collins Press, 2010).

Connolly, S. J. *Contested Island: Ireland 1460-1630* (Oxford: Oxford University Press, 2007).

Cosgrove, Art (ed.). *A New History of Ireland II: Medieval Ireland, 1169–1534* (Oxford: Oxford University Press, 1987).

Duffy, Seán (ed.). *Medieval Dublin* (Dublin: Four Courts Press, 2001).

Edwards, David, Pádraig Lenihan and Clodagh Tait (eds). *Age of Atrocity: Violence and Political Conflict in Early Modern Ireland* (Dublin: Four Courts Press, 2007).

Elliott, Marianne. *Wolfe Tone: Prophet of Irish Independence* (London and New Haven: Yale University Press, 1989).

Elliott, Marianne. *The Catholics of Ulster: A History* (London: Allen Lane, 2000).

Ferriter, Diarmaid. *The Transformation of Ireland, 1900–2000* (London: Profile, 2004).

Ferriter, Diarmaid. *Judging Dev: A Reassessment of the Life and Legacy of Éamon de Valera* (Dublin: Royal Irish Academy, 2007).

Foster, Roy (ed.). *Oxford Illustrated History of Ireland* (Oxford: Oxford University Press, 1989).

Frame, Robin. *Colonial Ireland, 1169–1369* (Dublin: Helicon, 1981).

Geoghegan, Patrick. *King Dan: The Rise of Daniel O'Connell 1775–1829* (Dublin: Gill & Macmillan, 2008).

Gillespie, Raymond. *Seventeenth-Century Ireland: Making Ireland Modern* (Dublin: Gill & Macmillan, 2006).

Hegarty, Shane and Fintan O'Toole. *The Irish Times Book of the 1916 Rising* (Dublin: Gill & Macmillan, 2006).

Jeffrey, Keith (ed.). *An Irish Empire? Aspects of Ireland and the British Empire* (Manchester and New York: Manchester University Press, 1996).

Kee, Robert. *Ireland: A History* (London: Weidenfeld & Nicolson, 1980).

Kelly, Ronan. *Bard of Erin: The Life of Thomas Moore* (Dublin: Penguin Ireland, 2008).

Keogh, Dermot. *Twentieth-Century Ireland: Revolution and State Building* (Dublin: Gill & Macmillan, 2005).

Lee, J. J. *Ireland 1912–1985: Politics and Society* (Cambridge: Cambridge University Press, 1989).

Lennon, Colm. *Sixteenth-Century Ireland: the Incomplete Conquest* (Dublin: Gill & Macmillan, 1994).

Lyons, F. S. L. *Charles Stewart Parnell* (Dublin: Gill & Macmillan, 1977).

McBride, Ian. *Eighteenth-Century Ireland: The Isle of Slaves* (Dublin: Gill & Macmillan, 2009).

McCracken, Thomas P. *Forgotten Protest: Ireland and the Anglo-Boer War* (Belfast: Ulster Historical Foundation, 2003).

Marley, Laurence. *Michael Davitt: Freelance Radical and Frondeur* (Dublin: Four Courts Press, 2007).

Moody, T. W., F. X. Martin and F. J. Byrne (eds). *A New History of Ireland III: Early Modern Ireland, 1534–1691* (Oxford: Oxford University Press, 1976).

Moody, T. W. and W. E. Vaughan (eds). *New History of Ireland IV: Eighteenth-Century Ireland* (Oxford: Oxford University Press, 1986).

Morgan, Austen. *James Connolly: A Political Biography* (Manchester: Manchester University Press, 1988).

Ó'Cróinín, Dáibhí. *Early Medieval Ireland, 400–1200* (London and New York: Longman, 1995).

Ó'Cróinín, Dáibhí (ed.). *A New History of Ireland I: Prehistoric and Early Ireland* (Oxford: Oxford University Press, 2005).

Ó'Siochrú, Micheál. *God's Executioner: Oliver Cromwell and the Conquest of Ireland* (London: Faber, 2008).

O'Toole, Fintan. *Ship of Fools: How Stupidity and Corruption Sank the Celtic Tiger* (London: Faber, 2009).

Richter, Michael. *Medieval Ireland: the Enduring Tradition* (Dublin: Gill & Macmillan, 1988).

Tóibín, Colm. *Lady Gregory's Toothbrush* (Dublin: Lilliput, 2002).

Vaughan, W. E. (ed.). *A New History of Ireland V: Ireland under the Union I, 1801–1870* (Oxford: Oxford University Press, 1989).

Vaughan, W. E. (ed.). *A New History of Ireland VI: Ireland under the Union II, 1870–1921* (Oxford: Oxford University Press, 1996).

Wills, Clair. *That Neutral Island: A Cultural History of Ireland during the Second World War* (London: Faber, 2007).

INDEX

378

PICTURE CREDITS

BBC Books would like to thank the following individuals and organisations for providing photographs and for permission to reproduce copyright material. While every effort has been made to trace and acknowledge copyright holders, we would like to apologise should there be any errors or omissions.

Abbreviations: *t* top, b bottom, *l* left, *r* right, *c* centre, *bl* bottom left, *br* bottom right, *tl* top left, *tr* top right.

Plate section 1: 1*tl* © Bridgeman Art Library / Getty Images; 1*tr* © The Print Collector / Alamy; 1*c* © Ken Welsh / Alamy; 1*b* detail of the Ardagh Chalice reproduced with kind permission from the National Museum of Ireland; 2*t* the tomb of Columbanus reproduced with kind permission from Bobbio Abbey; 2*c* © Mary Evans Picture Library / Alamy; 2*b* detail from Giraldus Cambrensis's *Pacata Hibernia* reproduced with kind permission of the National Library of Ireland; 3*t* Daniel Maclise, The Marriage of Strongbow and Aoife © National Gallery of Ireland; 3*b* courtesy of Oldirishmaps.com; 4*t* © Hulton Archive / Getty Images; 4*b* © Bridgeman Art Library / Getty Images; 5*t* © Alain Le Garsmeur / Alamy; 5*bl* from a picture by W. R. S. Stott. © Hulton Archive/Getty Images; 5*br* Oliver Cromwell © National Portrait Gallery, London; 6*t* © Mary Evans Picture Library / Alamy; 6*b* © Sotheby's / akg-images; 7*t* © Getty Images; 7*c&b* reproduced with kind permission of the National Library of Ireland; 8*t* Francis Wheatley, The Irish House of Commons © Bridgeman Art Library / Getty Images; 8*b* © Mary Evans Picture Library / Alamy.

Plate section 2: 1*tl* Thomas Moore by unknown artist © National Portrait Gallery, London; 1*tr* Arthur Wellesley, 1st Duke of Wellington by Juan Bauzil © National Portrait Gallery, London; 1*bl* © Hulton Archive / Getty Images; 1*br* Robert Stewart, 2nd Marquess of Londonderry (Lord Castlereagh) by George Dance © National Portrait Gallery, London; 2*t* Daniel O'Connell by George Hayter © National Portrait Gallery, London; 2*b* © The Print Collector / Alamy; 3*t* © Adam Burton / Alamy; 1*b* © Getty Images; 2*t* © Phil Seale / Alamy; 2*c* Photograph reproduced courtesy of National Museums Northern Ireland; 2*b* © Mark Phillips / Alamy; 3*t* Work by Ford Madox Ford © Manchester Art Galleries; 3*b* © Hulton Archive / Getty Images; 4*tl* © Pictorial Press Ltd / Alamy; 4*tr* © Hulton Archive / Getty Images; 4*bl* © World History Archive / Alamy; 4*br* © Pictorial Press Ltd / Alamy; 5*tl* © Mike Heaton / Alamy; 5*tr* © Irish Times images; 5bl © Hulton Archive / Getty Images; 5*br* © World History Archive / Alamy; 6*t&b* © Felix Rosenstiel's Widow and Son Ltd, courtesy of Dublin City Gallery The Hugh Lane; 8*b* © Colin McPherson/Corbis; 7*t&b* © BBC Worldwide Ltd; 7*c* © Homer Sykes Archive / Alamy; 8*t* © Bloomberg via Getty Images; 8*c* © Sipa Press/Rex Features; 8*b* © 2010 AFP.